THE HISTORY AND THEORY
OF INTERNATIONAL LAW

# Rewriting the History of the Law of Nations

# THE HISTORY AND THEORY OF INTERNATIONAL LAW

*General Editors*

NEHAL BHUTA

*Chair in International Law, University of Edinburgh*

ANTHONY PAGDEN

*Distinguished Professor, University of California Los Angeles*

BENJAMIN STRAUMANN

*Alberico Gentili Senior Fellow, New York University School of Law*

In the past few decades the understanding of the relationship between nations has undergone a radical transformation. The role of the traditional nation-state is diminishing, along with many of the traditional vocabularies which were once used to describe what has been called, ever since Jeremy Bentham coined the phrase in 1780, 'international law'. The older boundaries between states are growing ever more fluid, new conceptions and new languages have emerged which are slowly coming to replace the image of a world of sovereign independent nation states which has dominated the study of international relations since the early nineteenth century. This redefinition of the international arena demands a new understanding of classical and contemporary questions in international and legal theory. It is the editors' conviction that the best way to achieve this is by bridging the traditional divide between international legal theory, intellectual history, and legal and political history. The aim of the series, therefore, is to provide a forum for historical studies, from classical antiquity to the twenty-first century, that are theoretically-informed and for philosophical work that is historically conscious, in the hope that a new vision of the rapidly evolving international world, its past and its possible future, may emerge.

PREVIOUSLY PUBLISHED IN THIS SERIES

**The New Histories of International Criminal Law**
**Retrial*s***
Edited by Immi Tallgren and Thomas Skouteris

**Sovereignty**
**A Contribution to the Theory of Public and International Law**
Hermann Heller, edited and introduced by David Dyzenhaus

# Rewriting the History of the Law of Nations

*How James Brown Scott Made Francisco de Vitoria the Founder of International Law*

PAOLO AMOROSA

OXFORD
UNIVERSITY PRESS

OXFORD
UNIVERSITY PRESS

Great Clarendon Street, Oxford, OX2 6DP,
United Kingdom

Oxford University Press is a department of the University of Oxford.
It furthers the University's objective of excellence in research, scholarship,
and education by publishing worldwide. Oxford is a registered trade mark of
Oxford University Press in the UK and in certain other countries



First Edition published in 2019

Impression: 1



Published in the United States of America by Oxford University Press
198 Madison Avenue, New York, NY 10016, United States of America

British Library Cataloguing in Publication Data

Data available

Library of Congress Control Number: 2019941639

ISBN 978–0–19–884937–7

Printed and bound by
CPI Group (UK) Ltd, Croydon, CR0 4YY

*Rewriting the History of the Law of Nations: How James Brown Scott Made
Francisco de Vitoria the Founder of International Law.* Paolo Amorosa,
Oxford University Press (2019). © Paolo Amorosa
DOI: 10.1093/oso/9780198849377.001.0001

# Series Editor's Preface

The American jurist James Brown Scott, at one time, the main legal officer of the State Department, a founder of the American Society of International Law, and of the Carnegie Endowment for International Peace, was a central figure in the development and professionalization of international law in the United States in the early twentieth century. He was also very influential in the direction the historiography of the subject has subsequently taken, and in particular in its engagement with the so-called School of Salamanca of the sixteenth and seventeenth centuries, of which Francisco de Vitoria was the supposed "founder." For Scott, Vitoria's attempt to re-describe the earlier "law of nations" in such a way that while it remained firmly grounded in natural law, it became also a form of positive law was the foundational moment for modern international law. Vitoria had supposedly transformed what had earlier been only law between citizens and non-citizens of the Roman world into a truly global law which was both prior and superior to any form of civil law and thus equally applicable to both the Europeans and non-Europeans. But Scott's interest in Vitoria was not solely antiquarian. It was also crucial for his contribution to a series of debates over the future of international law, and international relations more widely, in the turbulent years after the end of First World War, a period which saw the rise of the United States as a global power and the creation of the first truly international legal and political institutions, the League of Nations and the Permanent Court of International Justice. For Scott himself, the two most pressing concerns, and the ones for which Vitoria's conception of the "law of nations" was central, were his bid to demonstrate the enduring significance of the Catholic natural law tradition for modern international law, at a time when positivism had seemingly diminished it forever, and, paradoxically perhaps, to support the increasing demands for an international recognition of equal rights for women.

But that was not all. Vitoria is, of course, best known for his intervention into the debates over the justification of the Spanish conquest of the Americas. His claims that prior to the arrival of the Spanish the American Indians possessed what he called full "public and private *dominium*"—that is sovereignty and property rights—in the lands they occupied, and that the only grounds upon which a just war might be made against them could be found in a universally binding law seriously undermined all of the Spanish crown's principal claims for the legitimacy of their conquest in the Americas. Ever since the early nineteenth century, this has led to him being looked upon, in Paolo Amorosa's words, as "a brave humanitarian ahead of his time." In the words of the English jurist Sir Travers Twiss, in 1856, he

*Rewriting the History of the Law of Nations: How James Brown Scott Made Francisco de Vitoria the Founder of International Law*. Paolo Amorosa, Oxford University Press (2019). © Paolo Amorosa
DOI: 10.1093/oso/9780198849377.001.0001

and the other members of the "School of Salamanca" were "the early streaks of dawn, the earnest of the coming dawn."

More recently a revisionist post-colonial literature has set out to demolish these comforting suppositions, arguing instead that Vitoria was merely pressing a revised version of the argument that Christians—and thus by implication all Europeans—always had the right to make war upon pagans as "barbarians" —and therefore all non-Europeans—and consequently to deprive them of both their sovereignty and their goods. This casts Vitoria not as the father of a truly *international* law, so much as the source of the claim, which was to be become central to the positivist international law of the nineteenth century, that the world is divided into "civilized" and "non-civilized" peoples, and that the former have not only a right but also a duty to rule over the latter. What is at stake in this dispute—and it is clearly of immense contemporary significance—is whether international law, and all forms of international justice, can ever be extricated from the history of European empire-building. Or as Paolo Amorosa phrases it here: "has international law been, since its birth, humanitarian or imperialist?"

Any attempt to answer this question, however, immediately lands us in the midst of a highly controversial methodological—and increasingly doctrinal—controversy. Is there really a continuous history of "international law" from the mid-sixteenth century until today? Can someone like Vitoria really be accused of contributing to the political agenda of imperial nations which lay far in the future? Can we, in other words, treat the questions which Vitoria attempted to answer as if they were substantially the same questions we might ask today? Or should we read all historical texts strictly in the terms, and the languages, provided by the contexts in which they were originally written? Does it make any sense to speak, as Scott did, of Vitoria as the "father" of anything so obviously remote from his conceptual grasp as modern "international law"?

This book addresses all three of these topics. It is a very substantial and original contribution to a central and still hotly contested moment in the evolution of both international law itself and of its historiography.

Anthony Pagden

# Acknowledgments

While this long, difficult, and rewarding journey draws to a close, I want to offer my most sincere thanks to all the people who have shared it with me. In the first place, the dissertation this book is based on could not have come to light without the attentive guidance of my supervisor Martti Koskenniemi. It has been a privilege to discuss and review my work with him, constantly learning from his sharp insights and vast knowledge. The quality of the present text has benefited immensely from this process but, most importantly, I personally have: it is said that a doctorate represents a rite of initiation into the academic profession and Martti has succeeded in offering me a thorough perspective of what it means to be a scholar. His technical observations always incorporated a careful consideration of the ethical and political stakes involved. He checked certain lapses of condescension I have had toward my subjects, while nurturing my ambitiousness. All those many teachings I will always treasure.

There have been other scholars who, during different phases of the work, have engaged closely with my drafts, providing me with invaluable advice. Especially in the initial phase of the research, when its framework was still far from defined, Walter Rech has been a fundamental support. During many long discussions, he has helped me clarify my own ideas and pointed me to ways through which I could best express them. Pamela Slotte has been of tremendous help over the course of the writing process. Beyond reviewing the texts I produced, she patiently listened to every doubt I expressed on the most disparate issues, ranging from the theoretical foundations of the dissertation to the administrative details of its submission. She unfailingly responded with prompt assistance and solutions, making the path toward completion of my doctoral studies considerably smoother. Rotem Giladi has kicked off the final review process by carefully going through the initial parts of the text. The latest reviewers have been the pre-examiners Karen Knop and David Armitage. I am thankful for their encouraging reports and pointed observations. They have given me a better understanding both of the contributions this work offers and of the avenues for its further improvement toward this final book form.

This work was conceived and researched in the context of the project "Intellectual History of International Law: Religion and Empire," funded by the Academy of Finland. Besides Martti, the project leader and initiator, Walter, and myself, our research group included Mónica García-Salmones Rovira and Manuel Jiménez Fonseca. With Mónica I shared the coordination of the "International Law and Religion Working Group," which resulted in the collective volume *International Law and Religion: Historical and Contemporary Perspectives*, published by Oxford

*Rewriting the History of the Law of Nations: How James Brown Scott Made Francisco de Vitoria the Founder of International Law*. Paolo Amorosa, Oxford University Press (2019). © Paolo Amorosa
DOI: 10.1093/oso/9780198849377.001.0001

University Press in 2017. Mónica's commitment to the long-term and large-scale endeavors we have worked on together has been exemplary, providing me with the motivation and enthusiasm necessary to overcome the many obstacles we faced. I am proud of the productive cooperation we built and of the achievements it led to. With Manuel I shared an office in the early years of my doctoral work. Together with our office mate Tuomas Tiittala, we spent long hours discussing our interests and views. At the time we considered those conversations as breaks from our solitary duties of reading and writing, but I now realize how much they contributed to the development of the basic ideas sustaining this text. Manuel has cared for my emotional health in a time of heavy personal loss, during which I doubted that I would ever be able to see the end of this project. The same goes for Tuomas. Our summer excursions into the nature of Middle Finland have been a source of inner peace and balance. I have similarly fond memories of a road trip from Salt Lake City to Las Vegas with Walter from that same period. The majestic views of the national parks we visited in Southern Utah gave me a new sense of perspective.

Since September 2012 up to the completion of the dissertation in late 2017 I have been based at the Erik Castrén Institute of International Law and Human Rights (ECI) at the Law Faculty of the University of Helsinki. I cannot think of another place where I could have pursued my research surrounded by such a diverse and inspiring community of scholars. In the first place I am thankful to the people who, alongside my supervisor, have brought us together: Jarna Petman and Jan Klabbers have been wonderful mentors and colleagues throughout my time at ECI. It is an impossible task to list all who have shared with me a coffee, small talk, one or several conversations on the politics of the day, or some obscure scholarly theory on the sixth floor of Porthania or somewhere else in the Law Faculty, but I am going to try anyway: Elina Almila, Arnulf Becker Lorca, Martin Björklund, Luca Bonadiman, Katja Creutz, Mehrnoosh Farzamfar, Joakim Frände, Nora Fabritius, Massimo Fichera, Elisabetta Fiocchi, Lorenzo Gasbarri, Janis Grzybowski, Lauri Hannikainen, Ville Kari, Hiva Khedri, Margareta Klabbers, Tero Kivinen, Magdalena Kmak, Paavo Kotiaho, Vesa Kyyrönen, Tero Lundstedt, Marja Luukkonen, Marta Maroni, Ketino Minashvili, Panu Minkkinen, Ilona Nieminen, Erman Özgür, Silvia Park, Eliska Pírková, Outi Penttilä, Santtu Raitasuo, Alberto Rinaldi, Semir Sali, David Scott, Sahib Singh, Ukri Soirila, Milka Sormunen, Diliana Stoyanova, Anna Suni, Immi Tallgren, Nadia Tapia, Reetta Toivanen, Taina Tuori, Guilherme Vasconcelos Vilaça, Maria Varaki, Claire Vergerio, Kangle Zhang. I want them all to know, including those I have missed to mention, that I am thankful because they have all contributed to the brilliant experience that produced this work. Of course, one could not think of the ECI community without mentioning the Institute's coordinator Sanna Villikka, a constant source of help and support for all of us. During her leave, I have seen Lauri Uusi-Hakala and Mari Taskinen rise, through ability and dedication, to the impressive task of filling her shoes. I owe a special mention to Maria José Belmonte Sanchez, research assistant for our project. Her constant moral support in the most difficult times of my doctoral studies is by itself a major contribution to this work. In addition, she has shared with me the tantalizing work of ordering and classifying the wealth of archival material that forms the backbone of this book. Also, the initial editing of the dissertation and the bibliography are the result of her skillful efforts.

Since my joining in April 2018, I have enjoyed the help and support of my current colleagues at the Centre of Excellence in Law, Identity and the European Narratives (funded by the Academy of Finland, funding decision number 312154) at the Faculty of Social Sciences of the University of Helsinki. The atmosphere at the Centre, collegial yet driven, relaxed yet creative, has proven ideal for the delicate process of turning the dissertation into a book manuscript. In particular, I would like to thank Kaius Tuori and Jacob Giltaij for reviewing the book proposal and for their advice on how to bring the best out of my work. I am also very grateful to Heta Björklund who has produced the final editing of the manuscript and the index.

Between September and November 2015 I visited archives in the United States, funded by the "Intellectual History of International Law" project. First, I spent a month at the Butler Library of Columbia University, examining the Carnegie Endowment for International Peace Records. I am thankful to the staff of the Rare Book & Manuscript Library for their professionalism and helpfulness, especially to Jennifer Comins, the curator of the collection. My access to the Butler Library was facilitated by the status of visiting scholar at Columbia's History Department, which I have been awarded thanks to Mark Mazower. The following month I was in Washington, D.C., studying James Brown Scott's personal papers at Georgetown University. I wish to thank the personnel of the Booth Family Center for Special Collections of the Lauinger Library. They kindly supported my work there beyond what duty required, answering my every question on the University and its history. In particular, Scott Taylor has been of tremendous help. Besides the project funding that made my archival research possible, for which I thank the Academy of Finland, I am grateful to the Ella ja Georg Ehrnrooth Foundation for the grant it awarded me for 2017.

I have presented parts of the work in several seminars and conferences. These included the Postgraduate Seminar in International Law at the Erik Castrén Institute, the Histories of International Law Conference (University of Utah, 2014), the Third World Approaches to International Law Conference (American University in Cairo, 2015), and the Conference Law in International Orders—Past and Present (Lauterpacht Centre for International Law, University of Cambridge, 2016). I am thankful to the organizers and to the participants of these events. The feedback I received on my papers and presentations in these contexts has been precious.

Last, but not least, I am grateful to my friends and family. Emanuele, Fabio, and Mario have been great company throughout my years in Helsinki. Laura, though not physically close, has always been present. I would like to thank my family for all their love and support. My relatives in Cerignola, my grandma Teresa, who has recently left us, her sister Nuccia, my aunts and uncles, my cousins and the little Antonio, Francesco, and Luigi have filled my holidays with joy. Through simple things, like providing me with the local food I so sorely miss, they keep me in touch with my roots. They know that I might live far away, but I have not forgotten where I come from. The past few years have brought to my sister Annamaria, my mother Rita, and me reasons for grief. Nevertheless, they have reacted with admirable strength. I always knew I could count on them for anything. They have taken care of so many shared responsibilities and never complained that I was not there in Italy to contribute. I am truly grateful, even if I do not show it enough. My mom has also instilled in me the passion for books and knowledge. She read to me about history and mythology much before I could be able to do it myself. From this *longue durée* perspective, she has been the earliest contributor to this work. If she has been the person closest to me at the very beginning, Hanna-Mari was there at the conclusion. I feel blessed to have her in my life. During the final months of feverish writing, she has forgiven my absence into James Brown Scott's world while gently holding me in the present. Her love has carried me through the finish line. Recently, in December 2018, she has also given me the best gift I have ever received by giving birth to our son Leone. While I type these last words with him sleeping close to me, I cannot but think at a long project that ends, this work, and a longer, even more challenging and rewarding that is just beginning, my life with him. Though the responsibility of fatherhood is great, he gives me strength and joy to face it with the same faith in the future I see in his trusting eyes and wide smiles.

This book is dedicated to the memory of my father, Alfonso Amorosa (1944–2014), a scrupulous lawyer with a genuine sense of justice. His example of integrity is a most powerful inspiration and compass, in research as well as in life.

Florence, May 2019

# Table of Contents



*Rewriting the History of the Law of Nations: How James Brown Scott Made Francisco de Vitoria the Founder of International Law*. Paolo Amorosa, Oxford University Press (2019). © Paolo Amorosa
DOI: 10.1093/oso/9780198849377.001.0001

# List of Abbreviations

| | |
|---|---|
| **AIIL** | American Institute of International Law |
| **AJIL** | American Journal of International Law |
| **ASIL** | American Society of International Law |
| **ASJSID** | American Society for the Judicial Settlement of International Disputes |
| **CEIP** | Carnegie Endowment for International Peace |
| **CU** | Congressional Union |
| **ERA** | Equal Rights Amendment |
| **IACW** | Inter-American Commission of Women |
| **IWSA** | International Woman Suffrage Alliance |
| **LEP** | League to Enforce Peace |
| **NAWSA** | National American Woman Suffrage Association |
| **NLWV** | National League of Women Voters |
| **NWP** | National Woman's Party |
| **US** | United States |
| **WILPF** | Women's International League for Peace and Freedom |
| **WPP** | Woman's Peace Party |

*Rewriting the History of the Law of Nations: How James Brown Scott Made Francisco de Vitoria the Founder of International Law*. Paolo Amorosa, Oxford University Press (2019). © Paolo Amorosa
DOI: 10.1093/oso/9780198849377.001.0001

# Introduction. An American Project

## 1. The Research Question and its Relevance to Current Debates on the History of International Law

In the mid-1920s, American international lawyer James Brown Scott (1866–1943) embarked on a campaign to prove that his discipline had been founded by the Spanish theologian Francisco de Vitoria in the sixteenth century and not by the Dutch Hugo Grotius in the seventeenth. International law was teeming with new ideas and experiments in the interwar years. Why would a leading scholar and political operator like Scott devote the last years of his career to a seemingly antiquarian endeavor?

This book provides an answer to that question. It describes how Scott's historical work was not antiquarian at all, but crafted as an intervention in vital debates over the changing nature of international relations following the Great War. In turn, I do not see my research as mere historical revision either. Understanding Scott's theory of the Spanish origin in context is useful to add depth to the conversations on international legal history of recent years, which have assumed the relevance of Vitoria for the discipline. Often, discussing the Dominican's thought in the context of international law has carried a larger, not always ostensible, meaning. Assessing the attitude of Vitoria toward his country's colonization of America has become a benchmark to evaluate the fundamental nature of international law itself. Was Vitoria using *ius gentium* to condemn colonial violence or was he ultimately justifying and enabling it? In other words, has international law been, since its birth, humanitarian or imperialist?

This debate has been sparked by Antony Anghie's seminal postcolonial history of the discipline. Anghie's *Imperialism, Sovereignty and the Making of International Law* makes the argument that Vitoria's was "a particularly insidious justification of [the] conquest precisely because it is presented in the language of liberality and even equality."[1] His treatment of the natives spearheaded the legal distinctions that would embed colonialist thinking in international law. These unequal structures, according to Anghie, are still present and are reproduced every time that international law renews and reforms itself.[2]

[1] Antony Anghie, *Imperialism, Sovereignty and the Making of International Law*, Cambridge: Cambridge University Press, 2004, p. 28.

[2] See ibid., pp. 312–13 and Antony Anghie, "The Evolution of International Law: Colonial and Postcolonial Realities," *Third World Quarterly*, 27, 2006, pp. 741–5.

*Rewriting the History of the Law of Nations: How James Brown Scott Made Francisco de Vitoria the Founder of International Law*. Paolo Amorosa, Oxford University Press (2019). © Paolo Amorosa
DOI: 10.1093/oso/9780198849377.001.0001

Anghie's assessment has been opposed by authors who still hold views substantially in line with Scott's: Vitoria's recognition of universal rights, applicable to both Spaniards and American natives, was a brave humanitarian stand, ahead of its time. Within this line of thinking, the Dominican's "moral cosmopolitanism" is considered "still an impressive feat,"[3] both in itself and because of the international legal tradition it originated. "Vitoria envisioned the 'rules of the game' for the world as a political community by reengineering the doctrine of the *ius gentium*. [He] gave birth to a big idea that many others, since then, have cultivated as a *discipline* and that has proved to be one of the most useful and now pervasive social artefacts of human progress."[4]

The debate on Vitoria and his international legal legacy includes a third point of view criticizing both Anghie and his opponents on the basis of considerations of historical method. To evaluate Vitoria's works in light of their later influence and use would be fallacious. To get a historically accurate account of the past, one should understand it in its own terms, without imposing our present concerns on it. In Martti Koskenniemi's characterization, this "type of critique claims . . . that we have no way of assessing Vitoria without committing the sin of anachronism and that viewing him as the 'origin' of something—of 'modern' international law—is a purely ideological move that provides no understanding of Vitoria in the temporal context where he lived and thought."[5]

The international legal scholar who has most vocally engaged in a rebuttal of this contextualist critique, in defense of Anghie's work, has been Anne Orford. I want to direct the reader's attention to a specific aspect of her rebuttal, which gives the measure of the importance of a full understanding of Scott's work on Vitoria and the Salamanca School to underpin current discussions on international legal history and the development of international law in the last century. Orford notes that Anghie "open[s] his reading of Vitoria . . . with the reclamation" of the Dominican "by James Brown Scott." While "Anghie does not deal with Scott in any detail in his history[,] the implications of [his] choice" to point at "Vitoria as received by Scott" are crucial. In so doing, "Anghie draws our attention to the special place that Vitoria played in the new American century."[6]

Indeed, as I noted at the outset, Scott was a major player in the international law and foreign policy establishment in the United States in the early twentieth

[3] Georg Cavallar, "Vitoria, Grotius, Pufendorf, Wolff and Vattel: Accomplices of European Colonialism and Exploitation or True Cosmopolitans?," *Journal of the History of International Law*, 10, 2008, p. 209.

[4] Pablo Zapatero, "Legal Imagination in Vitoria. The Power of Ideas," *Journal of the History of International Law*, 11, 2009, pp. 228–9.

[5] Martti Koskenniemi, "Vitoria and Us," *Rechtsgeschichte*, 22, 2014, p. 122. The article also features a fuller account of the debate I just outlined (see ibid., especially pp. 120–3). For the most recent and best articulated contextualist intervention in the debate see Andrew Fitzmaurice, "Context in the History of International Law," *Journal of the History of International Law*, 20, 2018, pp. 5–30.

[6] Anne Orford, "The Past as Law or History? The Relevance of Imperialism for Modern International Law," NYU Institute for International Law and Justice Working Paper Series, 2012/2, pp. 11 and 14.

century. A key founder of the American Society of International Law, Scott had been the main legal officer of the State Department before joining the leadership of the Carnegie Endowment for International Peace.[7] The picture of Vitoria he depicted reflected the "*practices* of international law developed for the American century . . . Scott was a believer in": in brief, "international administration" and "freedom of trade and commerce." That picture also worked "for the *rationalisation* of those practices and the new forms of international legal authority they brought into being."

Seen in this light, Orford argues, Anghie's work does not take Vitoria out of his sixteenth-century context. Rather, it tracks a series of more recent contexts for his reception. Beginning with Scott's historical work, "this series . . . suggests that the humanitarian critique of Spanish empire offered ideological innovators a means of rationalizing the form of empire that would triumph in the twentieth century. [E]arly modern *ius gentium* was systematically and carefully reconstructed in the United States of America . . . to make sense of practices that were already reshaping the world."[8]

This book expands on Orford's intuition and tells the story of Scott as an ideological innovator who adopted Vitoria as an historical subject and, at the same time, a proxy for his agenda. The nature of that agenda, after extensive investigation, turns out to be much more articulated and complex than a generic liberal internationalism and support for international institutions. Not only Scott's vision of the postwar international order, which he later associated with the Salamanca School, focused on adjudication, in direct contrast with that of Woodrow Wilson and of the younger up-and-coming generation of US international lawyers;[9] he also brought under Vitoria's umbrella causes that were highly controversial in US foreign policy circles but were invested by Scott with deep personal meaning. The last two chapters of the book are dedicated to two such causes: Chapter 5 describes how Scott used Vitoria to champion the enduring significance of a Catholic conception of international law; Chapter 6 tracks Scott's enlistment of Vitoria to support feminist activists seeking the international recognition of equal rights for women.

To serve his diverse goals, Scott deployed Vitoria in varied discursive functions that this book tracks and describes. In the first place, by successfully making the case for Vitoria as the founder of international law, Scott established the Dominican's work as belonging to the canon of the discipline. The canonization of Vitoria's arguments represented the logical basis of further moves. In Scott's progressive mindset the thought of canonical figures came alive as the foundation of present global legal arrangements and the blueprint for their future configuration. Therefore, for him,

7 For a detailed account of Scott's institutional and professional roles and initiatives, with an explanation of related political and ideological implications, see especially Chapter 1.

8 Orford, "The Past as Law or History?," pp. 11 and 15–16.

9 See especially Chapters 3 and 4.

the transition from establishing Vitoria as founder to deploying him as pedigree of current proposals was natural and organic. Scott employed the Dominican to lend authority either to specific international legal projects or to foundational visions of the international legal order as a whole. In the former mode, for instance, Vitoria could be enlisted in support of treaties prescribing equal rights for women and efforts of international codification. In the latter case, he became the intellectual father of a modern international law based on individual rights, equality, and global legal institutions. Scott's account was flexible and versatile not only when he cast Vitoria as pedigree but also when he sought to forge alliances. Indeed, Scott tailored the image of Vitoria he presented to the groups he sought to create common cause with. For instance, as a revered figure of the country's *siglo de oro*, Vitoria was the symbol of the alliance between Scott and the Spanish legal establishment; as a celebrated Scholastic theologian he buttressed Scott's approaches to the Roman Curia and the Catholic Church in the United States.

As the causes and the audiences he associated with Salamancan theology mirrored Scott's individual preferences and inclinations, a comprehensive account of the campaign for the Spanish origin of international law should necessarily cover his formative years and early career, drawing connections with his personal life and the development of his legal thinking and professional endeavors. In turn, these aspects can be better understood only against the background of a larger historical context. As a result, the book adopts a composite literary register and a multilevel analysis. It is both a professional biography and the account of a paradigm shift in international legal history. While, at its core, it is a story of Scott as an historian of international law, it necessarily features the exploration of larger interconnected trends and events taking place during his lifetime: the rise of the United States as a global power and related ideological developments; the social and religious changes the country went through in the period under scrutiny; the activity of hemispheric and global legal networks; the profound changes international law underwent between the late nineteenth century and the outbreak of the Second World War, including the creation of the League of Nations and the Permanent Court of International Justice.

## 2. Earlier Scholarship on Scott

With the renewed interest in international legal history of recent decades and the rising number of publications on the subject, a series of aspects of Scott's career has been researched and analyzed from varied and productive perspectives. There are valid texts that cover Scott's professional career generally or his historical work on Vitoria and the Salamanca School of theology. None covers both in a comprehensive way as this book does.

Two older texts still represent fundamental reading for anybody wanting to approach the study of Scott as an historical subject: the biography by Scott's right-hand man, George Finch,[10] and Ralph Nurnberger's *James Brown Scott: Peace Through Justice*.[11] They are both highly informative, but lack depth of analysis.

An author that has recently produced a series of excellent studies on Scott has been Juan Pablo Scarfi.[12] Scarfi's work sheds light on the role of international legal networks in the ascendance of the United States as the informal hegemonic power in the Americas. He has also given some consideration to the function of Scott's historical work on Vitoria within this hegemonic project.[13] Yet, the perspective Scarfi adopts, focused on international relations in the American continent, is only one among those I incorporate in my analysis of Scott.

In my opinion, the most detailed study on Scott's early career to date is Benjamin Coates' unpublished PhD thesis *Transatlantic Advocates*.[14] It is an impressive work, insightful and supported by extensive archival research. It pays attention to Scott's biography, education, and to the development of his legal thought. It draws a detailed picture of his institutional and professional relations, in the United States and globally. Coates' achieved purpose is to describe the legalist turn of US foreign relations in the first two decades of the twentieth century and its relation to the expansive policies that followed the Spanish-American War.[15] Yet, Coates does not focus on the religious and historical foundations Scott gave to his vision of international law. Moreover, he does not follow Scott's career into the 1920s and 1930s. This is when Scott, by that time perceived

[10] An abridged version of Finch's unfinished biography, mostly drafted in the late 1940s and early 1950s, has been published recently (George A. Finch, edited by William E. Butler, *Adventures in Internationalism. A Biography of James Brown Scott*, Clark: Lawbook Exchange, 2012). The biography includes a series of yet unpublished draft chapters found, together with the ones eventually published, in the James Brown Scott Papers, Booth Family Center for Special Collections, Lauinger Library, Georgetown University, Washington, D.C. (JBS Papers). Finch had also published an initial short version of the biography as a memorial article, shortly following Scott's death, on the AJIL ("James Brown Scott, 1866–1943," *American Journal of International Law*, 38, 1944, pp. 183–217).

[11] Ralph Dingman Nurnberger, *James Brown Scott: Peace Through Justice*, unpublished PhD dissertation, Georgetown University, 1975.

[12] See especially Juan Pablo Scarfi, *The Hidden History of International Law in the Americas: Empire and Legal Networks*, Oxford: Oxford University Press, 2017 and Juan Pablo Scarfi, *El imperio de la ley. James Brown Scott y la costrucción de un orden jurídico interamericano*, Buenos Aires: Fondo de Cultura Económica de Argentina, 2014.

[13] See especially Scarfi, *El imperio de la ley*, pp. 181–208 and Juan Pablo Scarfi, "Reconfiguraciones del saber jurídico. James Brown Scott reflota la obra de Vitoria desde Estados Unidos en años de entreguerras," in Ricardo D. Salvatore (ed.), *Los Lugares del Saber*, Rosario: Beatriz Viterbo Editora, 2007, pp. 269–93.

[14] Benjamin Coates, *Transatlantic Advocates: American International Law and U.S. Foreign Relations, 1898–1919*, unpublished PhD dissertation, Columbia University, 2010.

[15] Coates later published a book on the topic, giving Scott a smaller role than in his dissertation (Benjamin Coates, *Legalist Empire*, Oxford: Oxford University Press, 2016). Carl Landauer treats the same theme by analyzing the first issue of the *American Journal of International Law*: "The Ambivalences of Power: Launching the American Journal of International Law in an Era of Empire and Globalization," *Leiden Journal of International Law*, 20, 2007, pp. 325–58.

in the profession more as a noble father than a scholar at the cutting edge, turned more decidedly to history and developed his theory on the Spanish and Catholic origins of international law.

That later phase of Scott's career is the object of Christopher Rossi's *Broken Chain of Being*.[16] Yet, Rossi's book focuses on Scott's (mis)understanding of medieval and early modern ideas of law. Rossi looks at Scott's theory of the Spaniards as a political project to be situated within a specific timeframe merely to support the larger point of his book:[17] Scott was on a crusade to bring international law back to its moral foundations. While I share this conclusion, I find Rossi's narrative incomplete: his primarily philosophical outlook leads him to discount or misinterpret Scott's more immediate political projects like the promotion of international adjudication.

As I noted above, international critical legal scholarship by now assumes[18] that Scott's modern recasting of the work of the Spanish theologians allowed him to justify in universalistic terms the turn to imperialism of the United States following the Spanish-American War. In this sense, his historical reading has been a powerful ideological pillar of the liberal understanding of international law that has characterized the American century. Still, to my knowledge, no attempt has yet been made to produce a study dedicated to Scott's political uses of his international legal canon in context and in a deeper relation with the ideology of American exceptionalism. This book aims to be that study.

## 3. Scott's Spanish Origin, Equality, and the Canon of International Legal History

There is one large question I ask the past: could it be all so simple that Scott's redeployment of Vitoria was either a genuine humanitarian move or an imperialist, oppressive one? In other words, are there only two opposite ways to understand the humanitarian sensibility of liberal internationalism, selflessness on one side and rhetorical cloaking of power games on the other? In this book I strive to keep together both perspectives. On one hand, I argue extensively to prove the connection of Scott's theory of the Spanish origin with the rise of the United States as a global power and the resulting imperialist policies and practices. This includes pointing out flaws and inconsistencies in Scott's actions and thinking, evidence of a gap between his universalist, egalitarian aspirations and his nationalist and elitist prejudgments.

[16] Christopher Rossi, *Broken Chain of Being: James Brown Scott and the Origins of Modern International Law*, The Hague: Kluwer Law International, 1998.

[17] See ibid., pp. 21ff.

[18] Once again, the best example is Orford, "The Past as Law or History?," pp. 11–17.

On the other hand, I elaborate on my conviction that Scott could not be dismissed merely as a cynical apologist of power. His deep religious faith provided the foundations for his international legal scholarship. Putting aside for a moment any judgment on Scott's project and the policies he supported, he deserves recognition for his authenticity. After years of studying his work and life, I am convinced that his belief in international law as a force for good, determining the moral and social progress of mankind, was sincere.

I consider this last aspect particularly relevant. Taking Scott's moral stance in earnest allows a series of productive moves. At the outset, it aligns with a sociology of the international legal profession as a practice necessarily sustained by both cynicism and commitment, pragmatism and idealism.[19] This intellectual attitude allows us to evaluate and understand the success among international lawyers of the narrative of the Spanish origin from a more comprehensive perspective, more apt to capture its ambivalent legacy. This book provides a comprehensive description of Scott's project that serves the purpose of highlighting its shortcomings and contradictions without discarding its strengths and achievements. The relevance of this analysis for contemporary international law lies in the continuing significance of the liberal language of rights, free trade, and equality that Scott promoted through Vitoria.

Acknowledging Vitoria's contemporary relevance as the accomplishment of Scott's historical project also opens the avenue for a less direct but equally important critical perspective. Scott's narrative offers reasons for opposition, but also provides lessons to learn. Accepting his good faith allows us to take him as a useful model for renewal in international law, even while disagreeing with his politics and recognizing the flaws of his history writing. Indeed, the proof that Scott was a successful innovator is that, even though he was almost forgotten until recently, we have been accepting his version of the historical canon of international law. Without Scott, Anghie and many other international lawyers would not have given such a pivotal role to Vitoria in their historical work. Scott's narrative, though unpersuasive in historiographical terms, has endured. It still constrains the canon of authors associated with the development of international law and with it the self-understanding of the discipline. So, if the goal is to replace or, at least, demystify Scott's history and its political implications, it is important to think of the Spanish origin not just as the paradigm we need to move beyond. It is also the narrative that has performed that same transformative operation before and replaced a previous dominant paradigm. Indeed, before Scott's intervention, Hugo Grotius was given the title of founder of international law. His work

[19] See Martti Koskenniemi, "Between Commitment and Cynicism: Outline for a Theory of International Law as Practice," in *Collection of Essays by Legal Advisers of States, Legal Advisers of International Organizations and Practitioners in the Field of International Law*, New York: United Nations, 1999, pp. 495–523.

addressed the horror of the religious wars in Europe in the seventeenth century, ended by the peace of Westphalia and the rise of the nation-state. This perspective fit the Victorian understanding of international law as a tool regulating the external relations of European powers. By giving the title to Vitoria, Scott linked the inception of modern international law to the discovery of the American continent and the recognition of individual universal human rights. In the search of a newer transformative historical narrative of the discipline, moving away from Scott, learning what made him successful would allow to turn his skill against him. One key lesson that Scott's story teaches is that for an historical narrative to have a political impact it needs to be spread outside academia and employed in the service of practical immediate goals. Current international law projects on the left and within the eclectic label of critical legal studies[20] seem to have lost that kind of political ambition.[21]

What concrete political projects could be served by assessing critically Scott's international legal history and move beyond his account? I can think primarily of two. The first revolves around the concept of equality. If we have returned to pay attention to equality in global politics in recent years it is because of the increasing lack of it, especially in economic terms.[22] The recognition of this trend on a global scale runs against progressive narratives of modernity, predicting that globalization and the rise of international institutions could only lead to more equality, overall justice, and individual rights. Scott's was one such account: as I explain in detail in the *corpus* of the book, equality was a key concept in his theory of international law already before he started working on Vitoria and turned the Dominican into equality's prophet. Scott adopted equality as the distinctive principle of American political and legal culture, juxtaposing its progressiveness to the hierarchical societal arrangements of Europe. Yet, beneath the surface, Scott's understanding of equality proved to be based on an elitist and exclusionary logic. If the concept of equality is to return to a prominent place in sustaining transformative political

[20] According to Samuel Moyn, the problem with critical legal studies today is not only strategic but also theoretical. His diagnosis points to the lack of a common agenda shared by critical legal scholars, which, in turn, determined "the amorphous shape . . . of contemporary legal thought." (Samuel Moyn, "Legal Theory Among the Ruins," ssrn.com/abstract=2817067 (2016), p. 23, later published in Justin Desautels-Stein and Christopher Tomlins (eds.), *Searching for Contemporary Legal Thought*, Cambridge: Cambridge University Press, 2017.)

[21] "[W]here a generation and a half ago, most of the practical momentum in the international law leftwing projects came in the fields of international diplomacy and political activism, a vast majority of all leftwing efforts in international law today are limited to the field of academia." (Akbar Rasulov, "Bringing Class Back into International Law—A Response to Professor Chimni," ssrn.com/abstract=1675447 (2008), p. 6, later published in *Finnish Yearbook of International Law*, 19, 2008, pp. 243–94).

[22] For a review of recent studies addressing global inequality from an international legal perspective see Jochen von Bernstorff, "International Law and Global Justice: On Recent Inquiries into the Dark Side of Economic Globalization," *European Journal of International Law*, 26, 2015, pp. 279–93. For a historical account of the complex relation of equality and human rights see Samuel Moyn, *Not Enough. Human Rights in an Unequal World*, Cambridge: Belknap Press, 2018.

projects in international law, studying Scott can provide a series of warnings about its pitfalls and ambivalences.

The second project that can be helped by a better understanding of Scott's historical work in context is a rethinking of the canon of international legal history. The idea of canon has not been explored within the discipline and represents a valuable future research direction. The beginning of a conversation on canon could contribute to confront the Eurocentric nature of international law and its history. Indeed, canons of intellectual contribution are not fixed.[23] They derive from contingent decisions and projects, like Scott's. They can be questioned and problematized. On one hand, having a canon of seminal texts is an invaluable resource for an academic discipline. It helps to create a common tradition of intellectual exchange. Without it, it would be difficult to develop the shared sensibility necessary to have meaningful discussions around common themes. On the other hand, a canon can be a limit to renewal and originality. Restricting the analysis of intellectual traditions to a few important books or authors, understood in dialogue with each other, is problematic.[24] It may lead us to overlook the complexity of the intellectual and social milieu in which the canonical texts were produced. It also risks condemning texts and authors that are left outside as irrelevant on the basis of judgments made by early canon-setting authorities like James Brown Scott.

By perpetuating established canons without sustained self-reflection, international legal history risks failing to unlock its full transformative potential. A cursory focus on canonical names, even if just aimed at disproving or qualifying their contribution, could limit the space for renewal of the discipline. In particular, sticking with the canon, made almost invariably of Western white men, helps only in a limited way to deal with the key issue of Eurocentrism. "European stories, myths and metaphors continue to set the conditions for understanding international law's past as it does for outlining its futures."[25] Because of the attractive power of the canon, even historical projects with the explicit purpose of going beyond Eurocentrism often achieve their goal only in a limited fashion.[26] Going beyond the canon or attempting to widen its scope are difficult choices for at least a couple of reasons. Non-canonical work risks being considered irrelevant simply because it deals with an unconventional topic, especially if authored by a junior scholar. Moreover, the very fact that a topic is unconventional makes it more

[23] For a genealogical account of the idea of canon and a reconstruction of the debates it sparked in modern literature see Jan Gorak, *The Making of the Modern Canon: Genesis and Crisis of a Literary Idea*, London: Athlone, 1991.

[24] For a seminal explanation of this point in historiography, see especially Quentin Skinner, "Meaning and Understanding," *History and Theory*, 8, 1969, p. 3 and pp. 22–4.

[25] Martti Koskenniemi, "Histories of International Law. Dealing with Eurocentrism," *Rechtsgeschichte*, 19, 2011, p. 155.

[26] For instance, Rose Parfitt (see "The Spectre of Sources," *European Journal of International Law*, 25, 2014, pp. 297–306) has underlined this difficulty in relation to the *Oxford Handbook of the History of International Law* (edited by Anne Peters and Bardo Fassbender, Oxford: Oxford University Press, 2012).

difficult to acquire the needed expertise and sources to examine it. Going back to the complexity of Scott's historical project would help shed light on these issues in relation to the historical undertakings of today. It would do so by demystifying a canon that is difficult to put under serious challenge even while purposefully searching for new directions. I see the irony in my suggestion: one way to go beyond Vitoria and problematize his position in the historical canon of international law is a further focus on Vitoria, on how he entered the canon in the first place. But I do believe this is the proverbial step back one sometimes has to take in order to go forward. On one hand, I posit that we need to better understand how the canon is formed and reinvented, the nature and meaning of the powerful grip figures like Vitoria or Hugo Grotius have on our discipline's discourse. On the other hand, I aim to suggest, especially to early stage researchers, that looking at the past of international law does not necessarily mean looking at an already set list of names. There is exciting work to be made outside the current canon. Such work could, in turn, reshape the canon and determine new directions for international law, in the same way Scott's project did.

## 4. Descriptive Writing and Language Choices

As I have explained above, drawing from Orford, Scott's work on Vitoria can be understood as a justification and rationalization of a set of international legal practices and doctrines he supported. In another piece, Orford has developed a "praise of description . . . as a method for writing about law." Description, Orford argues, is particularly suited to track the emergence of normative discourses turning "practices into a coherent theoretical account."[27] She draws from the work of Michel Foucault in seeing description as the technique "to mak[e] visible those things that are already visible." The way we normally conceive the world and the societal structures around us is so embedded in our consciousness that achieving any larger awareness of it requires an investigative effort. "For Foucault, this involved first trying to analyse precisely the internal economy of a discourse and the systematic relations between the elements of that discourse." In other words, the complexity of social phenomena and the logic behind them obliges us to undertake an extensive mapping of their structure before there could be any sort of transformative explanation. "[O]nly by understanding the relations that existed within a language or a society . . . it [i]s possible to understand all the modifications that had to take place in order for one of the elements to change. This kind of descriptive work [i]s a necessary condition of theory."[28]

[27] Anne Orford, "In Praise of Description," *Leiden Journal of International Law*, 25, 2012, pp. 609 and 617.

[28] Ibid., pp. 617–18.

To be sure, this book is neither devoid of comment nor of the intention to possibly serve a larger transformative purpose, as I clarified in the previous section. But the nature of the task of providing a comprehensive account of Scott's historical project and its implications demand the employment of a primarily descriptive mode of writing. The social and political significance of marking Vitoria as the founder of international law requires the assemblage of an archive of knowledge encompassing the thought and action of international lawyers, religious leaders, feminists, activists, and government officials, active in the United States and globally, over the course of half a century. Laying out a description of the Spanish origin theory and its relations to other elements of political and social discourse contemporary with it is the main contribution of my research.

The adoption of such an intended descriptive mode of writing dictates certain linguistic choices. The language I employ has to align with the discourse I recount. I do not only resort often to direct quotes of my subjects but I also adopt their expressions and turns of phrase in my description. I should clarify that this, of course, does not mean that I share the implications of certain usages commonly employed by Scott and other characters in my story. I provide here two examples of such usages to elucidate this point: the use of "America" or "American" to refer to the United States and the expression "discovery of America" to define Columbus' expeditions and Spanish activities on the continent in the following decades.

With regard to the first, the usage of "America" as a substitute for United States or "American" to refer primarily to the culture or agency of US nationals or society, rather than in relation to the entire American continent, is as common today as it was in the early twentieth-century debates I describe in the book. I am careful to use "United States" in my own wording when referring, for instance, to the US government or national institutions while my subjects could have employed "American." I align to their use of "America" for United States when the ambivalence had a discursive value and was not a simple substitution. For instance, Scott and the other founders of the American Society of the International Law often used "American" as juxtaposed to "European" to underline the more modern and progressive nature of the values and the law put forward by the New World. However, that use of the word and the positive value associated would often collapse into referring to their own country, as reflected in their naming of the Society and its *American Journal of International Law*. When mentioning democracy and freedom as continental achievements, Scott would invariably go on and present, almost exclusively, US historical examples as corroboration.

Also the second example of expression I employ without sharing its implications, "discovery of America," is still in common use today. It could neutrally refer to the factual event of Columbus' expedition and the consequent knowledge the Europeans acquired of the existence of the American continent. But the word "discovery" has obvious implications in relation to America that should be highlighted. First of all, the verb "to discover" refers, in at least one of its meanings, to the first attainment of human knowledge of something, a process, a substance, or, in this case, a mass of land. According to Vitoria and Scott, the natives themselves were discovered by the Europeans. In light of these considerations, "discovery" indicates a hierarchical ordering placing the civilized Europeans, who are by that word recognized the agency to first gain knowledge of the American continent, above the natives who are blended with the land into objects of discovery. The constant association of the "discovery of America" and the humanitarian stance of Vitoria recognizing property rights on their lands to natives then signals, already on the surface, a contradiction in Scott's narrative of the foundation of modern international law. Its declared universal egalitarianism moves within a colonial logic. Secondly, beyond its general meaning, discovery was also an established legal concept of which Scott was well aware.[29] In legal terms, discovery was a title to territory traditionally opposed to conquest. Adopting the expression "discovery of America" to events later than the initial encounter with Columbus, as Scott did, implies the denial that the *conquistadores* were in fact, according to the meaning of the word itself, conquerors.

## 5. Structure and Outline of Chapters

The book begins with a short prologue, outlining James Brown Scott's life and education up to 1896, when he was thirty years old. That was the year during which Scott recited his first preserved public speech on international law in Los Angeles. The prologue ends with an analysis of the speech, which already contained many themes that Scott would rehearse for the rest of his career.

Following the prologue, the body of the book is divided in two parts, each made up of three chapters. The first part provides information on Scott's professional rise, tracking his activities and connections in the phase of his career preceding his work on Vitoria and the Salamanca School. The institutional links and networks described also provide a background for the explanation of the main elements in Scott's thought on international law and politics. In particular, Part I illustrates how both scientific reason and religious faith were fundamental bedrocks of his understanding of human interactions, the key role of adjudication in his theory of law, and the importance of a progressive reading of history to provide law with solid moral foundations.

[29] For a legal discussion of discovery and conquest by Scott see Chapter 3 section 1. To be fair, Scott wrote a single passage clarifying that Vitoria had not relied on discovery as a juridical doctrine (see James Brown Scott, *The Spanish Origin of International Law. Lectures on Francisco de Vitoria (1480–1546) and Francisco Suarez (1548–1617)*, Washington, D.C.: Georgetown University Press, 1928, p. 28). Still, he could not but be aware of the legal ambivalence of associating, on repeated occasions over the span of several years, Vitoria and the "discovery of America."

The first chapter, like all others in the book, is divided into three sections. Section 1 offers an analysis of the US foreign policy discourse at the turn of the century and connects it with the growing popularity of international law within the elites. This led to the foundation of the American Society of International Law in 1906, in which Scott played a crucial role. This event marked the successful end of an early phase in Scott's career: in just a few years he managed, through hard work and confident self-promotion, to position himself as a professional leader and a key foreign policy official. Section 2 follows Scott in his work as Secretary Root's legal advisor at the State Department, until the two moved together to lead the newly established Carnegie Endowment for International Peace. The highlight of Scott's government stint was the 1907 Second Hague Peace Conference, where he championed the project for an international court and made a large number of the transatlantic professional connections that would be crucial to his later projects. Section 3 describes how Scott, since 1910 a powerful administrator at the Carnegie Endowment for International Peace, deployed the massive resources at his disposal. Navigating through the turbulent 1910s, Scott built institutional structures in support of his main intellectual projects, international adjudication and Pan-Americanism, but lost the fight against the supporters of collective security.

The second chapter[30] illustrates the function of faith in James Brown Scott's theory of international law through an account of his understanding of the role of the United States in American continental relations. Section 1 introduces James Brown Scott's 1917 speech on the Platt Amendment around which the chapter is built. Starting from here, it traces the connection between the rise of international law and US–Cuba relations at the turn of the century. Section 2 describes the rise of humanitarianism in the United States in the late nineteenth century and its religious inspiration. This development would provide the ideological foundations for the narrative of the selfless empire that supported the 1898 US intervention in Cuba. Section 3 begins with a textual analysis of Scott's speech and connects it with the narrative of 1898. It continues by illustrating the ambivalent relationship of the narrative with concrete US policies toward Cuba and Latin America in the early twentieth century. I conclude the section by describing the collaboration of Scott with the leading Cuban international lawyers through the 1920s, in order to show how messianism acted for him as a thread of reconciliation of hegemonic attitudes and the principle of the equality of nations.

The third chapter[31] revolves around the series of books on US constitutional history Scott published at the closing of the Great War. Therein, he fleshed out his

[30] A shorter version of the second chapter was published as Paolo Amorosa, "Messianic Visions of the United States: International Law, Religion, and the Cuban Intervention, 1898–1917," in Martti Koskenniemi, Mónica Garcia-Salmones Rovira, and Paolo Amorosa (eds.), *International Law and Religion: Historical and Contemporary Perspectives*, Oxford: Oxford University Press, 2017, pp. 433–53.

[31] An earlier, shorter version of Chapter 3 has appeared as Paolo Amorosa, "James Brown Scott's International Adjudication between Tradition and Progress in the United States," *Journal of the History of International Law*, 17, 2015, pp. 15–46.

case for the creation of an international court as the best tool toward the achievement of a long-lasting global peace. The first section describes Scott's Armistice books and their background, explaining the foundations and development of the rationalist legal theory of adjudication that inspired them. The second section goes deeper into the content of the most significant of the books, *The United States: A Study in International Organization*, in order to contextualize it and relate it to the political debates in which it intervened. The third and closing section is centered on Scott's role in the debate over the League of Nations Covenant and collective security in the United States. I argue that that phase in Scott's career set the stage, in more than one way, for his work on Vitoria and the Salamanca School later in the interwar years. On one hand, the Armistice books represented a major research work on the historical foundations of international law built to influence current topical debates, a scheme he replicated with his various publications on the Catholic and Spanish origins of the discipline. On the other, the defeat of his positions in the postwar international organization debate at the end of the First World War signaled also his loss of influence in the scholarly legal discussions in the United States over contemporary hot-button issues. This circumstance led him to focus even more decisively on the past articulations of international law in his research work.

The second part includes Chapters 4 to 6. It provides a genealogical account of Scott's project on the Spanish origin of international law, exploring further its background, delineating the development of its elements, and describing in detail the main political purposes it served. It follows primarily the concluding phase of Scott's career, coinciding roughly with the interwar years, as he retired in 1940. Scott produced the earliest extended case for the Spanish origin in the form of lecture outlines for a course he held at Georgetown University in 1926. Since then, establishing Vitoria as the founder of modern international law became the main concern of his professional life.

The fourth chapter begins by tracking Scott's initial interest in the School of Salamanca, sparked by the work of Belgian international lawyer Ernest Nys. It proceeds to detail the conditions that led to the inception of the campaign for the Salamancan origin and describing its early phase.

The first section of the chapter describes the origin and planning of the series, Classics of International Law, edited by Scott, which occasioned his collaboration with Nys for the publication of Vitoria's lectures, in the original Latin and, for the first time, in English translation. In the closing part of the section, I have provided a brief outline of the historical significance of Vitoria, Francisco Suárez, and other authors usually associated with the Salamanca School, which offers a basic sense of the appeal they held for Scott. Indeed, before he claimed them they had been connected only sporadically with the tradition of international law. Nonetheless, they had been recognized intellectual authorities, in their lifetime and since, on an array of issues and disciplines ranging from theology to economics.

Section 2 tracks the most immediate conditions of possibility leading to Scott's earliest formulation of the Spanish origin. It details the reasons for the loss of academic relevance Scott suffered within the American Society of International Law (ASIL) in the early 1920s, at the same time as his star was rising further up in Europe, thanks to the ambitious projects he bankrolled there through the Carnegie Endowment for International Peace (CEIP) resources. Among these projects was the foundation of the Hague Academy of International Law. Collaboration for the establishment of the Academy brought Scott close to the Dutch international legal community, whose members, in 1925, took the lead in celebrating the 300th anniversary of the publication of the main work by their countryman Hugo Grotius, *De jure belli ac pacis*. Dutch international lawyers organized a follow-up visit to Spain, as recognition of the contribution of Francisco de Vitoria and Francisco Suárez to the discipline. These events led to a renewed interested in the history of international law, which Scott seized upon. In the 1926 Georgetown course, he explained in detail why Vitoria was the founder of modern international law and the work of the Salamanca theologians was crucial for global politics in his day.

Section 3 describes how Scott turned his theory of the Salamancan origin into a campaign, first by enlisting allies such as Camilo Barcia Trelles and José de Yanguas Messia among Spanish international lawyers and later by spreading his ideas within his network in Latin America. The chapter ends with an account of the publication and content of Scott's first book on the topic, titled, indeed, *The Spanish Origin of International Law*, which appeared in 1928.

The fifth chapter tracks Scott's fascination with Catholicism and his attempts to persuade the Vatican to endorse the brand of international law he championed as conducive to global peace. In the first section, I provide an account of why the Presbyterian Scott believed, since the beginning of his career, that the Pope and the Holy See could play a crucial role in sustaining the moral foundations of global politics. After explaining why this position was eccentric in the United States of the time, where Catholics were a minority considered undemocratic and disloyal to national institutions by the Protestant establishment, I move to detail Scott's early approaches to the Curia, marred by the outbreak of the First World War. Section 2 describes how, in the postwar years, Scott was influenced by a neo-Scholastic movement internal to US Catholicism, tracing modern democracy back to Thomist theology. Scott used these lessons to develop further his argument and enlarge the coalition promoting Vitoria as the founder of international law. In the United States, he enlisted scholars at Catholic universities, including his colleagues at Georgetown. To spread the idea further among international lawyers, he founded the Vitoria-Suárez Association, which found success especially—but not exclusively—with his Catholic colleagues. At the same time, through the late 1920s and 1930s, Scott's CEIP colleagues were preparing the ground for new proposals to the Holy See, by planning and funding an ambitious project of modernization of the Vatican library. Section 3 tells of Scott's last and best-prepared approach to the Holy See in favor of international law in the mid-1930s, once again marred by the deteriorating international situation, eventually leading to the Second World War. Scott formulated his argument for the Pope in the 1934 book *The Catholic Conception of International Law*, where he designed a narrative connecting Vitoria and Suárez to the fundamental theories of the discipline in the twentieth century. The implication was clear. The Church of Rome should not only have supported international law but also own it: after all it was the outgrowth of the Catholic theological tradition.

Chapter 6[32] tracks the story of an unlikely alliance between Scott and leading feminist activists Doris Stevens and Alice Paul. The first section provides a short history of the women's right movement in the United States and details how Paul and Stevens rose to become key figures for the achievement of women's suffrage in 1920. Section 2 begins by tracking the early interest by feminist activists in international politics. Eventually, in the mid-1920s, the National Woman's Party (NWP) too, which counted Paul and Stevens among its leaders, would decide to promote through international institutions its equal rights brand of feminism. As the NWP moved toward internationalism, Scott moved close to the positions of women's rights activists by becoming a supporter of the equality of sexes under nationality law. Section 3 follows the collaboration between Scott and the NWP leaders. Beginning in 1928, the collaboration would peak in 1933 with the approval at the Montevideo Pan-American Conference of what Scott called the Stevens treaties: one prescribing equality of rights between men and women in general was signed by four countries, the other, committing the parties to equal nationality laws, was unanimously accepted by the American republics. Scott connected the treaties with the egalitarian doctrines of Vitoria and Suárez, instructing Stevens on their crucial relevance for the inception of modern international law. In return, Stevens introduced him to the painter that would immortalize the bond between Scott and the Dominican theologian. Still visible today, a mural on the walls of the US Justice Department in Washington, D.C. depicts Vitoria; his features are modeled on James Brown Scott's appearance.

In the concluding remarks, I put forward a series of reflections on Scott's legacy and the significance of his work to articulate a responsible approach to the history of international law today.

[32] Parts of the chapter appear in Paolo Amorosa, "Pioneering International Women's Rights? The US National Woman's Party and the 1933 Montevideo Equal Rights Treaties," *European Journal of International Law*, 30, 2019, pp. 415–437.

# Prologue. The Education of James Brown Scott, 1866–1896

In 1876, a ten-year-old boy moved back to Philadelphia with his family. 1876 was not any year to return to the city: the eyes of the entire nation looked toward Philadelphia. The United States Declaration of Independence had been signed there one hundred years earlier. In 1870, Philadelphia's City Council had decided to celebrate the event with an international exposition, the first with global ambitions in the United States. The next year the United States Congress would endorse the project and pass a bill establishing an organizing commission. The Centennial International Exhibition[1] would open on 10 March 1876, with President Ulysses Grant attending, and closed six months later. It was, on most counts, a stunning success. Philadelphia, with a population of c. 800,000, was, at the time, the second largest city in the United States; yet it had to dramatically improve its infrastructure to manage and accommodate the almost ten million people that would visit the fair. The fairgrounds covered 285 acres. Thirty thousand firms from thirty-seven nations showcased in the over 250 individual pavilions.

The exhibition would leave an impression on the young James. The proud combination of patriotism and technological advancement that characterized the event would resonate in James' future work as an international lawyer.

The independence theme permeated the event material. The publications of the organizing commission featured famous depictions of the signing of the Declaration. Exhibitors branded their advertisements with images of American heroes and symbols such as the Founding Fathers, Abraham Lincoln, and the Star-Spangled Banner. Even many of the "curiosities" displayed stuck to the patriotic theme. They included a full-sized Liberty Bell made of soap and a Centennial medallion carved in butter.

Among the inventions first displayed were revolutionary devices such as Bell's telephone and the first Remington typewriter. The technological advancement boasted in Philadelphia spoke of a country at the cutting edge, ready to fully exploit its enormous natural resources.

[1] For factual information on the exhibition I rely primarily on Linda P. Gross and Theresa R. Snyder, *Philadelphia's 1876 Centennial Exhibition*, Charleston: Arcadia Publishing, 2005.

*Rewriting the History of the Law of Nations: How James Brown Scott Made Francisco de Vitoria the Founder of International Law*. Paolo Amorosa, Oxford University Press (2019). © Paolo Amorosa
DOI: 10.1093/oso/9780198849377.001.0001

The exhibition was a celebration of the resilience of the American project and the overcoming of the trials with which Providence had tested it. The Civil War had ended only a decade earlier, the consequences of the financial panic of 1873 were still being felt, yet the country was ready to take its place "among the powers of the earth," as the Declaration of Independence recited. The excited mood in the country found expression also in the religious revivals of those years. The United States had found self-confidence again: it embodied progress and showed the world it was on the right side of history.

But the events surrounding the fair also pointed to the steps yet to be made. For instance, the Centennial was a testing ground for women's rights claims, a cause that would be close to Scott's heart. The Women's Centennial Committee, led by Elizabeth Duane Gillespie (1821–1901), the great-granddaughter of Benjamin Franklin, was very successful in raising funds for the exhibition early on. However, many of their attempts to participate were frustrated. All works by women were banned from the Memorial Hall Art Exhibit. Women were also prevented from exhibiting in the Main Exhibition Building. This led to the decision to have an independent Women's Pavilion, the first of its kind at an international exposition. It showcased exclusively products of women's work, at Gillespie's insistence. They ranged from needlework and corsets to cutting-edge inventions such as emergency flares and model interlocking bricks.

Gillespie maintained a moderate position making sure that the Women's Committee did not touch on the sensitive issue of suffrage. However, it was the fair organizers who put their finger on the sore spot. Women's Day at the exhibition was celebrated on 7 November, Election Day. The reasoning for this was that men heading for the polls would not mind about missing the event. Still, the nation was changing, healing in a certain sense. The presidential elections returned another Republican former Civil War General, Rutherford B. Hayes. But the elections were highly contested, with Democrat Samuel J. Tilden winning the popular vote. This led to the so-called Compromise of 1877. In exchange for not challenging further Hayes' election, Democrats obtained the removal from the South of the federal troops that had been stationed there since the Civil War ended. One could see the Compromise as the beginning of the Jim Crow laws of racial segregation and a betrayal of Black Southerners. Most, though, partaking of the widespread optimism, decided that it was a key instance of national reconciliation. Scott himself would see it this way. The Civil War was only a bump on the road to progress.[2] The United States looked toward a bright future.

[2] See, for instance, James Brown Scott to Charles Francis Adams, February 28, 1914, in George A. Finch, edited by William E. Butler, *Adventures in Internationalism. A Biography of James Brown Scott*, Clark: Lawbook Exchange, 2012, p. 219.

## 1. Jimmy the Book Snatcher

John Scott and Jeannette Brown's youngest child was born in Kincardine, Ontario, Canada, on 3 June 1866. James' parents, both Scottish immigrants, had met in a New York church and married in 1853.

John Scott moved his family around often in those years, following chances of economic improvement. He was a stonecutter by trade, but also engaged in investments and worked his own land. James was born during one of the periods when John took care of his property near Kincardine. John and Jeannette had first moved to Canada shortly after the birth of their first child Mary to join John's sister Isabella who emigrated there.

John Scott was a devout Presbyterian and had several clergymen in his family tree. He made sure that religious education and the cultivation of piety were important aspects of the rearing of his children. Bible reading and time dedicated to praying were daily features of the Scott household's routine.

Between the births of Mary and James, John and Jeannette had three more children, Margaret, John, and Jeannette. John jr. died aged fifteen just before the family finally settled in Philadelphia in the year of the Centennial. John sr. also died there eight years later, in 1884, leaving James, then about to graduate from Philadelphia's Central High School, the only man in the household. James had always been very close to his mother and sisters and would continue to be for as long as they lived. Notwithstanding the volatility of his fortune, John Scott had managed to leave a substantial sum to guarantee his children's education. Jeannette sr. dedicated herself to that goal, for instance by joining their travels to pursue further studies in Europe. None of the Scott sisters married and all pursued very successful careers.

James' favorite sister was Jeannette, who was only two years older than him. "Scott always credited his sister with instilling in him a love for the classics and poetry."[3] She often read to him. Jeannette was the only one of the Scott children to follow professionally the artistic inclinations in the family. John sr. had been studying art and drew sketches but hid them from the family and discouraged his children from pursuing artistic careers. He was disappointed when Margaret enrolled in the Philadelphia School of Design, a path she later abandoned because of health issues that compromised her sight. Jeannette started her career only after her father's death.

The love of literature Jeannette instilled in James was manifested early on in the boy's passion for reading and books. Young James was a regular visitor to public libraries and spent most of his free time reading. He had the habit of checking bookshelves at friends' homes and wandering away absentmindedly with books he had started reading. He often did that in libraries before the staff could charge the loan,

[3] Ralph Dingman Nurnberger, *James Brown Scott: Peace Through Justice*, unpublished PhD dissertation, Georgetown University, 1975, p. 14.

also later in life. This earned him the nickname, molded on his initials, of Jimmy the Book Snatcher.[4] A distinctive sign for which Scott was remembered in later years was his carrying around a green bag overflowing with books.

Between 1881 and 1885, James studied at Philadelphia's public Central High School, where he excelled in science and the classics especially. In a sense, this prefigured the main tenets of his future scholarship. Scott believed in the importance of founding international law on rational and scientific principles while looking at past wisdom to keep infusing its content with morality. Following a desire of his late father, James decided to continue his education at Harvard. It would be there that he would meet international law for the first time.

## 2. "To Freeman Snow who first taught me to love International Law and, in doing so, to love him."[5]

James Brown Scott never attended law school. He practiced law very briefly at the end of the 1890s. Yet, being a lawyer defined his personal and professional identity. Even the green book bag he carried around was the traditional mark of the Anglo-Saxon lawyer.[6]

His first meeting with his life passion, international law, happened at Harvard College. At the time, international law was not taught in law schools, as it was not considered real, positive law, lacking a central authority that would enforce it,[7] a position Scott would fight against later in his career.

The international law instructor at Harvard was Freeman Snow (1841–94), a Civil War veteran and former pupil of the famous historian and intellectual Henry Adams (1838–1918). Scott and Snow developed a strong relationship. Scott would later remark to one of his closest students that Snow's "classes, his humanity and teaching ability in constitutional and international law made a deep impression upon"[8] him. Snow affectionately called Scott "man of the iron

[4] See ibid., p. 21.

[5] Dedication for the second edition of Scott's international law casebook (*Cases on International Law Principally Selected from Decisions of English and American Courts*, St. Paul: West Publishing, 1922). Both Nurnberger (*James Brown Scott*, p. 23) and Lewis Cochran Cassidy ("James Brown Scott: a Citizen of the World," *New York University Law Quarterly Review*, 9, 1931–32, p. 50) incorrectly claim the sentence to be the dedication of the 1902 first edition of Scott's casebook (*Cases on International Law Selected from Decisions of English and American Courts with Syllabus and Annotations*, Boston: Boston Book Company). Actually, both the 1902 edition and its 1906 reprint by West Publishing are dedicated to Andrew Sloan Draper, President of the University of Illinois.

[6] See Donald R. Richberg, "The Rise and Fall of the Green Bag," *Green Bag*, 18, 1906, pp. 465–7.

[7] In 1885, the same year Scott enrolled at Harvard, the Australian jurist Pitt Cobbett started the preface to his international law casebook by remarking: "There is a tendency on the part of English lawyers to regard that body of custom and convention which is known as International Law, as fanciful and unreal; as a collection of amiable opinions, rather than as a body of legal rules." (*Leading Cases and Opinions on International Law*, London: Stevens and Haynes, 1885, p. v) That sentiment was widely shared also within the American legal community.

[8] Lewis Cassidy to George Finch, July 8, 1948, quoted in Nurnberger, *James Brown Scott*, pp. 22–23.

memory."[9] Snow taught international law employing the case method that is still today associated with Harvard Law School and its dean Christopher Columbus Langdell (1826–1906). Teaching international law through cases implied a clear stance: international law was a technical and scientific discipline as much as the municipal legal subjects imparted in law schools. This stance would become one of the cornerstones of Scott's career.

Scott graduated from Harvard College in 1890 and spent a further year in Massachusetts obtaining a Master's Degree from the Graduate School. Having been awarded a Parker scholarship, Scott had the chance to make the first of the transatlantic trips that would become a constant feature of his life. Scott moved to Europe, where his mother and sisters had been living since around the time of his enrolment at Harvard. The Scott women had been based primarily in Munich but traveled around the continent to pursue education and training opportunities. For instance, in addition to studying in Munich, Mary, the eldest, a medical doctor, also studied in Berlin, Vienna, and Paris, where she was one of the first women to be admitted to the Pasteur Institute. Back in the United States, Mary would practice medicine focusing on children's diseases. Margaret, after being forced by her eye condition to abandon art, would study French and German, for the most part in Munich, living there with Jeannette sr. She would go on to graduate from the Sorbonne and become a professor of Romance languages, concluding her career at Syracuse University. Jeannette would conclude her working life as head of the Department of Painting at the same university. She also became a talented and well-respected artist, following her studies in Paris between 1889 and 1895.

James was based in Heidelberg, where he pursued a doctorate, but studied in Berlin and Paris as well. He traveled often to meet family members and also for health reasons. Indeed, while in Heidelberg, he developed lung issues that forced him to spend winters in warmer climates. He took this opportunity to make extended visits to North Africa, the Middle East, current-day Turkey, and Greece. During one of these tours, in 1893, Scott met Nicholas Murray Butler (1862–1947), future President of Columbia University, under curious circumstances. The two were in Egypt, on a ship sailing from Alexandria to Jaffa. Scott was used to feeling ill on boats, but, in his words, he had "never in [his] life . . . been so hopelessly seasick"[10] as that day. Butler tried to cheer up and help his fellow American in distress. This act of kindness was the start of a long-lasting friendship and productive professional collaboration.

In 1894, Scott concluded his studies at Heidelberg, obtaining the degree of *Doctor Utriusque Iuris*. During his time in Europe, he became fluent in German and French. Later in life he would learn also Spanish, a skill that would serve him

[9] See Finch, *Adventures in Internationalism*, p. 4 and H. U. Brandenstein to James Brown Scott, June 10, 1920, Folder 3, Box 71, James Brown Scott Papers, Booth Family Center for Special Collections, Lauinger Library, Georgetown University, Washington, D.C.

[10] Scott to Nicholas Murray Butler, August 31, 1933, quoted in Nurnberger, *James Brown Scott*, p. 27.

well in his Pan-American enterprises and his academic relations in Spain, primarily based on the promotion of the theologians of the Salamanca School as pioneers of modern international law.

Back in the United States, Scott would decide to move to Los Angeles because of the warmer climate more suitable to his health. There he started practicing law in 1895, but soon his inclination would lead him toward the tasks that would become his life trade. When a group of law clerks decided to come together to improve their knowledge of the theoretical aspects of the law, they asked Scott to be their preceptor. Over time, this study group would transform into the Law Department of the University of Southern California. It was Scott's first teaching job. During the Los Angeles years, Scott also gave his first public speech on international law. In 1896, he addressed the Sunset Club on international arbitration and its historical evolution,[11] a topic he had been interested in at least since his studies in Germany.[12] The speech contains several themes and arguments that would accompany Scott till the end of his career. I dedicate the next section to describing and analyzing the speech as an introduction to Scott's view of international law and, I believe, a useful guide for the remainder of the book.

## 3. "Between ourselves, I have been delivering that address ever since"

Even as a young professional delivering his first speech, Scott was certain about which direction history had taken. He expressed it confidently and unequivocally with the very first sentence of his first speech: "If we seriously consider the course of the world's history we shall at once see" that it was not only anymore "largely a record of battles . . . dominated by the individual will, whim or fancy of a sovereign or ruler." For centuries, "the people merely figure[d] as a spectator" but, according to Scott, by 1896, there had been "a permanent recognition of the claims of the many over the few[.] The ideal of a democracy" was "rapidly approaching."[13] The emergence of the people as a political actor had direct consequences on nations' resorting to war. "When war was the . . . affair of the most privileged classes, and affected them indirectly, if at all, it cannot be wondered at" that "war, with its attendant horrors and bloodshed, was of frequent occurrence. When, however, the

[11] James Brown Scott, "International Arbitration: Address of Mr. James Brown Scott before the Sunset Club, Los Angeles, California, 1897," MS 1207, Harvard Law School Library Special Collections. As Benjamin Coates has noted, while the manuscript is marked 1897, contemporary publications suggest that it was actually delivered in 1896 (see *Legalist Empire*, Oxford: Oxford University Press, 2016, p. 60 and fn. 7, p. 203).

[12] See Scott to Walter Schüking, April 6, 1933, vol. 335, Carnegie Endowment for International Peace Papers, Rare Books and Manuscripts Collections, Butler Library, Columbia University, New York City (CEIP Papers).

[13] The quotes in this section, unless otherwise indicated, are from Scott, "International Arbitration".

declaration of war as well as the conclusion of the peace rests with the classes who bear . . . the burden, it is natural to hope that they may devise some means whereby this acknowledged evil is averted. And the history of the past few decades shows conclusively that we are making substantial progress in this line." International arbitration had been emerging together with popular sovereignty, Scott reasoned.

To further clarify and develop the point, he resorted to social contract theory, which he would espouse also in the decades to come,[14] and then applied it to the international realm. "[L]et us consider man in a state of nature. . . . He is himself a law and his volition is the only guide of action." Yet, the encounter between men eventually required an organized society, either by surrendering to a sovereign monarch as in Hobbes' "classical apology of despotism" or through a democratically ascertained collective will, as Rousseau theorized. Still, these "fanciful" and "partial explanations" for Scott were "helpful" but not enough. To understand the evolution of law and society, one should have looked at it in its gradual unfolding, through its various steps. For example, in the state of nature, vengeance was permissible and killing was "a private matter between the slayer and the slained." But "[w]ith the germs of political organization, the loss of a member affected the public status of the community and the body politic intervened." The vengeance "system was not entirely abolished but restrained[;] hence we read of that called blood-money . . . to be paid for killing a member of the society. A community in which [such] customs prevail has indeed taken the initial step to advance from the rule of nature" but that "can be nothing but a transition." In fact, "[i]t is only with the entire subjection of the individual to the will of society that law and order are conceivable."

For Scott, this reasoning was "equally applicable to nations. . . . A nation existing in isolation, . . . would occupy the same situation as man in the state of nature. . . . Such was . . . the position of Rome for centuries." With the appearance of other nations, communities started relating with each other and find their way out of the rule of nature. "At such an early period it was possible for two states to settle their differences between themselves" without "unduly endangering . . . neutrals." Scott then quickly moved from "the origin of the diplomatic code in the Middle Ages" and the successive development of nationalities to the modern age. "The past hundred years has done more to bring distant countries into the family of nations than all previous ones." The shortening in time needed for travel and the speed of global circulation of news had fostered further global interdependence and made it "impossible . . .for our state to remain disinterested and neutral in any conflict of serious dimensions. [I]t is . . . childish to suppose that third parties will not be affected. . . . Nations like individuals cannot therefore stand idly by, and see two countries rush headlong with a struggle which . . . endangers their interests. Sooner or later they are drawn into the conflict and an international conference [in other words a mild

[14] "I am a believer in the social contract theory, which is a fact in America, although it might be a fiction elsewhere" (Scott to Doris Stevens, October 31, 1932, Folder 3, Box 48, JBS Papers.)

form of arbitration] is held to adjust the issues involved and to place the parties on a permanent basis of peace."

Scott continued the speech searching for traces of international organization in the earliest times of Western civilization and once again bringing together the threads of evolution to describe arbitration in modernity. He pointed to the early instances in which the destruction of war had been recognized as irrational and rudimentary mechanisms were devised to limit it. He also considered how the emergence of Christianity brought moral considerations to bear even more on how the effects of conflicts between polities were thought about. Also as a consequence of this trend, over the centuries the universal church came to stand as an authority that could sanction the legitimacy of temporal matters and the resolution of conflicts. "The State was to do the bidding of the Church in contradiction to the power of a single race or nation, mankind began to find themselves drawn into a closer union than they had ever known" under "the Bishop of Rome," "regarded as the messenger of Christ on Earth. [As] Christianity becomes an organized power," it seemed "natural to submit a temporal question to one whose judgment on things unfamiliar was deemed infallible." In Scott's account the Pope was the first proper international arbitrator.

But that first glimpse of international authority and organization provided by the unity of the *respublica christiana* under the Church of Rome disappeared as, with the Reformation, Europe descended into "the throes of a religious war." Paradoxically, Scott continued, it was in the midst of that apocalyptic turmoil that Hugo Grotius' *De Iure Belli ac Pacis* appeared in 1625 and laid the intellectual bases for international law to develop and flourish. "[S]ince the publication of the work diplomacy has become a science; . . . rights of nations in times of peace have been clearly laid down and defined and the rules and regulation of war have been stated, classified and reduced to first principles."

The next great advance in the rationalization and development of international law, in Scott's view, came by the hands of the German-American Francis Lieber in the context of the American Civil War. With his "Instructions for the Government of Armies of the United States in the Field," issued by Abraham Lincoln in 1863 and better known as the Lieber code, "Lieber indeed recognizes the legitimacy of war but seeks to limit hostile acts to the subjects in arms."[15] Scott continued his speech underlining the American contribution to the next phase of codification of international law, namely "the disposition of publicists to pick out those regulations common to all states and" use "them as a basis to draw up a code for the internation [sic] observance." His example for this phase is the 1873 "Outline for an International Code" by David Dudley Field, the lawyer and reformer from New York. The Field Outline and other similar projects at the end of the nineteenth

[15] For a recent in-depth analysis of the Lieber code and the context of its inception and early use see John Fabian Witt, *Lincoln's Code: The Laws of War in American History*, New York: Free Press, 2012.

century had one main thing in common: "they all advise an appeal to reason rather than to the sword" and "cite examples of arbitration[;] they all leave no doubt . . . that the domain of war may be restricted and the legitimate field of arbitration extended." But now, with the new century approaching, it was the time to push on and think even bigger: the projects "of the present day and generation go further and are so far advanced as to think and even dare hope that war maybe done away with altogether. . . . This doctrine," Scott cared to note, had been "championed [by the United States] in its weakness," until it was "respected of nations."

The remainder of the speech proceeds by going through examples of arbitration between the United States and the United Kingdom in order to identify the practical issues yet to face. Moving from the arbitration established by the 1814 Treaty of Ghent, through the resolution of the Alabama claims in 1872 and to the Bering Sea arbitration concluded just four years before that day, Scott pointed to the relations between to the two countries as an example of "good sense" and progressive thought. For instance, the convention concluded to solve the Bering Sea dispute provided for the members of the arbitration board "to be jurists" and "not mere diplomatic agents." This, for Scott, was an important marker of the move toward justice above mere national interest in international relations. The next steps in this move were clear to him: there should be a "permanent . . . tribunal" where "each member of the family of nations should be represented"; permanent should be also the "place of meeting" of the tribunal, "within a neutralized territory [like] Switzerland [or] Belgium" as "they are never liable to invasion and could always afford security."[16]

The build-up toward an effective use of arbitration as a rational and objective tool of international dispute resolution hinged even more decisively on the formulation of the disputed issue and the execution of the decision. The question submitted should be "carefully defined" by the parties so that arbitrators could apply their best legal judgment to it and the reasons and interests at the root of controversy would be clear to public opinion. In terms of applicable rules "judgments or awards should be based on international law and a code like that of D D Field or Bluntschli if adopted should be subject to interpretation like any other code[; i]n this way decisions would be based on precedent and interpretation and new questions would be met by analogy and decided in the light of international development."

The development of an international case law would be crucial also to support the authority of the permanent arbitration body and, therefore, guarantee the execution of its judgments. As the critics of international law argued, indeed, "no positive sanction exists," no mechanism of coercive enforcement for international legal arbitral decisions. But, for Scott, the coercive element would not even be desirable

16 Scott might have noted the involuntary irony in his early assertion when, almost twenty years later, the German violation of Belgian neutrality became one of the issues most debated by international lawyers in the context of the First World War.

in the international system. It would either provide a justification for the use of military force in pursuit of political goals or undermine the arbitration system by underlining the inaction of powers: "suppose that G[rea]t Br[itain] refused to abide by an international decision, would France or Germany forget their differences in a common war to enforce such judgment, . . . against a nation which each is anxious to have as an ally?"

The effectiveness of international arbitration was better protected by the widespread outrage that would be generated by the violation of the just decision of an authoritative body. "Couldn't be much affected by moral sanction? The sturdiest individual cannot be unmindful of the opinions of his neighbors . . . and a nation . . . cannot afford to be unmindful of its international standing [.] If nations . . . do not repudiate their debts it is not because they are scared, to use a popular expression, but it is due rather to that moral sense that impels us to do what is right, or better perhaps, not to do that which is flagrantly wrong, lest the international conscience be awakened."

Scott's conclusion is dedicated to the positive "probable consequences of the establishment of a Permanent Tribunal of Arbitration." The main one, for him, was that the "standing armies of Europe would have to go." His analysis of the issue was very much based on anti-militaristic lines of argumentation popular in the United States at least since the Revolution. In that line of thought, standing armies did not only represent a waste of public resources; their hierarchical structure would instill in large numbers of citizens attitudes and behaviors incompatible with the equality underpinning a democracy: in the mainstream political discourse in the United States militarism was necessarily linked to despotism.

Scott thought that international arbitration could save Europe from the pitfalls of militarism. Once disputes would not be solved through war anymore, "no nation will squander its wealth on rifles, cannons and uniforms." That might result in some industrial unrest in the short term, Scott admitted, because of the "time" required "to transfer labour and capital from one branch of industry" to others. But the advantages in the long run were unmistakable: "hundreds of thousands of men" could switch toward productive "employment [and the] country itself would be directly benefitted by the increased taxation."

With the last paragraph of the Sunset Club speech, Scott seemed to want to reassure his audience that all the positive consequences of cosmopolitanism he had described would not come at the expense of healthy patriotism and defense of the country. He tapped again into the traditional US anti-militaristic rhetoric to glorify the figure of the citizen-soldier; he even seemed to pre-figure his own participation in the Spanish-American War two years later: "it is hardly probable that the wartime rigor and the manly virtues would unduly suffer. The scholar is as good a soldier as the unlettered; an honest tradesman is as brave as a professional soldier which was abundantly proved by the Fr[ench] Rev[olution] and our own Civil

War." The internationalist future was not to be feared as "the home . . . would be as dear to us then as now and enlightened and generous patriotism would meet any sacrifice in order that the home, the family and the country might exist."

In 1937, when he was close to retirement, Scott sent the original text of his 1896 speech for preservation in Harvard law school's library. In the enclosed letter to his younger colleague Manley Ottmer Hudson, he reflected on the truth "of Longfellow's lines, 'The thoughts of youth are long, long thoughts.'" He also made a confession: "Between ourselves, I have been delivering that address ever since."[17] To someone accustomed to Scott's style in later years, his first speech rings, indeed, of a familiar vibe, which I tried to convey to the reader with the detailed sum and extensive quoting of the previous pages. That feeling of familiarity is not only about the recurrence of many of the themes in the speech in later publications and endeavors.[18] It is caused in large part also by the use of language and the structure of the argumentation. The long sentences punctuated by many subordinates and learned quotes were already there. So was the attention to historical detail, enjoyable and charming to the reader, especially at the beginning. However, as the reading and the familiarity with Scott's scholarship proceeds, those details feel more and more like minutiae and curiosities, rather than building pieces of a complex account. They seem to serve the function of creating a bond of trust between audience and author, by certifying the historical competence and expertise of the latter, without explicitly asserting it. The goal was to provide substance to an intentionally simple and linear narrative. Scott sought to convey a sense of self-evidence to the developments he described.

The 1896 speech represents the earliest preserved example of Scott's signature progressive historical account. Human relations naturally developed from being based on force to being regulated by law. This was the product of a rising egalitarian ethos, spreading globally through the new possibilities offered by technological advancements. Some key tropes Scott would use over the course of his career as evidence of that progress are central already in the 1896 Sunset Club speech. For instance, the parallelism of evolution occurring in the domestic and the international society found in the speech. Over the centuries, Scott argued, following British legal historian Henry Sumner Maine, court systems developed in civilized communities, guaranteeing order, justice, and equality. The growing use of legal settlement procedures between States was simply an example of the same evolution on a different scale. The future promised the full implementation of the principle of equality of nations through the judicial method. The already widespread use of

[17] Quoted in Finch, *Adventures in Internationalism*, p. 5.

[18] I will describe and analyze Scott's interventions on themes present in the speech later in his career several times in the remainder of this book. To give one example, in Chapter 3 I treat in detail Scott's view on the role of the moral sanction in the execution of international judgments at the closing of the First World War.

international arbitration, Scott made clear in the speech, was the stage that ushered the international judiciary soon to come.[19]

The key technique that Scott would keep employing in his work was the construction of a pedigree for international law based on a specific use of authorities and events. He invariably presented the authorities he chose to speak for him as enlightened prophets. The progressive developments they envisioned are laid in front of the reader's eyes. Scott's proposals then become just obvious and necessary further steps. They relied on the authority of past writers and common sense. Accordingly Scott did not ask his audience to trust him personally. He just humbly pointed to what was so clear that it was incontrovertible. One clear linguistic marker of this technique is the widespread use of the impersonal form in the beginning of sentences, pointing to what follows (or the debunking of it) as a matter of settled consensus or common sense.[20]

With this rhetorical artifice Scott made himself disappear leaving the authority from the past to deliver the message. Yet, the points made were still Scott's own. Through this practice Scott could claim a large and arguably idiosyncratic score of authorities in his camp. This is also how, later in his career, he could define Vitoria, a sixteenth-century Catholic theologian, as a liberal and the first modern international lawyer.[21]

In the same way Scott understood earlier thinkers through ideas of his age, he looked at and characterized historical events primarily through his direct concerns, even declaring his presentism openly at times.[22] So, for instance, in detailing the progress of international arbitration in the speech, Scott confidently found elements of it as far back as in the amphictyonic leagues of the obscure period of Greek history preceding the rise of the *polis*. Presenting thinkers as visionaries and historical events as origins of progressive institutions were the bases of Scott's pedigree-building for his vision of international law. This mode of reasoning is so central to all Scott's scholarship that, as I will argue through the book, it is impossible to disentangle the international lawyer from the historian and the believer.

[19] In Scott's mind, indeed, arbitration was the earlier stage in an evolution that culminated in a permanent court system, rather than an equivalent alternative form of adjudication. The continuity between the two is marked in the speech by Scott's interchangeable use of terms like "judges" for "arbitrators" or "judgments" for "arbitral awards" in reference to arbitral procedures he considered particularly advanced. Still in 1912, Scott would describe his recent publications to Belgian international lawyer Ernest Nys as "lay[ing] down the law of development from arbitration as a means of staying self-redress to a permanent judiciary which decides questions of right or wrong according to the principles of law" (Scott to Ernest Nys, May 31, 1912, Folder 14, Box 10, JBS Papers).

[20] I refer to formulas such as "it is easy to see how," "it is equally certain," "it is unnecessary to point out," "it is necessarily easier to," "it is natural to hope," "it is not only futile, but childish to suppose that".

[21] Scott's work on Vitoria and the Salamanca School in the interwar years and its uses by Scott in current political projects are the subjects of Part II of the book.

[22] See as an example James Brown Scott, *The Catholic Conception of International Law: Francisco de Vitoria, Founder of the Modern Law of Nations; Francisco Suárez, Founder of the Modern Philosophy of Law in General and in Particular of the Law of Nations—A Critical Examination and a Justified Appreciation*, Washington: Georgetown University Press, 1934, p. VII.

By that I mean that history and belief together were crucial, in Scott's mind, in order to both learn from the past and look toward the connected futures of the discipline and mankind. For him, a deep factual knowledge of historical events was necessary to perceive patterns of gradual social evolution and to predict and direct further steps. However, that could not be done without belief providing meaning to processes that would otherwise be soulless and unintelligible. Scott's belief in international law encompassed both science and religion, understood in a virtuous relation that went beyond accommodation and harmony. It was a relation of symbiosis. The authorities Scott revered the most—Grotius in the 1896 speech, Vitoria and the Spanish Scholastics later in his career—were the ones who had understood and shaped that relation. They had reached into the moral foundations of Christianity and brilliantly given them a scientific and rational legal shape. That was the miracle of modernity: reason and the Christian faith cooperating to bring about progress. Still, while progress was inevitable, Scott constantly underlined the importance of renewing the alliance of Christian morality and scientific thought in his day. On one hand, he denounced the cold and self-destructive rationalism of power politics, which overlooked any sense of justice. On the other, he pointed to the shortcomings of a large part of the Peace movement: their moral appeals could not bring peace about without the reasoned solutions provided by international law and the judicial method.

I find it important, in order to add context to the introduction of Scott's thought on the relation of science and Christian morality, to introduce also his peculiar relationship with organized religion. Throughout his life Scott would often remind his audiences and readers of his belonging to the Presbyterian denomination, a faith and affiliation that, as we have seen, he had inherited from his family. To be a member of a mainline Protestant church was overwhelmingly common in the US foreign relations establishment Scott would come to be a member of. Yet, in a much more uncharacteristic way for that social and professional group, Scott also displayed a positive opinion of and even a strong fascination with Catholicism. Even after a thorough research in Scott's archives I found it difficult to provide a univocal explanation for the circumstance. I believe the best contribution I have to offer on the topic is to give an account of Scott's several projects of cooperation with Catholic clergy and institutions that, to my knowledge, have not yet been the subject of academic publications. I tell those stories in Part II. Those projects of cooperation represent, in my opinion, one of the key lenses through which to analyze Scott's interwar work on the theologians of the Salamanca School.

In any case, I will not refrain from comments and certain circumscribed pieces of analysis related to Scott's unconventional relationship with Catholicism, especially when it comes to interact more directly with his general views on international law. The Sunset Club speech is, to my knowledge, the earliest instance witnessing Scott's positive association with Catholicism. Indeed, Scott's argument on the Pope as the first international arbitrator points to an ideal alignment between the Church of Rome and international law that would underpin Scott's attempts of cooperation with the Holy See. Indeed, Scott regarded the Catholic Church as a universal moral authority inspiring mankind to peace, the type of universal authority that was so often denied to international law by legal theorists looking at it through Benthamite, positivistic eyes. With his work on the Spanish and Catholic origins of international law, Scott aimed at influencing both the professional community of international lawyers and the Church of Rome. For the former, he portrayed Vitoria as the founder of an international law shaped by his own views: originating in the discovery of America and based on liberal politics, individual rights, and the judicial settlement of international disputes. Toward the latter, he made the point that Vitoria represented a somewhat lost inspiration in Church history: the Church should have directed its peace-making efforts to more concrete endeavors and explicitly support international legal solutions. After all, Scott argued, international law was of Catholic origin.

I find it easy to recognize the Scott of later years in the speech of the young professional of 1896, through many elements beyond the first expression of his Catholic sympathies. Yet, one could also find important differences. For one, in the Sunset Club speech Scott's account of global progress is still heavily Eurocentric. For instance, in 1896 Scott pointed to the French Revolution as the event through which the people appeared as a political and historical subject. In later years he would rather point to the American Revolution or to the development of English common law, carving a key role for American settlers in that story. In the same fashion, as I have already pointed out, after 1896 he would find the origins of modern international law in earlier authors rather than in the work of Grotius. This move had a strong political significance: it changed the context of the foundation of international law from the religious wars in Europe to the discovery of America and its autochthonous inhabitants.

To be clear, the Europhilia Scott displayed in 1896 would always be part of his mindset. Yet, it would turn into the admiration of an intellectual tradition rather than being the recognition of a moral and scientific leadership of the Old Continent. By the beginning of the twentieth century, in the mind of Scott and many other Americans of the North and the South, global leadership belonged in the Western Hemisphere, a change of perspective well served by the theory on the Catholic origins of international law. The Spanish-American War of 1898 spurred that shift in the US political discourse, a shift that had been in preparation for some time.

# PART I

# THE RISE AND FALL OF JAMES BROWN SCOTT AND THE TURN TO UNITED STATES HISTORY, 1898–1921

# 1
# Explaining Scott's Turn to American History

## 1. Young Professional, 1898–1906

### A Different Kind of World Power

The years covered in Part I were particularly eventful for the United States' international relations. Spanning from the Spanish-American War to the establishment of the League of Nations and the Permanent Court of International Justice, this period was marked by a growing interest of the American people in global issues and foreign policy. Notwithstanding the financial panic of 1893, a thrilling sense of novelty and engagement was running across the country already through the 1890s, the formative decade that saw Scott go from college student to dean of a law school. The extraordinary economic development experienced since the Civil War required new narratives and visions for the country's future. US strength was not just based on ideals and morality anymore; it could now count also on material power. More and more people believed it was time to project that power and those ideals outside North America. To do so the United States had to face a tough question: what did it mean to be a different and progressive kind of world power? Finding answers to that question required a deep rethinking of the United States' self-image. Excitement for the task prevailed over an underlying sense of uneasiness. These themes could be sensed in publications as diverse as utopian novels and studies in economics.

In her impressive survey,[1] Susan Matarese notes the explosion of utopian novels as a genre in the 1890s—"the single largest outpouring of utopian literature in U.S. history"[2]—and describes the recurring themes and widely shared conceptions in that wealth of literary material. Crucially, Matarese notes the literal rather than allegorical nature of this American utopian tradition.[3] The texts she studied describe in detail societies that are ideal yet are thought by the authors to represent a

[1] Susan M. Matarese, *American Foreign Policy and the Utopian Imagination*, Amherst: University of Massachusetts Press, 2001. The book "surveys more than two hundred works of utopian literature written by Americans in the period from 1888 to 1900 and presents a profile of their thoughts about the United States as a participant in world affairs" (p. 2).

[2] Ibid., p. 9.

[3] See ibid.

*Rewriting the History of the Law of Nations: How James Brown Scott Made Francisco de Vitoria the Founder of International Law*. Paolo Amorosa, Oxford University Press (2019). © Paolo Amorosa
DOI: 10.1093/oso/9780198849377.001.0001

realistic goal, reachable in a not too distant future. The work of these authors was utopian in the sense that it represented their vision of the good life for America. But this vision took most often the form of concrete practical plans. These sometimes-bizarre texts seem to acquire even further grounding when set against the historical context. They then really appear as a societal response to turbulent times and changing conditions: a search for a collective identity purposely geared toward the solution of a large array of tangible issues.

In this sense it is not surprising that an initial response was to look inward at the traditional self-understanding of the United States and at the values that were commonly said to have distinguished the New World from Europe.[4] "Every schoolchild could recite the catalog of American virtues: no kings, no aristocracy, no established church, no Inquisition." The utopian "writings reveal an aversion to European values and policies, both domestic and foreign, which further reinforced this sense of American singularity."[5]

That singularity had been perceived for a long time as something to be protected rather than spread. Yet, new approaches were quickly emerging. Matarese notes how utopian literature in the 1890s often mixed more established ideals of isolation and preservation of American uniqueness with the more recent aspirations of active world reform allowed by the new-found power. Indeed,

> messianic impulses... represent only the apparent opposite of the introversionism, feelings of singularity, and belief in America's moral superiority over other states that characterize the national image of its utopian authors. In fact, ... the view of the United States as a "Redeemer Nation" flows quite naturally from conceptions of Americans as God's chosen people, entrusted with a unique, divinely ordained mission on which the future of the world depends.[6]

As it transpires from the utopian literature, the self-understanding of the United States had a distinct religious dimension. One of my main arguments in the following chapter is that this circumstance would allow ministers and religious figures to be the main developers of the narrative that would make sense of the Spanish-American War for the American people. It was an exceptionalist narrative that explained the Cuban intervention of 1898 as the foundation of a new, altruistic way to wield national power and understand international relations. The pedigree of the United States as a different kind of world power rested on that "splendid little war." This narrative would fundamentally shape the thinking of key figures of the

[4] The most successful novel of this utopian tradition, to which many of the other works were a response or a rejoinder, is meaningfully titled *Looking Backward*, even if the "backward" referred to was actually the author's present (Edward Bellamy, *Looking Backward: 2000–1887*, Boston: Ticknor and Company, 1888).

[5] Matarese, *American Foreign Policy*, p. 20.

[6] Ibid., p. 24.

United States' foreign policy establishment for decades to come, James Brown Scott being one of them.

However, it is important to note that the changing conditions and new-found power were commonly addressed also with scientific language. For instance, US economists could rely on impressive statistical data to sustain their optimism and produce further visions of national greatness. Even an iconoclast like Brooks Adams (1848–1927), Henry's brother, eventually became a convert to the religion of optimism. A direct descendant of Presidents John and John Quincy Adams, Brooks used his first book to attack the foundations of the New England heritage of his patrician family. In *The Emancipation of Massachusetts* (1887),[7] he argued that the idealized Puritan society of the past had been a fierce theocracy rather than a beacon of freedoms, as the story usually went. Already then Brooks couched his resentment toward certain patterns and groups in the United States' society in an objectivist and factual language, as he would do over the course of his career.

In the 1890s, Brooks Adams would be one of the main intellectual contributors to the heated debates on currency that followed the 1893 financial crisis.[8] He attacked the backers of the gold standard, identified with a parasitic financial system that, in his opinion, was leading the country to ruin. This led him to larger reflections on the dangers faced by the American society. In *The Law of Civilization and Decay* (1895),[9] Adams described the scientific laws that he believed regulated the rise and fall of societies. This work fit with the prevailing academic mindset of the time, which recognized no necessary difference between the method of social and natural sciences,[10] also something that James Brown Scott would argue for.[11] As with *The Emancipation*, Adams' "continuing critique of American civilization . . . affected an air of disinterestedness by charging the volume with the language of physics and biology."[12] The main argument of the volume was, as suggested by the title, that the history of communities moved in alternating cycles of expansion and contraction. When the energy of a society grew toward civilization, this would be reflected in the type of people it produced: inspiring, forceful, and imaginative leaders. Once the economy reached a certain level of development, the energy toward civilization would dissipate. Society would produce a class of greedy, self-serving people who would stifle the positive productive forces and inaugurate

[7] Brooks Adams, *The Emancipation of Massachusetts. The Dream and the Reality*, Boston and New York: Houghton Mifflin Company, 1919 [1887].

[8] See e.g. Brooks Adams, *The Gold Standard. An Historical Study*, Boston: Alfred Mudge & Son, 1894.

[9] Brooks Adams, *The Law of Civilization and Decay. An Essay on History*, New York: MacMillan & Company, 1895.

[10] The seminal description of social sciences in the United States at the turn of the century is Dorothy Ross, *The Origin of American Social Sciences*, New York: Cambridge University Press, 1991.

[11] See James Brown Scott, "The Study of the Law," *The American Law School Review*, 2(1), 1906, pp. 3–4 and John Hepp, "James Brown Scott and the Rise of Public International Law," *Journal of the Gilded Age and Progressive Era*, 7, 2008, pp. 162–4.

[12] Gary Marotta, "The Economics of the American Empire," in *The American Economist*, 19(2), 1975, p. 34.

a phase of decay. That was what Brooks thought was happening to the United States of his time. The bankers supporting selfishly the gold standard were suffocating the farmers and producers who would need an expansive monetary policy to keep the country growing further. The win of the Wall Street-backed William McKinley against the Great Commoner William Jennings Bryan in the presidential elections of 1896 could not but confirm Adams' fears. The ideas expounded in *The Law of Civilization and Decay* were definitely ill-suited to please the prevailing mindset. Adams' "theory of history challenged the American belief in linear progress, voluntarism, and optimism."[13]

Then, suddenly, his outlook changed or, rather, found a working alignment with the mainstream. Brooks Adams' conversion had come at least by August 1898, the same month in which hostilities with Spain ended. In an article titled "The Spanish War and the Equilibrium of the World," Adams illustrated the impressive economic achievements of the United States, for instance by reference to the "iron trade, the basis of modern manufactures."[14] He compared the variation over the years in the output by several powers of pig iron, the intermediate product of the smelting of iron ore. In 1740, "France led the production of pig-iron" with 26,000 tons. The United Kingdom and Germany followed closely with 20,000 and 18,000 tons respectively. "America produced but little," just 1,000 tons. He then traced the intermediate steps that led to 1898. The pig iron output indicator showed that global economy was growing vertiginously and the hierarchy of European powers had changed. The United Kingdom had been the leading power since the early nineteenth century and Germany had distinctly overcome France after winning the 1870 war. Yet, the real jaw-dropping data was the incredible rise of the United States. In 1897, it had produced 9,652,680 tons of pig iron: almost as much as the United Kingdom and France combined. Adams' article went on to give further evidence on a number of economic indicators: steel exports, total exports, imports-exports balance, accumulated wealth, and more.

In Adams' view, scientific analyses of industry, public wealth, and financial markets all returned a clear verdict, consistent with his earlier theory of civilization and decay. Europe's civilization was in sharp decline; the United Kingdom's stint as leading global power, started after the battle of Waterloo in 1815, was already at an end.[15] "[T]he equilibrium then attained . . . now seems tottering to its fall."[16] Adams' data showed "not only that Great Britain is spending her capital, but that the flow of her money is toward America."[17] The only way for the United

[13] Ibid.

[14] Brooks Adams, "The Spanish War and the Equilibrium of the World," in *The Forum*, August 1898, pp. 641–51.

[15] See also, for instance, Brooks Adams, "England's Decadence in the West Indies" and "The Decay of England," in *America's Economic Supremacy*, New York: The MacMillan Company, 1900.

[16] Adams, "The Spanish War," p. 648.

[17] Ibid., p. 644.

Kingdom to avoid isolation by continental powers and further decline was to join an Anglo-Saxon alliance, taking advantage of and supporting "America's economic supremacy."[18] This would primarily happen by absorbing United States' exports and having joint control of maritime trade routes, especially in the Pacific, in view of the likely American seizing of the Philippines from Spain.

> The support of the United States may thus be said to be vital to England[.] Great Britain may, therefore, be not inaptly described as a fortified outpost of the Anglo-Saxon race, overlooking the eastern continent and resting upon America.[19]

The "equilibrium of the world" was shifting again. In Adams' reading, the Spanish war was a clear sign of the times. The dissolution of an old European empire had dragged the new global power into a confrontation that could only have one obvious result: a total victory for the United States.

How did this reading of the war relate to Adams' earlier bleak predictions for his country? According to him, the United States was saved by the alliance of the financial class with the patrician one. The latter, representative of the traditional values that had given the country the energy to grow, had been given the lead of government and foreign policy. This would allow the United States to keep rising as long as government was strengthened and centralized and foreign policy was aggressively expansive.

The patricians in government included some of Brooks and Henry Adams' closest friends and James Brown Scott's future collaborators: one of the most trusted foreign policy advisors was naval strategist Alfred T. Mahan, whose theories on the predominance of maritime power seem to have inspired much of Brooks' postwar work. John Hay became Secretary of State just after the war, in September 1898; the lawyer Elihu Root (1845–1937), Scott's mentor, set up the US colonial administration after the conflict as War Secretary; Theodore Roosevelt had resigned as Assistant Secretary of the Navy to go fight in Cuba with his Rough Riders. Once back home, his newly gained status of war hero earned him a place as Vice President for McKinley's second term. Roosevelt would suddenly succeed to the presidency in 1901 following McKinley's assassination. He would soon make Brooks Adams an important advisor. Even if he quit his frontal attacks on American capitalism, Brooks Adams would never become a favorite of Wall Street. Neither would he change his theory on the inevitability of eventual decline. Yet, his enthusiasm for imperialism made him sound much like one of the apostles of progress.

I have traced Brooks Adams' trajectory primarily to show how the messianic visions in turn-of-the-century United States contributed to the public discourse

[18] This is the meaningful title of Adams' 1900 collection of essays, the opening one being "The Spanish War and the Equilibrium of the World."

[19] Adams, "The Spanish War," p. 645.

seeping through extremely diverse types of languages and disciplines. I will make this point more specifically about international law and politics in the following chapter. In part, though, I also wanted to show how an unlikely suspect like Brooks Adams came to share the attraction of optimism and international engagement that was irresistible for most Americans in the period around the Spanish-American War. James Brown Scott was one of them, and he did not need to convert anyway. He had been a believer to begin with.

To be sure, anti-imperialists of various stripes were present and vocal in the public debate.[20] Among them were heavyweights such as Mark Twain, Andrew Carnegie, and former US President Grover Cleveland. Yet, over the course of the years preceding the Cuban intervention and immediately after it, one witnesses an irregular but steady conceptual shift in the country. Especially in the aftermath of the war, scores of skeptics jumped ship. It became more and more common to channel national self-righteousness and self-importance toward the international.

## Mainstreaming International Law

This growing awareness of international issues also meant that international law could become a relatively mainstream discipline. James Brown Scott was a key actor in this mainstreaming and took advantage of it to support his professional rise. Yet, this was hardly mere opportunism. The Spanish-American War had touched Scott profoundly: promoting international law turned even more forcefully into a life mission for him after it. He participated directly in it by volunteering as a soldier, even if he never saw action. More crucially for his career as an international lawyer, Scott fully transposed the religious narrative of altruism explaining the Cuban intervention into his scholarship. From then on his international law could be defined as outright exceptionalist, in a way it was not in his 1896 speech.

The war of 1898 was both an event Scott lived through and a key node of his historical account of international law. Scott was able to admit—mostly in private though—that US policies could be imperialistic[21] but would not let the narrative of 1898 be challenged. The Cuban intervention was the cornerstone of his progressive argument: it was the instance in which the United States, by supporting the struggle for freedom of another people, showed that international relations could be a matter of justice rather than force. Even a world power could rely on and respect international law and not simply use it as a cover for power politics when convenient. That explains Scott's continued defense of the Platt Amendment, the

[20] See, for instance, Warren Zimmerman, *First Great Triumph*, New York: Farrar, Straus and Giroux, 2002, pp. 313–61.

[21] For a rare example of public mild criticism of his country's actions toward Latin America by Scott see the 1915 Address in Folder 9, Box 47, JBS Papers.

piece of legislation that guaranteed a right of intervention for the United States in the Cuban Constitution. Its interpretation was a key issue for Scott: if the right of intervention was construed as a limitation of Cuban independence, then the whole foundational myth of the United States as a different kind of world power would collapse. The sacrificial reading of the Cuban intervention would be tainted by power politics and imperialism.[22]

What made the story even more compelling to sympathetic ears was the fact that it could genuinely be argued that the war of 1898 somehow created the United States as a world power: as I argue throughout this Part, the sense of triumph after victory over an European power overcame, at least for a time, the pre-war identity crisis. Now the country knew its place in the world. That included acting as a self-appointed role of guardian of international justice. As I will explain in the following chapter, triumphalism would soon recede somewhat because of the difficulties linked to the colonial administration of the territories gained from Spain. Yet, the perception of the further development of international law as an American project would persist. It is in this context that one should read the foundation of the American Society of International Law in 1906:[23] there was a distinct sense among the founders that having a professional class of foreign policy experts was a necessity for a world power. Oscar Straus, ASIL Vice-President and soon-to-be Secretary of Commerce and Labor, declared as much to the New York Times: "We are a world power and we must put world-power clothes on to meet the situation."[24]

While soon acquiring this hegemonic bent, the ASIL project had originated in a more traditionally pacifist context. Indeed, a preliminary plan for the Society was conceived in June 1905 at the Lake Mohonk Conference on International Arbitration. The Conference had been held annually since 1895, when Albert K. Smiley, a pacifist Quaker, had invited fifty prominent individuals to the Mohonk Mountain House, the summer resort he owned in Ulster County, New York, to discuss arbitration as a way to international peace.[25] Over the years, the attendance grew to around 300 people, including religious leaders, businessmen, members of the press, academics, and university officers. Like with other Peace Movement initiatives, lawyers were initially on the sidelines but gradually decided to get involved and give the project a pragmatic

[22] I will describe in some detail in Chapter 2 how different views of the Cuban question would draw lines and create oppositions between international lawyers in the Pan-American movement after the First World War. For instance, relations between Scott and Chilean international lawyer Alejandro Álvarez grew colder over the years in part because of a divergent interpretation of the Platt Amendment and, more generally, of the principle of non-intervention. The two had been close allies in promoting a Pan-American understanding of international law since the early 1910s.

[23] Scott's first-hand account of the ASIL foundation is "History of the Organization of the American Society of International Law," *Proceedings of the American Society of International Law*, 1, 1907, pp. 23–9; for a recent account see Frederic L. Kirgis, *The American Society of International Law's First Century 1906–2006*, Leiden/Boston: Martinus Nijhoff Publishers, 2006, pp. 1–17.

[24] "Root Heads New Body on International Law," *New York Times*, January 14, 1906, p. 4.

[25] The Conference would be held until 1916. The 1917 session had been planned but would never take place because of the United States' joining of the European War.

and technical turn. In the conferences of 1901 and 1902 there were only one or two international lawyers; by 1905 they had become thirteen, including James Brown Scott.[26] Scott had been among the invitees to the Conference since 1903, when he had accepted a professorship at Columbia Law School. He would later claim to have left University of Illinois because of the lack of support by President Draper to his plan of starting an international law journal;[27] he immediately saw in the new association a way to revive the journal project. At Mohonk, Scott, the dean of Columbia Law School George W. Kirchwey, and future Secretary of State Robert Lansing promoted a resolution in favor of a "movement to establish a society of international law in the United States and of an American journal of international law"[28] that was eventually approved by the Conference. In the remaining months of 1905, Scott carried most of the weight within the organizing committee. This included the drafting of the Society's constitution which set, at article II, the goal of the new organization: "to foster international law and promote the establishment of international relations on the basis of law and justice." On January 12, 1906, in the office of the New York Bar Association, the American Society of International Law was officially established and Scott was named as its Secretary, the main administrative officer. At the first meeting of the Society's executive board, on January 29, Scott was selected to be also the managing editor of the American Journal of International Law (AJIL). The AJIL's quarterly publication began in January 1907. Scott did not only take upon himself most of the editing work and the writing of the editorial comments for the first few issues; he also paid for their publication out of his own pocket.[29]

The Society and the Journal reinforced a key assumption shared among the ASIL founders and quite accepted in the whole establishment: the foreign policy leaders should be lawyers. As Koskenniemi has noted, "[b]etween 1889 and 1945 all US Secretaries of State were lawyers, and most of them were associated with the ASIL since its establishment."[30] The Society had within its initial ranks a number of extremely powerful players, who in most cases had built successful careers juggling political and judicial positions with legal practice on Wall Street and sometimes with academia. The first President of the Society, Elihu Root, represented such an archetypal establishment lawyer. He had temporarily left his corporate law practice to become Secretary of War in 1899. At the time the ASIL was founded, Root was the sitting Secretary of State. Vice-Presidents of the Society included Melvin Fuller,

[26] See Kirgis, *ASIL's First Century*, p. 6.

[27] See Scott, "Remarks at Luncheon in Celebration of the 25th Anniversary of the Society," *Proceedings of the American Society of International Law*, 25, 1931, pp. 242–3.

[28] See Scott, "History of the Organization," p. 23.

[29] See Ralph Dingman Nurnberger, *James Brown Scott: Peace Through Justice*, unpublished PhD dissertation, Georgetown University, 1975, p. 60 and fn. 13.

[30] Martti Koskenniemi, "The Ideology of International Adjudication and the 1907 Hague Conference," in *Topicality of the 1907 Hague Conference, the Second Peace Conference/Actualité de la Conférence de La Haye de 1907, Deuxième Conférence de la paix*, ed. by Yves Daudet, Leiden/Boston: Brill, 2008, p. 129.

the sitting Chief Justice of the Supreme Court, and two associate justices; William Howard Taft, sitting Secretary of War and future President of the United States and Chief Justice; influential former State Secretaries such as Richard Olney and John W. Foster; this to name just a few. In the words by Carl Landauer, "[t]he various officers of the society were part of the interlocking directorate of the US legal and international relations establishment, and very much part of what has been identified as a new American 'gentry' class."[31]

This gentry class expressed its commitment to American democratic values not only by adherence to formal institutional practices. They had a sense of duty toward the improvement of lower classes. Yet, that improvement was to happen in their own terms. This meant that they faced the quest for better working conditions with inflexible harshness. Strikes and protests were violently repressed. Legal action by workers for better treatment was routinely quashed with the fundamental contribution of the Fuller Supreme Court, in the name of formal freedom of contract.

Improvement for the lower classes had to come from philanthropy and programs of education.[32] In a sense, the founders viewed the ASIL as one such educational endeavor. They believed in the education of public opinion[33] as the main tool to render international law increasingly effective. The idea, considered democratic—and therefore American—was that the more global public opinion would be aware of the rules of international justice the more it would be able to identify and sway violating States and their governments. Of course, this also meant that for the lower classes to be "educated" they should see the world (and foreign policy) the same way the establishment—the "educators"—did.

The importance of understanding international law as a process of education, both within and outwith universities, was a theme James Brown Scott returned to very often and the main focus of his research in the opening years of the twentieth century. By the time he orchestrated the foundation of the ASIL, Scott's career had taken off in academia and beyond. In 1899, he left Los Angeles to become the first dean of the University of Illinois Law School. It was there that he met Adele Cooper Reed (1863–1939), the future Mrs. Scott, and married her on the first day of September 1901, just few months after the death of his mother. Three years older than James, Adele was a widow who was following courses in library science at the University. She would become a fundamental point of reference and support in

[31] Carl Landauer, "The Ambivalences of Power: Launching the American Journal of International Law in an Era of Empire and Globalization," *Leiden Journal of International Law*, 20, 2007, p. 327.

[32] See for instance Andrew Carnegie's article "Wealth" (*North American Review*, 148, 1889, pp. 653–64), that became a sort of manifesto for philanthropic endeavors in the Gilded Age, and the case for individualism and social Darwinism therein.

[33] For a deeper exploration of the concept of public opinion among US internationalists at the time see Stephen Wertheim, "Reading the International Mind: International Public Opinion in Early Twentieth Century Anglo-American Thought," in Daniel Bessner and Nicolas Guilhot (eds.), *The Decisionist Imagination: Sovereignty, Social Sciences and Democracy in the 20th Century*, New York: Berghahn Book, 2019, pp. 27–49.

Scott's life. She would accompany him on all of his many trips abroad, with a few exceptions for health reasons. Scott often remarked how much he relied on her for anything ranging from the most practical arrangement to trusted advice on his academic writings.[34]

As we have seen, in 1903 Scott went to teach at Columbia, called by Nicholas Murray Butler. Scott was happy to be back finally in the Northeast, at the center of the academic and political action. However, he was also very frustrated that he could not teach international law, as John Bassett Moore, the most renowned international lawyer in the United States at the time, held the chair at Columbia.[35] This was one of the reasons that led to a key event in Scott's career, his sudden move to the State Department in 1906. At the beginning of his tenure at the State Department, Root received a letter from Scott, containing an unsolicited application for the position of Solicitor, the main legal advisor to the Secretary.[36] Favorably impressed by the letter, Root, after making a few informal enquiries about him, decided to appoint Scott, although he had never heard of him before. It was the start a solid and fruitful collaboration.

## 2. Root's Legal Advisor, 1906–1910

### The American International Law Reshaping Foreign Policy: Scott at the State Department

Moving to Washington D.C., Scott had to leave his position at Columbia. However, even while in the highest echelons of government, he would always think of himself (and be perceived by others) first and foremost as an academic.[37] Indeed, he soon accepted some teaching work at George Washington University.[38] Yet, his

[34] On Scott's relationship with his wife see George A. Finch, "Rough: For Adventures in Internationalism," unpublished text meant for Scott's biography, Folder 1, Box 69, JBS Papers, pp. 9–11.

[35] At Columbia Scott taught courses on Equity Jurisdiction, Quasi-Contracts, Suretyship and Mortgages, Admiralty, Domestic Relations, and Criminal Law (see Nurnberger, *James Brown Scott*, p. 45).

[36] See Scott to Elihu Root, December 30, 1905, Folder 4, Box 7, JBS Papers.

[37] Scott's collaborators, both at the Department and at the Carnegie Endowment, normally referred to him as "Dr. Scott."

[38] There is evidence that some of Scott's collaborators had been complaining for a while about his neglecting of Department work in favor of academic commitments by the time he resigned the Solicitor position in 1911 (see Benjamin Coates, *Transatlantic Advocates: American International Law and U.S. Foreign Relations, 1898–1919*, unpublished PhD dissertation, Columbia University, 2010, pp. 301 and 303). One might speculate that the hostile environment at the Department may have prompted Scott's decision to leave. While this is likely, I do not believe it could have been a decisive factor. Scott was excited about joining the leadership of the generously funded Carnegie Endowment for International Peace. He immediately saw the unprecedented possibilities given by managing such large resources and jumped at the opportunity: "I shall be the chief administrative officer [of the Endowment] and shall devote my entire time to the work, and I . . . severed my connections with the Government in order to devote myself to the great task and the great opportunity which is before us" (Scott to Ernest Nys, March 27, 1911, Folder 6, Box 10, JBS Papers).

professional switch clearly influenced the direction of his research: his primary focus moved away from education back to international dispute settlement. To be sure, the two topics were very connected in Scott's mind. He believed that the authority needed for international judicial institutions to be effective could come only from the pressure of well-informed public opinion and not from coercive enforcement.[39] Scott focused more directly on the international court project because he was now in the position to promote it as government policy with Root's enthusiastic blessing; yet, in explaining the crucial function of an international justice system for global peace, he was educating the public as well.[40]

The peak of Scott's stint at the State Department was accordingly the 1907 Second Hague Peace Conference, an event that also represented an important benchmark for many of the historical trends I have been describing. For instance, one sees some obvious differences by comparing the First Conference of 1899 with the Second. "The 1899 Conference was still a European affair":[41] the United States was present with a small delegation that was at the margins of the negotiations. The 1907 one, on the other hand, starting from the way of its convocation, featured the United States acting as a leading power. Indeed, it was the initiative and diplomatic action of the US government that led to its organization. Theodore Roosevelt left to the Russian Czar Nicholas II the honor of issuing the official call, out of diplomatic courtesy.

Scott was an important protagonist of the Peace Conference. While the international court he envisioned would not be created until after the end of the World War, Scott believed he had achieved a milestone in his quest for an international judiciary in The Hague. Indeed, a court project was approved under US leadership. Yet, it could not be implemented as it fell short of providing a mechanism for the election of judges. The various proposals, entailing a weighted representation of countries on the bench based on population and/or wealth, failed to muster enough support. The responsibility was pinned on smaller countries and especially the Brazilian delegate Ruy Barbosa for not being able to compromise on that point. Barbosa insisted that his opposition was an obvious instance of defense of the principle of the sovereign equality. Interestingly, Barbosa drew from Root's formulation of the principle in Rio de Janeiro the previous year that had received the Brazilian's enthusiastic praise.

> Known later as "the Eagle of The Hague", Barbosa famously argued that each country, regardless its power and importance, should have equal representation in the projected court, opposing any distinction between great powers and small

[39] See Chapter 3.

[40] Indeed, Scott produced several popularizing pieces in those years. See for instance, James Brown Scott, "America and the New Diplomacy," *International Conciliation*, March 1909.

[41] Koskenniemi, "The Ideology of International Adjudication," p. 134.

> states. . . . The US delegates sent under Root's instructions did not back Barbosa's eloquent defence of sovereign equality among states in its full meaning, given its origins in Root's address at Rio de Janeiro. No doubt, Root's advocacy for sovereign equality at Rio de Janeiro was more formalistic and less committed than that of Barbosa at The Hague.[42]

Looking beyond the surface, though, it was clear that the European powers' support for an effective international judicial machinery was a façade. Germany and the United Kingdom, for instance, were formal co-sponsors of the US project. However, they would never have allowed the actual creation of a court with full judicial power and the level of unconditional jurisdiction that Scott envisioned. Engaged in an arms race against each other, both governments knew that the project was doomed to fail.

Still, the momentum for international adjudication in the United States was on the rise after The Hague. Scott would be a protagonist in many of the civil society initiatives for its promotion, especially after he joined the Carnegie Endowment for International Peace in 1910. Indeed, Scott would hold key operative positions within the Endowment that would allow him, for instance, to bankroll the American Society for Judicial Settlement of International Disputes he founded with Theodore Marburg, former US minister to Belgium.

These were busy years for Scott and Root. They marked the beginning of the implementation of several aspects of their internationalist project. Indeed, in 1906, with a South American tour by Root,[43] they laid the foundations of the Pan-American strategy they would pursue for the rest of their careers.

Root took advantage of the Third Pan-American Conference held in Rio de Janeiro that year to visit, in addition to Brazil, Uruguay, Argentina, Chile, and Peru. This was more than an ordinary diplomatic visit and not just because it was the first time that a sitting US Secretary traveled to South America. As noted by Juan Pablo Scarfi, Root's tour was "essential for understanding the process of US ideological legitimization of both Pan-Americanism and the missionary project of advancing international law and peace throughout the continent."[44]

The South American tour and the Second Hague Peace Conference can be considered as the most visible applications of the principles behind Root's two-pronged internationalist-legalist action as State Secretary. Regionally, he employed international legal language to improve relations on the American continent. Globally, international law was a key element of a larger strategy aimed at increasing American influence with European powers.

[42] Juan Pablo Scarfi, *The Hidden History of American International Law: Empire and Legal Networks*, Oxford: Oxford University Press, 2017, p. 28.

[43] See Editorial Comment, "Mr. Root's South American Trip," *American Journal of International Law*, 1, 1907, pp. 143–4.

[44] Scarfi, *Hidden History*, p. 3

On the former front, Root sought to develop a more multilateral approach in continental matters and inspire, with some success, a more amicable view of United States' hegemony among Latin American countries.[45] In order to do so, Root enlarged the scope of US exceptionalism in order to encompass the whole continent as a proponent of progressive and democratic values. The rhetoric he employed during his visit revolved around the idea of "Pan-American sameness" grounding "the binary opposition between a peaceful and civilized Western Hemisphere governed by democratic and republican institutions and an Old Continent governed by conflict, barbarism and war."[46] Indeed, at the global level, the promotion of international dispute settlement was to mark that fundamental difference between the old powers and the new one.

With regard to Root's legalist foreign policy, Scott was something between an implementing arm, an intellectual expounder, and a hardline militant.[47] On the side of international adjudication, Scott had made a prominent contribution already at The Hague Conference, as noted earlier. In relation to Pan-American action, however, Scott became more directly involved only once he and Root had left the State Department and went on to lead of the Carnegie Endowment for International Peace (CEIP).

## Jumpstarting a Powerhouse: Scott at the Carnegie Endowment for International Peace

Industrialist Andrew Carnegie (1835–1919) established the CEIP in December 1910. Born in Dunfermline in Scotland, he emigrated to the United States in 1848 when he was thirteen years old. By the 1860s, Carnegie had escaped poverty and built an enormous fortune as one of the main protagonists of the American steel and railroad-based industrial revolution. Carnegie was the main actor of the United States' exploding growth in metal output that Brooks Adams had taken as a benchmark for the changing "equilibrium of the world." Even if he is not mentioned in Adams' 1898 article, I imagine that no reader at the time could have read it without thinking of Carnegie. In the last two decades of the nineteenth century his ever-expanding empire reinforced its global leading position through constant technological innovation and increasing vertical integration of the supply chain.

Always vocal on political matters, Carnegie devoted himself almost completely to philanthropy after selling the Carnegie Steel Corporation to J. P. Morgan in 1901.

[45] On South American reactions to Root's visit see ibid., pp. 23–6.

[46] Ibid., p. 43.

[47] This should not be understood to mean that he did not develop and pursue his own independent agenda in several occasions and on varied issues. A clear example of this would be Scott's vocal and harsh opposition toward plans for collective security and peace enforcement in the postwar world order. Root's opposition would be much more ambiguous and nuanced. See Chapter 3.

His main goal was to promote culture and education at large. His donations would lead, to give just a few examples, to the establishment of over 3,000 public libraries in the United States and other English-speaking countries and to the Carnegie Institute of Technology, the precursor of today's Carnegie Mellon University.

Alongside a wide array of cultural enterprises, he focused on promoting world peace. Already in 1903, Carnegie would link his name permanently to the institutionalization of international law. The idea of providing stable headquarters to the Permanent Court of Arbitration (which was, famously, neither permanent nor a court) had been circulating since its establishment at the 1899 First Hague Peace Conference. The leader of the US delegation at the Conference, Andrew Dickson White (1832–1918), approached Carnegie and eventually convinced him to donate 1.5 million dollars for the project. There is some bitter irony in the fact that the Peace Palace, as the building would come to be known, would be inaugurated in 1913,[48] the year preceding the plunging of the world into the Great War. Today the Palace houses the International Court of Justice and its international law library. Among the other institutions seated there is the Hague Academy of International Law, one of the most ambitious and lasting projects James Brown Scott masterminded and brought to life at the Carnegie Endowment for International Peace.[49]

The inceptions of the two main international legal projects funded by Carnegie, the building of the Peace Palace and the CEIP,[50] bear more than one resemblance to each other. Indeed, in both cases, the proponent of the project was a man who owed his fame and prominence to a university presidency. White had been one of the founders of Cornell University. As its first president between 1866 and 1885, he took an important role in the modernization of higher education launched in those years in the United States. Nicholas Murray Butler, who insisted Carnegie should fund a research institute to rid the world of war, had ascended to Columbia presidency in 1902 and would remain in the position until his retirement over four decades later.

True, both White and Butler had Carnegie's ear as his "old shoes," part of the restricted circle of friends the philanthropist kept. Yet, the circumstance also says something about the different kind of figures university presidents were in turn-of-the-century United States. Their speeches were making the news, more often than not featuring on the front pages of newspapers. Their opinions would hold great weight in public discourse and the most prominent among them were easily recognizable by large audiences and referred to in media of popular culture. For

48 For contemporary accounts of the inauguration ceremony see "Queen at Opening of Peace Palace," *New York Times*, August 29, 1913, and "The Temple of Peace at The Hague," *The Advocate of Peace*, October 1913, pp. 200–1.

49 See Part II, especially Chapter 4.

50 For an account of the events leading to the creation of CEIP see Michael Rosenthal, *Nicholas Miraculous: The Amazing Career of the Redoubtable Dr. Nicholas Murray Butler*, New York: Farrar, Straus and Giroux, 2006, pp. 156–68.

instance, Woodrow Wilson, initially less known than White or Charles W. Eliot of Harvard, famously reached to the New Jersey governorship and then to the US presidency exploiting the fame as an anti-elitist reformer gained as President of Princeton. Butler, instead, tried but failed more than once to gain the Republican nomination for President of the United States. However, he managed to become the quintessential university president.[51] Under his presidency, Columbia went from a traditional elite college to become a powerhouse of modern education, renowned globally. And, whatever one thinks of his polarizing figure, everybody in the United States of the first half of the twentieth century was compelled to identify Columbia University with Nicholas Murray Butler.

When he first met Carnegie in 1891, though, Butler was not yet the universally known (and often reviled)[52] "Dr. Butler" or "Nicholas Miraculous," as Theodore Roosevelt and many others liked to call him behind his back. He was just an ambitious young member of Columbia's philosophy department searching for funding to implement his many ideas for educational enterprises. The two men clicked. They not only shared the value they put on education but also an enthusiasm for social Darwinism and the idea that success in life went hand in hand with moral fiber.

Butler first became directly involved with Carnegie's philanthropist endeavors when he was named, along with many other star university presidents including Eliot and Wilson, among the trustees of the Carnegie Foundation for the Advancement of Teaching in 1905. The Foundation's president, astronomer Henry S. Pritchett, who also presided over the Massachusetts Institute of Technology, would go on to become a precious collaborator for Scott and Butler and a trustee of the CEIP.

In January 1908, Carnegie wrote to some of his "old shoes," including Butler, soliciting further ideas to productively employ his fortune. The memo Butler sent as a reply essentially contained a range of projects Columbia could implement with Carnegie's funds. Carnegie did not go for it, as he believed that elite universities already had enough resources of their own. But he did pick up on one idea in the memo. Butler suggested that Columbia could use the funding to create "a great body of international opinion which would not tolerate the brutalities and the immoralities of war, with all that war means and involves."[53] Carnegie liked the idea of a research institution devoted to peace, but before committing he wanted

[51] For an insightful analysis of Butler's cultural significance in his time see Rosenthal, *Nicholas Miraculous*, pp. 3–26.

[52] See ibid., pp. 8–10. Author Upton Sinclair, among Butler's most vocal critics, painted a damning portrait in his investigative book on education in the United States and attacked him for his unabashed elitism. For Sinclair, Butler, "the intellectual leader of the American plutocracy," was the most "complete Tory . . . ever been in" US public life. (*The Goose Step: A Study of American Education*, Pasadena: published by the author, 1923, p. 33).

[53] Nicholas Murray Butler to Carnegie, January 30, 1908, Carnegie Papers, Library of Congress, quoted in Rosenthal, *Nicholas Miraculous*, p. 162.

his doubts on the disorganization and lack of pragmatism of the American peace movement addressed.

> "I feel too much is in the air", he responded to Butler . . . . "Much talk about bringing people together, and all this sort of thing, and nothing of a definite character." Carnegie . . . wanted to know exactly how [his money] would be used: "The avenues of expenditure should be distinctly stated[".][54]

Although that clashed with his eagerness to have the funds at his disposal, Butler shared, at least in principle, Carnegie's preoccupations.[55] With the crucial cooperation of Hamilton Holt, editor of New York's weekly *The Independent* and peace activist, he developed a more detailed course of action based on the promotion of international institutionalization, including plans for a world parliament and a world court.

When Carnegie finally became convinced, the project moved quickly yet with impressive efficiency, along the lines of Butler and Holt's proposals. On December 14, 1910, Carnegie stood in front of the press and a number of invited dignitaries in the conference room of the Carnegie Institution in Washington. He read a short statement announcing the foundation of the Carnegie Endowment for International Peace through his donation of ten million dollars.[56] The task he entrusted to the organization was to "hasten the abolition of international war, the foulest blot upon our civilization."[57] Root and Butler made sure, since the earliest preparatory phase, that the Endowment would be dedicated to scientific research of the causes of war and practical methods to remove them, setting itself on a different path than the earlier peace movement.[58] Root made it clear at the first meeting of the trustees: "We must do what scientific men do" acting on "that deeper insight" that could be "attained only by long and faithful and continuous study."[59]

[54] Ibid., p. 165.

[55] Butler was actually more distant than Carnegie from the positions of the peace societies. Meaningfully, he tried, without success, to convince Carnegie to remove the word peace, too associated in his view with the radical and unscientific endeavors of the peace activists, from the name of the Endowment. Instead, he proposed the more "academic" Carnegie International Institute (see David S. Patterson, "Andrew Carnegie's Quest for World Peace," *Proceedings of the American Philosophical Society*, 114, 1970, p. 381).

[56] According to Benjamin Coates' calculations, based on a comparison "of the figures as a shares of income (GDP/capita)," ten million dollars in 1910 would be equivalent to more than one billion dollars today (see Coates, *Transatlantic Advocates*, p. 80). A few years later, Lassa Oppenheim would refer to the CEIP as having "the budget of a small state" (Oppenheim to Scott, January 22, 1915, Box 566, CEIP Papers).

[57] Quoted in "Andrew Carnegie's Announcement of His Great Peace Fund," *Advocate of Peace*, January 1911, p. 7.

[58] The relation of the Endowment with the peace societies would be a source of controversy in the board of trustees for decades to come (see, as examples, Frederic A. Delano to Nicholas Murray Butler, January 13, 1931, Box 19, CEIP Papers and "Memorandum in regard to the Endowment Policy toward other Peace Organizations," 1937, Box 9, CEIP Papers).

[59] Carnegie Peace Fund, "Stenographic Report of Proceedings, First Meeting of the Board of Trustees," December 14, 1910, p. 21, Box 19, CEIP Papers.

On that day, Carnegie was surrounded by twenty-seven of the twenty-eight original trustees of the Endowment. The roster was packed with prominent lawyers, businessmen, and politicians. No leader of the peace societies was appointed.[60] Among the trustees were, of course, Nicholas Murray Butler, Elihu Root, and James Brown Scott. The three went on to form the leadership of the organization. Root had been named the first president of the Endowment, a position he accepted after an insistent work of persuasion by Carnegie. Butler would lead the Division of Intercourse and Education, the propaganda machine of the Endowment, and its main "avenue of expenditure." Scott would be Director of the International Law Division and the top administrative officer of the organization as its Secretary.

## 3. Powerful Organizer, 1910–1917

### Scott's Early Projects at CEIP

I agree with Michael Rosenthal that Butler's "assertion in *Across the Busy Years* [his autobiography] that he 'had persuaded Andrew Carnegie to establish the Carnegie Endowment' is too facile."[61] Carnegie was most likely swayed by intervening political events and, by that time, many "old shoes" and influential figures had joined the advocacy for the peace institute.[62] Yet, Butler definitely had some influence. His early plans shaped the philosophy behind CEIP at its establishment. Moreover, the story tells something about the perseverance, the energy, and the capacity Nicholas Murray Butler employed for the promotion of himself and the institutions he was associated with. Indeed, the Endowment gave Scott and his collaborators unprecedented resources and infrastructure to implement their internationalist projects. But, as will be clear from my accounts, what they achieved was owed in large part also to their skills, clout, influential international networks, and vision.

Scott did not lose time in redesigning the lines of action of his main projects to match the new possibilities granted by the Endowment. During the early years he would do much groundwork for many projects that would come to full fruition only in the 1920, after the end of the Great War.[63] Other endeavors of those years would acquire even more urgency because of the war, furthering the promotion of

[60] One arguable exception was Democratic Congressman from Texas James L. Slayden. He was a peculiar figure in the peace movement to begin with, considering that his pacifism was based more on economic than moral considerations.

[61] Rosenthal, *Nicholas Miraculous*, p. 164

[62] See Patterson, "Carnegie's Quest," pp. 377–8 and Rosenthal, *Nicholas Miraculous*, pp. 166–7.

[63] Two examples are the correspondence with TMC Asser on the establishment of the Hague Academy of International Law (see Chapter 4) and the initial contacts that would lead to the cooperation between CEIP and the Holy See from 1926 on (see Chapter 5). Both took place during the earliest years of CEIP but the related plans had to be momentarily abandoned because of the outbreak of the First World War.

adjudication and Pan-Americanism that Scott and Root had already set as priorities at the State Department.

Already in that same year of 1910 Scott had been among the founders of the American Society for the Judicial Settlement of International Disputes (ASJSID). The Society would soon turn into Scott's propaganda arm in the advocacy for a permanent international court, composed of independent professional judges. In the days immediately following the inauguration of CEIP, on December 15–17, the ASJSID held its first National Conference, with Scott as its President. Root, Carnegie, and US President Taft were among the speakers. Scott used considerable Endowment resources to print and disseminate the Conference proceedings. This scheme would continue until 1917 when the ASJSID's activities[64] were discontinued because of the United States joining the war: the Endowment sustained the expenses for establishment members to come together and speak in favor of a world court and for their arguments to be spread around, through Scott's facilitation and organization. Those arguments were not novel; they were the same Scott had developed much earlier and sustained forcefully at the Second Hague Peace Conference.[65] Yet, their hold in the United States was growing and with that the hope that they would be accepted elsewhere as well. Indeed, as Scott believed and often explained, progress was a process of gradual social and cultural growth: it needed both work and patience.

Soon also the American Society of International Law started receiving funding from CEIP. The various organizations Scott led would support and advertise each other's endeavors, also thanks to the fact that they shared the same leadership beyond Scott's operative guidance.[66] The next step Scott took was to use the CEIP resources to create an international research association that would further the ideals that had inspired Root's 1906 South American visit: promoting the continental cooperation between American countries and their shared values through international law. The inception of the American Institute of International Law (AIIL) owed much to the crucial cooperation of Chilean diplomat Alejandro Álvarez.[67] The two international lawyers had first met while working for their respective governments. In 1908 Álvarez had been sent to Washington by the Chilean government to try to settle an investment dispute and found Scott, then Solicitor at

[64] Other than the organization of the National Conferences and the publication of their proceedings the ASJSID also published a series of twenty-nine pamphlets. Generally on ASJSID see Finch, *Adventures in Internationalism*, pp. 79–80 and Coates, *Transatlantic Advocates*, pp. 117–23.

[65] For an in-depth analysis of Scott's case for international adjudication see Chapter 3.

[66] Just to give a couple of examples out of the many possible, Root was president of both the CEIP and the ASIL and would also be Vice-President of the ASJDID for the year 1916. Joseph H. Choate, one of the original Vice-Presidents of the ASIL and head of the US Delegation at The Hague in 1907, and Charles W. Eliot, former President of Harvard, would both become president of the ASJDID. They were both also among the original trustees of CEIP.

[67] For an insightful analysis of Álvarez's Americanism see Arnulf Becker Lorca, "Alejandro Álvarez Situated: Subaltern Modernities and Modernisms that Subvert," *Leiden Journal of International Law*, 19, 2006, pp. 879–930.

the State Department, as his counterpart.[68] They became friends, based on their common will to universalize the American experience.

Álvarez visited Washington once again in the spring of 1911 and spent two days in intense discussions with Scott. They envisioned an organization, modeled on the *Institut de Droit International*,[69] which would focus on regional issues and would allow the international lawyers of the Americas to cooperate on a more stable basis. Contrary to what happened in the *Institut*, the members of the AIIL would be organized in national societies. Álvarez promised to use his contacts in Latin American countries to jumpstart the organizing of the local societies and get possible members involved.

The American Institute was to give independent expert support to the action of the Pan-American Union in bringing the countries of the continent closer. The practical goal was a regional codification of international law of a scientific rather than political nature. The AIIL would "draw leaders of thought together [to] discuss scientific questions of international law . . . so that, little by little, a code . . . might be drafted which would represent the enlightened thought of American publicists and be the result of their sympathetic collaboration." Such a code "would stand a better chance of adoption" than one prepared by governmental delegates that "would not represent international law but the views of the Governments appointing them."[70]

Root's 1906 visit had been designed to counteract the setbacks on continental cooperation caused by Roosevelt's Big Stick policy. Similarly, during their spring 1911 planning meeting Scott and Álvarez agreed that the aggressive policy of the United States was limiting the influence of the Pan-American Union. They saw the AIIL and international law more in general as part of the solution. This coincidence of views was possible because Álvarez accepted and considered beneficial, under certain circumstances, the continental hegemony of the United States. This was so as long as the United States "protect[ed the region] from external threats [or] intervene[d] to secure the internal order of a state affected by chaos and misgovernment."[71] However, United States' actions had often gone beyond, violating the principles of sovereign equality and non-intervention. For Álvarez, the codification of a regional international law would serve the purpose of containing the hegemon to a benevolent role.

So, one could say, by way of simplification, that the idea of an American international law was for Scott a tool to enlist the whole continent in support of the United States' global vision. For Álvarez, however, it was a way to underline Latin

[68] See Becker Lorca, "Álvarez Situated," fn. 155 p. 917.

[69] Founded in Belgium in 1873, the *Institut* was the first professional organization of international lawyers. While open to non-European lawyers (Scott had been a member since 1908), the *Institut* at the time was still dominated by European lawyers and European issues. The standard account on the *Institut* and its early history is Martti Koskenniemi, *The Gentle Civilizer of Nations*, Cambridge: Cambridge University Press, 2001, pp. 39–97.

[70] Scott to Root, June 3, 1911, quoted in Finch, *Adventures in Internationalism*, pp. 143–4.

[71] Becker Lorca, "Álvarez Situated," p. 917.

American specificity and protect it from the negative sides of the policies of its northern neighbor.

While diverging, especially on the content of the principle of non-intervention, their agendas overlapped enough to keep their collaboration solid until after the Great War. In October 1911 they met again in Paris, where Álvarez lived and Scott was attending a meeting of the *Institut de Droit International*. They drafted a joint letter explaining the American Institute project and proceeded to send it to potential members in the Americas. Receiving enthusiastic feedback and promises of involvement, they asked for the advice of European members of the *Institut*. The main criticism returned was directed at the idea that there could even be a regional international law. International law was one and universal. Scott was quick to tone down almost to the point of denial the claims of regional exceptionalism, in order to smooth things over, with a letter to European colleagues:

> The name "American" has been used for geographical reasons, to distinguish this Institute from the (international) Institute of International Law, of which you are an honored member, not to suggest that there is or can be an American International Law. There are indeed American problems to be solved by the application of the generally-recognized principles of international law[.] I make this statement, in order that there may be no mistake as to our purpose, which is to contribute, to the full extent of our abilities, to the development and the dissemination of a system of international law, as it has been created by the weight and wisdom of European publicists.[72]

Following the approval of the Constitution and By-laws by the prospective members, Scott and Álvarez declared the American Institute of International Law officially founded. Consistently with Scott's fancy for symbolic dates, they did it on October 12, 1912, Columbus Day.[73] It would still take a few more years to have the organization up and running, though. At first, it was difficult to get the national societies founded. Indeed, one of the functions of former Secretary of State Robert Bacon's[74] 1913 South American visit[75] as Endowment representative was to engage national establishments and governments to support that task.

[72] Scott, letter November 7, 1912, quoted in Finch, *Adventures in Internationalism*, p. 145.

[73] See "Report of the Director of the Division of International Law," *Year Book of the Carnegie Endowment for International Peace*, 1915, p. 129.

[74] Bacon (1860–1919) had been Assistant Secretary of State under Root and succeeded him as Secretary for a brief period in 1909. He and Scott met at the Department and became very close friends. They went on to edit together a series of volumes collecting Root's speeches and writings. The news of Bacon's sudden death in 1919 reached Scott in Paris, where he was participating at the post-First World War Peace Conference. Scott would later publish Bacon's biography: Scott, *Robert Bacon, Life and Letters*, Garden City, NY: Doubleday, 1923.

[75] For a detailed account of Bacon's tour see Scarfi, *Hidden History*, pp. 41–7. According to a letter written by his wife, Scott was the actual author of all the addresses Bacon delivered in Latin America: see Adele Scott to James Brown Scott, June 25, 1913, Folder 1, Box 70, JBS Papers.

Whatever enthusiasm Bacon had achieved in that respect waned because of the outbreak of the World War. Once again it was up to Álvarez and Scott to employ their efforts to convince their colleagues that international law mattered more because of the war, not less. "Today, when Europe is passing through a formidable crisis, [Latin America] must organize, in order to become the spokesman of law and justice in international relations."[76]

It was time for the Americas to take the lead and teach the authoritarian and monarchic powers of Europe to go beyond the use of force to settle political rivalries. Peace could be achieved by pursuing the democratic and progressive values of the Western Hemisphere, justice by a scientifically sound legal codification of those values. That was the "stupendous task"[77] the international lawyers of the Americas were called to perform by history.

Scott, with the Endowment's backing, accelerated the preparatory work and took any chance to push the charter members to be ready for the Institute's first meeting. The meeting would take place in Washington in December 1915, in connection with the Second Pan-American Scientific Congress. Scott did everything he could to ensure it would be a success. Governments were exhorted to help and, as a result, were heavily involved in the creation of the local societies, somewhat contradicting Scott's striving for scientific independence. For instance, the Uruguayan Society of International Law was created through a committee appointed by the President of the Republic and given an official standing by presidential decree.[78] Indeed, the US diplomatic missions in Latin American countries were also enlisted to participate in the promotion. To address the economic concerns of both governments and potential participants, the Carnegie Endowment decided to cover the expenses for three delegates from each Latin American country. Moreover, through the good offices of the newly appointed Secretary of State Robert Lansing—as we have seen a prominent member of the ASIL since its foundation—Scott was essentially put in charge of the organization of the whole Congress. Finally, on December 29, the members, coming from twenty-one countries, met in the building of the Pan-American Union, itself a gift from Andrew Carnegie. The highlight of the session was the approval by the American Institute of a Declaration of the Rights and Duties of Nations, drafted by Scott and modeled on the United States Declaration of Independence. In his remarks at the meeting, Scott made the point even more explicit: the constitutional traditions of Latin American countries derived from the US one. That was why the "conception of the Latin American State is the same as the North American conception."[79] The Declaration of Independence had provided

[76] Álvarez and Scott, "Note Concerning the American Institute of International Law and Affiliated National Societies of International Law," CEIP Year Book, 1915, p. 129.

[77] Ibid., p. 127.

[78] See "Report of the Director of the Division of International Law," CEIP Year Book, 1915, p. 119.

[79] Scott, *The American Institute of International Law: its Declaration of the Rights and Duties of Nations*, Washington, D.C.: The American Institute of International Law, 1916, p. 35.

the basis for the ideals of equality and self-government throughout the American Continent. Not only the legal guarantee for equality among individuals sprang from it: so also did sovereign equality as a principle of American international law.

With the Declaration of the Rights and Duties of Nations, Scott gave concreteness and articulation, relying on US legal sources, to the ideals of Pan-American sameness expressed earlier by Root. As Scarfi has put it, "[t]he declaration was a more explicit and sophisticated projection of US exceptionalism into the Western Hemisphere than anything earlier."[80] The first meeting had made clear, if there were any doubts, that Scott's model would prevail over Álvarez's in the AIIL: the elaboration of a continental international law would be based on a strong imprinting of US hegemony.

At the second session of the Institute in January 1917, Scott would press the point in the most symbolic way with his presidential address.[81] Returning to one of his favorite international legal foundational myths, he would take the stage in Cuba and declare the Spanish-American War the prime example of US selflessness and brotherhood toward Latin America.

## Scott's Turn to History and the New World Order

The war years meant for Scott advocacy for his internationalist views, to secure a postwar world order based on law and adjudication. But they also meant patriotic duty, since before the United States became one of the belligerent powers in April 1917. Since its creation in August 1914, he chaired the Joint State-Navy Neutrality Board, the organ that provided official legal opinions to the administration on behavior toward belligerents in the Great War.[82] As soon as the United States declared war, Scott enrolled again in the Army, once more churning legal opinions, this time on the conduct of the hostilities. He would also find a government-appointed role in the peace negotiations, participating to the Paris Conference as a legal advisor to the American delegation.

While co-opted by the administration, Scott was one of the most vocal opponents of collective security, the key element of President Woodrow Wilson's plans for a League of Nations.[83] Indeed, the idea, spurred by the European war,

[80] Scarfi, *Hidden History*, p. 49.

[81] Chapter 2 revolves around an analysis of this speech.

[82] For an interesting analysis of the activity of the Neutrality Board see Benjamin Coates, "'Upon the Neutral Rests the Trusteeship of International Law': Legal Advisers and American Unneutrality," in *Caught in the Middle: Neutrals, Neutrality and the First World War*, ed. by Johan Den Hertog and Samuël Kruizinga, Amsterdam: Amsterdam University Press, 2011. Scott had been appointed by Lansing, then counselor at the State Department. Scott had also given Lansing the idea to create the Board in the first place (see Martin David Dubin, "The Carnegie Endowment for International Peace and the Advocacy for a League of Nations, 1914–1918," *Proceedings of the American Philosophical Society*, 123(6), 1979, p. 363).

[83] For a comprehensive and insightful account and analysis of the various arguments on the creation of international institutions as a guarantee for the postwar global order and their reproduction in

that international law should be backed by military sanctions had broken the US internationalist movement into factions since before Wilson endorsed it. Scott saw collective security as a step back in the progress of international relations. Indeed for him, an international institutional system based on coercive enforcement was a way to facilitate the starting of wars rather than to prevent them. International disputes would keep being solved by "might" rather than by "right," as Scott would put it. The only way to have a peaceful international system was to create a judicial power and let it gradually build up case law and credibility. That is why, as the momentum for adjudication slipped away during the war years, Scott felt he had to keep pursuing the case he had made since the beginning of his career, and strengthen it. Characteristically, he did not attack the administration head on. His criticism was couched as advice and support rather than taking a polemical form. He would show through a careful reading of American history that judicial settlement was key to the US constitutional tradition and it embodied the egalitarian and progressive ethos of the New World. At a moment that he perceived as decisive in every possible sense, Scott turned to the past and to the trusted techniques he had used since his first speech. To convince the public and, especially, the administration[84] that adjudication was the obvious way forward in the progress of mankind, he would lay out in front of them the whole historical process that led to that conclusion. On one hand, he would focus on and deepen his explanation of US 1898 intervention in Cuba as an almost mystical moment that marked the beginning of a new way to understand international relations.[85] On the other, he would publish several books delineating the inception of the US Constitution and the role of the Supreme Court in the federal system. As the action of the Supreme Court had brought stability and peaceful dispute settlement to reign among the previously confrontational American former colonies, so an international court would for the Society of Nations.[86]

Scott's advocacy was unsuccessful. He failed to sway the administration: the Covenant of the League of Nations would be based on collective security in the form of a territorial guarantee against aggression. He also failed to return his judicialist views to the place of prominence they held among US international lawyers in the early 1910s.

later scholarship, providing context for my discussions of the topic throughout this work, see David Kennedy, "The Move to Institutions," *Cardozo Law Review*, 8, 1987, pp. 841–988.

[84] Scott placed two quotes by Woodrow Wilson in the inscriptions of one of his books on the US Constitutional Convention in a clear attempt of *captatio benevolentiae* (see Scott, *James Madison's Notes of Debates in the Federal Convention of 1787 and their Relation to a More Perfect Society of Nations*, New York: Oxford University Press, 1918, p. vi). Years later, he would admit that the book was primarily an attempt to sway Wilson (Scott to Nicholas Murray Butler, October 13, 1930, Folder 6, Box 60, CEIP Papers).

[85] See Chapter 2.

[86] See Chapter 3.

True, Scott would participate in the establishment of the Permanent Court of International Justice in 1921.[87] In public, he would salute the coming into existence of the Permanent Court as a milestone of human civilization: "We should not criticize the defects of the plan. We should fall upon our knees and thank God that the hope of ages is in the process of realization."[88] In private, he would admit to being unsatisfied by it, even if it was indeed one of his proverbial steps forward.[89] To begin with, the United States would not be part of it as it was not a member of the League of Nations. Moreover, Scott believed its jurisdiction was too limited and more should be done to guarantee the full independence of its judges. Above all, he was convinced that the Court could not flourish while connected to the League of Nations system, which favored the use of force: collective security simply denied the primacy of law.

Notwithstanding the defeat of his effort, Scott would continue on the path he set for himself with his first turn to history at the closing of the First World War. Not only did he remain convinced that to make his case in the present stronger he should focus on explaining the past of international law and its evolution; he decided that he would track the rules and principles of the discipline back to its founders: the sixteenth-century Salamanca theologians and especially Francisco de Vitoria. This clear continuity of purpose is one of the main reasons why I think it is crucial to understand and look closely at Scott's first turn to history, as I will do in the following chapters. Only by fleshing it out does one get to comprehend fully his later historical work, his second turn to history starting in the mid-1920s. Moreover, it is also a convenient vantage point to provide a wide-ranged analysis of Scott's cultural and ideological background before moving to Part II and the main focus of the book: Scott's work on the Catholic and Spanish origins of international law and its political uses.

[87] Elihu Root was one of the ten experts appointed by the Council of the League of Nations in 1920 to form the Advisory Committee of Jurists tasked with the drafting of the Permanent Court's statute. Scott joined the Committee as Root's secretary and technical advisor but, according to the British member Lord Phillimore, he "was almost treated as an actual member of the Commission" ("Scheme for the Permanent Court of International Justice," *Transactions of the Grotius Society*, 6, 1920, p. 89). On the Advisory Committee of Jurists see Ole Spiermann, "'Who Attempts too Much Does Nothing Well': the 1920 Advisory Committee of Jurists and the Statute of the Permanent Court of International Justice," *British Yearbook of International Law*, 73, 2003, pp. 187–260.

[88] Scott, "Editorial Comment—A Permanent Court of International Justice," *American Journal of International Law*, 1921, p. 55.

[89] See, for instance, James Brown Scott to Henry Cabot Lodge, April 30, 1924, Folder 1, Box 12, JBS Papers.

# 2

# International Law as Faith. The Cuban Intervention and the Narrative of 1898

On December 17, 2014, Presidents Obama and Raúl Castro announced a new phase in the relationship between Cuba and the United States, re-establishing diplomatic relations after fifty-three years of severance. In his statement,[1] Obama acknowledged the serious differences that would still divide the two countries, especially on human rights issues. Yet, he depicted the harsh Cuban policy conducted by his predecessors as the counterproductive relic of a global war against communism the United States had already won. Obama, indeed, did not look further back than the 1959 Castrist revolution, focusing on Cold War events and themes.

In his speech, however,[2] Raúl Castro employed a different frame of reference. He made a brief remark commending the loyalty of the Cuban people to its principles since the beginning of independence wars in 1868. Castro was referring to the various attempts by Cubans to topple Spanish colonial power on the island. When in 1898 Spain was finally forced to leave, Cuba was formally independent but occupied by the United States Army. Historians have often pointed out that recovering events and the related narratives from the turn of the century is crucial to understand how the United States and Cuba have mutually contributed to shaping each other's political identity long before their Cold War confrontations.[3] I contribute to that enterprise with a related claim. The narrative of 1898, depicting North Americans as selfless helpers of the Cuban people, has contributed to the articulation of international law as a professional discipline in the United States and to the tightening the discipline's ties to religious discourse. That narrative had its most powerful and popular expounding in the theological terms used by preachers across the country when commenting on the Cuban intervention. The grip of this narrative was not only in the influence it had in framing the 1898 war and its immediate aftermath. It persisted in the exceptionalist understanding of the role of the United States in the international legal system maintained by James Brown Scott and the other founders of the American Society of International Law (ASIL) up to the end of the First World War and beyond.

[1] Available at http://www.whitehouse.gov/the-press-office/2014/12/17/statement-president-cuba-policy-changes (last accessed July 2, 2019).

[2] Available at https://www.voltairenet.org/article186231.html (last accessed July 16, 2019).

[3] See for instance Louis A. Pérez, *Cuba in the American Imagination: Metaphor and the Imperial Ethos*, Chapel Hill: University of North Carolina Press, 2008, especially pp. 1–23.

*Rewriting the History of the Law of Nations: How James Brown Scott Made Francisco de Vitoria the Founder of International Law*. Paolo Amorosa, Oxford University Press (2019). © Paolo Amorosa
DOI: 10.1093/oso/9780198849377.001.0001

Recognizing the religious matrix of this narrative helps to make sense of the rhetoric of the early generation of US international lawyers to which Scott belonged. They insisted on understanding law as science, proposing a specific kind of legal formalism as the guarantee of justice and equality. At the same time, their faith in the United States and international law as messianic forces helped them to dismiss anxieties and unfavorable events as momentary setbacks in an inevitable providential plan. In this chapter I set to show how, through faith, these international lawyers reconciled imperial ambitions and democratic values. This composite mindset presented international law as a political theology: metaphysically founded but with clear pragmatic implications for the direction of international relations.

## 1. James Brown Scott in Havana: International Law and the Selfless Empire

On the evening of January 22, 1917, James Brown Scott, President of the American Institute of International Law, took the floor at the Institute's Second Annual Meeting in Havana, in the presence of Cuban president Mario García Menocal. Scott remarked at the outset that he had waited nineteen years to be there in Cuba, but the moment had finally come. He was referring to the 1898 Spanish-American War. At the time a volunteer private in the United States Army, Scott was about to leave for the island. His regiment was instead finally attached to the forces on the Pacific front, tasked with the operations in the other Spanish colony of the Philippines. Yet the United States won the war faster than anyone could have expected. The soon-to-be Secretary of State, John Hay, would call it "a splendid little war." Scott's regiment would never leave California.

The year before he finally reached Havana, Scott had published a volume entitled *Military and Colonial Policy of the United States*. The book was part of a series, edited by Scott and Robert Bacon, collecting the speeches and writings of their mentor Elihu Root. In the book's foreword, Scott remarked how the texts therein addressed issues to be seen "as consequence or aftermath of the war with Spain in 1898."[4] He continued by telling the story of how Root was involved in colonial administration and the spirit with which he carried out his task. It all started in July 1899 with an unexpected phone call. The President's office was calling to tell Root he had been chosen to be the new Secretary of War. Root had been involved in Republican Party politics for a long time. He was especially known as an anti-corruption reformer in his home State of New York, where his thriving corporate

[4] Elihu Root, *The Military and Colonial Policy of the United States: Speeches and Reports*, collected and edited by Robert Bacon and James Brown Scott, Cambridge: Harvard University Press, 1916, p. xi.

law practice was based. He had never held office before;[5] neither did he believe he was suited for the position. "Thank the President for me, but say it is quite absurd, I know nothing about war," Root replied. But President McKinley did not want an army man. He wanted a lawyer to set up administration in the newly acquired territories and the lawyer he wanted was Root. At that point, for Root, "there was but one answer to make." He "went to perform a lawyer's duty upon the call of the greatest of all our clients, the Government of" the United States. None other than Root himself painted this neat recollection of the conversation in a public speech almost seventeen years after it happened.[6] One might speculate on whether Root had "adjusted" the exchange for storytelling purposes and an audience of lawyers. Yet, the message he wanted to relay was clear. It was not about war. It was about law, justice, and efficient administration. That was Root's task: to export and spread American freedom through law.

Scott in Havana was still carrying out the American world-civilizing mission Root had undertaken when he accepted McKinley's cabinet position offer. This mission had a broad scope, not restricted to the US imperial enterprises that followed the Spanish-American War. International lawyers had been at the forefront of a revolution. A country that had understood since its independence its foreign relations as being aimed at maintaining isolation and avoid entanglements, now felt ready to assume an active role of primary importance in international politics. Of course, such a momentous change came with anxieties and ambiguities.[7] It was the entire identity of the United States as a nation that was under discussion. On that evening of 1917 in Cuba, Scott was giving his take on that change. It was the view of an idealist international lawyer who believed that the values on which the United States was founded could and would redeem the whole world.

Scott began his address reminding the audience how the United States became the occupying power in Cuba in 1898. The Spanish-American War was one of humanitarian intervention on behalf of the Cuban people to stop the barbarities being perpetrated by the Spanish government. Indeed the United States Congress, in declaring war, had affirmed through the Teller Amendment that there was no

[5] Root had been a delegate-at-large, designated by the Republican caucus, at the 1894 New York Constitutional Convention, where he was the major force behind the reform of the state judicial system (see Philip C. Jessup, *Elihu Root*, vol. 1, New York: Dodd, Mead & Company, 1938, pp. 175–7). Yet, he saw this and other institutional tasks he would perform as technical and professional rather than political. Root, notwithstanding continued party pressures to run for various positions including President of the United States, would seek office only once and late in his life. In 1909, he was elected United States Senator for the State of New York, a position he would hold until 1915.

[6] Root held the speech before the New York County Lawyers' Association on March 13, 1915. Scott had published the text of the entire address in another volume of the series ("The Lawyer of Today," in Elihu Root, *Addresses on Government and Citizenship*, collected and edited by Robert Bacon and James Brown Scott, Cambridge: Harvard University Press, 1916, pp. 503–9), as he noted when referring to it in the preface to *The Military and Colonial Policy*. For a political background and an account of the reactions to Root's nomination as Secretary of War see Jessup, *Elihu Root*, vol. 1, pp. 215–19.

[7] See Chapter 1, subsection "A Different Kind of World Power."

intention to exercise any control beyond the temporary one necessary to pacify the island. "That was," according to Scott, "the intention of the United States":[8] to keep Cuba free from foreign intervention and under a republican government that would truly represent the Cuban people. Scott pointed to the Platt Amendment, drafted by Root, as the primary means with which the United States pursued the goal of a free and independent Cuba. This statement exposes the depth of the contradictions international lawyers in the United States faced in order to recreate a viable national identity for their country as a world power. The Platt Amendment, indeed, represented the US legislative step toward insertion in the Cuban Constitution of a right of intervention for the United States in Cuban affairs.

Scott, in his speech, recounted the details of the Amendment's legislative history. After being adopted by Congress on March 2, 1901 as an amendment to the Army Appropriation Bill, the text of the Platt Amendment also became part of the then draft Cuban Constitution on the following June 12. In 1903, Cuba and the United States entered into a bilateral treaty that reproduced the text of the Amendment.[9] Scott made sure to underline that the Amendment originated in the instructions given by Root on February 9, 1901 to the military governor of the island, Major General Leonard Wood, as preparation for the withdrawal of the United States' troops. The instructions contained a series of measures that would be replicated, with slight modifications, in the text of the Amendment. Such measures would greatly restrict the room for maneuver for the future Cuban government, ranging from constitutional limitations on treaty-making with countries other than the United States to restrictions on the taking on of public debt. Yet the key provision "the people of Cuba should desire," according to Root, was indeed the constitutional recognition of the right of intervention of the United States in Cuban affairs. In the discursive part of the instructions, Root switched often in considering Cuban independence as desirable because of United States' interests or because of democratic values, as it would give the chance to Cubans to rule themselves with a republican form of government. However, when formulating the draft provisions that would end up in the Platt Amendment, Root made use only of a language of selflessness and duty. The US right of intervention would serve the "preservation of Cuban independence and the maintenance of a stable government, adequately protecting life, property and individual liberty."[10]

[8] James Brown Scott, "The Platt Amendment—Recommendations of Habana Concerning International Organization," in American Institute of International Law, *The Recommendations of Habana Concerning International Organization. Address and Commentary by James Brown Scott*, New York: Oxford University Press, 1917, p. 3.

[9] Cuban-American Treaty of Relations, signed May 22, 1903, in Charles I. Bevans (ed.), *Treaties and Other International Agreements of the United States of America 1776–1949*, vol. 6 Canada-Czechoslovakia, Washington D.C.: Department of State Publication, 1971, pp. 1116–19.

[10] This formula is used by Root in the Instructions (see Scott, 'The Platt Amendment', p. 6) and then replicated in the Platt Amendment (see Scott, 'The Platt Amendment', p. 10).

This second line of reasoning, the one focused on US selflessness, was the one followed by Scott in his Havana speech. Scott explained the US-Cuban relationship as regulated by the Platt Amendment as an anti-imperialist model of equal relations. Yet an occupying power had dictated into the Constitution of the occupied country a right of intervention in its own favor. How could that be called equality and serve the achievement of self-government for the Cuban people?

This seemingly specific question is an inspiring starting point to reflect on a key moment for the study of international law in the United States. As I argued in the previous chapter, the Spanish-American War and the unexpected ease of its victory led to a renewed focus on international law, partly in order to reconcile the new leading global role of the country with its democratic tradition. Scott, Root, and the other founders of the ASIL recast even the formal colonialism in the Philippines and the tutelage of the newly independent Cuba as an expression of egalitarian values, American and universal at the same time. This ambiguous nationalist/cosmopolitan identity was based on a narrative of progress: the peak of civilization reached by the United States would gradually expand worldwide through example and benevolent assimilation. In the eyes of these international lawyers, if this was to be called imperialism it had nothing to do with the predatory attitude of European mold. The American civilizing mission was geared toward the selfless goal of creating "a new imperialism—the imperialism of liberty."[11] The natural American adherence to international law and its underlying liberal values was considered as the *trait d'union* between the colonial policy of the United States and its global promotion of international institutions and adjudication.

## Science, International Law, and the Social Context: The Platt Amendment as Equality[12]

There are aspects of the interaction between US identity and the development of international law that are understudied. For instance, historians acknowledge the close ideological connection between Christianity and Western values underwriting international law and its imperial aspirations in the second half of the nineteenth century and the early twentieth century. Most scholarship seems, however, to assume that the international lawyers of the age, cosmopolitans often on the liberal side of the political spectrum, were not people living intense religious experiences but rather were shallow cultural Christians sharing a secularized rationalist identity. Such an assumption would definitely be incorrect in relation to many key founders of the ASIL. James Brown Scott, as we have seen, had been a fervent

[11] Congregationalist theologian Lyman Abbott (1835–1922), quoted in Andrew Preston, *Sword of the Spirit, Shield of Faith: Religion in American War and Diplomacy*, New York: Alfred A. Knopf, 2012, p. 225.

[12] For a deeper exploration of this subsection's themes see Chapter 3.

religious believer since his childhood. A Presbyterian of Scottish strain, he would base his career on the American exceptionalism with an internationalist flavor that emerged primarily in the mainstream religious discourse in the key year of 1898.[13] While he insisted on the scientific nature of international law, Scott also underlined the importance of its egalitarian moral foundations and found its origin in the theology of the Salamanca school. In this aspect Scott seems to represent a tension that has been present throughout the various expressions of US national identity over the course of history. To this day, the Enlightenment roots of the Revolution keep clashing and melting with the messianic visions of American civil religion.[14]

The Havana speech represented a telling example of Scott's composite sensibility and of the way it shaped his international legal scholarship and activism. Moreover, it established a direct link between the Spanish-American War and the new egalitarian era of international relations that Scott envisioned as emerging under the influence of the United States. The "splendid little war," with its preparation and its aftermath, has received more and more attention by scholars as a catalyst for fundamental changes in the political imagination and the foreign policy of the United States. Yet its implications for the development and professionalization of international law have been largely ignored.[15]

James Brown Scott was at the forefront of international lawyers striving to provide the discipline with scientific status and professional dignity. The mindset linked to this enterprise would be crucial in shaping Scott's understanding of the Platt Amendment. International lawyers, pressured by the Austinian challenge, felt even more than other legal scholars the necessity to establish law as a science. This led them, at least in rhetorical terms, to relegate religious values to the foundations of international law and exclude them from its operation. However, this hardly meant that they perceived a problematic tension between science and Christian faith. Indeed, one distinctive trope in the intellectual milieu in the United States at the time, accepted by most theologians, was the theorized harmony (or at least non-contradiction) of science, including Darwinism, and religion.[16]

In the academic milieu of the turn of the century, social sciences' main aspiration was to achieve a level of objectivism comparable to the one of natural sciences. In law schools, the drive for scientific systematization took the shape of Langdellian formalism. Christopher Columbus Langdell, Dean of Harvard Law School, is known to

[13] See Matthew McCullough, *The Cross of War: Christian Nationalism and U.S. Expansion in the Spanish-American War*, Madison: The University of Wisconsin Press, 2014.

[14] See, for instance, Paul T. McCartney, *Power and Progress: American National Identity, the War of 1898, and the Rise of American Imperialism*, Baton Rouge: Louisiana State University Press, 2006, pp. 27–43.

[15] One notable exception is Carl Landauer, "The Ambivalences of Power: Launching the American Journal of International Law in an Era of Empire and Globalization," *Leiden Journal of International Law*, 20, 2007, pp. 325–58.

[16] For a description of the debates that led to the adoption of the harmony position in the Presbyterian denomination see Bradley J. Longfield, *Presbyterians and American Culture: a History*, Louisville: Westminster, John Knox Press, 2013, pp. 120–7.

have revolutionized the teaching of law in the United States through the use of the case method. For Langdell, judicial decisions were the raw material that lawyers should empirically study. From them, lawyers would be able to induce principles and systematize them. In turn, solutions for further legal questions could be deduced from these principles. Such a rationalist and formalist understanding of law was strongly connected with the idea of the United States as a messianic project. The constant evolution toward systematization meant the removal of arbitrariness in court decisions, so realizing the ideal of "a government of laws, not of men." Leading at the peak of civilization, the US legal system had realized equality before the law for everyone.

Scott was a self-professed follower of Langdellian scientism.[17] Yet, as the 1902 introduction to his first international law casebook made clear, his goal was not only to provide law students with material, but also to sustain his nationalist and, at the same time, internationalist project. Scott underlined how the status of international law as a legal discipline could not be denied because of a basic observation: international law was applied in courts. Therefore, it could be studied and developed in scientific terms. Crucially for Scott, it had been "English and American courts of justice" that had been acting to "enforce international law . . . repeatedly . . . for the past two centuries."[18] This seemingly technical point underwrote a whole series of implications. International law was of Anglo-Saxon origin, in itself a valid pedigree of civilization for a discipline in the turn-of-the-century United States. It was also American, part of the United States' municipal law and developed within its judicial system with the Supreme Court at its top. For that reason international law was universal as well, as the Supreme Court, with its effective jurisdiction over sovereign States, was the only tested and viable model for a future international court. Alongside this procedural point ran the substantial one: formalist law as developed by US courts meant the realization of freedom and equality. If the Old World wanted progress and the peace that came along with it, it just had to learn from the United States. The tables had turned.

Freedom and equality within the Langdellian strain of formalism concretely meant absolute freedom of contract. The rejection of any form of constraint on freedom of contract as a progressive affirmation of individualism would be for decades a cornerstone of the United States' legal system. American courts, especially the Supreme Court of the Lochner era, systematically intervened to void, for instance, legislation for the protection of workers,[19] using freedom of contract in the interest of employers. As union leader John L. Mitchell put it, workers seemed

[17] See Scott, "The Study of the Law," *The American Law School Review*, 2(1), 1906, pp. 3–4 and Hepp, "James Brown Scott and the Rise of Public International Law," *Journal of the Gilded Age and Progressive Era*, 7, 2008, pp. 162–4.

[18] James Brown Scott, "Preface," in *Cases on International Law Selected from Decisions of English and American Courts with Syllabus and Annotations*, Boston: Boston Book Company, 1902, p. v.

[19] For the discussion of an example of stricken-down social legislation under the described ideology see Jonathan Zasloff, "Law and the Shaping of American Foreign Policy: From the Gilded Age to the New Era," *New York University Law Review*, 78, 2003, pp. 269–70.

to be "guaranteed the liberties they do not want and denied the liberty that is of real value to them."[20] Law and freedom were construed as blind to insuperable disproportions in bargaining power. This individualist and formalist posture was commonplace within the US establishment. Progress, for the elite, did not entail redistribution. Freedom was political, not social or economic. The equality to be guaranteed was formal, not substantial.

It is easy to read a similar formalist understanding of equality in Root and Scott's theorization of the Platt Amendment.[21] The representatives of the Cuban people had agreed to it and that manifestation of will was all that mattered in order to create a legal obligation. Equality meant absolute freedom of contract. Therefore, the circumstance that the contracting parties were in a relation of occupying and occupied, and the importance of the object, the constitutional document of a party, could be deemed irrelevant. With a legal theory that considered a legal obligation as neutral and just by definition, it was possible to mask the contradiction between democratic ideals and imperial uses of American power.

## 2. The Narrative of 1898: The Religious Foundation of the Cuban Intervention

### Before the War: Public Opinion, Humanitarianism, and Religious Discourse

The intrinsic 'diversity' of American imperialism was an article of faith in more than one sense. It was often assumed and only thinly argued. Actors in the US public discourse did not feel the need to support the dogma of the selfless empire, but rather preferred to continue expounding it with slight variations. The progressive credentials of the New World and the evident success of the United States as a country, especially after the triumphant war, sufficed. But, more pointedly, the exceptional moral nature of the American empire was constructed in explicitly religious terms because the narrative of the 1898 war came largely from the pulpits. Historians underline the role of the "yellow press" in exciting the public opinion toward war. But what is too often forgotten is that at the time texts of popular diffusion were hardly limited to the secular press, which itself made use of religious imagery and printed sermons. The religious press was widespread and influential at both national and local level. In 1898 it featured sermons and editorials that framed a comprehensive and quite uniform Christian understanding of the war.

[20] John L. Mitchell, "The Workingman's Conception of Industrial Liberty," *American Federationist*, 17, May 1910, pp. 406–7, quoted in Eric Foner, *The Story of American Freedom*, New York: W. W. Norton, 1998, p. 123.

[21] See, for instance, Scott, 'The Platt Amendment', pp. 14–16.

The 1890s represented a period of unprecedented interest and involvement of the American people in foreign policy debates. Information traveled much faster between continents thanks to the recently laid-out web of transatlantic telegraphic cables. The "sensationalist 'yellow press', seeking to increase daily circulation, found foreign affairs to be an ideal source of provocative headlines."[22] US public opinion had already been inflamed about international crises before the Cuban rebellion that led to the 1898 war took the stage. Some of those crises particularly resonated with the American public, anticipating the themes of humanitarianism and exceptionalism that would come together in the narrative of 1898.

Humanitarian demands first took the form of requests for governmental support of international relief actions. In 1892, the American people, informed of a famine in Russia that threatened the life of millions of peasants, pressured for institutional action. After much infighting and indecisiveness, both Congress and President Grover Cleveland refused to get directly involved, even refusing to ship privately collected relief goods to Russia. Yet, press campaigns led the Iowa governor, Horace Boies, to create the Iowa Famine Relief Commission. With the refusal of Congress to get involved, the Red Cross took charge of delivering the Iowan aid to Russia. The American Red Cross had been founded in 1881, thanks to the lobbying of Clara Barton, still at the helm during the Russian famine relief effort. A veteran nurse and relief organizer of the American Civil War and the Franco-Prussian War, Barton had eventually convinced President Chester Arthur to support the creation of a US branch of the organization, which since then had already dealt with domestic crises.[23] "[T]he entire Russian famine relief effort raised Barton's and the American Red Cross's visibility further convincing humanitarian activists of their ability to mobilize voters and move government to ameliorate the world's ills."[24] The pattern repeated itself a couple of years later when newspapers and magazines started reporting the Turkish persecution of Armenians. Cleveland claimed not to have the constitutional authority to act and it was once again Barton and the Red Cross who traveled to provide the help offered by American private relief organizations.

In 1895, a diplomatic crisis of a more traditional kind brought strong public support to the Cleveland administration's reassertion of the Monroe Doctrine. A slow-burning dispute over the boundary between Venezuela and the colony of British Guyana escalated to the point that the United Kingdom seemed on the verge of military intervention. The United States did not show much interest in intervening until the Venezuelan government put William Scruggs on its payroll. A former United States minister to Venezuela turned lobbyist, Scruggs published a

[22] Frank Ninkovich, *The United States and Imperialism*, Malden: Blackwell Publishers, 2001, p. 14.
[23] See Jeffrey Bloodworth, "For Love or for Money?: William McKinley and the Spanish-American War," *White House Studies*, 9, 2009, p. 140.
[24] Ibid., p. 141.

pamphlet titled *British Aggressions in Venezuela or the Monroe Doctrine on Trial* in October 1894 and ensured its wide distribution. The point he made was simple: the United States had both a moral duty and interest to protect self-government in the continent against the despotic greediness of European empires.[25] While the controversy dragged on, the Royal Navy occupied a Nicaraguan port in April 1895 to protect British nationals over an unrelated matter. The US "public opinion was violently outraged. The Cleveland Administration was vigorously attacked for its supineness in the face of British brutality and aggression; and Scruggs, in his campaign on behalf of Venezuela, found a powerful if unexpected ally in the Royal Navy."[26] In July, the new Secretary of State Richard Olney sent a provocative diplomatic note to London. It contained a sentence that would go down in history as the Olney corollary to the Monroe Doctrine. While crafted in language "undoubtedly of the bumptious order,"[27] as Olney himself would later admit, it represented the growing self-confidence and self-righteousness of the United States in international matters. According to the note, "today the United States is practically sovereign on this continent and its fiat is law."[28] Eventually the British government agreed to resolve the dispute through arbitration. American public opinion rejoiced in what was perceived as an historic victory against European imperialism and recognition of the United States' leadership in the New World.

The religious press was very active in reporting and taking position on these crises, as it would be in the context of the 1898 war. Moreover, the interest of US religious denominations and their clergy in international issues predated by decades the one of the yellow press. Indeed, the idea to substitute force with law in international relations, by resorting to international adjudication rather than war, had been advocated by American religiously inspired organizations much before it became a project of lawyers and of the United States government. The early American peace societies grew out of the idea that war is incompatible with Christian religion.[29] Following the foundation of the New York Peace Society in 1815, other local ones quickly appeared in the rest of the United States, even if the center of the movement would remain in the Northeast.[30] David Low Dodge (1774–1852), the force behind the creation of the New York Society, ascribed even this organizational success to divine intervention. He suggested that the independent way in which societies were "formed, without any correspondence or knowledge of each other"

[25] See Robert Arthur Humphreys, "Presidential Address: Anglo-American Rivalries and the Venezuela Crisis of 1895," *Transactions of the Royal Historical Society*, 17, 1967, pp. 142–6.

[26] Ibid., p. 148.

[27] Richard Olney to Philander Knox, January 29, 1912, Knox Papers, Library of Congress Manuscript Division, no. 16, quoted in Ninkovich, *The United States and Imperialism*, p. 13.

[28] Quoted in Ninkovich, *The United States and Imperialism*, p. 13.

[29] See James Brown Scott, "Introduction," in William Ladd, *An Essay on a Congress of Nations*, New York: Oxford University Press—American Branch, 1916, pp. v–vii.

[30] See Mark Janis, *The American Tradition of International Law: Great Expectations, 1789–1914*, Oxford: Oxford University Press, 2004, p. 98.

was due to "providence having paved the way." For him, it was "the spirit of God" that "had moved on the hearts of many of his children to consider the subject" of peace.[31] The man who more decidedly led the pacifist effort toward the promotion of international institutions was William Ladd (1778–1841), a Maine landowner turned preacher and activist. He succeeded in his effort to unite the local peace societies under one banner, founding the American Peace Society in 1828. Ladd's leadership was also connected to a shift in the movement from the radical pacifism of Dodge to a more gradualist approach and the refusal to condemn all wars in the present. Gradualism brought with it pragmatism, a connection of peace with concrete plans rather than simply high-minded religious claims. Ladd published *An Essay on a Congress of Nations* in 1840. His proposal envisioned a Congress made of "Christian and civilized nations," enjoying equal voting rights and a permanent Court of Nations modeled on the US Supreme Court. Indeed, James Brown Scott would advertise those early American efforts by re-publishing the *Essay* in 1916. Ladd figured well in Scott's international law pedigree as he claimed that the originality of his institutional proposal lay in the Langdellian theme of the separation between political (the Congress) and judicial functions (the Court). Moreover, the publication reinforced Scott's strong ties with the American Peace Society. Indeed, by the time of the foundation of the American Society of International Law in 1906, the Peace Society had become moderate enough to ally on a steady basis with pragmatist, establishment international lawyers.[32]

The pre-1890s international activism of religious leaders that inspired the narrative of 1898 hardly stopped at the peace movement, however. Shaping the world through direct action rather than just by American example was crucial in the mindset that led to the impressive growth of foreign missionary work in the nineteenth century. Missionaries spearheaded expansionism outside the American continent. Indeed, they exported American values long before Frederick Jackson Turner's theory of the frontier in 1893 would certify that expansion now could and would only happen beyond the United States' boundaries. It is important to note that US missionary enterprises went beyond evangelization. For instance, missionaries built and managed schools and hospitals. This focus on good works was in line with the growing influence of Darwinism and biblical criticism. Progressive Protestant ministers argued for the compatibility of Christian faith

[31] David Low Dodge and others, *Memorial of Mr. David L. Dodge*, Boston: S. K. Whipple & Co., 1854, p. 99.

[32] International lawyers of Scott's generation still strove to distinguish themselves from radical groups in the peace movement. For lawyers peace was a worthy objective obtainable in the long run through science-based institutional plans and the education of the public opinion. That is why they deemed plain appeals to abolish war on the basis of its immorality as irrational and counterproductive. Scott found a precious ally for his gradualist and judicialist project in the American Peace Society. With the progress of the First World War, Scott's ideas came to be challenged by the growing popularity of collective security as the cornerstone of the postwar world order. The American Peace Society was one of the few institutions to remain on Scott's side when, while still influential, he was firmly on the losing side of international legal debates in the United States (see Chapter 3, section 3).

and science. This modernist turn resonated with many secular intellectuals who, like Scott, strove to combine their enthusiasm for evolutionary theories and scientific progress with providential and millennialist Christian beliefs. The success of the missionary movement also meant that missionaries were one of the primary sources of information for Americans about the rest of the world. The United States' diplomatic missions were few and scarcely staffed: a comprehensive reform and strengthening of the State Department structure would come only under the tenure of Elihu Root as Secretary, starting in 1905. Missionary presence abroad prevailed not only through sheer numbers: missions were often placed in remote areas where no US diplomat had the chance to set foot. While the coexistence of diplomats and missionaries often led to turf frictions, in many cases diplomats too, like Americans at home, had to rely on missionaries as their only source of information.

No wonder, then, that religious leaders felt so well placed to tell Americans the true meaning of a Cuban intervention. Their organizations had been aiming at shaping the world in the United States' image and told back home about their efforts long before the rest of the country also became ready to cross the oceans. In the initial phases of the Cuban crisis, most religious leaders stood by President McKinley, praising him for his restraint and opposing intervention. Indeed, before 1898, calls by religious leaders for US full-blown foreign military intervention had been rare and isolated. Social Gospeler Josiah Strong's invocation of intervention in response to the Armenian crisis had been a notable exception to the general trend. It was in 1895, while the Armenian atrocities were garnering attention, that rebellion in Cuba broke out again. Indignation in the United States rose up when the Spanish military governor Valeriano Weyler enacted a reconcentration policy on the island. To deprive the rebel guerrilla groups of support, Weyler ordered the concentration of the inhabitants of rural areas in guarded camps. The lack of adequate provisions and sanitation in the camps led to the eventual deaths of approximately 100,000 Cubans by early 1898.[33] The yellow press reports stirred outrage in the US public. The Christian press joined the condemnation of Weyler's policies, depicting them as an expression of the barbaric rule of Catholic Spain. Yet the support for the Cuban rebellion did not turn into a call for intervention. "Even as ministers, editors, and denominational resolutions called for an end to Spanish rule on the island, they also continued to insist on American neutrality in the conflict."[34]

Even after the sinking of the USS *Maine* in the Havana harbor on February 15, 1898, the opinion of the religious establishment stood firmly against intervention. McKinley had sent the battleship, with the reluctant permission of the Spanish government, to monitor the situation and ensure the safety of US citizens. When

[33] See McCullough, *The Cross of War*, p. 15.
[34] Ibid.

the *Maine* suddenly sank because of an explosion, causing the death of 266 US sailors, the already angry public immediately blamed the Spanish government. Restraint was once again the watchword of religious leaders. Support for the president was coupled with accusations against the sensationalist press, blamed by a sermon preached on February 27 of "the strain and the nervousness and nationwide exasperation of the past two weeks." In that same sermon, Charles Parkhurst of the Madison Square Presbyterian Church went on to explain how the press and its "lying" was exploiting the "vast population" and compromising its "moral marrow." It did so by impressing "hundreds of thousands of inconsiderate ones who are not necessarily without conscience, but who are childishly fascinated by its flamboyancy and who become in time so debilitated, intellectually and morally debilitated, by its stimulated piquancy as to come in time really to love a lie well sell seasoned better than the truth."[35]

This paternalistic view of public opinion points to another point of contact between religious leaders and secular intellectuals of the time. They considered the universal project of modernity, in which the United States, providence, reason, and democracy had become one and the same, endangered by the unreflective nature of the people. As Paul Kahn notes, this type of "argument . . . animated the jurisprudence of the [Supreme] Court" at the time, under Melvin Fuller as Chief Justice between 1898 and 1910. The "deep skepticism of populist movements" is a constant contradiction of modern democracies.[36] This is reflected in the idea of Langdellian international lawyers that progress is a process of education. It is not by chance that the article opening the very first issue of the *American Journal of International Law*,[37] authored by Root, is titled "The Need of Popular Understanding of International Law." Education, though, meant primarily learning from and listening to the ones who knew better, the establishment. This ambiguity is well reflected in the expression Root used when he first penned the provisions that would become the Platt Amendment: those were the provisions that "the Cubans should desire" in their Constitution. In the same way as the domestic public opinion was reasonable only within the parameters set by the establishment, the Platt Amendment was conceived not as that which the United States government or the Cuban people desired, but as that which Root believed the Cubans should desire.

[35] Charles Parkhurst, "The State of the Country," printed in the Presbyterian *Evangelist* (10 March 1898): pp. 11–12, quoted in McCullough, *The Cross of War*, pp. 17–18. McCullough also notes that on 3 March "the Nation, a prominent secular periodical highly critical of rampant jingoism, confirmed that the tone" of moderation "was typical of the ministerial response" to the sinking of the *Maine* "nationwide" (p. 18).

[36] Paul Kahn, "Law of Nations at the Origins," in Martti Koskenniemi, Mónica Garcia-Salmones Rovira, and Paolo Amorosa (eds.), *International Law and Religion: Historical and Contemporary Perspectives*, Oxford: Oxford University Press, 2017, p. 418, fn 18.

[37] Elihu Root, "The Need of Popular Understanding of International Law," *American Journal of International Law*, 1, 1907, pp. 1–3.

## International Law as Civilization and the Religious Discourse: The Platt Amendment as Selflessness

How, then, did the religious leadership come to support the intervention and give it its meaning? In the weeks immediately following the sinking of the *Maine*, Congress was pushing for war. The representatives of big business instead in this phase still believed that their economic interests in Cuba would be further prejudiced by a US military intervention. The president strove to keep his options as open as possible while several powerful forces required him to take a stance. On March 21, the inquiry ordered by McKinley in the immediate aftermath of the sinking did not assign blame, but concluded that the explosion was external to the ship.[38] The belief that there had been Spanish foul play grew stronger in the United States. The vengeful slogan "Remember the *Maine*" quickly spread in the yellow press and on the streets.

The sinking of the *Maine* is one of the most remembered events of the Spanish-American War and is often assumed to have been the last straw that pushed the United States to intervene. Yet several historians point at a different event that might have swayed the skeptical voices in US society to support intervention. A few days before the release of the *Maine* inquiry, on March 17, Senator Redfield Proctor of Vermont delivered a speech in Congress about his recent trip to Cuba. Proctor was known as a cool-headed pro-business conservative, skeptical of the reports of the yellow press. However, his direct experience convinced him that the reality was even worse than how it had been described in the newspapers. "Reporters noted that Proctor read his speech describing the starvation of tens of thousands without any trace of dramatic flourish. The calm, deliberate manner in which he offered his testimony to Congress made for a striking contrast with the sensational claims of the 'yellow' journalists. In short, when this man described what he had seen in this way, conditions of mass starvation and widespread Spanish brutality, people believed him."[39]

Proctor's speech swayed Wall Street, now convinced by one they saw as their own that the situation was too dire, also in relation to their business interest, for the United States not to act.[40] Finally, on April 11, McKinley asked Congress for the authorization to intervene. On April 25, Congress declared the existence of a state of war with Spain. Matthew McCullough, author of the most complete study to date of 1898 sermons and religious editorials on the war,[41] argues that Proctor's speech coincided with what he calls "the great reversal" for religious leadership too. He

[38] Later investigations would prove the explosion to be accidental, due to the ignition of powder charges stored in the ship.

[39] McCullough, *The Cross of War*, p. 19.

[40] See Mike Sewell, "Humanitarian Intervention, Democracy, and Imperialism: The American War with Spain, 1898, and After," in *Humanitarian Intervention: A History*, edited by Brendan Simms and David J. B. Trim, Cambridge: Cambridge University Press, 2011, pp. 310–11.

[41] McCullough, *The Cross of War*.

claims that "[i]n the religious press, in the wake of this report, focus shifted over resistance to jingoes over possible retaliation for the *Maine* to wholehearted support for intervention."[42] With this swift reversal, ministers took up the responsibility to frame the intervention as Christian, motivated only by selfless and humanitarian considerations. The United States would sacrifice lives and resources to help the Cubans in their struggle for freedom without any desire for territorial or financial gain. According to McCullough, two main biblical *topoi* were used to explain the intervention in Christian terms: the parable of the Good Samaritan[43] and the sacrificial death of Jesus Christ.[44]

The biblical parable exemplified the love for one's neighbor the United States was showing in intervening in favor of Cubans. The Samaritan intervened to help a robbed and wounded Israelite, with whom he shared no other bond than common humanity. Before him two religious leaders had passed by and left their fellow Israelite in his misery. In the same way as the Samaritan, ministers argued, the United States was ready to change course from the previous fear of entanglements and intervene, fulfilling its role of a chosen Christian nation. The passers-by would be made to symbolize the isolationist voices within the United States or the selfish European nations that would not help those in need.

Even more powerful was the evoking of the sacrificial death of Christ. Sacrifice for national values had been the most recurring characterization of the Civil War, a still open wound Americans hoped to finally heal through the unity inspired by the 1898 war. Ministers would, for the first time, use the category of sacrifice not to understand purely national events but as those made to benefit another people. To those who protested that Cuban lives were not as worthy as North American ones, New York Presbyterian David Gregg reminded, in a sermon delivered on April 24, that Christ had sacrificed himself for sinful human beings. Gregg did not challenge the notion of the Cubans' lesser value: social Darwinism and racist theories had a strong hold on liberal Protestants then. But he argued that sacrifice for them was still the Christian thing to do. Fellow New York Presbyterian Henry Van Dyke would add, in his May 1 sermon, that intervention was a providential necessity, an act of submission to God. Resorting to war to fulfill God's will was the cross that the nation was called to bear. On the same day, modernist minister Thomas Dixon argued that only from now on there could be a new Christian understanding of international relations. The "old law of nations" was based on self-interest as the "supreme standard of life." The US intervention on behalf of the Cubans represented "the first time in modern history" that "a great nation ha[d] accepted the Spirit of Jesus Christ as the motive power of life" and "the law of Christ" as

[42] Ibid., pp. 19–20.
[43] See ibid., pp. 28–31.
[44] See ibid., pp. 31–6.

"sacrificial and redemptive love."[45] The ministers made a strong case to convince American society and the world at large that the United States was truly the "Good Samaritan among nations," as Texas Baptist B. H. Carroll put it.[46]

## 3. "The Best Friend of Cuba": Scott's Messianism between Hegemony and Equality

### Messianism and Ingratitude

The rhetoric of Scott's Havana speech of 1917 came straight from 1898. To frame the Platt Amendment as just, as I argued above, he resorted to Langdellian legal themes, widespread in the establishment thought of his generation. But the speech and Scott's scholarship in general went further, evoking eschatological themes. Through his numerous works, Scott weaved together events like the discovery of the Americas, the Mayflower Compact, the adoption of the United States Constitution, and the Second Hague Peace Conference. Such linear narrative did not only merge science and religion, progress and providence. It also identified international law with the United States: the United States was the chosen nation, the Messiah, and the new egalitarian international law was its Word of Salvation.

In the Havana speech, Scott evoked the Christ-like nature of the United States by referring to the self-sacrifice of both the Cuban intervention and the Platt Amendment. The right to intervention was a burden the United States accepted to keep Cuba free. In general, Scott "regard[ed]" the Amendment "as a protection against an assault from without, as a bulwark against misgovernment from within, and as a shield and a buckler even against the great republic to the north."[47] It had originated from the meeting of "two nations . . . upon a plane of equality [and] just terms[;] each has observed the spirit as well as the letter of its obligation." The relations between the two countries ("friendly, confidential and without a trace of suspicion as to the motives of either") set an example toward the global achievement of peace. If all powerful nations, the argument went, interacted through law with the less powerful, like the United States had done with Cuba, all international controversies would eventually be solved peacefully through adjudication. "When, however, [nations do] not meet upon the plane of equality, and the sword of Brennus is thrown into the scale, and they do not arrange their relations . . . in accordance with the principles of justice, but in accordance with the desire of the strong under threat of force, they can not expect to live in peace and harmony, and, if they did, all

45 Thomas Dixon, "The Battle Cry of Freedom," *Dixon's Sermons: A Monthly Magazine*, June 1898, pp. 4–6, quoted in McCullough, *The Cross of War*, p. 35.

46 B. H. Carroll, "Sermon on John 15:13," quoted in McCullough, *The Cross of War*, p. 28.

47 Scott, "The Platt Amendment," p. 52.

history would give them the lie."[48] To reinforce the point Scott resorted to biblical imagery and quoting Christ: "If we are not our brothers' keeper, we are, or at least we should be, the conservators of the law. . . . 'Inasmuch as ye have done it unto one of the least of these, my brethren, ye have done it unto Me.' "[49]

After outlining the "concrete example" of brotherly love through law shown by the United States toward Cuba, Scott went on to define "the methods whereby justice may enter into the practice of nations"[50] it was an expression of:

> I consider three things indispensable in any consideration of this subject, and, without an agreement upon them, it is in my opinion a waste of time to discuss international questions and plan for a happier future. The first is that we regard all nations as equal. The second is that the relations of nations be based upon principles of justice; and the third, that the promises of nations, whether they be embodied in formal documents, such as treaties or conventions, or preserved in informal agreements, be scrupulously kept.[51]

Through these three themes, Scott drew a direct connection between the Platt Amendment and the creation of a court of international justice he had been advocating for years. With the Amendment, Cuba and the United States had set their relations on the path of equality, justice, and respect for international legal agreements; but that was based on the benevolent use of its power by the United States. For that to become the new normal on the global scale, Scott pointed to the "necessity of a court for the [S]ociety of [Nations] in order to administer justice between and among the civilized states forming the society, by defining, by interpreting and applying the rule of law to disputes between and among them."[52] International dispute resolution was the way forward and, for Scott, that it would come was not a question of "if," but a question of "when." Progress was moving from politics to law and the United States was the providential force that would make sure to drive history and civilization further.

With the messianic narrative of selflessness underlying the speech Scott seemed to refute the accusation, coming from many quarters, that the United States might, instead, be enforcing "the desire of the strong." The point was extremely delicate for him. Indeed, the allegation of imperialism in relation to Cuba was so sensitive that Scott did not directly acknowledge it, even as it loomed silently over the speech and, I assume, occupied the mind of his audience in Havana. As I noted above,[53] Scott could admit at times that the United States' policies toward Latin America

[48] Ibid., p. 14.
[49] Ibid., p. 39.
[50] Ibid., p. 15.
[51] Ibid., pp. 15–16.
[52] Ibid., p. 47.
[53] See Chapter 1.

could be imperialistic, though mostly in private communication and speaking abstractly rather than in relation to a specific incident. But he was not ready to accept any alternative reading to his own on the Platt Amendment; that is how I explain the lack of any reference to different views in the speech. The recognition of the North American selflessness embodied in Scott's account of the Spanish-American War represents a fundamental building stone of his life's work: the description of and the advocacy for a progressive international law based on the principle of equality and championed by the United States. Without it, the whole intellectual edifice would crumble. The simultaneous emergence of the United States as a different kind of world power and of the new international law based on right rather than might is the key event from which Scott looked both into the past and into the future. Looking back, the Cuban intervention was the culmination of historical processes that had placed America at the center of the development of modern international law. In those years at the closing of the World War, Scott would focus on the advent of the United States as a political and legal project.[54] In later years, he would direct his attention to the discovery of America and the recognition of rights to the natives by Francisco de Vitoria as the origin of universal equality.[55] Looking forward, the war of 1898 was the inspiration for the further evolution of international law in egalitarian terms, chiefly through the establishment of an international court.

Scott's silences about the US–Cuba relations went beyond the lack of mention of the opposition to his narrative of selflessness. The speech referred to events later than 1898 and the adoption of the Platt Amendment, yet it failed to acknowledge the anxieties lived by US society in consequence of the Spanish-American War. The bloody repression of the rebellion that broke out in 1899 in the Philippines against the United States as colonial power would leave scars. The rebellion was officially quashed in 1902 but hostilities continued for close to a decade in many areas of the archipelago. Congressional hearings and investigative press informed the US people that their army had been using the so-called water cure to extract information on the rebel forces from Filipinos. Important public figures who had reluctantly supported intervention turned into vocal anti-imperialists.[56] The triumphalism did not disappear from political discourse, but the claim of purity of the motives of the US colonial enterprise receded as the new president, Theodore Roosevelt, insisted on his country's military power more than his predecessor did. The succession in the White House and its tragic circumstances[57] marked another symbolic change: McKinley would be the last Civil War veteran to hold presidential

[54] Scott's works on that topic are the main focus of the following chapter.

[55] See Part II.

[56] One of them was magnate Andrew Carnegie, the man who would generously fund the Carnegie Endowment for International Peace, the powerhouse managed by Scott and Root.

[57] McKinley was shot by an anarchist on September 6, 1901 and would die eight days later. Roosevelt, as his vice-president, would succeed him, before being elected in his own right in 1904.

office. The restraint caused by the trauma of the Civil War would leave place to more confident muscular politics.

In this political climate, the United States would occupy Cuba for a second time in 1906, the same year in which Scott and Root would be at the forefront of the foundation of the ASIL and Root would visit South America.[58] By this time, Cuba had become a nuisance more than a place of world redemption. The United States reluctantly heeded the call of Cuba's political factions, both of which hoped to gain advantages by the US presence. Both President Estrada Palma and the rebelling Liberals forced the hand of the United States,[59] voluntarily creating conditions under which Roosevelt had to intervene. This time the objectives of the intervention were much less ambitious. The main goal was to protect US investments, primarily in sugar estates and sugar mills, and to do so without firing a shot. Roosevelt dispatched to Cuba as provisional governor Secretary of War William Howard Taft. Taft was clear in his mind that a Cuban question would hurt his presidential ambitions. When it was time to find a longer-term solution the choice was, at the suggestion of Root, now Secretary of State, Nebraska lawyer Charles E. Magoon, former governor of the Panama Canal Zone. Magoon did what he had to in order to keep Cuba stable, thereby setting a precedent for future US policy. He resorted heavily to patronage and gave in to the requests of the Liberals in order to keep them from resorting to arms again, thus creating the conditions for an unfair electoral process. Yet the goal of a quick normalization was achieved and Magoon could leave Cuba in the hands of newly elected President Gomez in January 1909. Cuban political leaders learned their lesson: as long as a semblance of order was maintained, they could continue with personalist politics, rigging elections and making use of public money for patronage purposes. Until the unrest in the late 1920s that would lead to the rise of Fulgencio Batista and the military in the early 1930s, Cuban politics maintained a semblance of democratic process. Anytime investors felt threatened, the United States government would send Cuba a reminder in the form of battleships or marines.[60] The bottom line set by the 1906–09 occupation was that reform and democratic values did not matter to the United States as long as Cuba kept quiet.

Scott not only failed to acknowledge the complications brought to the 1898 narrative by the postwar reality in the United States' discourse: he also ignored the

[58] In an unsigned editorial in the 1907 first volume of the AJIL, Scott would rush to point out that the US occupying administration of governor Magoon was as constitutionally legitimate as any elected Cuban one, by virtue of the constitutionalization of the Platt Amendment: see "The Nature of the Government in Cuba," *American Journal of International Law*, 1, 1907, pp. 149–50.

[59] See José M. Hernández, *Cuba and the United States: Intervention and Militarism, 1868–1933*, Austin: University of Texas Press, 1993, p. 150.

[60] The main example of these "softer" forms of American military presence on the island, which would come to be known as the "sugar intervention," began in August 1917. It was caused by tensions starting in March, just two months after Scott delivered his speech. See Louis A. Pérez Jr., *Intervention, Politics and Revolution in Cuba, 1913–1921*, Pittsburgh: University of Pittsburgh Press, 1978, pp. 79–92.

Cuban resistance to it and the subsequent North American accusations of ingratitude. Cuban rebels had been suspicious of the United States' possible motives since before intervention became a concrete possibility. Their fears came true when they realized that the United States wanted to keep tight control over the postwar political arrangements. Contrary to the United States' narrative, Cuban rebels believed they would have won the war even without external intervention. Seeing their powerful neighbor sweeping in to reap the fruits of their three-year-long fight and then ignore them created resentment. Yet the United States, convinced of its sole merit for ousting Spain and its selfless motives, required gratitude.[61] Lack of appreciation for the United States' sacrifice of lives and resources became entangled with racial themes. "The realization that the armed ranks of *Cuba Libre* included large numbers of Cubans of color immediately had a sobering effect on American enthusiasm for independence"[62] and dissolved the early parallels between the revolutionary struggles of Cuba and the United States.

Gratitude became the measure of Cuban readiness for self-government. Cubans appeared to North Americans less civilized than initially thought and the ingratitude they showed toward their self-appointed liberators was construed as definite proof that they did not deserve full independence. The New York Times feared "an irresponsible government of half-breeds." Governor General Leonard Wood claimed that "[t]he only people who are howling for [self-government] are those whose antecedents and actions demonstrate the impossibility of self-government at present."[63] When the United States posed the enshrining of the Platt Amendment into the Cuban Constitution as the condition for self-government, Cubans protested that both their war efforts and the official promise of independence for Cuba in the Teller Amendment had been betrayed. In June 1901, the Cuban Constitutional Convention would accept the Platt Amendment by one vote. Even Tomás Estrada Palma, soon to become the first president of the Cuban Republic and widely considered pro-American, would harshly protest the "brusque and precipitous manner in which the Platt resolution was imposed"[64] while also remarking the necessity to accept it to express gratitude to the United States.

Once the occupation ended in 1902, commentators in the United States jumped at the chance to present their country as faithful to its promise of Cuban independence and a civilizational mission achieved. Yet, as Leonard Wood had admitted in

[61] For an exploration of this theme see Louis A. Pérez Jr., "Incurring in a Debt of Gratitude: 1898 and the Moral Sources of United States Hegemony in Cuba," *American Historical Review*, 104 ,1999, pp. 356–98.

[62] Ibid., p. 365.

[63] New York Times (1 August 1898), p. 6; Leonard Wood to William McKinley, 6 February 1900, Special Correspondence, Elihu Root Papers, Manuscript Division, Library of Congress; quoted in Pérez, 'Incurring in a Debt of Gratitude', p. 365.

[64] Tomás Estrada Palma to Gonzalo de Quesada, March 14, 1901, in Gonzalo de Quesada, *Archivo de Gonzalo de Quesada*, vol. 1, Havana: Gonzalo de Quesada y Miranda, 1948, pp. 151–2, quoted in Pérez, "Incurring in a Debt of Gratitude," p. 374.

a letter to Roosevelt, "[t]here is of course, little or no independence left in Cuba under the Platt Amendment."[65]

## The Platt Amendment and the Soul of America

Notwithstanding these and further political developments, Cuba remained a place of redemption for Scott, maintaining its pivotal role in his US-centric account of international law. The trip to Havana of January 1917 was just the first of many. During the 1920s, Scott would try to make Cuba the center of the Pan-American international law project. In this endeavor, the idealistic symbolism of the narrative of 1898 met with the political expediency of the US postwar Cuban policies. Scott allied with Cuban despotic President Gerardo Machado (1925–33)[66] to build a grandiose seat in Havana for the American Institute of International Law, modeled on The Hague's Peace Palace. The project would never be fully realized because of the growing political tensions in Cuba and the declining interest in law as a tool of foreign policy within the US establishment in the late 1920s. Yet, it is a concrete illustration of the place Cuba had in Scott's international legal narrative and the politics underlying the American international law project in its development. Since 1922, Scott sought to revitalize the AIIL, in response to the renewed rise of anti-Yankee sentiment in Latin America. To pursue this goal, he found allies that would be closely aligned to the hegemonic direction he advocated for the Institute.[67] That meant sidelining even a moderate anti-interventionist like Alejandro Álvarez,[68] who was, let's not forget, an enthusiastic supporter of the Monroe doctrine as a continental achievement. Coherently with this move, Scott would become more personally attached to Cuba and to its most prominent international lawyers Antonio Sánchez de Bustamante y Sirvén (1865-1951) and Cosme de la Torriente y Peraza (1872–1956). Bustamante had been elected as a judge in the Permanent Court of International Justice since its establishment in 1922. He had close links to US corporations and to President Machado, who he supported by presiding the 1928 Constitutional Convention that allowed him to stay in power without elections.[69] De la Torriente was a veteran of the War of Independence against Spain, who would become President of the Assembly of the League of Nations (1923–24)

[65] Leonard Wood to Theodore Roosevelt, October 28, 1901, Leonard Wood Papers, Manuscript Division, Library of Congress, quoted in Pérez, "Incurring in a Debt of Gratitude," p. 375.

[66] After a first term as a result of open elections, Machado sought to change the Constitution in order to remain in power, after he had promised that he would not seek re-election. His attempt caused unrest that he exploited to retain the presidency without elections in 1928. He would manage to maintain power amidst growing opposition until 1933, when he was deposed by a military coup.

[67] Juan Pablo Scarfi tells this story in detail in Chapter 4 of his *The Hidden History of International Law in the Americas: Empire and Legal Networks*, Oxford: Oxford University Press, 2017.

[68] On the *de facto* exclusion of Álvarez from the AIIL management see, for instance, the correspondence in vol. 298, 1924, CEIP Papers.

[69] See Scarfi, *Hidden History*, p. 100.

and State Secretary in the Cuban government (1913–14 and 1933–35). Between 1923 and 1925 as first Cuban Ambassador to the United States[70] he worked successfully with Scott on the restitution to Cuba of the Isles of Pines, which had had an unclear legal status since the 1898 war. Both men agreed with Scott's view of the Platt Amendment and its positive value for Cuba. They were Cubans showing the gratitude the northern neighbors thought they deserved.[71] By putting the AIIL in the hands of Bustamante, de la Torriente, and the Cuban Society of International Law, Scott gave a prominent voice to Latin American lawyers who would promote the version of international law more congenial to the US continental hegemony. But putting Cuba and Cubans at the center also had a highly symbolic role in the ideological battle over the soul of the continent. Throughout the 1920s, the nature of the Platt Amendment remained one of the major—if not the major—technical topics over which international lawyers in America clashed over the relations between the United States and Latin America. In other words, recognizing Cuba as a fully independent and sovereign nation, as Scott and the "loyalists" Bustamante and de la Torriente did, meant considering the US hegemonic policies not only as beneficial for the continent but also as morally and legally sound. In opposition, considering Cuban sovereignty as curtailed by the Platt Amendment meant criticizing the United States as a violator of the international legal principles of equality of nations and non-intervention. Scott and his Cuban allies made sure to curb all such criticism. Their reactions were directed both at more moderate accounts, like Álvarez's, and at those more directly accusing the United States of imperialism in Cuba, like the account of Peruvian international lawyer Alberto Ulloa Sotomayor (1892–1975).

On November 28, 1924, de la Torriente wrote to Scott to bring to his attention two statements in *The Monroe Doctrine*,[72] a book by Álvarez just published by the Division of International Law of the Carnegie Endowment, which Scott directed:

> Page 20. –
> In the course of the nineteenth century the policy of hegemony of the United States passed through various phases, which it may be useful to indicate:
> III. Intervention at the birth of a new state on the continent, by emancipation or secession, afterwards restricting its external sovereignty. This is what happened in the case of Cuba and of Panama.

[70] Prior to de la Torriente's appointment, Cuba was represented in the United States through a legation: see James Brown Scott, "Cuba and the United States: Exchange of Ambassadors and of Views," *American Journal of International Law*, 18, 1924, p. 119.

[71] See, for instance, Cosme de la Torriente's speech, "Cuba, the United States of America and the League of Nations," March 5, 1922, Folder 8, Box 39, JBS Papers.

[72] Alejandro Álvarez, *The Monroe Doctrine: Its Importance in the International Life of the States of the New World*, New York: Oxford University Press, 1924.

> Page 215. –
> In May, 1902, Cuba was evacuated by the United States and on May 23, 1903, it entered into a perpetual treaty with the latter which amounted to a considerable restriction of Cuban independence. Among other provisions the United States is authorized to protect the independence of Cuba, which can not enter into any treaty with other countries that might affect its independence.

The only comment de la Torriente added was a sentence at the closing: "Opinions of this sort are responsible for such informations [sic] as that which appears in the Almanach de Gotha."[73] He was referring to a discovery Scott himself had made by chance the previous summer while in Paris, and which he had shared with his network. He had "noticed in a book-store the Almanach de Gotha for 1924." Scott remarked that the Almanach had "always been considered as a work of authority," "not official[lly] issued by the German Government, but . . . looked upon as a semi-official publication." He "picked it up and turned, as an American would, to the section on the United States" only to learn "to [his] astonishment, [his] amazement and . . . horror, that the United States [was] credited with a series of protectorates": Santo Domingo, Haiti, Panama, Liberia, and, most importantly to Scott, Cuba. He checked the previous editions of the Almanach and confirmed that the attribution of protectorates to the United States was a new addition. For him, that was the sign that Latin American accusations, doing "injury to the good name of the United States"[74] had recently found influence in Europe; he had to step up his efforts to thwart them, both through international legal scholarship and by promoting conciliatory gestures by the US government.

On the first front, for instance, he replied the next day to the letter from de la Torriente, thanking him "for calling attention to [the] passages" in the book by Álvarez claiming that the United States had been and was still restricting Cuban sovereignty: that "ha[d] given [him] the opportunity of condemning unofficial statements of this kind wherever found." Scott also informed him that "action ha[d] been taken" to "neutralize" such statements:

> I have prepared for insertion in the volume a supplementary note[.] It will be printed, with mucilage on the left edge so that it may be attached and become a part of the volume, without interfering with the table of content or the text. [A] copy of the supplementary note will be sent to every library and person receiving the volume, with the request to insert it between pages vi and vii and all copies not yet distributed will likewise contain the insert.[75]

[73] Cosme de la Torriente to Scott, November 28, 1924, Folder 5, Box 8, JBS Papers.
[74] Scott to William E. Borah, November 26, 1924, Folder 28, Box 11, JBS Papers.
[75] Scott to Cosme de la Torriente, November 29, 1924, Folder 28, Box 11, JBS Papers.

The note, titled "Supplemental Preface," is marked November 29, 1924, the same date as Scott's reply to de la Torriente. Interestingly, it did not address Álvarez's statements in the book directly. The text's explicit goal was to debunk the attribution of protectorates to the United States by the Almanach de Gotha. Scott argued that the "official utterances on the Monroe Doctrine" by US officials "contained in the . . . volume" as annexes "show that these statements in the *Almanach* are devoid of foundation." Essentially, Scott was attempting to turn Álvarez's book against his author to defuse his assertions on Cuban limited sovereignty without even acknowledging them. The wider argument was a typically formalist one: the US government had always recognized the principle of equality of nations and no official document, domestic or international, including the Platt Amendment, had sought to limit the independence of the American Republics. "Any expression to the contrary, by whomsoever made and wherever found, is personal opinion without the authority of the United States."[76]

Scott also used the Almanach de Gotha statements in the second front of his strategy to improve the reputation of his country, the lobbying of the US government. As I noted above, Scott joined de la Torriente in urging the relinquishment of US claims on the Isle of Pines. Scott believed that the ratification of the treaty to that effect would "remove the one outstanding difficulty with Cuba, and, therefore, with Latin America."[77] During 1924, Scott wrote several letters to powerful players in his network to call their attention on the issue. To Senator William E. Borah, the Republican Chairman of the Senate Committee on Foreign Relations, Scott wrote that "were it not for" the Almanach de Gotha "incident," he "would not [have] even" asked his "time to read [the] letter." But Scott pointed out to Borah that if "the attitude of the United States . . . ha[d] convinced the German scholars . . . that Cuba [was] dependent . . . to a degree . . . justifying . . . the term 'protectorate,'" the formal renunciation of US claims on the Isle of Pines was the costless act that could change that perception.[78] Scott approached both Republicans like Borah[79] and Democrats like the former Secretary of State (1913–15) and presidential candidate (1896, 1900, and 1908) William Jennings Bryan.[80] He also made sure that the sitting Secretary of State Charles Evans Hughes knew of these approaches, "as the best way to call the matter to his attention without seeming to interfere with his conduct of our foreign affairs."[81]

[76] James Brown Scott, "Supplemental Preface," in Álvarez, *Monroe Doctrine*, unnumbered page between pp. vi and vii.

[77] Scott to William Jennings Bryan, January 19, 1924, Folder 26 Box 11, JBS Papers.

[78] Scott to William E. Borah, November 26, 1924.

[79] Other than the November 26 letter see also Scott to Borah, January 21, 1924, Folder 26, Box 11, JBS Papers.

[80] "Could you be good enough to write to your Democratic friends in the Senate—especially those of the Foreign Relations Committee . . . advocating the prompt ratification of the treaty? Anything you can do would be in the interest of good relations, and will greatly please our Cuban friends" (Scott to Bryan, January 19, 1924). See also Bryan's positive reply, 13 May 1924, Folder 2, Box 2, JBS Papers.

[81] Scott to Bustamante, November 29, 1924, Folder 28, Box 11, JBS Papers. Around a month later, Hughes sent a letter to a leading Democratic Senator advocating the ratification of the treaty and

To explain the question to his correspondents, Scott pointed them to his publications on the subjects and, especially to an editorial comment he had published on the AJIL in January 1923.[82] There he explained how the issue came to be: a provision that was not present in the original Root formulation, Article VI, had been added into the Platt Amendment, and therefore became part of the Cuban Constitution and of the 1903 general treaty regulating US–Cuba relations.[83] It provided "[t]hat the Isle of Pines shall be omitted from the proposed constitutional boundaries of Cuba, the title thereto being left to future adjustment by treaty." According to Scott, this was due to a misunderstanding by North American investors on the terms of the Treaty of Paris, which closed the war with Spain. Its first article provided for Spain to relinquish "all claim of sovereignty over and title to Cuba." Now, the Isle of Pines had always been considered as part of Cuba by the Spanish administration. The United States government shared that understanding upon signing the treaty. But many investors and new residents believed instead that the Isle of Pines had passed under US sovereignty by virtue of Article 2 of the treaty, ceding "the island of Porto Rico and other islands now under Spanish sovereignty in the West Indies." Moreover, "[s]ome color was lent to this contention by the statement under date of August 14, 1899, made by . . . the then Assistant Secretary of War, 'that this island . . . was ceded by Spain to the United States, and is, therefore, a part of our territory, although it is attached at present to the division of Cuba for governmental purposes.' "[84] Root would deny that statement on several occasions.[85] Eventually, in 1907, even the Supreme Court would declare in unequivocal terms Cuban sovereignty over the Isle of Pines.[86] Yet, the treaty with the purpose of adjusting the island's status according to the Platt Amendment, had "slumbered in the Senate,"[87] to use Scott's words, awaiting ratification from 1904 until the mid-1920s.[88] On March 13, 1925, the Senate finally provided its advice and consent and the treaty could be ratified. That this political development became possible was mostly due to the need of appeasing Latin America, on one hand, and the decreased interest in a possible annexation of the Isle of Pines, on the other; yet, the joint efforts of Scott and de la Torriente were certainly instrumental to raise awareness on the issue within the political establishment in the United States. This

arguing, as he had been consistently doing during his time in office, that the United States had no valid claim to the Isle of Pines (see Hughes to Joe T. Robinson, January 2, 1925, 837.014P/324, in *Foreign Relations of the United States*, vol. II, 1925, pp. 1–3).

[82] James Brown Scott, "The Isle of Pines," *American Journal of International Law*, 17, 1923, pp. 100–4.
[83] See section 1 of this chapter.
[84] Scott, "The Isle of Pines," p. 103.
[85] See ibid., pp. 103–4.
[86] *Pearcy v. Stranahan*, 205 US, 257, in *American Journal of International Law*, 1, 1907, p. 784.
[87] Scott, 'The Isle of Pines', p. 100.
[88] A first treaty on the issue had been signed on July 2, 1903, but it failed to achieve ratification before expiring. The second treaty, without expiration terms, was signed on March 2, 1904 and reported favorably twice, in 1906 and 1922.

positive result reinforced Scott's alliance with the Cubans; the resolution of the Isle of Pines question became their go-to evidence of US benevolence toward the rest of the continent.[89] In fact, the Isle of Pines issue has a prominent part in the book that most represents Scott's cooperation with Bustamante and de la Torriente: *Cuba, la America Latina, los Estados Unidos*.[90] The volume is a collection of essays by Scott, translated into Spanish by Bustamante,[91] who also wrote a preface. De la Torriente penned an afterword in which he referred to Scott as the *mejor amigo de Cuba*, the best friend of Cuba.[92] Scott reciprocated by dedicating the book to his two Cuban friends.

It should not come as a surprise then that the book is built as an elaborate defense of the Platt Amendment and US continental policies, addressing Latin American criticism. The use of the Spanish language itself pointed to the intended goal and audience: "to incline the hearts and minds of the Americans to the South of our boundary line to the ideals of Americans above that line. . . . This little book is an attempt to explain each to the other and unite us in a common American ideal."[93] Once again, like in the 1917 Havana speech, Scott employed a selective account of Cuban history. In a letter to Bustamante, he surveyed his earlier publications on Cuba he had decided not to include in the volume. Scott explained that his criterion was to exclude texts that did not hold "more than passing value."[94] Yet, it is conspicuously clear, going through the excluded publications, that they are the ones treating events of US direct interference in Cuban affairs after the war of 1898 and the occupation resulting directly from it—events like the Second Occupation and the Sugar Intervention, which reinforced the idea of Cuba as a US protectorate. *Cuba, la America Latina, los Estados Unidos* became the occasion for Scott to face the protectorate argument head on, in an uncharacteristically confrontational way.[95]

Indeed, even if de la Torriente connected Álvarez's passages in *The Monroe Doctrine* to the attribution of protectorates to the United States by the Almanach de Gotha, the Chilean had stopped short of using the word. Other Latin American international lawyers had not. Scott dedicated the longest article in the Cuba section of the book, previously unpublished, to debunk the arguments of one of them, Alberto Ulloa Sotomayor. The article, titled "La Enmienda Platt: Lo que

[89] See for instance James Brown Scott, "The Isle of Pines and the Solidarity of Pan-America," *Advocate of Peace through Justice*, 87(4), April 1925, pp. 228–32.

[90] James Brown Scott, *Cuba, la America Latina, los Estados Unidos*, Havana: El Siglo XX, 1926.

[91] According to Scott, Bustamante also paid personally for the publication of the volume, while the initial idea for it was de la Torriente's: see Scott to Robert E. Olds, July 7, 1926, Folder 33, Box 11, JBS Papers.

[92] Cosme de la Torriente, "La Obra del Mejor Amigo de Cuba," in Scott, *Cuba, la America Latina, los Estados Unidos*, pp. 397–424.

[93] Scott to Olds, July 7, 1926.

[94] Scott to Bustamante, April 23, 1925, Folder 29 Box 11, JBS Papers.

[95] "I dislike to engage in controversies, and when I do not agree, I prefer to dissent in silence." Scott to Bustamante, April 9, 1925, Folder 11, Box 29, JBS Papers.

es e lo que no es," took issue with the section on protectorates of Ulloa's *Derecho Internacional Publico.*[96] The Peruvian dedicated paragraphs 203–8 to Cuba, classified as *el caso tipíco de protectorado parcial.*

After describing the relevant norms, Ulloa devoted paragraph 208 to analysis and seemed to refer to Scott's Cuban allies:

> Espíritus optimistas pretenden en Cuba interpretar su situación internacional respecto de los Estados Unidos como una alianza en beneficio reciproco. La interpretación es notoriamente forzada. La Enmienda Platt ha creado a Cuba una situación de dependencia y tutela, en beneficio exclusivo de los Estados Unidos.

Ulloa argued that it was unlikely that Cuba would at some point gain full sovereignty, given the disparity of power with the northern neighbor and its geopolitical interests. Yet, he called the rest of the continent to sympathize with and support Cuba, hoping for change:

> La América debe a Cuba, sacrificada por una fatalidad geográfica, el aliento moral de su simpatía y el concurso de su influencia internacional para redimirla.[97]

Rather than developing new arguments, Scott characteristically asserted that the factual evidence supported his conclusion in an obvious fashion. Therefore, if scholars like Ulloa still contended that Cuba was a protectorate, what he could do was to clarify further. He proceeded to supplement the history of the Platt Amendment with lesser-known documents and he explained the eight articles of the text one by one. Yet, the level of detail did not change the core of his reasoning. First, the fact that the Platt Amendment had become the object of a bilateral treaty in itself showed that the United States treated Cuba as an equal. Second, the history of the Amendment proved that the right of intervention was a burden for the United States in favor of Cuba, more than the other way around:

> La Enmienda Platt no crea una tutela sobre Cuba. Si crea un deber, éste parte de los Estados Unidos para garantizar la independencia y soberanía de la Isla que creó con su intervención. Y la garantía no es en interés exclusivo de los Estados Unidos, como afirmó el doctor Ulloa, si han de aceptarse en su verdadero valor las opiniones del Secretario Root, y si ha de tenerse en cuenta la acción subsecuente de los Estados Unidos. . . . Sostener que esta obligación asumida por los Estados Unidos y este permiso otorgado por Cuba, es con detrimento de la independencia y soberanía de Cuba, sería en efecto sostener que un tratado o protocolo de los

[96] See Alberto Ulloa Sotomayor, *Derecho Internacional Publico (Curso Universitario)*, Lima: Sanmartí y cía, impresores, vol. I, 1926, Section 10, Chapter 5.
[97] Ibid., p. 93.

> Estados Europeos garantizando su independencia y soberanía, constituye un menoscabo de esa independencia o de esa soberanía, que el tratado o protocolo se celebra para mantener. La declaración misma es su propia refutación.[98]

Scott concluded by remarking once again that the accusations made about the United States were not only technically incorrect but also unfair. The good faith shown in liberating and protecting Cuba rather than annexing it was to be commended and met with gratitude:

> La verdad sobre este asunto es que en vez de ser Cuba objeto de "simpatías", debe ser envidiada. Hay muy pocos pequeños países adyacentes a otros poderosos y cuya independencia se deba a la intervención del vecino grande, en que el país poderoso, en vez de anexarse el territorio, como sucedía con tanta frecuencia en el pasado, empeñe su buena fe para mantener la independencia del vecino pequeño contra todas las potencias extranjeras, incluyendo la misma más grande y vecina. Si toda potencia más grande garantizase la independencia y soberanía de su vecina menos fuerte, y cumpliese su palabra empeñada como lo ha hecho el Gobierno de los Estados Unidos, ninguna potencia pequeña del mundo estaría viviendo bajo la amenaza de sus vecinas poderosas.[99]

In his eventual reply, Ulloa noted how Scott gave "*una importancia excesiva a las formas*"[100] by insisting on US official documents recognizing Cuban independence. Looking at reality beyond form, the treaty of 1903 had been unilateral as it set the conditions Cuba had to accept for the occupation to end.

And indeed the controversy over Cuba was more than one between a formalist and a more realist approach to international law. The different accounts of the Platt Amendment found themselves in a battle for the soul of America, by qualifying the moral nature of US hegemony through legal discourse. It was about deciding if the regional power was benevolent and progressive or tyrannical and imperialist. And all the factual and legal evidence employed seemed to matter less in reaching the decision than the political belief of the actor. For Scott at least, as I tried to show, it would always be a matter of faith in the redemptive, messianic role of the United States in history. Among growing pressure and need for political expediency, he would not abandon the narrative of the selfless empire.

Scott's work on Francisco de Vitoria and the legacy of the Salamanca School can be seen as a continuation of that effort to redefine the moral foundations of the continent in US terms. The principle of equality that, in Scott's view, the United

98 Scott, "La Enmienda Platt: Lo que es e lo que no es," in *Cuba, la America Latina, los Estados Unidos*, pp. 114 and 116.

99 Ibid., p. 116.

100 Alberto Ulloa, "El Profesor Brown Scott y la situación de Cuba," in *Revista de Ciencias Juridicas y Sociales*, 1, July 1927, p. 12.

States had championed through the Platt Amendment had found its origin in the conceptualizing of the discovery of America by Vitoria. By "appl[ying] the doctrines of Augustine . . . as elaborated by St. Thomas Aquinas, to the barbarian principalities" of America, the Dominican had "replac[ed] a divided Christendom by the international community composed of all states, irrespective of race, religion, language or geography."[101] This historical point was the pedigree Scott wanted to provide to the progressive international law embodied by the United States. 1926 was not only the year in which Scott published, as we have seen, his most articulate defense of the Platt Amendment; it was also the year in which the task he "devoted [him]self almost exclusively to"[102]—explaining and popularizing the Spanish and Catholic origin of international law—fully began.[103]

The shortcomings of Scott's grandiose construction of the American equality through the Platt Amendment were well symbolized by Cuba and its deferential establishment. Bustamante and de la Torriente were elitists whose political views favored a formal view of equality that left space for hierarchy and privileges. Their country was so powerless in front of the United States that a full independence *de iure*, even if limited *de facto*, was the best situation to realistically aspire to for many; and then how things would concretely play out would have to be left to the goodwill of the US government. Of course, if one was outside this specific mindset, like Álvarez and Ulloa, the relations between the United States and Cuba could not be deemed equal. But if one had a solid belief with a religious foundation in the United States as the redeemer of mankind, as I argue Scott did, the picture changes. Accepting that assumption provided the narrative of the selfless empire upholding the equality of nations with an internal coherence that it would not have had otherwise. Indeed, in this Chapter I have put the 1917 Havana speech in context and described its aftermath as a key example of the providential streak in Scott's thought. He could dismiss events countering his narrative and internal contradictions exactly because he was a man of faith. He believed in the saving power of international law and science, that they were tools of God to bring about the millennium. Considering the workings of providence through history, certified by the evident progress of mankind, embodied by the United States, even major conflicts and contradictions could be considered as minor obstacles on a road to peace otherwise well traced. For Scott the 1906 Second Occupation was at worst a bump

[101] Scott to Monsignor Eugène Tisserant, undated, estimated December 1934, Folder 4, Box 52, JBS Papers.

[102] Ibid.

[103] Between March and May 1926 Scott delivered at Georgetown a course titled "The Founders of International Law" in which he gave a prominent role to Vitoria and Suarez (see Thomas H. Healy, "Notice to Students. Re: Founders of International Law," January 28, 1926, Folder 3 Box 53, JBS Papers and Edmund A. Walsh, "Foreword," in James Brown Scott, *The Spanish Origin of International Law. Lectures on Francisco de Vitoria and Francisco Suarez*, Washington, D.C.: Georgetown University Press, 1928, p. 9.) From that moment until the end of his career, the Salamanca School became the main subject of his scholarly work.

in the road of progress; even the still raging First World War was one. Indeed, as we have seen, Scott in Havana was speaking not only about United States–Cuban relationships or American continental politics but also about the global post-World War order and the need for an international court.

Scott was a Wilsonian in the vague meaning we give to the word today: one who aimed at reforming the world by exporting American values and a believer in international institutions. This does not, however, tell us much about the stakes involved in the US foreign policy at the end of the First World War. Scott was also, arguably, the staunchest opponent of Wilson's plans on collective security. In that January of 1917, the idea of collective security had already gained traction in foreign policy discourse and took over the dominance Scott's judicialist plans had previously enjoyed. A few months later, in April, Scott would be challenged for the first time within the ASIL on this point.[104] From then on, Scott would be honored and remembered as a noble father, but a younger generation would take control of the Society's academic directions.[105] Yet, Scott's religious-like belief in US values and the need to spread them globally would prove to be a long-standing feature of subsequent international legal scholarship in the United States even through the years in which the realist critique was at its peak.

[104] See Chapter 3 section 3.
[105] I tell this story in the following chapters, 3 and 4.

# 3

# International Law as Science. Scott's Historical Case for Adjudication and the Fight against Collective Security

One remarkable feature of international law in the last few decades has been the staunch opposition of the government of the United States of America to the jurisdiction of international courts.[1] Observers have been tempted to regard the United States' confrontational posture as a mere product of egoistic political realism. Often, the story goes that this realism is at odds with the "authentic" spirit of cosmopolitanism and internationalism proclaimed by President Woodrow Wilson and international lawyers such as James Brown Scott one century ago. And yet, it would be simplistic to characterize today's defiant attitude of the United States toward international adjudication as a realist, nationalistic degeneration of an originally cosmopolitan ideal. Looking beneath the surface, both old and current approaches to international law in the United States reveal themselves as sharing crucial assumptions, all expressions of the traditional American regard for democracy and the rule of law.

Indeed, the current critique of international adjudication is not simply a realist attempt to oppose politics to law and the judicial method. Critics specifically attack international law and adjudication, whereas they maintain a strong faith in the domestic rule of law and revere the Supreme Court. Often, these critics do not reject international courts as such, but as a threat to the United States' popular sovereignty that the Supreme Court represents. They denounce international adjudication whenever they assume that it restrains the rule of law in the United States.

This attitude is not entirely different from that of James Brown Scott and the other "idealists" who founded the American Society of International Law (ASIL)

[1] The most symbolic example is the 1986 United States' withdrawal of acceptance of the International Court of Justice's jurisdiction, following the Court's judgment in the *Nicaragua v. United States* case. More recently, the United States government has actively opposed the activity of the International Criminal Court and of the International Tribunal on the Law of the Sea. A paradigmatic critique of international criminal adjudication has been provided by Henry Kissinger ("The Pitfalls of Universal Jurisdiction," *Foreign Affairs*, July/August 2001, available at http://www.globalpolicy.org/component/content/article/163/28174.html) (last accessed July 4, 2019). Paul Kahn, on the other hand, has explained the opposition of the United States to the International Criminal Court in political theological terms ("Why the United States is So Opposed," *Crimes of War*, December 2003, available at http://web.uncg.edu/dcl/courses/humanright/paul_kahn.pdf) (last accessed July 4, 2019).

*Rewriting the History of the Law of Nations: How James Brown Scott Made Francisco de Vitoria the Founder of International Law*. Paolo Amorosa, Oxford University Press (2019). 
DOI: 10.1093/oso/9780198849377.001.0001

in 1906. Both generations shared similar goals, though they implemented diverse strategies to attain them. The men of 1906 wished to strengthen the rule of law at home, and believed that the best means to achieve this was to make the United States' version of it universal and export it. They came to appreciate the establishment of an international judiciary as a suitable institutional tool to spread American democratic values and civilize the world. The project of James Brown Scott and his colleagues in academia and at the State Department was to endorse international adjudication as shaped in the United States' image. This chapter explores Scott's historical work in view of the aftermath of the First World War as a paradigmatic example of that American project.

## 1. The Armistice Books and the Science of International Adjudication

James Brown Scott had a penchant for anniversaries and meaningful dates. Each introduction of his main works of 1918, revolving around the constitutional history of his country, the United States, are all, with one exception, dated November 11, the day of signature of the armistice at the conclusion of the First World War.[2] With the First World War reaching its end, opening the possibility for the creation of a new world order, such a "patriotic" choice of topic might sound somewhat odd for someone of his profession, influence, and commitment toward the advancement of international law. By describing the work of the Federal Convention of 1787 that produced the United States Constitution, Scott believed that he was providing his audience with the most instructive and successful example of an international conference. In Scott's mind, the problems faced by the international community of his time were similar to the ones faced by the thirteen States of the North American continent in achieving their "more perfect Union," and therefore the solutions adopted by the Founding Fathers could be imitated. Scott's main argument was that the creation of the Supreme Court, "in its origin, and in fact, an international

[2] The exception is represented by the introduction of *Judicial Settlement of Controversies between States of the American Union. Cases Decided in the Supreme Court of the United States*, ed. by James Brown Scott, in 2 vols., Oxford: Oxford University Press, 1918, marked September 30, 1918. The works bearing an introduction by Scott dated November 11, 1918 are: James Brown Scott, *James Madison's Notes of Debates in the Federal Convention of 1787 and Their Relation to a More Perfect Society of Nations*, New York: Oxford University Press, 1918; James Brown Scott, *Judicial Settlement of Controversies between States of the American Union: An Analysis of Cases Decided in the Supreme Court of the United States*, Oxford: Oxford University Press, 1919; James Brown Scott, *The United States: A Study in International Organization*, Oxford: Oxford University Press, 1920; Gaillard Hunt and James Brown Scott (eds.), *The Debates in the Federal Convention of 1787 which Framed the Constitution of the United States of America reported by James Madison*, Oxford: Oxford University Press, 1920, which includes also an introduction by co-editor Hunt, also dated November 11. That this is no coincidence is reinforced by the 1920 postscript added to the preface at the time of actual publication of *The United States*, in which Scott remarked that "The text . . . speaks from Armistice Day, 1918" (p. x).

tribunal,"[3] had brought the controversies of the American States within the realm of law. A permanent international court could serve the same purpose for the rest of the world. The United States was the living proof that the judicial settlement of disputes between sovereign States was not just possible: it was the definitive means to avoid the resort to war. Scott's understanding of the history of the United States was also his institutional plan for world order. In such a "period of international transition," "men . . . minded to create a more perfect Society of Nations" would "be heartened by the history" and "profit by the labors of th[e] Federal Convention."[4]

Scott's convictions on the exceptionality and exemplariness of the history and the special destiny of the United States[5] were commonplace in his cultural context, as we have seen already. In particular, Scott was not the only legal professional or member of the United States' foreign policy establishment to propose the Supreme Court as the ideal model for a future international court.[6] However, Scott deserves particular attention, as the international lawyer who engaged most in detail with the creation of the Supreme Court and its relevance for international relations at the crucial moment of the Great War's end. Moreover, he enjoyed a unique position among international legal professionals. As we have seen in Chapter 1, as Director of the International Law Division of the Carnegie Endowment for International Peace, he had an extensive budget to produce and disseminate publications, of his own and of others, and to fund meetings, conferences, and organizations. Scott was, indeed, "holding the purse" and enjoying the influence that came with it within the transatlantic community of international lawyers.

In 1918, Scott produced a series of complementary books on US history aimed at designing a progressive correlation between American independence and the establishment of an international judiciary. In this project, Scott relied heavily on James Madison's *Notes on the American Constitutional Convention*. By general agreement the *Notes* represent the most detailed and complete surviving first-hand recollection of the proceedings of the Convention. Scott set out to comment on them to enlighten the general audience about the international implications of the American constitutional development. The "little book,"[7] as defined by Scott himself, was followed by a new edition of the *Notes*.[8] As hinted at above, in Scott's description the crucial contribution offered by the delegates to the Convention was the devising of a court able to settle judicially the controversies between sovereign

[3] James Brown Scott, "Prefatory Note," in *Judicial Settlement of Controversies between States of the American Union*, vol. I, p. vii.

[4] Scott, *James Madison's Notes of Debates*, p. 3.

[5] The classic text on destinarian thinking in the United States is Anders Stephanson, *Manifest Destiny. American Expansionism and the Empire of Right*, New York: Hill and Wang, 1995.

[6] See, as one of many possible examples, George W. Wickersham, "The Supreme Court of the United States, a Prototype of a Court of Nations," in *Proceedings of the American Society for Judicial Settlement of International Disputes*, 3, 1913, pp. 17ff.

[7] Scott, *James Madison's Notes of Debates*. The expression "little book" is used both in the beginning of its preface (p. vii) and in the dedication of it to Arthur Deerin Call of the American Peace Society.

[8] Hunt and Scott (eds.), *The Debates in the Federal Convention of 1787*.

States, setting aside force in favor of law. He also wanted to show and explain the success of the US Supreme Court in the exercise of its inter-State jurisdiction by publishing a collection of cases[9] and his analysis of them.[10]

But the book at the center of Scott's historical effort of 1918 was definitely *The United States: A Study in International Organization*. With it, Scott set out his grand narrative of law as a fundamental element of the identity of the American people and, at the same time, a global factor of progress and peace. Differently than in the educational book on *Madison's Notes*, in the lengthy volume *The United States*, Scott designed in detail and with a technical use of legal concepts the successful trajectory of the political communities that would come to form the United States, since the Mayflower Compact up to the most recent case-law of the Supreme Court. Consistently with its main claim, the largest part of the book was dedicated to an analysis of the principles governing the judiciary power in US constitutional law and their interpretation by the Supreme Court.

As already noted by contemporary scholars,[11] Scott's understanding of history was riddled with contradictions and shortcomings, mainly aimed at taming historical reality so as to fit the narrative of a harmonious development of US law along individualistic and judicialist lines. Still, his views illustrate a peculiarly American cultural sensibility that, as underlined above, would enjoy substantial influence in the shaping of international law in the American century. Scott's remarkably stable convictions on the evolution of law and its nature[12] relate deeply to the larger context of social sciences in turn-of-the-century United States, all infused with a sense of national mission.[13] What distinguished him from other university professors acting within the same ideological framework was the fact that his specialization, professional position, and contacts made him much more capable of practical action toward the goal they all shared: governing the world through an American understanding of science and liberal politics.

## James Brown Scott and the Politics of the American Constitution

*The United States* opened on the image of a ship carrying what Scott called "with . . . pride the American spirit" to the New World. The initial expression of that spirit was law: lacking a royal charter for the land they arrived at, the Pilgrims "entered into . . . the Mayflower Compact, . . . believing that government . . . derives its just powers from the consent of the governed."

[9] Scott, *Judicial Settlement of Controversies between States of the American Union*.

[10] Scott, *Judicial Settlement of Controversies between States of the American Union: An Analysis*.

[11] See Edward S. Corvin, "Book Review. The United States of America: a Study in International Organization," *University of Pennsylvania Law Review*, 69(4), 1921, pp. 393–4.

[12] See Scott's confession to Manley O. Hudson, in the Prologue.

[13] See Dorothy Ross, *The Origin of American Social Sciences*, New York: Cambridge University Press, 1991.

*In nuce*, the elements of Scott's description of human progress were all present as the Pilgrims reached the American soil. This was in the nature of a Big Bang: "the spirit which pervaded these newer Pilgrims, and which today pervades the western world"[14] created a whole universe of political meaning. The exception that determined the new course of history lay far in the past, in the discovery and settlement of America. Since then, in Scott's narrative, law was at the center of the American stage.

To confirm the gradual growth of American law, Scott commented on a remark by William E. Gladstone (1809–98), four times British prime minister. He underlined that the US Constitution could not be reduced to the momentary expression of a revolution: it was the product of time and experience in the same way as the British one. Gladstone's opposition of the "British Constitution" as "the most subtile [sic] organism . . . proceeded from . . . progressive history" and "the American" as "the most wonderful work struck off at a given time by the brain and purpose of man"[15] prompted Scott to disagree:

> With the Saxon Conquest of England, progressive history began in England, and with the advent of the first English settler to America, progressive history began in America, and the culminations were the unwritten Constitution of Great Britain on the one hand and the written Constitution of the United States on the other.[16]

Common law was brought to the United States[17] where it started an independent path of organic development. The common law traveling on the Mayflower enjoyed the pedigree of a slow and gradual evolution in the mother country as well as the possibility of a novel, emancipatory growth as the embodiment of a new American spirit, thanks to the lack of an imposing tradition in the New World.

Scott's point against Gladstone related strongly to his understanding of the nature of law and his liberal political preferences. Accordingly, the foundational freedom of the American experiment was, in his view, of English origin and not of a radical revolutionary character. The settlers were British subjects, endowed with the related rights and duties, who organized the life of their body politic through the institution of assemblies, just like Englishmen. Scott, accordingly, described

[14] Scott, *The United States*, pp. 3–4.

[15] William E. Gladstone, *Gleanings of Past Years, 1843–78*, vol. 1, London: John Murray, 1879, p. 212.

[16] Scott, *The United States*, p. 64.

[17] Scott was aware that his assumption of original application of the common law to the American colonies was problematic, even if carefully contextualized historically (see ibid., pp. 97–9), as it was clearly established within the English legal system that the colonial institutions operated under Royal Prerogative up to the Revolution. To make the point, Scott intervened in the old debate on the mode of acquisition of the colonial territories, by conquest (granting Royal Prerogative) or through discovery and occupation by Englishmen (providing them and their offspring with common law rights). To support the latter position, Scott relied on John Marshall's opinion in the *Johnson v. McIntosh* Supreme Court case (1823) against the classic formulation of the British conquest argument by William Blackstone (see ibid., pp. 90–3).

in detail the development of colonial institutions in British America. He depicted the colonists' struggle for independence as a reaction to a violation of their natural rights by the Crown and not as the will for a change of regime. Scott considered the US Constitution as a legal tool based on the continuity of the achievements of generations. "It is a development, under a new environment, of old forms of government. Everything in it that was new was a 'conservative innovation.'"[18] Thus read a quote that Scott meaningfully placed on the first page of *The United States*.

Scott elaborated on the ideology of US independence by describing its European influences in terms of political thought. His analysis took the form of a rather clichéd opposition between Lockean liberalism and Rousseauian republicanism, resolved in absolute favor of the former. While he conceded that Thomas Jefferson, who drafted the Declaration of Independence, "may have been influenced by French ideas" later in life, Scott affirmed that "Jefferson was, in his earlier days, influenced by English liberal writers, for the purpose of the colonists was to show that as Englishmen they were entitled to English liberty as laid down by English writers of repute." Scott pointed out that the language of the preamble of the Declaration, which affirmed the "unalienable Rights" of "Life, Liberty and . . . pursuit of Happiness," was directly borrowed from Locke's writings. Crucially, in his opinion, "the United States [wa]s the first country which ever put . . . these doctrines . . . into effect in the form in which they were stated."[19]

The introductory chapters of *The United States* aimed at building up for the country and its law the solid political credentials of a democracy based on an individualistic conception of freedom. American liberty was accordingly constructed on negative rights, the enjoyment of which counted on the State not to interfere. Justice as respect of negative liberties required the separation of powers and procedural guarantees to constrain State power and avoid its abuse. "A government of laws, not of men,"[20] in the wording of the traditional formula Scott employed often. The described political credentials reinforced, in Scott's view, the evident success of the United States as a political community, grown into a world power in a relatively short time. These circumstances constituted the political and factual justification

[18] W. T. Brantly, "Of the Influence of European Speculation in the Formation of the Federal Constitution," *Southern Law Review, New Series*, vi, 1880, p. 351, quoted in Scott, *The United States*, p. 1.

[19] Scott, *The United States*, pp. 35–6.

[20] John Adams (1735–1826), who would later become the second President of the United States, gave currency to the formula by inserting it into the Bill of Rights of the Massachusetts Constitution (Art. 30) in 1780. Adams himself (see *Novanglus Papers, No. 7*, in *The Works of John Adams*, ed. by Charles Francis Adams, vol. 4, Boston: Charles C. Little and James Brown, 1851, p. 106) attributed the modern use of it to English theorist James Harrington (in his formulation the word "empire" substituted "government." See Harrington, *The Commonwealth of Oceana*, London: F. Streater, 1656, *passim*). Scott, in *The United States*, wrote of Adams' use of the sentence and quoted one of Harrington's passages containing it (p. 169). Ironically, in so doing, Scott highlighted, if in a limited way, the very connection he strongly denied between a leading founding Father and a political theorist of communitarian views. For an articulated discussion of the dialectic of liberalism and republicanism in the thought of the American revolution see Paul W. Kahn, "Reason and Will in the Origins of American Constitutionalism," *Yale Law Journal*, 98, 1989, pp. 449–517.

for proposing the United States as a legal model to the world. However, to understand more deeply the theoretical basis of Scott's adjudication project and his use of US constitutional history it is necessary to take a closer look at the formative years in which he developed his legal theory.

## The Case Method and the Ideology of Legal Evolution

As I explained previously,[21] Scott had encountered international law and the case method of legal education as an undergraduate at Harvard in the 1880s. That experience marked him profoundly: Christopher Columbus Langdell, the Harvard law professor who popularized the case method, would remain his ideal model of educator and legal theorist. I have also briefly outlined already the connection between Langdellian legal theory and several aspects of Scott's mindset: his favor for case-based education and the judicial method, his elitist understanding of formal equality, and the progressive role he believed the United States to have in global politics.[22] However, since my aim in this chapter is to focus on the rationalist, scientific side of Scott's thinking underscoring his historical work, it is important to provide a deeper explanation and contextualization of the case method and its relation to evolutionary ideology and narratives of progress. And I see no better starting point than Christopher Columbus Langdell himself.[23] Langdell was a figure of significant impact: "During his tenure as dean of Harvard Law School . . . from 1870 to 1895, [he] conceived, designed, and built the system of academic meritocracy that became the normative model of professional education in the United States."[24]

It is easy to draw parallels between the principles that shaped his pedagogy and legal thinking and his biography. Langdell overcame the poverty of his youth to excel as a law student at Harvard and, later, as a Wall Street corporate lawyer. His humble beginnings on a New Hampshire farm meant he had to work hard since boyhood, undertaking both manual and intellectual work, first to survive and then to establish himself professionally.[25] That led him to pursue academic meritocracy over the gentlemanly values that regulated US universities of the mid-nineteenth century. Around meritocracy he built a theoretical framework that went beyond a restructuring of professional higher education,[26] envisaging its effects on the legal

[21] See Prologue.

[22] See Chapter 2 section 1.

[23] The deepest and most convincing examination available, among a massive wealth of material on Langdell's life and intellectual contribution is Bruce A. Kimball, *The Inception of Modern Professional Education. C.C. Langdell, 1826–1906*, Chapel Hill: The University of North Carolina Press, 2009. I am deeply indebted to it for the writing of this subsection.

[24] Ibid., p. 2. On the success of Harvard Law School and the spreading of its model see ibid., pp. 2–4.

[25] On Langdell's early years until his graduation from Harvard Law School see ibid., pp. 10–41.

[26] Langdell's reforms outside the classroom revolved around the setting of higher and objective standards for the evaluation of students. They included the requirement of a bachelor's degree for admission to law schools and the designing of a curriculum of courses that had to be taken in sequence, lasting

system and society at large. Indeed, "Langdell maintained that the just working of the legal system relies on the effectiveness of the legal profession, which depends on lawyers' expertise derived from their academic achievement in law school."[27] He reached this conclusion through his years of practice in New York City (1855–70), during which he witnessed a class of legal professionals he considered to be unskilled, amass fortunes through complicity with the Tammany Hall corrupt political machine.[28] In short, it was the ingraining of meritocracy in legal education that best guaranteed "a government of laws, not of men." Being a successful lawyer would become not only financially but also morally and intellectually rewarding. In fact, Langdell considered his system democratic in a double sense: on one hand, it guaranteed objective fairness in society; on the other, it provided opportunities of professional and social advancement to the most skilled and the hardest-working.

In terms of classroom pedagogy, Langdell's legacy is tied to the case method.[29] Bruce Kimball has traced the intellectual sources and biographical circumstances that led Langdell to abandon the dominating scheme of the lecture and study from textbooks to employ the Socratic method of class discussion and induction from court decisions:

> He had read Locke's recommendations that teachers should present students with original sources rather than textbooks, work from the particular to the general, challenge students with the competence of those more advanced, encourage students' autonomy, and impart not content but a method of learning. . . . The reading of Locke's education . . . , the exposure to specimens in his natural history course, the intellectual influence of scientific taxonomy in the mid-nineteenth century, the intense discussion of cases with [Harvard Law School] students outside of class, the research for Parson's treatises [on contract law], the shift to Code Pleading in New York that entailed new emphasis on appeal to precedents, the predominance of Langdell's legal practice in equity, and the increased reporting of cases throughout the United States [were] his reasons for choosing to teach from cases.[30]

three years instead of the previous two. At the same time he ensured a more qualified faculty by setting an academic career track and hiring younger scholars, trained in the new method and familiar with his ideas, rather than already established judges and lawyers.

---

27 Ibid., p. 2.

28 On Langdell's time in Wall Street practice see ibid., pp. 42–83.

29 Some argue that a case method of legal teaching had been developed and used in the United States before Langdell did, for instance by John Norton Pomeroy, Elihu Root's teacher at the Law School of New York University (see Jonathan Zasloff, "Law and the Shaping of American Foreign Policy: From the Gilded Age to the New Era," *New York University Law Review*, 78, 2003, p. 252). Bruce Kimball has rejected this thesis, convincingly in my opinion (see Bruce Kimball, "The Langdell Problem: Historicizing the Century of Historiography, 1906–2000s," *Law and History Review*, 22(2), Summer 2004, pp. 335–7). In any case, the case method became widely spread only following its successful employment at Harvard Law School by Langdell.

30 Kimball, *The Inception*, pp. 87–8 and 140–1.

Upon his return to Harvard as Dane Professor of Law and Dean of the Law School in 1870, Langdell embarked in the production of his first teaching casebook. The first half of his *Cases on Contracts* appeared already at the end of that year, in November.[31] The following year, Langdell would publish a larger, complete version of the first edition of the casebook[32] containing what would go on to become a famous preface outlining his method.

The model of casebook Langdell trail-blazed was revolutionary. The details of its composition perfectly mirrored its editor's pedagogic ideas.[33] In the first place, it was characterized by the attention it put in favoring autonomous intellectual work in the extraction of legal principles. To pursue that goal, Langdell omitted any headnotes or commentary to the cases. The traditional legal treatise, instead, aimed at leaving reference to cases in the footnotes or completely omitted, so not to deflect attention from the exposition of legal doctrines by the author. Secondly, he took measures to historicize the decisions and make evident the process of evolution of legal doctrines. For the first time, cases were arranged in chronological order and indicated with full information including the judging court, its location, and the accurate date. Moreover, Langdell added superseded cases, pointing to the relevance of reasoning above existing rules and to the understanding of the slow and complex process from which legal principles originated and were refined.

Following Langdell's example, the case method spread quickly among US law schools and with it the production of casebooks, covering a wide range of legal branches. Freeman Snow, Scott's instructor at Harvard, would be the first American author to produce a casebook on international law.[34] In 1902, Scott would be the second.[35]

The case method responded both to practical and theoretical needs. It was the most efficient training tool for students but it also represented the educational side of a specific theory of law as a science.[36] A scientific approach would reside in the

[31] *A Selection of Cases on the Law of Contracts with References and Citations . . . Prepared for Use as a Text-Book in Harvard Law School*, ed. by Christopher Columbus Langdell, Boston: Little, Brown, 1870.

[32] *A Selection of Cases on the Law of Contracts with References and Citations . . . Prepared for Use as a Text-Book in Harvard Law School*, ed. by Christopher Columbus Langdell, Boston: Little, Brown, 1871.

[33] See Kimball, *The Inception*, pp. 88–9.

[34] Freeman Snow, *Cases and Opinions on International Law with Notes and a Syllabus*, Boston: Boston Book Co., 1893.

[35] *Cases on International Law Selected from Decisions of English and American Courts with Syllabus and Annotations*, ed. by James Brown Scott, 1902, re-issued in 1906. The second edition was released in 1922 (*Cases on International Law Principally Selected from Decisions of English and American Courts*, St. Paul: West Publishing) and the third and last (*Cases on International Law*, co-edited with Walter H. E. Jaeger, St. Paul: West Publishing) in 1937, three years before Scott's retirement from public life. It would be the most widely used casebook in the teaching of international law in the United States at least until the 1930s, when it had to compete with Manley O. Hudson's *Cases and Other Materials on International Law*, St. Paul: West Publishing Company, 1929.

[36] Langdell's pedagogical innovations went hand in hand with his legal theory but the two had diverging fortunes. While the case teaching method became by the end of his career, in 1900, the standard for the developing US law schools, the background formulation of law as an apolitical science that had led to its devising was close to disappearing from the academia. On the separate fortunes of the case method and Langdellian theory see Thomas C. Grey, "Langdell's Orthodoxy," *University of Pittsburgh*

discovery of the principles underlying law's concrete data. Legal "doctrines could be inducted from the study of cases; the solution to any particular legal problem could be in turn deducted from the principles."[37] Langdell would put it so in the preface to his first casebook:

> Law, considered as a science, consists of certain principles or doctrines. To have such a mastery of these as to be able to apply them with constant facility and certainty to the ever-tangled skein of human affairs, is what constitutes a true lawyer; and hence to acquire that mastery should be the business of every earnest student of law. Each of these doctrines has arrived at its present state by slow degrees; in other words it is a growth, extending in many cases through centuries. This growth is to be traced in the main through a series of cases; and much the shortest and best, if not the only way of mastering the doctrine effectually is by studying the cases in which it is embodied.[38]

Langdell and his followers, including Scott,[39] compared the proposed "scientific" legal methodology to taxonomy as employed by mid- and late nineteenth-century natural sciences. Langdell's knowledge of the subject derived primarily from the natural history course he attended as a sophomore during the academic year 1848–49, the only formal scientific education he ever received. His teachers, the botanist Asa Gray and the Swiss zoologist Louis Agassiz, were leading scholars in their respective fields. It would be incorrect to think of taxonomy as simple classificatory work that would be surpassed by Darwin's evolutionism.

> [A]s known and practiced by such sophisticated scientists as Gray, taxonomy was more subtle and complicated, as was its relationship to evolutionary theory. In fact, "far from discrediting the old taxonomy, Darwin consummated it and vindicated its essential validity." Gray, in particular, recognized that *The Origin of the Species* depended on "the quest for a natural system of classification," without which "the *Origin* would have lacked that connection with empirical evidence which gave it most strength." . . . Gray thus understood that one needed taxonomy in order to recognize evolutionary change.[40]

*Law Review*, 45(1), 1983–84, p. 2 note 3. On Langdell's immediate legacy see Paul D. Carrington, "Hail! Langdell!," *Law and Social Inquiry*, 20, 1995, pp. 691–3.

---

37 Benjamin Coates, *Transatlantic Advocates: American International Law and U.S. Foreign Relations, 1898–1919*, unpublished PhD dissertation, Columbia University, 2010, p. 28.

38 Christoper Columbus Langdell, "Preface," in Langdell (ed.), *A Selection of Cases* (1871), p. vi.

39 Scott, "The Study of the Law," *The American Law School Review*, 2(1), 1906, pp. 3–4 and Hepp, "James Brown Scott and the Rise of Public International Law," *Journal of the Gilded Age and Progressive Era*, 7, 2008, pp. 162–4.

40 Kimball, *The Inception*, p. 26.

This was the scientific understanding that helped to shape Langdell's legal thought: one in which classification and evolution, the static and the dynamic element, were combined and mutually elucidating. However, Kimball warns not to make too much of Langdell's analogies between law and science. They appear only a few times in his large body of work. Also, they were probably primarily a way to endear his vision to Harvard President Charles W. Eliot, who had wanted Langdell as dean and was a chemist by training.[41] Yet, legal scholars picked up the idea enthusiastically. It became commonplace to think that improvements in the law required a systematization of the legal principles through the analysis of court decisions and their relation to each other. The evolution of science, including legal science, was part of the general progress of human civilization. Scott expressly acknowledged his debt to Langdell.[42] Both shared the organic view transpiring from Langdell's preface, understanding law in constant evolution into a better functioning autonomous system of formal rules. Both hoped to remove arbitrariness in the application of legal rules as a way to a more just and democratic society. However, Scott's legal science incorporated, in addition, an ethnocentric understanding of the growth of law as an outcome of American national spirit.

The organic growth metaphor for law had been for more than a century a *topos* of conservative political thinking. The legal scholar who combined organic growth with the romantic idea of a national spirit of the people, was Friedrich Carl von Savigny (1779–1861), the leading figure of the German historical school. Scott, who had completed his studies in Heidelberg and had the utmost respect for German legal scholarship, was indebted to Savigny's theories. In his view, an American spirit had operated in the development of law even before the country's independence.

Over his many years of professional activity, Scott would keep emphasizing both the scientific, logical element necessary for the discovery and application of legal principles and the spiritual element embedded in a conception of law as evolution of custom in society. He was particularly indebted to British legal historian and imperial administrator Henry Sumner Maine (1822–88),[43] who, as we have seen, had influenced already Scott's first speech. Maine's goal was to recast, through an empirical and inductive method, historicist ideas on the progressive development of legal concepts and social institutions. In this way he also sought to oppose the dominating Benthamite view that law was the command of a legislator moved by utilitarian considerations. The influence of *Ancient Law* (1861),[44] his

[41] See ibid., pp. 349–51.

[42] See Scott, 'The Study of the Law', p. 2 and 5–6.

[43] For an exposition of Maine's evolutionist theories of law and the influential legacy of *Ancient Law* see Peter Stein, *Legal Evolution: The Story of an Idea*, Cambridge: Cambridge University Press, 1980, pp. 86–115.

[44] Henry Sumner Maine, *Ancient Law: Its Connection to the Early History of Society and Its Relation to Modern Ideas*, London: John Murray, 1861.

most renowned work, would prove to be long lasting. The effort therein for a scientific analysis of the evolution of social institutions was in tune with the interest of the time, already accustomed to evolutionary thinking through the publication of Darwin's *Origin of Species* in 1859.

For Maine, the change in human relationships within progressive societies could be exemplified as a movement from status to contract based on the affirmation of individualism. As Peter Stein noted, "those who saw history as the gradual attainment of an ideal like freedom recognised in [Maine's] exposition the gradual unfolding of the idea of the self-determination of the free individual, projected on the plane of law."[45] Maine's theorization was, in practice, taken to the extreme by rejecting any form of constraint to freedom of contract. This individualist trend would dominate much longer in the United States than in Europe.

As I briefly noted in the previous chapter,[46] this formalist understanding of freedom was the main legal tool used by the US elites to frustrate the efforts of the labor movement at the turn of the century.[47] Notwithstanding the steady rise of real wages during the massive economic growth of the gilded age, the working class mostly remained in a state of profound destitution. This was a period of massive economic inequality, in which the continuing plight of workers co-existed with the amassing of fabulous fortunes, Andrew Carnegie's being an example. However, the growing establishment of large factories and the specialization of industrial workers created the conditions for the organization of a strong labor movement. One of the main goals of the movement was to obtain legal reforms ensuring fairer working conditions. The typical example of legislation sought was a maximum limit to daily working hours. Some reforms pursued protection for the general working population, others focused on children and women. The movement often scored legislative successes. However, courts became the line of last resistance for the elites. They repeatedly struck down protective legislation, claiming it violated freedom of contract. Paradoxically, courts claimed that they were guarding the autonomy of workers as much as that of the employers: for instance, an eight-hour working day limit would prevent a worker willing to work more—and earn more—to do so, the argument went. As the journalist and financial expert Horace White put it, "the right of each man to labor as much or as little as he chooses, and to enjoy his own earnings, is the very foundation of free government."[48] This idea had purchase, considering the country was still facing the consequences of slavery and the Civil War. But of course, this was an extremely formalist reasoning that overlooked the

[45] Stein, *Legal Evolution*, p. 101.

[46] See Chapter 2 section 1.

[47] For a detailed analysis of the political struggles of the time around the concept of freedom of contract and its ideological foundations see Eric Foner, *The Story of American Freedom*, New York: W. W. Norton, 1998, pp. 115–37.

[48] Quoted in Nancy Cohen, *The Reconstruction of American Liberalism, 1865–1914*, Chapel Hill: The University of North Carolina Press, 2002, p. 40.

reality that workers hardly had any negotiating power in industrial relations. By the 1880s, the application of the freedom of contract principle to suppress labor legislation was commonplace. It affected a wide variety of measures, ranging from prohibitions on production in dangerous or unhealthy environments to requirements to pay salaries in money rather than merchandise. Courts also used freedom of contract to ensure that the growing influence of the labor movement would be curbed, alongside their routine injunctions against strikes. For instance, the Supreme Court upheld the validity of so-called yellow-dog contracts,[49] which prescribed as a condition of continuing employment that the worker was not or would not become a union member. Another Supreme Court case, decided in 1905, would give to the freedom of contract doctrine of this period the name with which it will go down in history: Lochner-era or Lochnerism. In *Lochner v. New York*,[50] the Court invalidated a New York State law that set a limit of working hours for bakers.

The concept of freedom of contract was one key example of how the elites used the doctrine of legal evolution in the pursuit of conservative political goals. In general, "the idea of legal evolution appealed to conservative legal thinkers, especially perhaps to academic conservatives who liked to think of themselves as progressive."[51] Such consideration seems to apply to Scott, in particular in relation to the individualist corollaries of legal evolution just described. This individualist and formalist stance of Langdellian mold was shared by most of the American legal elite of the time. The realist and pragmatic critique of scholars like Oliver Wendell Holmes Jr. (1841–1935),[52] aimed at keeping law opened to social considerations and communitarian arguments, would remain a minority voice for a few more decades. The language preferred by this individualist elite constantly mixed claims of a progressive character for the American experiment and references to the stability offered to it by its law. The same language would form the basis on which Scott built his international law.

## International Law as Law

Scott explicitly employed the authority of Maine to oppose the evaluation of international law made by a disciple of Jeremy Bentham, the jurist John Austin. In 1899, Scott obtained his first academic appointment as first dean of the newly founded College of Law of the University of Illinois. His main project then was to give academic and professional dignity to international law within the US legal community against the persistent popularity of Austin's famous

[49] See *Adair v. United States*, 208 US 161 (1908).

[50] 198 US 45 (1905).

[51] Stein, *Legal Evolution*, p. 122.

[52] On the complicated relationship between Holmes and Langdell, see Kimball, *The Inception*, *passim*.

pronouncement of 1832 that denied its legal nature and considered it, at best, positive morality.[53] As a consequence of the positivist atmosphere reigning in legal academia, Scott had to struggle even to bring the teaching of international law to the law school he directed. David Kinley, dean of the College of Literature and Arts, where the courses on international law were traditionally offered because they were "associated with a liberal education rather than a technical one," opposed his endeavor.

Kinley could count on the support of several legal authorities, including Oliver Wendell Holmes, soon to become an influential and long-serving (1902–32) Justice of the Supreme Court of the United States: "International Law, of course, has little to do in any sense, with the practice of the profession. I should almost as soon require chemistry." Scott managed to prevail but his success did not survive his departure from Illinois in 1904, which resulted in the College of Law excluding international law from its curriculum.[54]

Scott's main gesture to affirm international law's legal and scientific nature in his early career was represented by the first edition of his casebook, published in 1902. The case method suited his ideas on legal evolution and historical progress. These ideas would lead him toward the research of the intellectual origins and the foundational myths for legal structures more suitable to his political beliefs. The use of this technique would become a constant feature of Scott's professional activity, as we have seen in relation to the Platt Amendment and the introductory chapters of *The United States*.

As made clear by the short preface to the casebook and by its full title, Scott was aiming, already in 1902, to provide international law with an Anglo-American pedigree:

> The idea underlying this volume is that international law is part of the English common law; that as such it passed with the English colonists to America; that when, in consequence of a successful rebellion, they were admitted to the family of nations, the new republic recognized international law as completely as international law recognized the new republic.[55]

For Scott, the history of the United States was by then, following the triumph of the Spanish-American War, evidently the ultimate political success, the highest stage of human civilization. In his view, the history of international law ran parallel to the destiny of America as the standard bearer of a new diplomacy, more advanced than the traditional European one and based on the sharp division of law and politics. International relations would lead toward progress and justice if put in the

[53] See John Austin, *The Province of Jurisprudence Determined*, London: John Murray, 1832, p. 208.
[54] The recounting of the episode is based on Coates, *Transatlantic Advocates*, pp. 29–30, where also the related quotes are from.
[55] *Cases on International Law* (1902), ed. by Scott, p. v.

hands of the lawyer and not of the "diplomatist" who "does not and cannot consider the question at issue with the impartiality of a judge, for he is influenced by the interests of his country."

At this stage, Scott decided not to delve into the "vexed question whether [international law] is law in the abstract." What mattered, in relation to the goal of founding its teaching and study on a scientific basis through the collected cases was that "municipal law it was in England; municipal law it remained and is in the United States." The fact, substantiated by the casebook, that "English and American courts of justice enforce international law, and have repeatedly done so in the past two centuries," made it part and parcel of the fundamental knowledge of "the American student or practitioner." Moreover, for Scott, the resulting "mass of judicial decision"[56] represented a solid foundation for the codification and development of international legal principles in Langdellian scientific terms and a clear representation of the progressive trajectory of international law and history.

Scott took a similar approach when he addressed the American Bar Association at its Annual Meeting in August 1903, in order to make the case for international law to be taught in law schools. His speech, titled "The Place of International Law in Legal Education"[57] started by proving, once again through cases, the claim of international law as a proper legal discipline. In his rather technical discussion, geared toward an audience of legal professionals, Scott reviewed a series of Supreme Court prize cases, finding once again a key moment of awareness originating out of the Spanish-American War. During the war, two Spanish fishing vessels, the *Paquete Habana* and the *Lola*, had been captured by the United States. In delivering the majority opinion for the Supreme Court in the resulting case, Associate Justice Horace Gray performed an exercise that mirrored Scott's. He affirmed, by looking at the Court's precedents, that the law of nations and its doctrines had been always upheld as law of the land, and that was true in particular of customary international law.

> International law is part of our law and must be ascertained and administered by the courts of justice of appropriate jurisdiction as often as questions of right depending upon it are duly presented for their determination. For this purpose, where there is no treaty and no controlling executive or legislative act or judicial decision, resort must be had to the customs and usages of civilized nations.[58]

Once he had established the legal nature of international law to his audience of professionals through the authority of the Supreme Court, Scott moved on to explain why its knowledge was necessary to both the student and the practitioner.

[56] Ibid., pp. v–vi.

[57] James Brown Scott, "The Place of International Law in Legal Education," in *Transactions of the Twenty-Sixth Annual Meeting of the American Bar Association, held at Hot Springs, Virginia, August 26, 27 and 28, 1903*, Philadelphia: Dando Printing and Publishing Company, 1903, pp. 583–94.

[58] *Paquete Habana v. United States*, 175 US 677 (1900).

Obviously, as he had affirmed in the introduction to the casebook, it was because courts used it in reaching their decisions. But would it be necessary also to the everyday lawyer that would probably never argue a prize case in front of the Supreme Court or become a diplomat or a Congressman? While conceding "that cases" primarily "of international law [we]re rare in comparison,"[59] Scott replied in the affirmative, listing a series of legal issues involving international law that could easily appear in small-time, everyday practice.[60] Having established that proper knowledge of international law was needed by every legal professional, Scott explained his proposals to make it part of formal legal education in the United States. The most important and obvious for him and the basis of every meaningful reform would be the offering of an international law course in every law school. International law could not be understood in its technical value if it stayed only in departments of liberal arts; it could "well be taught" there "[f]or purposes of citizenship and general culture." It would "cease, however, to be law when so taught; for a layman . . . does not, grasp legal technicalities and the nice reasoning that obtain in the discussion of legal distinctions and subtleties, so that . . . international law [in his hands] becomes a hodgepodge of diplomatic history."[61] That is where the crux of the problem was: international law was not perceived as a legal subject by most lawyers primarily because of where and how it was taught; that made them overlook the professional usefulness it had for them, especially in court litigation. The "technical knowledge require[d]" in cases involving international law entailed "legal training, previous legal study, and can only be acquired, it is submitted, in a law school. Unless technically taught these are only insignificant service to the technical lawyer. . . . The professional man . . . must seek the professional school—in this case the law school—for his law."[62]

Later, in 1907, now an established professional thanks to the association with Root and his work at the State Department, Scott would finally formulate a direct response to the Austinian objection, in the first volume of the *American Journal of International Law*.[63] His article on "The Legal Nature of International Law" focused on the nature of sanction, also a key concept in Scott's analysis of the American Constitutional Convention.

[59] Scott, "The Place," p. 594.

[60] See ibid., p. 590–1. Among the topics involving international legal issues cited by Scott were: "the right of asylum in legations and ships of war and merchant vessels; jurisdiction over offenses committed abroad or on the high seas; extradition and interstate rendition; domicile, expatriation and naturalization[;] the effect of war upon trade, ordinary contracts, insurance, agency, partnership, and the statute of limitations."

[61] Ibid., p. 591.

[62] Ibid., p. 592.

[63] James Brown Scott, "The Legal Nature of International Law," *American Journal of International Law*, 1, 1907, pp. 831–66.

## 2. The United States as Universal History: Scott's Recurring Themes in Legal Progress

### Public Opinion as Sanction: The Case for Adjudication against Collective Security

The gist of Scott's argument was that the Austinian conception of law as command was inaccurate in positing force as the exclusive element to characterize a legal system as such. Austin had simply failed to consider law in its various stages of evolution. In a fashion reminiscent of his first speech given ten years earlier, Scott wrote of the stages of progressive growth of judicial systems. He referred to historical examples of courts that developed remarkable procedural complexity without enjoying enforcing powers, so as to underline his point that law consisted simply in rules of conduct, which did not require a specific sanction to be legal. Sanction as direct enforcement was, in his opinion, only one of the many possible means to an end, the observance of the law.

Scott's reasoning did not only serve the purpose of legitimizing international law, in opposition to the restrictive Austinian definition of legal rules. He also wanted to introduce another key idea shared by many leading US jurists of his time. There was an effective moral sanction embedded in legal rules, exercised through the pressure of public opinion.

Elihu Root provided a clear formulation of the argument in 1908 with his presidential address at the second annual meeting of the American Society of International Law, entitled "The Sanction of International Law."[64] In municipal legal systems, Root argued, "in the vast majority of cases men refrain from criminal conduct because they are unwilling to incur . . . the public condemnation . . . which would follow a repudiation of the standard of conduct prescribed by . . . the community in which they live . . . for its members." Root deemed compliance based on coercive enforcement or its direct deterrence as exceptional:

> [I]t is only for the occasional nonconformist that the sheriff and policeman are kept in reserve[.] For the great mass of mankind laws established by civil society are enforced directly by the power of public opinion, having, as the sanction for its judgments, the denial of nearly everything for which men strive in life.[65]

Applying the same reasoning to relationships between States, Root argued that compliance with international law derived from the awareness of the governments of the

[64] Elihu Root, "The Sanction of International Law," in *Addresses on International Subjects by Elihu Root*, collected and edited by Robert Bacon and James Brown Scott, Cambridge: Harvard University Press, 1916, pp. 25–32.

[65] Ibid., pp. 27–8.

most civilized countries that respect for the law was in their long-term interest: "nonconformity to the standard of nations means condemnation and isolation." Strategic considerations of the potential advantages brought by the "influence exercised by the general opinion of the world regarding the nation's character and conduct" would operate "independent[ly] of any calculation upon a physical enforcement of the opinion of others." Root admitted the difficulty of explaining rationally the operation of public opinion as the embedded moral sanction in international legal rules. Still, he affirmed it as a "universally recognised" empirical truth: "the nation which has with it the moral force of the world's approval is strong, and the nation which rests under the world's condemnation is weak, however great its material power."[66]

As the world became more and more interdependent through the improvement of technology, Root argued, the increase of means of communication and travel favored the spread of "a just appreciation of international rights and duties and a knowledge of the principles and rules of international law"; it strengthened as well the sphere of action for an international public opinion. At the same time, the influence of public opinion would require a judicial systematization and clarification of legal principles, as its "force . . . can be brought to bear only upon comparatively simple questions."[67] Therefore, in Root's argumentation, the progressive development of institutions of international adjudication would bring with it a virtuous circle of mutually supportive trends. The technical improvement of international law would increase the trust States have in it. In turn, this trust would convince governments to enlarge the realm of disputes they considered justiciable rather than eminently political. Closing the circle, the solution through adjudication of disputes touching vital interests of nations would increase the interest and knowledge of the public in matters of international justice, thus strengthening the influence of the moral sanction represented by public opinion.

The importance of public opinion for the international legal order as conceived by Scott and Root represented the thread between international law as a science of adjudication and international law as a moral system based on the "indefinite and almost mysterious influence exercised by the general opinion of the world."[68] This synthesis is, as I explained above, the linchpin of an exceptionalist discourse of progress: global peace and free trade would be achieved by the universalization of the American rule of law. Root, in his short speech to the ASIL, did not fail to refer to the US Declaration of Independence and its call to a "decent respect to the opinions of mankind." He remarked "that the first public national act in the New World [had been] an appeal to that universal international public opinion, the power and effectiveness of which the New World has done so much to promote."[69]

66 Ibid., pp. 30–1.
67 Ibid., pp. 31–2.
68 Ibid., p. 30.
69 Ibid., p. 28.

Scott's description of the American foundation as a milestone in the progress of international law in *The United States* also featured the issue of sanction. He approached it through the opposition in the Constitutional Convention between the delegates supporting coercion of States by force and those who wanted the American Union to be bound purely by law. Scott, once again, aimed at presenting a narrative featuring the solution of a political issue through a legal compromise suggested over time by experience. In the bigger picture of progressive history, the Articles of Confederation represented for Scott a necessary "step to a more perfect Union"[70] of particular significance from an international point of view. Indeed, Scott offered the Confederation as a rudimentary and initial model of organization for the Society of Nations, should it decide to proceed toward institutional integration, as it seemed clear it would at the time of writing in 1918. During the War of Independence, the former colonies could agree, out of the necessity of coordination of the war efforts, only on a loose union incorporated in the Articles of Confederation. Entered into force in 1781, the Articles contained only what Scott defined as "a suggestion of a judiciary."[71] Rather than focusing on the defects of the Articles as an institutional system, Scott suggested to look at the cause of their shortcomings. He found it in the "defective vision of the [revolutionary] statesmen." Even the Founding Fathers, praised and revered by Scott at every opportunity, could not see at once, in their historical context, the advantages of a stronger central government for the protection of commerce and the strengthening of the country. This was understandable, as they feared the creation of "a domestic tyrant in the place of the imperial Parliament"[72] they were revolting against.

Scott saw the final institutional goal for the international community in the universalization of the American rule of law and separation of powers embodied in the US Constitution. In Scott's narrative of the passage from the Articles of Confederation to the Constitution, one key issue was that of compliance and sanction. Under the Articles, a treaty of alliance in nature, compliance with its obligations was a responsibility of the States. Congress found itself powerless in front of repeated violations by the States that were jeopardizing foreign relations, weakening commerce, and creating internal tensions. The experience derived from the implementation of the Articles provided the Founding Fathers with two shared considerations difficult to reconcile: on one hand, there was need of a closer union, still based on the idea of limited government but endowed with larger centralized powers; on the other, it was clear that it would be hard to reach a compromise in that direction for States that were already failing to comply under less demanding obligations.

[70] Scott, *The United States*, p. 46.

[71] Ibid., p. 45. Scott referred to the power of Congress under the Articles to decide boundary disputes between States and to create courts to determine prize cases.

[72] Ibid., p. 46.

Scott underlined how the calling of the Constitutional Convention, promoted by Madison and the State of Virginia, was ultimately motivated by the necessity for a common regulation of commerce. Indeed, the free exercise of commercial activity was, in his view, both the incentive and the consequential reward of legal progress and the growing interdependence of communities. While Madison initially proposed a sanction for States' violations of the Constitution, the final constitutional compromise relied on a doctrine of limited government and dual sovereignty. The national laws would apply directly to individual citizens, "without the intervention or agency of the State,"[73] and the Supreme Court would represent the guarantee against the overstepping of legal boundaries by constitutional subjects. The Supreme Court was then construed as the lynchpin of the "government of laws, not of men," providing the legal solution also to the controversies of States between themselves and with the Federal Government:

> [T]he judicial power of the United States was not meant to be and is not the agency of the General Government, to maintain its supremacy at the expense of the States. It maintains the powers which the States, in their common interest, freely granted to the agency of their creation, which we call the United States, and protects it from assault by one of the States in its own interest.[74]

The Supreme Court would speak the law, representing both an organ of independent judges applying rational legal principles and the voice of Scott's mystic American spirit: "We the People," in the words of the preamble of the Constitution. Paul Kahn has described the connection between Supreme Court judgments and the popular sovereign in the American political imagination in Schmittian terms, as a manifestation of will, a decision on the exception.[75] Scott's description of the nature of the United States' judiciary is at the opposite end of the spectrum. His aim was the presentation of the US constitutional system as the triumph of liberalism, of law over politics, of reason over will, of coercion of law over coercion by force. Faith and the American spirit operated at a pre-political level. The deity was not the popular sovereign but the rule of law itself. The measure of the people's sovereignty was in the individual rights each and every citizen could claim.

In terms of sanction, the "sheriff and the policeman" having the power to enforce both federal and State law on Root's individual "occasional nonconformist" would suffice as insurance of order. The possibility of the use of force against States was expunged from the legal system as counterproductive: it would trigger hostilities and split the Union rather than lead to compliance. In this respect, Alexander

[73] Scott, *James Madison's Notes of Debates*, p. 27.

[74] Scott, *The United States*, p. 370.

[75] Paul Kahn, *Political Theology. Four new Chapters on the Concept of Sovereignty*, New York: Columbia University Press, 2011.

Hamilton's words in arguing for ratification of the Constitution in front of the New York Convention, quoted by Scott, sound almost prophetic:

> It has been observed, to coerce the states is one of the maddest projects that was ever devised. A failure of compliance will never be confined to a single state. This being the case, can we suppose it wise to hazard a civil war?[76]

Yet, in *The United States*, the one occasion in which the Federal Government and a group of States faced themselves in open hostilities was relegated close to irrelevance. The Civil War was underscored by omission. It was referred to only *en passant* in a very limited number of occasions, without any explicit attempt of historical analysis, and with two clear instrumental purposes. On the one hand, the Civil War was referred to simply as the background for facts at the basis of Supreme Court judgments, relevant for the operation of the Federal judiciary power Scott aimed to illustrate.[77] On the other, he underlined how the conflict did not disrupt the continuity in the constitutional development of the Union.[78] The American Civil War came out as a momentary setback in the inevitable road to progress, as a crisis of lesser relevance than the historical advancement it stimulated. Based on the analogy between US constitutional history and international history, the same consideration applied to the Great War. After a brief period of desolation at its outbreak,[79] Scott would soon come to see the First World War primarily as an opportunity to infuse the promotion of international judicial institutions with new strength.[80]

The core of Scott's argument was in this optimistic view of the use of force as retreating in an increasingly law-governed world. The United States achieved over time a prosperous union between sovereign States through the development of a court-based rule of law. A key aspect of the successful progress of American law was, in Scott's assessment, that the trust inspired in the States by the activity of the Supreme Court resulted in a voluntary increase of its jurisdiction and, therefore, of questions considered judicial rather than political. Scott concluded that "the judicial power of the United States . . . render[ed] the use of force against the States a stranger to the American system."[81] In the same way, the Society of Nations should have worked toward creating an international judiciary with the goal of developing a global rule of law, rather than designing a system of collective security,

[76] Quoted in Scott, *The United States*, p. 205. See also the quote by Madison at p. 204, repeated at p. 281, and the one by Oliver Ellsworth at 281–2.

[77] See ibid., pp. 382–4 and 459ff.

[78] See ibid., pp. 334–5.

[79] See Coates, *Transatlantic Advocates*, pp. 337–8.

[80] Scott's book of 1916, *The Status of the International Court of Justice* (Oxford: Oxford University Press) was the reprint of a pamphlet for the American Society for Judicial Settlement of International Disputes "published but a few weeks . . . before the outbreak of the great war in August 1914" (p. iii). In the preface to the reprint, Scott remarked how Root had urged that the text appear "in a permanent book form" in view of "a new departure after the war . . . of peaceable settlement" (pp. iii–iv).

[81] Ibid., p. 278.

as proposed by President Wilson, resulting only in increased instability. The US process of constitutionalization indicated a third way, distinct from

> the time-honored method of settling controversies between States sovereign, free and independent . . . either by diplomatic negotiation or by armed conflict; . . . the Revolutionary statesmen interposed between . . . the two, the judicial method . . . They had in mind a court of justice . . . that . . . to have jurisdiction over the States and bind their actions, could only be created by them directly . . . as they had no superior.[82]

## Universal Rule of Law and American Expansionism

Scott's narrative recast the history of the foundation of the United States as a case for the creation of an international court. In his story, the 1787 Constitutional Convention ("an international conference") at times looked like a more successful version in facing rather similar problems of the 1907 Second Hague Peace Conference. In The Hague, in Scott's probably oversimplifying view, the plan for an international judiciary he advanced was blocked precisely by a short-sighted disagreement between large and small States over representation in the court.[83] Analogously, as depicted in *The United States*, American conventional debates were marred by the opposition between large States, proposing proportional representation in the Congress under the Constitution, and small States, insisting on the equality of voting rights. At the end of the day, the issue found a solution in the provision of a representation quota based on the number of inhabitants of the State in the House of Representatives and equality of votes in the Senate.

The effort of conveying the dramatic nature of the moment transpires from the text. As for the international community of Scott's time, the risk of failure of an institutional project on the verge of making history was very present and could be overcome only through "the necessary spirit of concession." His description of how "the difference was adjusted by a concession of the extreme views of each, resulting in a compromise which made the Constitution a possibility"[84] paired up with his faith that the Society of Nations will soon be able to reach a similar result and fulfil "the promise of an international judiciary."[85]

The identification of parallel progressive paths for the American union and the international community was based on the assumption of universality of the rule of

[82] Ibid., p. 211.

[83] See in this sense James Brown Scott, "Aim and Purpose of an International Court of Justice," *Annals of the American Academy of Political and Social Science*, 96, 1921, p. 100–2. For a different account on the issue, see Chapter 1.

[84] Scott, *The United States*, p. 172.

[85] Ibid., p. 269.

law, for which Scott provided, at the same time, a distinctively North American (or, at most, Anglo-Saxon) pedigree. This ambivalence framed a fundamental objective of Scott's project: the reconciliation through law of the aspirations and the actions of the United States, finally ready to engage with the world in a position of leadership.

The Spanish-American War had brought the United States' identity crisis to the fore, as I have argued above. The arguments for intervention had a clearly ambivalent character.[86] Imperialists like Theodore Roosevelt and Alfred Thayer Mahan had been supporting an attack on Spain as necessary to build up the sea power the United States would need to fulfil its military potential since before the advent of the more congenial McKinley Republican administration in 1896. Still, the building up of sufficient momentum to convince a sceptical President to declare war reached the tipping point only when anti-imperialists also joined the fighting camp in view of a humanitarian intervention to stop the Spanish repression of a widespread Cuban rebellion. At the end of a war justified "in the cause of humanity" in order "to put an end to . . . barbarities, bloodshed" and "starvation,"[87] the United States was in control of Cuba, the Philippines, Puerto Rico, and Guam. In that same year of 1898 it had also annexed Hawaii. Carl Landauer has skilfully described the discomfort with turn-of-the-century expansionism in the political debate of the time in the United States.[88] The fate of the Philippines became for many inextricably intertwined with the fate of the American soul. Racial, constitutional, and geopolitical arguments would cut across usual political, class, and cultural divides and inform the reasoning of both the imperialist and the anti-imperialist camps.[89]

Focusing on the contextual analysis of the first volume of the *American Journal of International Law*, published in 1907, Landauer underlines how the journal "expressed itself in such a homogenized voice" and displayed "an attitudinal cohesion," notwithstanding the "discernable . . . cultural ambivalence in [its] pages" and "despite the presence" as contributors "of Republicans and Democrats, prominent imperialist and anti-imperialists." In order to explain away the circumstance, Landauer turns to "the cohesiveness of the US elite at the end of the 19th century and beginning of the 20th."[90] Law was but one expression of the larger cultural paradigm that united the establishment and supported it in leading the country to an enlarging role on the global scene, even in the presence of harsh disagreements over fundamental concrete political issues. The point becomes clear through the close analysis of the debates of the time on expansionism.[91] Arguments and

86 I have treated this debate in more detail in Chapter 2.

87 McKinley's war message to Congress, 11 April 1898, quoted in Warren Zimmerman, *First Great Triumph*, New York: Farrar, Straus and Giroux, 2002, p. 262.

88 See Carl Landauer, "The Ambivalences of Power: Launching the American Journal of International Law in an Era of Empire and Globalization," *Leiden Journal of International Law*, 20, 2007, pp. 345–51.

89 See Zimmerman, *First Great Triumph*, pp. 313–61.

90 Landauer, 'The Ambivalences of Power', pp. 351–2.

91 See, for instance, the description of the arguments used in the Congress debates on the fate of the Philippines by Thomas B. Reed, George Frisbie Hoar, and Albert J. Beveridge, in Zimmerman,

counter-arguments move within the same linguistic register, framed by liberal political assumptions and a constant deployment of the modern social sciences (including law), which provided the supposed rational basis of North American superiority. The criticism of overseas expansionism took in most cases the form of a jeremiad denouncing the risk of decay of US society and institutions as consequence of militarism and/or of the inclusion of uncivilized people. Every opposition represented at the same time an exceptionalist celebration of US civilization.

## Imperialism and Equality

More than a decade after the publication of the first volume of the *American Journal of International Law*, Scott still grappled with US expansionism through his liberal vision of history and legal science. This became clear in *The United States* as Scott described the Founding Fathers battling and defeating the corrupting temptations of imperialism in relation to the Northwest Territory. This contest arose in consequence of the Revolutionary War, as Great Britain had ceded to the United States an area north of the Ohio river and west of the Appalachians, still to be settled and lacking government structures. In 1787, the need to provide a political organization for the Territory made concrete the constitutional issue of admitting new States into the Union at the Federal Convention.

Scott highlighted how certain Founding Fathers, naming Gouverneur Morris as the most outspoken example, were already willing to betray the democratic principles at the basis of US independence, looking at the issue "rather from the standpoint of imperialists on the other side of the water than as statesmen of the new world recognizing the equal rights of the parts of the Empire."[92] Morris and other likeminded members of the Convention achieved the goal of avoiding an express provision of the principle of equality of States in the letter of the Constitution. However, the admission of new States on equal footing soon became accepted practice, consistently sanctioned over the years by the Supreme Court. Indeed, Scott depicted in parallel the proceedings of the Federal Convention with the contemporary ones of the Congress under the Articles of Confederation. With the Northwest Ordinance, the latter established the practice of expansion of the Union through the creation of new republican and equally participating States, confirmed in 1789 by the Congress under the Constitution. This allowed Scott, once again, to produce a narrative of complicated yet gradual legal progress, an inevitable trajectory dictated by the American spirit: "equality is the very life and breath of American institutions."[93]

*First Great Triumph*, pp. 343–9, or the intellectual debate on social Darwinism depicted ibid. at pp. 339–42.

92 Scott, *The United States*, p. 291.
93 Ibid., p. 294.

"No other solution of the problem is conceivable in this more perfect union of the western world; no other solution should be possible in a perfected Society of Nations."[94] Yet, the account Scott offered as background for such a sweeping argument for equality is, at best, selective. Indeed, Scott remarked how James Kent, in the first volume of his *Commentaries on American Law*,[95] published in 1826, warned of another potential risk under the Constitution "that the evils of the old system would reappear in the new."[96] The provision providing for control of Congress over Territories before their admission to statehood could leave the "colonists . . . in a state of the most complete subordination, and as dependent upon the will of congress as the people of this country would have been upon the king and parliament of Great Britain, if they could have sustained their claim to bind [Americans] in all cases whatsoever."[97]

Scott dismissed Kent's preoccupation in hindsight by briefly asserting that the Congress had acted with wisdom and rapidly conceded statehood to Territories. His few concrete remarks, elsewhere in the book, on the treatment of Territories by Congress, did not offer more recent examples. He referred again to the 1787 Northwest Ordinance, praised as a compact between the original States and the people of the Territories, providing the latter with a "declaration of rights" and "the threefold distribution of power."[98]

But what about control of Congress of "other Property belonging to the United States"[99] not destined to statehood? The only instance in which Scott referred to the topic in *The United States* is as well the only one in which he referred obliquely to the US colonial venture following the Spanish-American War. In the chapter on constitutional amendments, Scott described how the first ten integrations to the Constitution, collectively known as the Bill of Rights, came to be left out of the original text only to be approved by Congress already in 1789, entering into force following ratification by three-fourths of the States in 1791. Most delegates, in the rush of the closing days of the Convention, "considered nugatory" a declaration of rights embedded in the Constitution, when "the people" would have "evidently retained every thing, which they did not in express terms give up."[100]

In what could seem simply one of his usual arguments for codification, Scott penned a brief paragraph entitled *Value of the Amendments*. To prove its worth beyond the American context, Scott affirmed that the Bill of Rights embodied "universal truths and therefore susceptible of universal application."[101] The only

94 Scott, *James Madison's Notes of Debates*, p. 61.
95 See James Kent, *Commentaries on American Law*, Vol. I, New York: O. Halsted, 1826, pp. 360–1.
96 Scott, *The United States*, p. 295.
97 Kent, *Commentaries*, pp. 360–1.
98 Scott, *The United States*, pp. 288–9.
99 United States Constitution, Art. 4 Section 3, Clause 2.
100 George Washington, Letter to Lafayette, 28 April 1788, quoted in Scott, *The United States*, p. 329.
101 Scott, *The United States*, p. 330.

factual background offered for universality, though, was the US unilateral imposition of selected Bill principles by Root in his capacity as Secretary of War in 1900 in the Philippines. At the time, the country was still torn by a war between the US occupying forces and the Filipino independence fighters who had initially supported the United States against Spain. The paragraph lacked any reference to the conflict and was built on two lengthy quotes.

The first one is from the April 7, 1900 Instructions, drafted by Root and signed by McKinley, to the Philippines Commission, then the highest civilian authority on the archipelago. It contained the motivation Root provided for the restatement of American rights in the new possession: "it is evident that the most enlightened thought of the Philippine Islands fully appreciates the importance of these principles and rules, and they will inevitably within a short time command universal assent."[102] The sentence is a manifesto of the ideas that Scott proclaimed with *The United States*: the progress of civilization was set in the direction shown by the example of American democracy and the justice embodied in the formality of its law. Such values could not but spread with the growing interdependence of the world and the growing education of peoples. Consent of the governed to power would also spread gradually from the educated elites ("the most enlightened thought") to the whole of the people. In the same instructions, Root, true to his views on the relation of custom and popular sovereignty, insisted with the Commission that their rule was to be based on local habit for the sake of stability and the general benefit of the Filipinos. Yet, he made clear that local custom had to yield to the fundamental principles and individual rights enshrined in US law if the "high mission" of "substituting the mild sway of justice and right for arbitrary rule" envisioned by President McKinley was to be accomplished.[103]

The second quote in Scott's paragraph was from the opinion of Justice Day in the Supreme Court case of *Kepner v. United States*, decided in 1903. Commenting on the instructions, the quoted text simply recognized the American origin of the rights prescribed for Filipinos by Root as "the safeguards of [the United States Constitution] for the protection of life and liberty."[104] The case belongs to the series known as the "insular cases,"[105] which determined the status of the newly acquired overseas possession under the Territorial Clause of the Constitution. The Supreme Court reflected the anxieties and ambivalences of the establishment over expansionism since the early insular cases decided in 1901: it denied the full automatic protection of the Constitution to the Territories, yet obliquely

[102] Elihu Root, *The Military and Colonial Policy of the United States*, ed. by Robert Bacon and James Brown Scott, Cambridge: Harvard University Press, p. 291, quoted in Scott, *The United States*, p. 330.

[103] See Elihu Root, *The Military and Colonial Policy*, pp. 290–2. The quote is from McKinley's Presidential Proclamation, 21 December 1898.

[104] Scott, *The United States*, p. 331.

[105] For a recent analysis of the insular cases and their persisting relevance see *Reconsidering the Insular Cases: the Past and Future of the American Empire*, Gerald L. Neuman and Tomiko Brown-Nagin (eds.), Cambridge: Harvard University Press, 2015.

acknowledged the extension of unspecified basic rights.[106] Root explained the judgments to the press with one of the witty comments he was known for: "the Constitution follows the flag—but doesn't quite catch up with it."[107] The sentence caught the tension embedded in the narrative of liberalism as progress, its promise of the good life always in the making, and in the civilizing struggle of law and justice to overcome power politics. Scott celebrated the success of the American Union by highlighting the expansionism of its law, the Constitution, instead of its territorial expansion, symbolized by the flag. *The United States* traced the birth and development in US history of several different but interconnected trends of expansion for the democratic rule of law Scott pointed to as the path for global progress.

Equal rights were expanding to groups of individuals previously excluded. Democratic government was spreading and would receive new strength as a consequence of the Great War. More and more questions of political sensitivity were coming to be considered justiciable with the development of international mechanisms of dispute settlement, as it had happened in the United States under the influence of the Supreme Court. What Scott narrated was the unfolding of the *telos* of history, in which he believed both as a man of science and as a man of faith. International law was the gospel based on reason with which the American chosen people through its educated elite would lead the world toward the messianic goal of the common law of humanity:

> [T]here will be a single law, with a single and impersonal application in every one and all of the states forming the international community, and the citizens or subjects of these states will be co-terminous and identical with humanity, which always was, which is and ever should be above and beyond any nation or any group of nations, however great, however powerful, however civilized.[108]

The scientific profile of international law Scott embraced since the time of his Langdellian training and his insistence on the centrality of its moral foundations were to co-exist over the span of a career longer than four decades. Indeed, with the importance placed on the harmonization of reason and faith as fundamental to the theory and practice of government, Scott was placing himself within an American tradition of thought traceable to the Founding Fathers he so much revered.[109] Yet, there is a noticeable trend in Scott's primary interest over the years switching from the rational operation of law, on the fore when he needed to establish himself as

[106] See *Downes v. Bidwell*, 182 US 244 (1901).
[107] Quoted in Philip Jessup, *Elihu Root*, vol. I, New York: Dodd, Mead & Company, 1938, p. 348.
[108] James Brown Scott, "The Progress of International Law during the last Twenty-Five Years," *Proceedings of the American Society of International Law*, 25, 1931, p. 33.
[109] See Gregg L. Frazer, *The Religious Beliefs of America's Founders*, Lawrence: Kansas University Press, 2012.

a professional in the scientist atmosphere of the turn of the century, to the moral basis and historical origin of the law of nations at the center of his research in the interwar years. At the crucial time of the First World War's end, *The United States* and the other Armistice Day books represent a key step toward Scott's later work, showing that he was equally engaged with the future and the past, with law as universal morality developed through professional expertise.

## 3. The Losing Quest against Collective Security and the Decline of Scott's Legalism

### The Emergence of Collective Security and the League to Enforce Peace

In 1966, Charles Fenwick (1880–1973) published in the *American Journal of International Law* an editorial comment distinguishing the new (and improved) international law from the old one.[110] With affection, he recalled the faith of his mentor James Brown Scott in the significance of the results of an "old" international legal event such as the Hague Conferences. Yet, Fenwick regarded the Hague system as an expression of an archaic international law, tainted by the naiveté of international lawyers who prescribed rules without sanctions regulating the conduct of hostilities rather than directly act "to put an end to war itself." In opposition to Scott, Fenwick pointed at "collective security" as "the cornerstone of any effective system of peace" and at its championing by Woodrow Wilson at the Paris Peace Conference "to have marked a line, however inconclusively, between the old international law and the new."[111] Collective security represented for Fenwick both the practical premise and the intellectual corollary of an international law based on cooperation, rather than only on the rights and duties of States as it had been for Scott.

Fenwick had already expressed his differences with Scott several decades before. In April 1917, they both intervened at the annual meeting of the American Society of International Law, which happened to be held just a few days after the United States had declared war on Germany and intervened in the Great War. Fenwick spoke quite conventionally on the organization of an international judiciary after the war. Yet, he kept returning to the necessity of an "international executive arm" to be "the authority behind the international court" and "to enforce the decision of the court when rendered."[112] Other participants challenged Scott more harshly

[110] Charles Fenwick, "International Law: the Old and the New," *American Journal of International Law*, 60, 1966, pp. 475–83.

[111] Ibid., pp. 476–7.

[112] Charles Fenwick, "International Organization—Judicial," *Proceedings of the American Society of International Law*, 11, 1917, p. 72.

with interventions and questions assuming that "law is not enough; behind law there must be power."[113] Scott replied insisting on his settled progressive narrative. Force in international relations was doomed to disappear and be replaced by justice through a long process of education of public opinion.[114]

That sparring at the ASIL meeting of 1917 marked the emergence of a younger, innovative generation of international lawyers, including Quincy Wright (1890–1970), Edwin Borchard (1884–1951), Manley Ottmer Hudson (1886–1950), and Fenwick himself, that would soon take over the academic direction of the Society.[115] Apart from Hudson, they did not have a primarily legal background but one in political science.[116] Indeed, they all rejected any stark distinction between law, politics, and force, the very cornerstone of Scott's Langdellian formalism. This ideological difference is what allowed them to accept and support institutionalized collective security while Scott could not.

In any case, the breaking into factions of the US internationalist movement over proposals of collective security had begun much earlier than the ASIL 1917 meeting and Scott's writing of the *United States*. Scott began the decade criticizing sanctionism from a position of power, enjoying the success of his brand of judicialism within the establishment and the leadership position he had recently acquired at the Carnegie Endowment for International Peace. Yet, as Benjamin Coates has noted, "if in 1910 Scott's legalism represented an advanced internationalist vision, by the end of the decade it had become a refuge of unilateral nationalists."[117]

Already in May 1911 Scott would clarify to Theodore Marburg why the American Society for the Judicial Settlement of International Disputes they had recently founded together would betray its goals by supporting a league of peace as the one advocated by Hamilton Holt. Holt had already suggested the creation of an international police to punish aggressor States and enforce international law in the early plans for the CEIP he had drafted with Nicholas Murray Butler,[118] before being left out of the organization's leadership. He went on to campaign for the creation of a league or an alliance that would be able to maintain peace by using force against wrongdoers. At this early stage, rather than directly disparaging the league's idea, Scott explained to Marburg that it was "unwise" to support it as it followed a whole different philosophy than the one of judicial settlement, "the cause in which" they were both "so deeply interested."

[113] Lord Arthur Balfour, quoted in William C. Dennis, "International Organization: Executive and Administrative. Some Supposed Objections to a League for Peace," *Proceedings of the American Society of International Law*, 11, 1917, p. 96.

[114] James Brown Scott, "International Organization: Executive and Administrative," *Proceedings of the American Society of International Law*, 11, 1917, pp. 101–18.

[115] Hatsue Shinohara tells their story in her *US International Lawyers in the Interwar Years. A Forgotten Crusade*, Cambridge: Cambridge University Press, 2012.

[116] See ibid., p. 36.

[117] Coates, *Transatlantic Advocates*, p. 383.

[118] See Chapter 1.

> The thing to do is to build up international institutions, to negotiate treaties binding nations to submit their international differences to judicial or arbitral settlement, leaving the enforcement of the awards in such cases to the good faith of the countries already pledged by the submission of the controversy. Year by year, public sentiment is becoming stronger, and it will accomplish our purpose, I am quite sure, without forming a league as is proposed. My experience at the Second Hague Conference and in the Department of State leads me to the belief that nations are exceedingly sensitive about the organization of leagues which may, in any way, seem to question their sovereignty and its untrammelled exercise.[119]

Scott used every occasion to let his correspondents know of his negative opinion of sanctionism and the league of peace project.[120] But it was not until the First World War started that the sanctionist movement gained wider traction and the fracture between internationalists became more evident. As we have seen, soon after its outbreak, Scott would come to see the World War as an opportunity to relaunch the advocacy for international judicial institutions. Instead, many American supporters of international adjudication no longer believed that the United States could simply teach the world by example. The raging of the Great War, seen as the definitive proof of the instability of European politics, brought them to conclude that international law had to be sustained by the sanction of force. Holt, for instance, wrote to Scott in May 1915 that he agreed with him, but only "in the long run": "certainly the time will come when no force will be used to compel obedience to decisions of courts and legislatures." Yet, he continued, "this war . . . has made me feel that we have not arrived at that happy state where we can afford to ignore force."[121]

The sanctionist evolution of US internationalist legalism led, in June 1915, to the creation of the League to Enforce Peace (LEP). Its leadership featured Holt and close associates of Scott such as former US President William Howard Taft and Theodore Marburg, who had not been convinced by Scott's arguments against collective security. The LEP would quickly gain impressive support and influence. Its first annual national meeting, in May 1916, attracted an audience of over 2,000 people, cutting across political affiliations. On that occasion, President Woodrow Wilson argued, for the first time in public, for the creation of a postwar "association of nations" in which the United States would participate.[122]

[119] Scott to Theodore Marburg, May 2, 1911, Folder 7, Box 10, JBS Papers.
[120] See, for instance, Scott to Alfred Vanderpol, December 23, 1912, Box 560, CEIP Papers.
[121] Hamilton Holt to Scott, May 3, 1915, Folder 3, Box 4, JBS Papers.
[122] Wilson's speech can be found in *Enforced Peace: Proceedings of the First Annual National Assemblage of the League to Enforce Peace*, New York: League to Enforce Peace, 1916, pp. 159–64.

Yet, the program of the LEP[123] did not move much beyond the one Taft and Marburg had sustained, together with Scott, within the American Society for the Judicial Settlement of International Disputes (ASJSID). Of the four proposals composing the program three fit nicely with orthodox judicialist theory. The first two envisioned an international court to settle justiciable disputes and a council of conciliation to settle non-justiciable ones. The fourth called for periodical conferences between the league members to codify rules of international law, with clear inspiration from the Hague model. The novelty was in the third proposal. According to it, the league member nations "shall jointly use forthwith both their economic and military forces against" any other party threatening or starting war without submitting the controversy to the court or the council of conciliation.

The success of the LEP was due in large part to the vagueness of this provision. It is significant that both Wilson and Henry Cabot Lodge, the Republican Senator who would lead the opposition to US participation in the League of Nations, participated in the 1916 LEP meeting and there expressed their support for the organization.[124] For traditional legalists like Taft, it was possible to argue that collective security represented a practical mechanism to reinforce the ambition of an effective international adjudication, rather than a radical change of philosophy. James Brown Scott strongly disagreed and became the LEP's staunchest opponent.

To many it came as a surprise that Scott fought harshly against an organization that adopted all the main elements of his project for international law. Yet, this was consistent with his settled legal theory, which he would later try to elucidate in relation to US constitutional history with the Armistice Day books. Scott believed that mankind was on a path of gradual evolution from force to justice as the basis of human relationships. As he would argue also through *The United States*, the insertion of any recognition of force, such as a mechanism of collective security, within an international adjudicative system would impair its effectiveness and recreate the instability of a balance of power structure. The only sanction law needed was the reprobation of public opinion for violators.[125] Indeed, the education of public opinion to justice would be the key factor to bring about progress toward the judicial settlement of disputes and peace. Collective security, rather than a panacea, was for Scott a counterproductive shortcut.

By early 1916, Scott was aware that the sanctionists were gaining support. He felt that his was "a voice crying in the wilderness." Scott often argued that his brand of legalism was the rational solution tested by practice and supported by people professionally qualified when it came to foreign policy. But it was being overshadowed by two louder and dangerous voices in public discourse: on one hand, the radical pacifists with their vague moral outcries and, on the other, the LEP. The latter's

[123] Ibid., pp. 189–90.
[124] The text of Lodge's speech for the occasion is ibid., pp. 164–7.
[125] See section 2 of this chapter.

proposals "experience ha[d] either rejected or . . . would be condemned by a better knowledge of international relations and the principles which underlie them." The sanctionists' goal was essentially to replace a "genuine international court and genuine international sanctions" with "an ex parte tribunal and armed alliances." Their league was "a Holy Alliance to use force, and to cut throats if need be."[126]

As Wilson's and British support for a postwar league became stronger and more explicit, Scott's battle for a non-coercive international system seemed to grow more and more desperate, even as he used the CEIP resources to muster support.[127] His defeat was definitely not due to lack of trying. In the second half of 1916, following Wilson's pronunciation at the LEP meeting and amid growing political controversy over postwar plans, Scott stepped up his efforts and "laid out a broader program designed to undercut sanctionism."[128] The program was based on Scott's traditional recipes: in the first place, a resumption of the Hague Conferences to adopt fundamental principles of international law, such as the ones he had written into the AIIL's Declaration of the Rights and Duties of Nations. A "juridical union" of all civilized nations would provide the apparatus for the judicial settlement of justiciable disputes around those principles, while a council of conciliation would "consider, discuss and report" on non-justiciable controversies.[129] This program was designed to reunite around it the limited number of organizations that Scott had been able to keep faithful to his ideas, essentially the AIIL, the World's Court League, and the American Peace Society. Even this limited support had to be obtained through CEIP's subsidies and direct intervention in the organizations' governance. For instance, in April and May 1916, Scott had been heavily involved in the rewriting of the constitution of the American Peace Society, with the goal of its gaining tighter control over its local chapters in order to steer them away from sanctionism and radical pacifism. Paradoxically, among Scott's few allies now were the pacifists he despised as irrational, unpractical people and unilateralists who saw judicialism as a limited form of internationalism that could preserve the United States from long-term entanglement in European issues.

But also the LEP's internationalist agenda was less far reaching than it seemed. As Scott argued for an international court by describing the United States as a model of judicial union, Hamilton Holt declared "the United States itself is the greatest League of Peace known to history."[130] This nationalistic stance reflected the belief that the league could be steered by the United States and the United

[126] Scott to W. I. Hull, February 11, 1916, Hull Papers, quoted in Martin David Dubin, "The Carnegie Endowment for International Peace and the Advocacy for a League of Nations, 1914-1918", *Proceedings of the American Philosophical Society*, 123(6), 1979, pp. 364–5.

[127] For a detailed discussion of the activity of Scott and his associates against sanctionism see Dubin, *The Carnegie Endowment*, pp. 344–68.

[128] Ibid., p. 365.

[129] See ibid.

[130] *Enforced Peace*, p. 56.

Kingdom or, in any case, that the autocracies of central Europe would be marginalized. Once again there is a parallel to be drawn between the supporters of international adjudication and the LEP. The common conviction that the United States was, by its democratic creed and advanced political system, a naturally law-abiding country led to the consideration that an international court could never find it on the losing side of an important dispute. In the same way, the sanctionists could not think of the United States ever being punished as the aggressor within a league of nations. Despite the disagreements on the form and level of involvement, the common ground of the discussion between internationalists was that the United States would determine and oversee the new world order based on the ever-growing global interdependence.

## Fighting Collective Security within the Administration: Scott and Lansing versus Wilson

Once the United States entered the war in April 1917, Scott involved the CEIP in his scheming with Secretary of State Robert Lansing, aimed at dissuading President Wilson from fully embracing collective security over judicial settlement. At the same time, the CEIP would join the war effort. Already in early 1917 the CEIP leadership took measures to distance the Endowment from peace activists in the anti-preparedness movement.[131]

With the blessing of Root and the Endowment's Board of Trustees and Executive Committee, Scott placed resources at the disposal of the State Department. First, the Board of Trustees clarified the Endowment's position in relation to the war in a meeting held on April 19. With a first resolution "the Trustees . . . declare[d] their belief that the most effectual means of promoting durable international peace [wa] s to prosecute the war against the Imperial German Government to final victory for democracy." The second adopted resolution, suggested by Scott,[132] authorized "the Executive Committee . . . to take such action and at such time as it may deem proper" in order "to overcome the remaining obstacles to the establishment of an International Court of Justice."[133] Shortly after, on April 21, Scott gave execution to the resolution by contacting Lansing. Five days later, the Secretary of State accepted "very grateful[lly]" on "behalf" of the "Government the services of the Division of International Law, its personnel and equipment." He remarked the importance of "adding to the active force of the Department at a time when the burden of work [wa]s heavy and increasing from day to day."[134] During the

131 See Dubin, *The Carnegie Endowment*, p. 359.

132 See ibid., p. 366.

133 The resolutions are retrievable in "Memorandum for the Information of the Board of Trustees in the Semi-Annual Meeting—December 16, 1918," vol. 425, CEIP Papers.

134 Robert Lansing to Scott, April 26, 1917, vol. 425, CEIP Papers.

following months, Scott worked both for the Army, as judge advocate with the rank of major, and for the State Department together with the staff of his CEIP Division. Between late 1917 and early 1918, the State Department would also gradually take over the Washington offices of the Endowment at Jackson Place, across the street from the White House.[135]

On January 8, 1918, with the Fourteen Points speech Woodrow Wilson developed his peace plans and renewed his commitment to a postwar association of nations. During that same month Lansing and Scott also stepped up their efforts. Lansing requested the War Department to detail Scott with State for special research work. The nature of the work was made official the next month with a letter by Lansing. Scott and the Division were supposed to analyze "the effect of the present war on the principles and rules of international law, with respect to the proposals which have been made for a world organization after the termination of this war."[136] This was a pretty wide mandate that allowed Scott to push judicial settlement over collective security within the limits of the President's indications. Scott prepared the Armistice Day books during 1918 as part of that effort.

In February Lansing also created an advisory committee on international law that would liaise between the Department and the Inquiry, the study group led by Colonel Edward House and set up by Wilson in September 1917 to research and advise in view of the peace negotiations. The committee members were the then Solicitor of the Department, Lester H. Woolsey,[137] the Inquiry's main international lawyer David Hunter Miller, and Scott. On March 2, the CEIP's Executive Committee authorized an appropriation of 10,000 dollars to fund the Division of International Law's work for the State Department, which would be doubled on September 30. On the same March day the Committee also approved the engraving of the sentence "Peace through Victory" on all Endowment stationery to make sure that occasional correspondents could not doubt the organization's patriotism and commitment to the war effort.[138]

Preparations continued intensely over 1918, with Scott and Lansing still conspiring and searching for ways to change the president's mind, notwithstanding the growing difficulty of the task.[139] After the November 11 armistice, Lansing managed to convince Wilson to let Scott and his Endowment staff participate in the Paris Peace Conference. Scott would be named one of the two technical advisors in international law of the US delegation, the other being David Hunter Miller.

[135] See Executive Committee Resolutions November 1, 1917 and January 11, 1918, vol. 425, CEIP Papers. Since the establishment of the CEIP to his retirement in June 1940, Scott's main office would be in the Endowment Secretariat at Jackson Place.

[136] Robert Lansing to Scott, February 28, 1918, vol. 425, CEIP Papers.

[137] See James Brown Scott, "Lester H. Woolsey, the New Solicitor for the Department of State," *American Journal of International Law*, 11, 1917, pp. 645–6.

[138] For the relevant resolutions see vol. 425, CEIP Papers.

[139] On the development of Wilson's League of Nations Covenant proposal and Root's reaction to it, see the following subsection "Defeating the Covenant in the Senate."

Wilson, together with Lansing and Scott, left for Europe on December 4, 1918 on the ship S. S. *George Washington*. On December 27, Lansing made one last attempt by tasking Scott and Miller with the preparation of a draft peace treaty that would reflect their common positions, without the president's knowledge. The resulting text, in addition to prescribing the arbitral and judicial settlement of international disputes, offered alternatives to an obligation to go to war or, in general, employ military sanctions against violating governments. Miller and Scott proposed, instead, the automatic suspension of diplomatic and consular relations and treaties between league members and violators, resulting in high economic, rather than military, pressure.

To say that Wilson was not pleased when, on January 10, in presence of the other US Peace Commissioners, he learned of the Miller-Scott project from his Secretary of State would be an understatement. Lansing recorded in his diary that the terms of the argument were so confrontational to make him consider resigning.[140] He remarked that "the President's sweeping disapproval of members of the legal profession participating in treaty-making seemed to be, and I believe was, intended to be notice to me that my counsel was unwelcome."[141] Not surprisingly, "this incident ended for practical purposes" Lansing's and "Scott's involvement in matters touching closely upon the drafting of the Covenant of the League of Nations."[142]

## Defeating the Covenant in the Senate: Root versus Wilson

Differently than Scott, Elihu Root, acting as the consummate politician he was, maintained an open position on the postwar plans until 1919, when he developed a constructive response to President Wilson's plan.[143] He made sure that the Carnegie Endowment steered clear of sanctionism, despite the involvement of a few trustees, including Oscar Straus, with the LEP. Yet, he reacted ambiguously to the courting he received by the LEP through Harvard president A. Lawrence Lowell. Root praised the LEP for further popularizing international issues in the United States but never gave it his full endorsement. In the years leading to the end of the war, he often declared that as long as international law was advanced, the mechanisms of its enforcement were of secondary importance.

But when, in April 1919, the Paris Peace Conference agreed on the text that would become the League Covenant, a divided Republican party turned once again

[140] See Dubin, *The Carnegie Endowment*, p. 367.

[141] Robert Lansing, *The Peace Negotiations, A Personal Narrative*, Boston: Houghton Mifflin Company, 1921, p. 107. In general on the issue see ibid., pp. 106–8 and 198–201.

[142] See Dubin, *The Carnegie Endowment*, p. 367.

[143] See especially Root's public letter of June 19, 1919 to Henry Cabot Lodge in *American Journal of International Law*, 13, 1919, pp. 596–602.

to Root to develop a coherent common position. That legalism did not have any role in Wilson's view of the new world order had been clear at least since July 1918. Then, the President finalized his proposed Covenant. "Significantly," he "stripped from an earlier draft" by his main advisor Colonel House "a resolution calling for an international court."[144] Wilson purposefully kept lawyers on the sidelines of the peace negotiations and resisted all pressures to have Root as a peace delegate.[145]

Despite Wilson's opposition, the Covenant contained limited provisions on voluntary arbitration and the creation of an international court. Its text, though, maintained Wilson's diplomacy as main inspiration, especially in its most crucial and controversial element, the territorial guarantee of Article X. The lynchpin of the collective security system in the Covenant, the article provided that League members "undertake to respect and preserve as against external aggression the territorial integrity and existing political independence" of other members.

Was this the mechanism capable of providing the global stability needed for American ideals to thrive and expand? Would Article X provide security for the United States or simply turn "it into the world's policeman"?[146] Was then Wilson's territorial guarantee an open door for militarism to destroy from within the democratic nature of American society? The conflict on US ratification of the Paris Peace Treaty came down to the answers Root and Wilson provided for this type of questions. Indeed, Senate rejection of the Treaty was due to Wilson's refusing to accept the reservations around which Root had managed to reunite the Grand Old Party, primarily aimed at neutralizing the obligation created by Article X.[147]

Interestingly, an analysis of their intellectual background indicates fundamental commonalities. As most within the intellectual political elite of their generation, Scott included as we have seen, both Root and Wilson had an organic view of society. Polities evolved naturally over long periods of time, developing bonds responding to the unfolding of history. For both, history followed an inexorable progressive pattern toward civilization. They agreed that the peoples of England and, especially, the United States represented the pinnacle of human development. Their difference concerned the role of law within this frame.

[144] Coates, *Transatlantic Advocates*, p. 413.

[145] "I have absolutely no faith in Mr. Elihu Root and feel sure that he would do something to prove his falseness if we delegated him to act" (Wilson quoted in Richard William Leopold, *Elihu Root and the Conservative Tradition*, Boston: Little, Brown and Company, 1954, p. 35). The lack of esteem was mutual. Root was reported to have said in a private conversation: "we had had weak and wrong-headed presidents, but never until Wilson had we had an unscrupulous and dishonest president" (Chandler P. Anderson Diary, 6 November 1916, Chandler P. Anderson Papers, Library of Congress, quoted in Dubin, *The Carnegie Endowment*, p. 335, fn. 74).

[146] Zasloff, *Law and the Shaping of American Foreign Policy*, p. 353.

[147] See ibid., pp. 341–56. The Senate rejected the Treaty of Versailles, which contained the League of Nations Covenant, with three votes on two separate occasions. On November 19, 1919, Wilson ordered Democrats to vote against the Treaty with the Republicans' reservations. The second vote, on the Treaty without reservations, saw the Cabot Republicans and the irreconcilables, who would vote against any version of the Treaty, in opposition. The final rejection came on March 19, 1920, with a negative vote on a version with reservations.

The political theorist "Wilson believed laws and institutions must never strangle the spontaneous growth of society . . . through the legislation and the enforcement of abstract rules."[148] For the lawyer Root, instead, legal formalism was a crucial product of social progress. Through formalism, a civilized community would achieve justice and freedom by removing arbitrariness in the application of legal rules. In this sense, legal formalism was America's gift to the world. What kind of obligation, then, was the one toward the international society enshrined in collective security under Article X? Wilson, to counter the argument that the United States would be forced to constant interventions abroad, remarked that the article would be "binding in conscience only, not in law."[149] But what would this mean in practical terms for the United States? Wilson never made it clear: "a moral obligation is of course superior to a legal obligation, and, if I may say so, has a greater binding force; only there always remains in the moral obligation the right to exercise one's judgment as to whether it is indeed incumbent upon one in those circumstances to do that thing."[150] Such vagueness was not only political expediency. For Wilson, once the moral bonds of the community of nations had been created through the establishment of the League, the practical details would be determined by time and progress.

Yet, that same vagueness was also the weak point a skilled lawyer like Root was perfectly equipped to respond to, in order to create a common sentiment toward the League within the Republican Party. For Root, the idea of collective security could in principle be agreed upon if construed as a practical reinforcement of the only worthy goal toward global security: an effective and trusted international legal system. Wilson had not only curbed all plans for the development of legal institutions. By voluntarily leaving a key obligation like Article X open to interest-based manipulation, he was destroying the "system of international good faith." "I can imagine no proposition more demoralizing and destructive than this," Root wrote to Republican Senator Colt. In the legalist view, "the certainty of the obligation to do the thing agreed upon," not "the existence or non-existence of a sanction" guaranteed compliance. Wilson's watered down construction of international obligation was for Root "fatal to the maintenance of peace and the rule of international right."[151]

Wilson ended up defeated in his most cherished endeavor: a League of Nations participated in and led by the United States. Yet, the displacement of legal formalism from its key role in US foreign policy operated by his administration contributed to change in the study of international law. The challenge to Scott's views at the ASIL meeting of 1917 would be only the early sign of an increasing trend. Scott

[148] Stephen Wertheim, "The Wilsonian Chimera: Why Debating Wilson's Vision Hasn't Saved American Foreign Relations," in *White House Studies*, 10, 2011, p. 345.

[149] Wilson quoted in Zasloff, *Law and the Shaping of American Foreign Policy*, p. 353.

[150] Wilson quoted ibid., p. 354.

[151] Letter from Elihu Root to Senator LeBaron Colt, August 28, 1919, quoted ibid.

would later have a long spell as ASIL president (1929–39), but he would never gain back the tight control he had on the Society and its Journal in the years immediately following its foundation.

Scott had become a revered mentor for many younger international lawyers, but he was no longer considered a scholar at the cutting edge in the United States. In connection to this one can register, over the course of the 1920s, the strengthening of tendencies already present in Scott's professional interests. In the first place, he devoted more and more time, and the CEIP resources he managed, to international projects of cooperation rather than to the American Society. Key examples of such international projects were the re-launching of the AIIL, the foundation of the Hague Academy of International Law, and a greater involvement in the activities of the *Institut de Droit International.* All three institutions would obtain their funding almost entirely from CEIP through Scott.

Secondly, but most crucially for the present work, James Brown Scott launched himself into a significant, new research project on the history of international law, after the one centered on US constitutional history explained in this chapter. As we will see in Part II, he had had an interest in the early classics of international law and the predecessors of Hugo Grotius since the turn of the century. But only in the mid-1920s he would focus on two theologians of the Salamanca School, Francisco Suárez and, especially, Francisco de Vitoria, and lay out in a large body of work his theory of their respective roles in the inception of international law in its modern form. Scott depicted them as the pioneers of a law of nations based on the principles of equality and progressive thinking, the same kind of legal evolution that the United States embodied and for which he advocated in his era. Over the course of a relatively short amount of time, Scott published several books and articles outlining the intellectual greatness of the two Spaniards and the relevance in his time of the Spanish and Catholic origins of the discipline. Indeed, as the Armistice Day books were strongly connected to the judicial settlement versus collective security debate at the closing of the First World War, so too the Spanish origin works would try to achieve concrete and current political goals, obtaining a papal endorsement for international law and the recognition of equal rights for women.

# PART II

# REWRITING INTERNATIONAL LEGAL HISTORY: VITORIA AND THE NEW WORLD, 1925–1939

# 4
# The Spanish Origin of International Law

## 1. The Spanish Origin's Background

### Setting the Canon: The Inception of the Classics of International Law Series

James Brown Scott had had an interest in legal history at least since his studies at Harvard and in Germany. As I noted in the Prologue, the historical evolution of judicial institutions and constitutional theories had had a key role already in his 1896 first public speech. The eventual turn to the Salamanca School as his main research interest in the mid-1920s was long in the making. The development of Scott's thought on the history of the discipline can be observed through the story of the Classics of International Law Series project. Like many other events in Scott's career, the inception of the Classics was linked to his move from the University of Illinois to Columbia and the Northeast in 1903.

Scott had received from Ira C. Baker, a professor of civil engineering at his former university, a letter of introduction for Robert S. Woodward (1849–1924). Woodward had obtained a degree in civil engineering in his home State of Michigan, before branching out to astronomy, mathematics, and physics. In 1893 he joined Columbia to teach mechanics and mathematical physics. Two years later he became dean of the Faculty of Pure Science.

Scott and Woodward struck up a friendship, but the latter soon had to leave New York City and move to Washington, D.C. In 1904 he had been called to the presidency of one of the many charitable endeavors of Andrew Carnegie, the Carnegie Institution of Washington, founded two years before. The goal of the Institution was to support basic scientific research in the widest sense. Initially it awarded grants to individual researchers, but Woodward enacted a change of philosophy: the Institution started funding departments and larger projects, focusing its efforts on areas of research that could be supported over longer periods of time.[1]

As we have seen, Scott would soon follow Woodward to the capital city, in order to join the State Department as Solicitor. The two rekindled their relationship, enjoying conversations encompassing science and the humanities. With regard to international law, they agreed in rejecting the positivistic view of it being "a

[1] See, for instance, F. E. Wright, "Biographical Memoir of Robert Simpson Woodward, 1849–1924," *National Academy of Sciences of the United States of America—Biographical Memoirs*, XIX, 1937, p. 14.

*Rewriting the History of the Law of Nations: How James Brown Scott Made Francisco de Vitoria the Founder of International Law*. Paolo Amorosa, Oxford University Press (2019). © Paolo Amorosa
DOI: 10.1093/oso/9780198849377.001.0001

thing of treaty and convention . . . instead of an inevitable system based upon principles of justice expressed in rules of law, with reason as guide."[2] Scott explained to Woodward that the law of nations would exist even "if treaties and conventions should go by the board": positive agreements "were but the present form of older principles, . . . universal and persisting through the ages."[3] Natural law provided the fundamental content and structure of international law.

Woodward was interested in the resemblance between his conception of science and Scott's theory of law, built around rational principles. Scott went on to describe the law of nations in his historical development. He affirmed that, while he was not one of the great early discoverers of international legal principles, Grotius was definitely crucial in his role of systematizer. Woodward offered in return that he ascribed a similar role in the evolution of science to Isaac Newton and his *Principia*.

According to Scott, the Classics project grew out of these friendly talks during Sunday afternoon excursions in Woodward's car in the summer of 1906.[4] While their two wives sat together in the back, Scott would join the driver Woodward on the front seat, "where Grotius and Newton contended for mastery."[5] Woodward explained to Scott that, unfortunately, it was difficult for contemporary scientists to approach Newton's masterpiece. Indeed, while he had recently invented calculus, Newton had used instead the language of geometry, generally employed in his era. "Therefore astronomers of our day had to brush up their geometry in order to find their way through Newton's text."[6] In yet another parallel between international law and science, Scott replied that Grotius' work represented the same kind of obstacle because of an "excess of classical learning" and reliance on scores of Greek and Latin authors. "Today it seems to many a wearisome process to find a way through a text of the three books on the Law of War and Peace, so entangled is the reader in the brambles of Greece and Rome." Scott concluded that "the beneficiaries of the Twentieth Century who have profited by [Grotius' and Newton's] labors" in any case "prefer[red] a more direct method, instead of an excess of classical illusion or geometrical demonstration."[7]

The discussion must have left an impression, as in one of the next Sunday drives Woodward asked Scott to draft an outline for a project of republication of the canonic texts in international legal literature.[8] The Classics series would also please the voices within the Carnegie Institution pushing to devote resources to research

[2] Scott, untitled document, undated (written in 1925 or later), Folder 12, Box 36, JBS Papers.
[3] Ibid.
[4] Ibid., pp. 3–4.
[5] Ibid., p. 3.
[6] Ibid.
[7] Ibid., p. 4.
[8] Elsewhere, Scott is credited with the initial idea for the series: see, for instance, *Memorandum Concerning the Initiation of the Project for a Series of Publications Comprising the Classics of International Law, Adopted by the Carnegie Institution of Washington. Based on Notes Taken from the Minutes of the Meetings of the Board of Trustees of the Carnegie Institution*, November 6, 1949, Folder 12, Box 36, JBS Papers.

in international law. For instance, Andrew D. White had forcefully made that case at the meeting of the Board of Trustees in December 1905; this resulted in a resolution promising a report, within the next year, on possible forms of support to "investigation, codification and publication of results" in the discipline.[9]

According to Scott, it was Woodward himself who suggested the main goals of the series:[10] the new editions should be loyal to the original text and, at the same time, ease the approach for the contemporary reader. In the opening of his letter to Woodward of November 2, 1906, detailing the project, Scott would sum up the key elements of his proposal:

> that the texts be edited in the original without note or annotation; that suitable introductions be contributed to each text by specialists of standing; that the texts be accompanied by translations when the originals are in foreign languages; that the individual texts selected for publication be edited by specialists in international law; and that the series as a whole be under the supervision of a editor-in-chief.[11]

In the letter, Scott explained further how the series would represent a valuable public service. He told of his personal experience and how it had been impossible for him to find works on the law of nations by authors preceding Hugo Grotius in libraries in the United States. At best, one could find extracts in later "books of authority"; "students of international law" could "not, as science demands, go to the source itself, examine it, and master it." The publication of the classics "would perhaps not popularize international law, but it would bring international law to the people."[12] Indeed, the chance to study the discipline back to its origins was, for Scott, crucial for "an adequate knowledge of the system at present and to predict with certainty the future development of the science."[13] In the letter, he made the point that, as we have seen, he had made before and would make again: international law, like the US Constitution, was a product of organic growth and the evolution of centuries.

Understanding the growth of international legal thinking also meant understanding the respective roles of Grotius and his predecessors. In this respect, Scott showed a more articulated stance in the 1906 letter to Woodward than in his Sunset Club speech ten years before. In the speech, he had credited the Dutch with turning diplomacy into a science and laying down the principles of the law of

[9] See ibid.

[10] See Scott, untitled document, pp. 4–6.

[11] *The Classics of International Law. Letter from James Brown Scott, Solicitor for the Department of State, to R. S. Woodward, President of the Carnegie Institution of Washington, relative to a Project for the Republication of the Classics of International Law*, Carnegie Institution of Washington, January 1907, p. 3.

[12] Ibid., p. 6.

[13] Ibid., p. 5.

nations, without referring to any intellectual precursor. In the letter, he proceeded to add qualifications to the label of founder of international law Grotius had been commonly receiving. For Scott, "[t]his, like many general statements, [wa]s true enough, but likely to mislead. . . . The individual greatness of the work of Grotius" was precisely "in the fact that he built upon the past with full knowledge of the writings of antiquity and of the Middle Ages."[14] Grotius deserved to be considered the "first and . . . greatest expounder" but not the founder of international law, which was "rooted in a more remote past." One of the main purposes of the Classics of International Law Series was indeed to return to the spotlight "the predecessors" who were "well-nigh invisible in the shadow of [Grotius'] presence."[15]

To identify the predecessors, Scott relied on literature dating from the mid-nineteenth century to the time of writing. The authors mentioned in the project outline, all eventually published in the series, ranged chronologically from the fourteenth-century canon lawyer Giovanni da Legnano to Alberico Gentili, whose lifespan overlapped with Grotius'. Between them were two authors of the Salamanca School of theology: Francisco de Vitoria and Francisco Suárez. They are just mentioned in the letter: Scott did not give them any special role in the development of international law at this stage, other than that of Grotius' predecessors. It is also interesting that the one sentence dedicated to Vitoria justifies his relevance to international law with his work on the law of war; there is no specific reference to the *Relectio de Indis noviter inventis* (Lecture on the American Indians recently discovered), the key text Scott would later use to link the discovery of America and the founding of international law.

Scott also suggested the names of some of Grotius' successors whose work should appear in the series. Almost all of those mentioned (Richard Zouche, Samuel Pufendorf, Cornelius Van Bynkershoek, Christian Wolff, Emer de Vattel) would be published in the Classics. It is also easy to discern the criteria Scott would later use to leave out a few other suggestions made in the letter. On one hand, he suggested the publication of collections of the relatively recent opinions and decisions on international law by British and US judges like Lord Stowell and Joseph Story. Yet, records of their court cases were reasonably available in the United States; moreover, their most important pronouncements on international legal issues were already widely featured in the international law casebook Scott had published in 1902 and just reissued in that same year of 1906. On the other hand, Scott had proposed scholarly texts published in the late eighteenth and nineteenth centuries—for instance, Georg Friedrich Von Martens' *Précis du Droit des Gens Moderne* and Richard Wildman's *Institutes of International Law*—that would surely be more available and accessible to the contemporary readership than older ones. Interestingly, the only nineteenth-century book that would eventually be

[14] Ibid., pp. 3–4.
[15] Ibid., pp. 4–5.

part of the Classics was *Elements of International Law* by Henry Wheaton, first published in 1836.[16] It is not surprising that Scott would make such an exception for Wheaton, who had been a US diplomat in Europe between 1827 and 1846. Wheaton's message fit nicely with Scott's narrative. *Elements* was the first legal treatise entirely dedicated to international law in the English language. Therein, Wheaton defined international law as the "law of the civilized, Christian nations of Europe and America";[17] Christianity was the common cultural heritage that supported the claim of the then young and still fragile American republic to a rightful participation as a subject of the *ius publicum Europaeum*.

Wheaton was also one of the only three authors—together with Samuel Rachel and Johann Wolfgang Textor—not mentioned in the letter that would be included. All considered, it is remarkable how much of a series that would continue producing publications until 1950, even after Scott's death in 1943, was already laid out in the 1906 letter. I believe this circumstance is relevant, as the Classics of International Law Series has had an enormous influence in setting the canon of fundamental texts in international legal history.[18] It also seems that Scott had such an ambition at the outset: in the letter he proposed to call the series *Corpus iuris gentium*, envisioning it as a complement to the centuries-old legal monuments of the *Corpus iuris civilis* and the *Corpus iuris canonici*. The publications did not only, as intended, raise the availability and ease of access to the volumes included, many of which still reach today's reader primarily in their Classics edition: it also raised their prominence in intellectual discourse above the less available works of excluded authors. For instance, the impressive work of Peter Haggenmacher shows in detail how rich the pre-Grotius tradition was,[19] much more than the Classics would lead us to believe. As I noted, Scott partly relied on other authors and specialist literature for his choices. Yet, his 1906 letter, only eleven pages long, lacked

[16] Henry Wheaton, *Elements of International Law with a Sketch of the History of the Science*, Philadelphia: Carey, Lea & Blanchard, 1836. *Elements* would appear in the Classics of International Law Series in 1936, on the centenary of the first edition. However the text reproduced in the Classics would be the one of the 8th edition, edited by Richard Henry Dana (*Elements of International Law*, Boston: Little, Brown, and Company, 1866) after Wheaton's death.

[17] Wheaton, *Elements*, 1st edn, p. 45. On Wheaton's theory of international law see Luigi Nuzzo, *Origini di una Scienza: Diritto Internazionale e Colonialismo nel XIX Secolo*, Frankfurt am Main: Klostermann, 2012, pp. 18–21.

[18] For instance, historian David Armitage has credited James Brown Scott with creating, through the Classics series, "the earliest historical canon of works of international thought" (David Armitage, "The International Turn in Intellectual History," in Darrin M. McMahon and Samuel Moyn (eds.), *Rethinking Modern European Intellectual History*, Oxford: Oxford University Press, 2014, pp. 236–7).

[19] See Peter Haggenmacher, *Grotius et la Doctrine de la Guerre Juste*, Geneva: Graduate Institute Publications, 1983. Another exemplary study of the pre-Grotian tradition is Ernest Reibstein's *Die Anfänge des neueren Natur- und Völkerrechts. "Studien zu den Controversiae illustres" des Fernandus Vasquius (1559)*, Bern, Verlag Paul Haupt, 1949. To be fair, in a letter of 1913 Scott asked his colleague Ernest Nys' opinion about which predecessors of Grotius should be published in the Classics, beyond the ones listed in the initial 1906 plan, in order to reflect a larger section of that literary tradition (see Scott to Ernest Nys, January 14, 1913, vol. 346, CEIP Papers). Yet, to the best of my knowledge, no further action was ever taken in that respect.

proper argumentation and leaves its reader with a sense of arbitrariness. It is true that it was just the initial outline of a project on which Scott and many others would invest impressive intellectual and economic resources over the next forty-four years: there is definitely a risk of reading too much into it. But, at the same time, the remarkable similarity of its selection with the one of the final product makes it, arguably, one of the single most important interventions in the determination of what we consider to be the canon of international law today.

## Turning to Salamanca: Scott's Evolving Thought and the Early Classics

Scott's project outline was discussed in December 1906 at the Annual Meeting of the Board of the Trustees of the Carnegie Institution. The Board left the matter to the Executive Committee, which, in turn, asked the trustee William W. Morrow, a federal judge, to produce a report. During 1907, Morrow met several of the main authorities in international law both from the United States, like John Bassett Moore, and Europeans, such as Thomas Erskine Holland, Lassa Oppenheim, Ernest Nys, and Georg Jellinek. He approached many more by letter. At the next Annual Meeting, on December 10, 1907, Morrow reported that all the experts consulted had approved the project. He also added that he was "gratified by the interest 'all these great man' took in this proposed publication, and the value they thought it would be to the world, and 'above all stood out the interesting fact that in every instance they said that if Professor Scott was to be the sponsor, it would at once receive very cordial reception in Europe.'"[20]

The final approval of the project came on December 8, 1908. Elihu Root was not able to attend the Annual Meeting. However, he had sent in advance the proposal for a resolution appropriating the initial 10,000 dollars to start work on the Classics of International Law Series. It would be Woodward, White, and Seth Low, predecessor of Nicholas Murray Butler as President of Columbia University and former Mayor of New York City, who carried the day. They swayed the Board of Trustees and managed to prevail in the meeting over the voices that argued for a further postponement of the project. James Brown Scott was officially named general editor of the series, a role he had already offered himself for in the 1906 letter, on the condition that he would be allowed to do it without compensation.

Yet, the first publication in the series only came in 1911, with Richard Zouche's 1650 *Juris et judicii fecialis*, edited by Thomas Erskine Holland.[21] George Finch,

[20] *Minutes of the Annual Meeting, Carnegie Institution, 10 December* 1907, quoted in Memorandum *Concerning the Classics of International Law*, p. 2.

[21] Richard Zouche, *Juris et judicii fecialis, sive juris inter gentes, et quaestionum de eodem explicatio*, edited by Thomas Erskine Holland, English translation by James Leslie Brierly, 2 vols., Washington, D.C.: Carnegie Institution, 1911 [1650].

Scott's right-hand man from the State Department for many years till the end of his career, explained, in hindsight, "the many difficult and time-consuming problems involved in carrying out the project." First of all, it was complicated finding out "the location of and obtaining access to the best text to be reproduced (preferably the last edition completed in the author's lifetime)." Secondly, every book required the cooperation of more than one kind of specialist and expert. These included "competent translators who had to be not only thorough Latinists but familiar with the technical subjects as discussed several centuries ago, . . . the most eminent authorities in each field to write the biographical and analytical introductions that accompanied every number in the series, not to mention the painstaking and arduous work required of the editorial staff in preparing the manuscripts and accompanying data for the press."[22]

Notwithstanding the practical difficulties inherent in the nature of the project and a complicated historical context, including two World Wars and the consequences of the 1929 financial crash, Scott and his collaborators produced a series worthy of the ambition of the initial project. Between 1911 and 1950 they edited and published twenty-two works for a total of forty volumes.

As we have seen in Part I, the 1910s were busy years for Scott, who participated in several large projects and endeavors: the establishment and the initial steps of the Carnegie Endowment for International Peace (CEIP); the management of a still young and under-staffed American Society of International Law (ASIL) and the editing of the *American Journal of International Law* (AJIL); the foundation, promotion, and organization of the American Institute of International Law (AIIL); the constant propaganda effort in favor of the establishment of an international court; the government assignments in relation to the First World War; keeping in mind also how prolific he was as a writer. All of this considered, it is surprising how productive the Classics project would be in its early years. Working on it allowed Scott to reflect further on the role of the Spanish School and the origins of international law. The developing of his thoughts on the subject can be tracked through gradual and often small changes in the language employed across different types of textual material: correspondence, public speeches, and published writings. Taken together, these changes provide a strong sense of Scott's growing consideration for the authors of Salamanca school, especially Vitoria and Suárez.

Already in 1912 the Classics series produced its second issue, the first one featuring the work of an early modern Spanish author: Balthazar Ayala's *De iure et officiis bellicis et disciplina militari*.[23] Writing to a colleague at the end of that year, Scott placed Vitoria and Suárez "among the founders of international law,"[24] rather

[22] George A. Finch, *History of the Carnegie Endowment for International Peace, 1910–1946*, unpublished manuscript, pp. 365–6, Folder 3, Box 67, JBS Papers.

[23] Balthazar Ayala, *De iure et officiis bellicis et disciplina military libri III*, edited by John Westlake, English translation by John Pawley Bate, 2 vols., Washington, D.C.: Carnegie Institution, 1912 [1582].

[24] Scott to Alfred Vanderpol, December 23, 1912, Box 560, CEIP Papers.

than simply remarking their importance as predecessors of Grotius. In the same letter, Scott showed a specific interest in Vitoria's *De Indis* he had not expressed in outlining the Classics project. The letter was addressed to Alfred Vanderpol, president of the *Ligue des catholiques français pour la Paix* and expert of just war theology in the Middle Ages and early modernity. Vanderpol had recently published a book on the history of the Catholic doctrine on war, including his translation to French of Vitoria's *De iure belli*;[25] Scott remarked how important it would be to have a translation in a language accessible to the modern reader also for such a significant text as *De Indis* was.

Characteristically, Scott did not limit himself to suggesting a course of action to his French colleague; he also took initiative. Less than a month after his letter to Vanderpol, Scott would ask Belgian international lawyer Ernest Nys to edit and to write the introductions for works of Vitoria and Suárez for the Classics; he expressly mentioned *De Indis* as key content for the Vitoria collection.[26] This was the occasion for Scott to return to the topic of the Spanish origin and elaborate.

While "not wish[ing] to detract from the great and commanding position of Grotius in the domain of international law," this time Scott did not simply add qualifications to his title of founder: he asserted that it was "unjust to call him" so. Indeed, it was Vitoria who "define[d] accurately the reasons which have led to a society of nations and the creation of rules for the society in the same way as d[id] Suárez and Grotius at a later date."[27] Nys would accept Scott's offer. Work toward the publication of a volume collecting two public lectures by Vitoria, *De Indis* and *De iure belli*, began immediately. By May 1914, the texts had been translated to English[28] and Nys had delivered his introduction.[29]

In the same period, Scott was also working to acquire tighter control over the Classics of International Law Series. By mid-1914, the Carnegie Institution had agreed to transfer the project—and the large expenses that came with it—to CEIP.[30] The outbreak of the World War over the summer slowed down but did not stop progress with the Classics until 1917, when the United States entered the conflict. On the first day of that year, the project passed officially from the responsibility of the CEIP and was assigned to the Division of International Law directed by Scott; from now on he would have wide autonomy not only in relation to the academic side but also with regard to the budgetary and administrative aspects of the series.

1917 was also the year that saw the last two Classics issues—taking the total to eight in six years—before a break that would last until 1921. One of them was,

25 Alfred Vanderpol, *La guerre devante le Christianisme (ouvrage suivi d'une traduction du "De jure belli" de François de Vitoria)*, Paris: A. Tralin, 1911.

26 See Scott to Nys, January 14, 1913.

27 Ibid.

28 See Scott to Ernest Nys, November 24, 1913, vol. 346, CEIP Papers.

29 See Scott to Ernest Nys, May 18, 1914, and Ernest Nys to Scott, May 27, 1914, Box 564, CEIP Papers.

30 See Robert Simpson Woodward to Scott, July 27, 1914, vol. 346, CEIP Papers.

finally, Vitoria's two *relectiones*, edited by Nys.[31] In his short preface, Scott made his strongest affirmation to date of Vitoria as the founder of international law and added, for the first time, an oblique connection between the discipline's inception and the discovery of the American continent. He wrote that he could not "allow the volume to go to press without a tribute in passing to the broad-minded and generous-hearted Dominican." Unfortunately, "Victoria's claim as a founder of the Law of Nations" had to "be based upon these two readings taken down by a pupil and published after his death[.] They [we]re sufficient, however, to show that International Law is not a thing of our day and generation or of the Hague Conferences, nor indeed the creation of Grotius, but that the system is almost as old as the New World."[32] Reinforcing this last point in his introduction, Nys elaborated on the context of Vitoria's work. His lectures were centered on "that event, the greatness of which can not be exaggerated, the discovery of the New World—in other words the addition of an immense field to the theatre of human activity and the inclusion of the whole globe within the scope of man's political activity."[33]

As we have seen, with the end of the war approaching, Scott's historical work was dedicated to US constitutional history as a model of international organization. Yet he started hinting at the direction his research would take in the interwar years: connecting the values expressed in Vitoria's work with international law in his present and the United States' global moral leadership. In his 1918 report as Division Director of CEIP, in order to reaffirm the practical significance of the Classics series, Scott decided to use Vitoria's thought to show the relevance of centuries-old expressions of the law of nations even in relation to the ongoing war.

Quoting the closing passage of *De iure belli*, Scott pointed to three "rules . . . for rulers . . . enunciated by the learned professor of Salamanca" and "deal[ing] respectively with conduct before war is declared, during the war itself, and after the war has been finished."[34]

> First, granting that a ruler has the authority to wage war, he ought not to seek occasions and causes of war, but ought to have peace with all men. Secondly, granting that a war has arisen from just causes, the ruler ought to wage it not for the destruction of the opposing nation, but for the prosecution of his own right and the defense of his own country, and in such a way that peace and security may eventually be obtained. Thirdly, at the end of the war, the victor should use his

[31] Franciscus de Victoria, *Relectiones: De Indis and De Jure Belli*, edited by Ernest Nys, English translation by John Pawley Bate, Washington, D.C.: Carnegie Institution, 1917 [1696]. The other issue in the same year was Giovanni da Legnano, *De bello, de repraesaliis et de duello*, edited by Thomas Erskine Holland, English translation by James Leslie Brierly, Washington, D.C.: Carnegie Institution, 1917 [1477].

[32] James Brown Scott, "Preface," in Vitoria, *Relectiones*, p. 5.

[33] Ernest Nys, "Introduction," in Vitoria, *Relections*, p. 64.

[34] James Brown Scott, "Report of the Director of the Division of International Law," in CEIP Yearbook, 7, 1918, p. 140.

victory with moderation and Christian modesty and ought to consider himself as a judge between the wronged nation and the nation doing wrong, and not as a prosecutor.[35]

To Scott, these rules of just war doctrine had "an exact counterpart in the policy of our President" and the United States' conduct in the conflict to date and not by chance. "It [wa]s difficult to imagine how more prudent and more equitable rules than these could be formulated." Vitoria's rules represented an early formulation of basic principles of justice, which were "the very fount . . . international law" sprang from. In that situation of global crisis the Classics had a crucial role to play. They were essential to the process of education that would achieve just relations and stability: through the volumes, "those principles of international law which have come to being in response to the needs of the nations . . . , by creating an international opinion in favor of international law, [would] persuade where force can not compel the nations to accept its just principles and to dwell in peace." In short, a "series" that had been "[d]esirable . . . in 1906, when it was first suggested," had become "necessary in 1918."[36]

## Scott and the Salamanca Scholars

This short survey shows how, between the inception of the Classics project and the late 1910s, Scott's thought had come to feature, if in an embryonic form, the main elements of the narrative of the Spanish origin he would fully explore from the mid-1920s on. His views evolved from acceptance of the mainstream idea of Grotius as the forefather of international law to the recognition of Vitoria as the founder of the discipline. With this move he was able to connect the roots of international legal discourse with the discovery of the American continent. This, in turn, added a further layer of pedigree to the idea of an American newer and better international law that Scott had been exploring in those years with Alejandro Álvarez through the AIIL. As we have seen, especially in Chapters 1 and 2, the American international law project was based on the idea of making equality of nations the guiding principle of universal legal relations. Now, one of the reasons of Vitoria appealed to Scott was that the Dominican's recognition that *ius gentium* (law of peoples or nations) applied to the autochthonous peoples of America and that they had *dominium*—a concept encompassing the rights of both jurisdiction and ownership—could be construed as the first affirmation of universal equality of individuals and human societies. To my knowledge, Scott had not yet made this connection explicitly by 1918; but his insistence on the significance of *De Indis*, the

[35] Vitoria, *Relectiones*, p. 197.
[36] Scott, "Report of the Director of the Division of International Law," 1918, pp. 140–1.

main text in which Vitoria analyzed the status of the natives, seems meaningful. After all, Scott had already shown a keenness to turn to Vitoria to make sense of the pressing matters of US foreign policy and international law of his day. He had used him to describe the morality and justice of the involvement of the United States with the First World War; in the same way Vitoria's words could be easily made into support for an extensive variety of twentieth-century political projects. Hailed as the apostle of equality, Vitoria could become the prophet for any project that would fit under that vague umbrella. And, as I argued in the earlier chapters, the ideal of equality, in the hands of Scott and the legal establishment of his time, could easily turn into a formalistic justice for the most powerful, both within domestic societies and in international relations. Moreover, Vitoria's language offered itself to produce varied meanings for practical reasons. The only testimonies of his thought we have are notes from lectures taken down by his students, as he did not publish any text in his lifetime. Even if we assume the notes as proper reflections of Vitoria's opinion on a subject, which is far from being a given, there would still be a serious obstacle between the mindset of the modern reader and the Dominican's scholastic teaching style. Vitoria's lectures revolved around a specific text or issue (*quaestio*). His pedagogy, focused on the reasoning process, required that he would walk his student through the various arguments applicable to the subject at hand, even the ones to be eventually discarded, rather than providing right away a straightforward solution. As any of the contrasting arguments fleshed out could be extracted as Vitoria's opinion, it is clear to see how his work could easily be subjected not only to diverging plausible interpretations but also misinterpretation in good faith and willful manipulation.[37]

This last consideration points to the importance of understanding the openly presentist nature of Scott's interpretations of the work of Vitoria and the other authors of the School of Salamanca. As I mentioned earlier and will describe in detail later in the text, he would attach to Vitoria labels and opinions completely outside the intellectual horizon of a sixteenth-century theologian. For instance, to paint the Dominican as a theorist of liberal politics or of nationality on the basis of *ius soli*, as Scott did, linked Vitoria to political concepts and social movements that appeared centuries after his lifetime.

Scott might have been responsible for spreading the idea that the foundation of international law rested with the sixteenth-century Spanish theologians, but he definitely did not create them as intellectual authorities. Figures like the Dominicans Vitoria and Domingo de Soto and the Jesuits Suárez and Luis de Molina were

[37] This might be one of the reasons why the legacy of Vitoria is still open to widely diverging interpretations today. The status of Vitoria's legacy in current international legal literature is, in my opinion, so closely connected to Scott's legacy that I have treated the two topics together both in the Introduction and the Concluding Remarks.

influential thinkers and political operators already in their lifetime.[38] As advisors to kings, Emperors, merchant guilds, and Popes, they provided articulated analyses on disparate, complex, and sensitive topics.[39] Indeed, "[i]n the early modern world, theology, the 'mother of sciences', because it dealt directly with first causes, was considered to be above all other modes of inquiry, and covered everything that belongs to what today is called jurisprudence, as well as most of moral and political philosophy, and what would later become the human sciences." This implied that "[j]urists were members of a distinct and, in the opinion of most theologians, inferior faculty,"[40] as their purview was limited to human law; theologians, instead, were able to deal with the higher sources of divine and natural law.

Vitoria claimed as much at the opening of *De Indis*.[41] He warned jurists that describing the status of the American Indians was not a matter of human statutes, but required an expertise they did not have, involving the realm of conscience and the divine. In his quest to claim the authors of the Salamanca School as founders of international law, Scott would often disregard their self-identification with the theological rather than the legal tradition. He referred to Vitoria as "a theologian and jurist," at the same time a "churchman" and a "man of law."[42] To Suárez, he repeatedly referred as the "prince of modern jurists."[43] Scott's representation was not due to lack of knowledge of the primary sources and their historical context, nor did he fail to give account of Vitoria's stance at the beginning of *De Indis*. But

[38] For a recent history of the School of Salamanca and its later influence see Miguel Anxo Pena González, *La Escuela de Salamanca. De la Monarquía hispanica al Orbe católico*, Madrid: Biblioteca de Autores Cristianos, 2009. Juan Belda Plans (*La Escuela de Salamanca y la renovación de la teología en el siglo XVI*, Madrid: Biblioteca de Autores Cristianos, 2000) provides an analysis of the theological innovation by the School's authors and a periodization into different phases of development. His criterion of direct linkage with Vitoria and Salamanca leads him to exclude Suárez, who never taught in that University. For further reading, see the work of the leading historian on the Salamanca School's conceptualization of the New World, Luciano Pereña (see, for instance, his *La idea de justicia en la conquista de América*, Madrid: Mapfre, 1992). Pereña also directed through the 1980s and 1990s the publication of the *Corpus Hispanorum de Pace*, a vast collection of sixteenth-century Spanish primary materials about the colonization of the Americas and the related debates.

[39] "Vitoria was asked about the justice of the Portuguese slave trade, the validity of clandestine marriages, and the legitimacy of increasing the price of corn during a poor harvest, to name but a few. Melchor Cano advised Philip II in his struggle with Pope Paul IV, and was even consulted as how best to defend the Canary Islands against attacks by French pirates. Francisco Suárez . . . was questioned innumerable times on the Immaculate Conception, the election of the pope, on benefice, marriage contracts, and the preaching rights of the Dominicans." (Anthony Pagden, "The School of Salamanca," in George Klosko (ed.), *Oxford Handbook of the History of Political Philosophy*, Oxford: Oxford University Press, 2011, p. 247.

[40] Ibid., p. 246.

[41] See Francisco de Vitoria, "On the American Indians," in *Political Writings*, edited by Anthony Pagden and Jeremy Lawrance, Cambridge: Cambridge University Press, 1991, p. 238.

[42] James Brown Scott, *The Spanish Origin of International Law: Francisco De Vitoria and his Law of Nations*, Oxford: Oxford University Press, 1934, p. 102.

[43] James Brown Scott, *The Catholic Conception of International Law*, Washington D.C.: Georgetown University Press, 1934, p.vii; James Brown Scott, *Law, the State, and the International Community*, vol. I, New York: Columbia University Press, 1939, p. 558; James Brown Scott, "Introduction," in Francisco Suárez, *Selections from Three Works*, translations by Gwladys L. Williams, Ammi Brown, and John Waldron, with revisions by Father Henry Davis, Oxford: Oxford University Press, 1944, vol. II, p. 12a.

even that passage he translated into debates relevant and contemporary to him. In Scott's hands, Vitoria's warning to the jurists became a general statement about the nature of "law," which "should be moral, instead of a mere command of an artificial superior."[44] With this simple move, Scott had weaponized Vitoria against his adversaries, twentieth-century positivist lawyers.

Still, theologians they were,[45] proudly claiming to be disciples of Thomas Aquinas (1225–74), whose immensely influential work provided, indeed, the starting point and the inspiration for many of the Salamancans' reflections. As theologians, the authors of the Salamanca School were entitled to grapple with the deeper foundations of civil and spiritual rule, highly contested in their lifetime. Even if their texts reached at times a high level of abstraction, they were dealing with high-stakes issues bearing direct consequences in the struggles for power of sixteenth-century Europe. This does not mean that their continuing influence has been limited to what international lawyers today would define as matters of sovereignty. Current readers are stricken by the insight of their economic thought and the complexity of their views on property and trade. Indeed, Martti Koskenniemi has argued that "the principal legacy of the Salamanca scholars lay in their development of a vocabulary of private rights . . . that enabled the universal ordering of international relations by recourse to private property, contract, and exchange."[46] Yet, let's not forget that they were all university professors of theology, despite the fact that they treated topics today in the realm of technical experts like lawyers and economists; by this I mean that their main job was to teach priests and monks how to administer the sacrament of penance and absolve from sin.[47] Sinfulness was the yardstick against which they measured behavior, even when discussing the legitimacy of the actions of kings or of the interventions of Popes in civil matters.

Vitoria, Suárez, and the other Spanish theologians were grappling with times of fast and complex change, putting strain on traditional ways of thinking about politics and conceptualizing society. It is historically questionable to point at smoking guns of intellectual development as Scott did, but one can say, without a doubt, that the thinkers of the Salamanca School were able to face baffling issues with creative pragmatism and brilliance of thought. Therefore, it is not surprising that their legacy is still so widely discussed. Yet, the fact remains that their revival among international lawyers in the twentieth century would be the result of one man's "self-imposed mission"[48]—it was because James Brown Scott would come to assert that Francisco de Vitoria had "formulated the modern law of nations" and Francisco

[44] James Brown Scott, "The Modern Law of Nations and its Municipal Sanctions," *Georgetown Law Journal*, XXII, 1934, p. 144.

[45] It is to be noted, though, that the more inclusive accounts have associated jurists such as Fernando Vázquez de Menchaca (1512–69) to the School.

[46] Martti Koskenniemi, "Empire and International Law: the Real Spanish Contribution," *University of Toronto Law Journal*, 61, 2011, p. 1.

[47] See ibid., p. 13.

[48] James Brown Scott, untitled document, undated (most likely 1935), Folder 4, Box 52, JBS Papers.

Suárez had later "set forth . . . the philosophy of international and the philosophy of law in its entirety."[49] This was the "Spanish origin of international law."

## 2. Conceiving the Campaign: Scott's Long Road to Salamanca

### The Dutch Connection: From The Hague to Salamanca

Once the urgency of weighing in the creation of the postwar world order wore down, the CEIP management would finally take a breath and look at the future of the organization in the new global landscape.

As Nicholas Murray Butler wrote to Scott in 1922, "[s]omething ha[d] got to be done to stir American public opinion on sounder lines"—read more internationalist—"than those followed" at the time. After all, "[e]verywhere" he went, Butler found "the people hungry for leadership."[50] Scott, ever the optimist, made the point that "[i]n the United States," the CEIP might be "preaching to the converted."

> Our people are permeated through and through with the idea of international peace. They are born in a union of States, and they can not see why the world can not be organized in some way which will give to the peoples of different countries the liberty which we all enjoy, and that peace which is the perfected fruit of justice.[51]

Accordingly, Scott argued that CEIP efforts should be concentrated on Europe, which was still suffering the consequences of the war and its nationalistic divides. The Endowment's seat in Washington was "like the Church Triumphant, which has the center of its authority in [an] atmosphere of peace." The new focus should have been elsewhere: "the aggressive branch of the Endowment, like the Church Militant, should be firmly established, outwardly and visibly among the children of men, who most need its ministrations." Scott was referring to the CEIP Paris office, whose activities had been stunted early on by the outbreak of the war. "[T]he Paris

[49] Scott, *The Catholic Conception of International Law*, p. vii.

[50] Nicholas Murray Butler to Scott, December 27, 1922, Folder 10 Box 2, JBS Papers.

[51] This assertion failed to take into account the steady shift of US political discourse in the early 1920s away from any possibility of membership in an international institution, be it the League of Nations, a similar association of nations, or the Permanent Court of International Justice alone: see, for instance, Warren F. Kuehl and Lynne K. Dunn, *Keeping the Covenant. American Internationalists and the League of Nations, 1920–1939*, Kent: The Kent State University Press, 1997, especially pp. 1–41 and Richard W. Leopold, *Elihu Root and the Conservative Tradition*, Boston: Little, Brown and Company, 1954, pp. 152–8. The shift was partly connected with the association of internationalism with Bolshevism that had become common among conservatives (see Benjamin Coates, *Legalist Empire*, Oxford: Oxford University Press, 2016, p. 171).

branch should . . . be the center of Europe" and "radiate propaganda" to the rest of the continent and beyond. It was to "be regard[ed] as the very hands of the organization for executing projects in partibus infidelium," to "be determined upon," of course, "in the general headquarters, in the United States."[52]

The work at home continued, but the CEIP would indeed step up considerably its operations abroad and especially in Europe in the 1920s.[53] This came in the form of both completely new projects and the resurfacing of plans abandoned because of the war. One particular endeavor that was particularly close to Scott's heart belonged to the latter group: the foundation of the Hague Academy of International Law. The Academy would not only be one of the lasting legacies of Scott and the CEIP; it would also be one of the main tools Scott used to exercise his influence among international lawyers. And, as an unintended consequence, it would help Scott to forge the Spanish connections crucial for key events in Scott's recovery of the Salamanca School to happen.

The Academy project originated from the earliest days of the Endowment. The first approach from Tobias M. C. Asser, co-founder of the *Institut de Droit International* in 1873,[54] reached Elihu Root in February 1911, asking for funding. Asser, who had also participated as a Dutch delegate to both the Hague Peace Conferences, was by then a noble elder within the transatlantic community of international lawyers. Once he had received a preliminary manifestation of interest in the proposal from Root, he sent detailed plans on March 19. Asser was writing on behalf of a committee of twenty-one Dutch notables, including Bernard Loder, who would go on to be the first president of the Permanent Court of International Justice, and Pieter Cort van der Linden, the future war-time prime minister. The committee had picked up on an idea launched at the 1907 Conference by the prime minister of Romania, Dimitrie Sturdza.[55] Sturdza's basic proposition already contained the key elements that characterized the Academy from its foundation up to the present day: it would offer a series of lectures on international law over the summer, during universities' annual summer break. This would mean the most renowned authorities in the discipline would be free of other academic commitments and thus be available to deliver courses in The Hague. The same was true for interested students, who could then attend the Academy, alongside their regular studies, to specialize in international law. Asser and his collaborators had added other features that would prove durable, such as the entrusting of the academic

[52] James Brown Scott to Nicholas Murray Butler, May 29, 1923, Folder 1, Box 60, CEIP Papers. Underlining in the original.

[53] On the CEIP activities in Europe between the wars see the work of Katharina Rietzler, for instance, "Before the Cultural Cold Wars: American Philanthropy and Cultural Diplomacy in the Inter-war Years," *Historical Research*, 84, 223, February 2011 and "Philanthropy, Peace Research, and Revisionist Politics: Rockefeller and Carnegie Support for the Study of International Relations in Weimar Germany," *GHI Bulletin Supplement*, 5, 2008, pp. 61–79.

[54] On Asser's role in the foundation of the *Institut* see Martti Koskenniemi, *The Gentle Civilizer of Nations*, Cambridge: Cambridge University Press, 2001, pp. 12–19.

[55] See T. M. C. Asser to Elihu Root, March 19, 1911, Box 558, CEIP Papers.

direction of the institution to a collective organ named Curatorium and the invitation of lecturers for *ad hoc* courses, rather than appointing them for a longer time.[56]

The idea of an international educational institution solely devoted to give resonance to the most advanced theories in international law could not but catch the growing interest of the CEIP leadership.[57] Accordingly, the idea that the courses should be published as monographs emerged early on. In June, Root instructed James Brown Scott to take over the project on the Endowment side.[58] In his next letter, Asser expressed the hope that the Academy would offer the first series of lectures in the summer of 1913, in concomitance with the inauguration of the Peace Palace.[59]

Asser's wish would remain unfulfilled. The beginning was promising. Scott continued corresponding with Asser, tweaking details and sharing memoranda, over the remainder of 1911. By December, he was able to announce to Asser that the Board of Trustees of the Carnegie Endowment had authorized an appropriation not exceeding 40,000 dollars to fund the Hague Academy.[60] Yet, before giving the final green light the Trustees wanted reassurance on the viability of the project and the breadth of its support. They wanted to kickstart the Academy but also to know that it would be able to stand on its own feet financially soon enough. The Dutch committee spent 1912 trying to overcome those doubts. In March 1912, they sent a circular letter on the Academy plans to the most eminent European international lawyers,[61] receiving back forty letters of approval and support.[62] Following further intercession by the Dutch Minister of Foreign Affairs René van Swinderen, the Trustees finally relented.

By February 1913, though, Asser knew that the goal of opening the Academy that coming summer had become unrealistic.[63] In the event, he would not even be able to attend the Peace Palace inauguration in August, as he died on July 29, aged seventy-five. Asser's death was a big blow to the Hague Academy plans, but Scott did not lose courage. In October, he confirmed to the new Dutch Foreign Minister, John Loudon, that all problems had been resolved and the Academy would open in 1914.[64] Indeed, its official incorporation took place on January 26, 1914. But growing political tensions in Europe got in the way of the preparations. For instance, Loudon reported to Scott the protests of Johannes Kriege, head of the legal

[56] See ibid.

[57] See, for instance, Elihu Root to James Brown Scott, August 10, 1911, Box 558, CEIP Papers.

[58] See James Brown Scott to Elihu Root, June 9, 1911, and James Brown Scott to T.M.C. Asser, June 9, 1911, Box 558, CEIP Papers.

[59] T.M.C. Asser to James Brown Scott, July 26, 1911, Box 558, CEIP Papers.

[60] James Brown Scott to T.M.C. Asser, December 16, 1911, Box 558, CEIP Papers.

[61] See untitled document filed as "Circular letter to Dr. Scott by Provisional Committee of The Hague," Box 560, CEIP Papers.

[62] See "List of Letters Received by the Provision [sic] Committee of the Proposed Academy of International Law," Box 560, CEIP Papers.

[63] See T.M.C. Asser to James Brown Scott, February 25, 1913, Box 560, CEIP Papers.

[64] See James Brown Scott to John Loudon, October 21, 1913, Box 561, CEIP Papers.

department of the German Foreign Office, who had also been a delegate at the Second Hague Peace Conference. According to Loudon, Kriege "fear[ed] that only pacifists [would] be asked to lecture in the Academy" and, in that case, "German students" would not be encouraged "to attend the courses." To avoid inconveniences, Kriege suggested "that a man like Prof. Niemeyer" could "be asked to lecture."[65] Even if Scott's closest colleagues in Germany were among the most eminent pacifists,[66] he eagerly promised "to overcome the scruples Dr. Kriege properly expressed."[67] Not only did he agree to invite Niemeyer, he also made a complete turnaround from the language he used in those same years with his pacifist friends.[68] "I share your wish that 'that word pacifist did not exist', and I also agree with your conclusion that 'the meaning it has acquired harms the great cause,'" he replied to Loudon. However, there was nothing to worry about: the founders of the Academy did not "create an organ of pacifism," but a "scientific . . . organ of . . . enlightened international practice." "[T]he subject of war [would] receive ample consideration, because, whether we object or not to war as a method of settling international disputes, war exists as a recognized agency in the practice of nations, and . . . must therefore be required in an Academy devoted to the exposition of international law."[69]

Scott's proactive and accommodating attitude was not enough to smooth over all troubles though. A further postponement became indefinite once the Great War broke out that summer. Soon after the end of the hostilities, work toward the opening of the Academy restarted. Charles Lyon-Caen was named President of the Curatorium, in place of Louis Renault, who had died in 1918. Scott, writing to Lyon-Caen in 1921, saw the formal opening as an approaching reality.[70] Finally, in July 1923, when the Academy had been for more than twelve years in the making, he could excitedly cable from The Hague to the CEIP headquarters: "OPENING WONDERFUL STUDENT BODY UNEXPECTEDLY LARGE."[71] With another about-face, Scott tried to please the Dutch crowd and the local hosts with his speech at the ceremony. Between the many reasons he gave to praise the country and the city, there was one in which he did not believe in anymore: "It is a great

65 John Loudon to Scott, February 7, 1914, Box 569, CEIP Papers.

66 Scott worked on several projects, both after and before the war, with international lawyers and peace activists Walter Schücking, Alfred Fried, the Swiss-German Otfried Nippold and the younger Hans Wehberg. When, in 1912, they asked for CEIP funding for an international law journal in German, it was Scott who named as a condition that the editor would be a "progressive"; the journal, as Scott made clear, should promote the "modern international law" he and his corresponding friends represented, rather than a "militaristic," "retrogressive," and "reactionary" one (see correspondence in Box 559, CEIP Papers).

67 James Brown Scott to John Loudon, February 27, 1914, Box 569, CEIP Papers.

68 See ibid. Scott's positioning in relation to the peace movement was always strategic and uncomfortable not only in the United States, as we have seen, but also on the international scene.

69 Scott to Loudon, February 27, 1914.

70 James Brown Scott to Charles Lyon-Caen, July 3, 1921, vol. 282, CEIP Papers.

71 James Brown Scott to George Finch, July 18, 1923, vol. 292, CEIP Papers.

pleasure, . . . to be again at The Hague, . . . where Grotius, 'the Miracle of Holland', laid the foundations of international law."[72]

Yet, it would be the Netherlands and Grotius who would lead Scott back to Salamanca. 1925 would be a key year leading up to Scott's full dedication to the theory of the Spanish origins of international law. Marking the 300th anniversary of the publication of Grotius' main work, *De jure belli ac pacis*, it spurred a series of celebratory events and publications that renewed the interest of international lawyers in the past of their discipline.

Between July 29 and August 4, the *Institut de Droit International*'s annual meeting took place in The Hague in the Peace Palace, following an invitation by the Dutch government motivated by the upcoming anniversary.[73] Bernard Loder, who we have already met as a member of the Dutch committee tasked with the foundation of the Hague Academy, was then President of the *Institut*. Loder's opening address could not but be dedicated to celebrating the achievements of his countryman Hugo Grotius.[74] The anniversary of *De jure belli ac pacis* was not the celebration of "*un fait purement historique*," Loder pointed out. The work was the "*expression des vrais sentiments de droit et de justice dans la sphere de ce jus gentium*" which Grotius erected "*en système et par cela meme, créer comme science.*"[75] The ideas expressed by Grotius were ahead of their time but, according to Loder, he would also have looked with pride at the progress achieved in the next 300 years in terms of both rules and institutions. To claim their right to celebrate the work of Grotius, the international lawyers of the day simply had to pick up the mission and accept the call of the international community. "*La Société des Nations a fait son appel à votre science, à votre experience et votre dévouement*."[76]

The organizing committee also included in the program a visit to Grotius' tomb in the *Nieuwe Kerk* (New Church) of Delft, his native city, on July 30. After Loder had placed a bronze palm on behalf of the *Institut* on the funerary monument, Baron Édouard Descamps, the Belgian veteran of international conferences, took the floor to honor again "*l'immortel batave*."[77] What had brought the members of the *Institut* before his tomb that day was the ideal they shared: Grotius' "*grande conception, à la fois si naturelle et si chrétienne, d'une justice plus haute dans une paix moins précaire qui remue et enflamme notre temps.*"[78] A few days later, at the

[72] James Brown Scott, *Address delivered July 14, 1923, by Mr. James Brown Scott at the formal opening of the Academy of International Law at The Hague, established with the cooperation of the Carnegie Endowment for International Peace*, vol. 292, CEIP Papers.

[73] See "Avant-propos," *Annuaire de l'Institut de Droit International*, Paris: A. Pedone Editeur, 32, 1925, p. v. For a brief contemporary account of the session see Hans Wehberg, "The Institute of International Law," vol. 300, CEIP Papers.

[74] See *Annuaire de l'Institut de Droit International*, 1925, pp. 433–45.

[75] Ibid., p. 434.

[76] Ibid., p. 445.

[77] Ibid., p. 455.

[78] Ibid., p. 464.

closing of the meeting, James Brown Scott would be elected as new President of the *Institut*. He was the first American to hold the position.

The committee for Grotius' centenary decided to add another leg to the celebrations. In April 1926 a delegation of Dutch lawyers, led by the former Minister of Finance Willem Treub, visited Spain, then under the military dictatorship of Miguel Primo de Rivera, to commemorate the theologians of the Salamanca School.[79] Their first destination was Granada, birthplace of Francisco Suárez, where they laid a wreath upon the monument dedicated to the Jesuit theologian. Next they traveled to Madrid, where they were received by the Minister of Foreign Affairs, José de Yanguas Messia (1890–1974), himself a professor of international law at the Central University of Madrid, today named Complutense. During an official reception at the Academy of Jurisprudence, the guests presented their Spanish hosts with an exemplar of the Grotius gold medal coined the previous year for the tercentenary celebrations, once again in honor of Suárez. Between April 21 and 23, the Dutch delegation was in Salamanca, accompanied by the Spanish Minister of Education and former professor of natural law in Valladolid, Eduardo Callejo de la Cuesta.[80] Here the Grotius medal was given to the University of Salamanca for the merits of Francisco de Vitoria and accepted by the Rector Enrique Esperabé de Arteaga.[81] The Dutch delegation also participated in the unveiling of an inscription in the convent of San Esteban, to which Vitoria belonged. The plaque celebrated the fourth centenary from the 1526 coming to Salamanca of the "*Maestro Fr. Francisco de Vitoria, glorioso Patriarca del renacimiento intelectual salmantino y defensor acérrimo del Derecho de Gentes.*"[82]

Between banquets, sightseeing, ceremonial moments, and speeches of circumstance, the hosts found time to offer an academic event to the Dutch delegation. Camilo Barcia Trelles (1888–1977), professor of international law at the University of Valladolid, gave two lectures titled *Los orígenes ibéricos del derecho internacional* (the Iberian origins of international law). At the opening of the first lecture, he noted that, while he had been invited on occasion of the bestowal of the Grotius medal, his lectures would be based on the work of Vitoria. He then proceeded briefly to draw distinctions of biography and method between the two figures, but did not touch on their respective roles in the foundation of international law. Yet, the title of the lectures had already pointed to where Barcia Trelles stood. In the first lecture, he gave an account of and commented on the *Relectio de Indis*, in the second on *De iure belli*.[83] His conclusion was that the values embodied in the just

79 A short report of the visit drafted by Scott, dated 1927, is in Folder 2, Box 63, JBS Papers.

80 The Salamancan leg of the visit was announced and reported in detail, including transcriptions of the main speeches, in the local newspaper *El Adelanto*, issues of April 20, 21, 22, and 23, 1926.

81 See *El Adelanto*, April 22, 1926, p. 4.

82 See *El Adelanto*, April 23, 1926, pp. 4–6.

83 The first lecture is transcribed in *El Adelanto*, April 21, 1926, pp. 1–2, the second in *El Adelanto*, April 22, 1926, pp. 4–5.

war doctrine of Vitoria had not yet found expression in the present world, and certainly not in the Peace of Versailles, where some of the victors acted vindictively and not as guardians of the objective law of nations. That is why it was worthwhile to be in Salamanca and remember its great scholars of the sixteenth century: there was still a lot to learn from "*el gran espíritu de Francisco de Vitoria: amor a la paz; amor a la verdad; amor a la justicia.*"[84] In that glorious past, Barcia Trelles believed, was the future of Spain and the whole world.

Minister Callejo proceeded to close the Salamancan celebration. He shared his idea that the event had a more than a passing value and should result in something more permanent. His suggestion was immediately followed up on, with the support of the Spanish government, through the foundation of the *Asociación Francisco de Vitoria*. Members of the *Asociación* would be public figures and academics hailing from Spain, Portugal, and Latin American republics, its purpose the promotion of the work and the values of the theologians of the Spanish *siglo de oro*. Yanguas Messia and Barcia Trelles, founding members of the *Asociación*, would be instrumental in bringing James Brown Scott to Salamanca for the first time in November 1927.

## The Making of Founders: From Grotius to Vitoria

The third centenary of the publication of *De iure belli ac pacis* was also a cause for celebration among international lawyers and peace activists in the United States. Together with many other organizations,[85] the ASIL played its part. Articles on Grotius, including one by Scott,[86] appeared in all four issues of the AJIL in 1925. During the opening day of the annual meeting of the Society, Jesse S. Reeves of the University of Michigan delivered a speech on Grotius' life and work.[87] Two days later, on April 25, the Society had its formal dinner. Its program bore the image of Grotius,[88] who was honored with a speech by the Dutch Minister to the United States De Graeff.[89]

The events of 1925 did not mark the first occasion in which members of the US foreign policy establishment had enthusiastically celebrated Grotius' role in the development of international law. One could even argue that they had a role

[84] *El Adelanto*, April 22, 1926, p. 5.

[85] See for instance, Cornelis Van Vollenhoven, *Grotius and Geneva, lectures delivered in Columbia University, July 1925*, in *Bibliotheca Visseriana*, vol. VI, Leiden: Brill, 1926, p. 38.

[86] See James Brown Scott, "Grotius' De Jure Belli ac Pacis Libri Tres: The Work of a Lawyer, Statesman and Theologian," *American Journal of International Law*, 19, 1925, pp. 461–8.

[87] Jesse S. Reeves, "The Life and Work of Hugo Grotius," *Proceedings of the American Society of International Law*, 19, 1925, pp. 48–58.

[88] See Van Vollenhoven, *Grotius and Geneva*, p. 38.

[89] His remarks can be found in *Proceedings of the American Society of International Law*, 19, 1925, pp. 145–9.

in creating his fame as the founder of the discipline.[90] In 1899, Andrew D. White, acting as head of the US delegation at the First Hague Peace Conference, sent a peculiar request back to the Secretary of State John Hay.

On May 28, White had visited the New Church of Delft, in order to attend religious service. While he was not pleased by the quality of the service—"very crude and dismal, . . . consisting of two long sermons separated by hymns, and all unspeakably dreary," White appreciated seeing Grotius' tomb, which "stirred many thoughts." He reflected, not sparing hyperbole, on how "clear" it was "that of all books ever written—not claiming divine inspiration—the great work of Grotius on 'War and Peace' has been of most benefit to mankind." The work of the Conference, White continued, "at the end of the nineteenth century, [wa]s the direct result of his, at the beginning of the seventeenth."[91]

The following June 7, White wrote a letter to Hay. He suggested that the US delegation could lay a silver wreath on the tomb. This would not be simply to honor Grotius and the hosting Dutch government "but also . . . a sign of good-will toward the older governments of the world on the occasion of their first meeting with delegates from the new world, in a conference treating of matters most important to all nations."[92] As soon as Hay gave the green light, White started arranging the event; it would take place on a highly symbolic date, July 4, the US Independence Day. White also obtained local cooperation: the head of the Dutch delegation at the Conference, Abraham Van Karnebeek, would chair the ceremony; the Minister of Foreign Affairs Beaufort and T. M. C. Asser would deliver speeches.[93] After the morning event in the New Church, the guests would enjoy a luncheon hosted by the US delegation. The menu included *filets de sole à la Grotius* and *poulardes à la Washington*.[94] It would be truly "a Dutch-American party."[95]

Notwithstanding the rainstorm that hit Delft that day, "[c]arriage after carriage rolled up to the door of the church, and gayly dressed ladies and profusely decorated men entered the crumbling old portals."[96] The event had attracted a diverse audience:

> The entire Dutch government arrived to participate in the ceremony, as did most of the peace conference delegates, and nearly all ambassadors resident in The

[90] See in this sense Martine Julia Van Ittersum, "Hugo Grotius: The Making of a Founder of International Law," *Oxford Handbook of the Theory of International Law*, Oxford: Oxford University Press, 2016, pp. 82–100.

[91] Andrew Dickson White, *Autobiography*, vol. II, New York: Century Co., 1905, p. 274.

[92] Ibid., p. 291.

[93] For the respective speeches see *Proceedings at the Laying of a Wreath on the Tomb of Hugo Grotius*, The Hague: Martinus Nijhoff, 1899, Van Karnebeek at pp. 5–10, Beaufort at pp. 34–37, Asser at pp. 38–44.

[94] See M. Hanken-Parker, "A Tribute to Hugo De Groot," *New York Times*, July 30, 1899

[95] Van Ittersum, "Grotius: The Making of a Founder," p. 90.

[96] Hanken-Parker, "A Tribute to Hugo De Groot."

> Hague. In addition, the pews filled with faculty members from Dutch universities, Leiden in particular, and a large crowd of American tourists.[97]

Among the attendees was also Descamps, who would lead a similar celebration for the *Institut* twenty-six years later.

After opening speeches and the performances of a 150-strong choir, the main event, the oration by White, took place. He started the speech by reminding his audience of the debt owed by the United States and the whole world to Grotius' work. It was to develop the principles the Dutch had first expressed that the first truly global conference was then assembled. A celebration of the US Independence Day in Delft was symbolic also because "[f]rom its Haven . . . sailed the 'Mayflower'—bearing the Pilgrim Fathers who, in a time of obstinate and bitter persecution, brought to the American Continent the germs of that toleration which had been especially developed among them during their stay in the Netherlands, and of which Grotius was an apostle."[98] That spirit of toleration Grotius had also translated in the political "doctrine which founds human rights upon an early social compact" and "out of which sprang the nationality" of the United States, "embodied in th[e] Declaration of Independence."[99] White went on to describe this special relation more specifically through international law. Indeed, the widespread study and appreciation of international law in the United States could not but be, at the same time, a debt owed and a tribute to Grotius.[100] To reinforce the argument of his crucial role, White also touched upon the relation between Grotius and earlier writers. Indeed, White conceded without mentioning Vitoria, Grotius had a debt toward thinkers like Isidore of Seville, Suárez, Ayala, and Gentili. Yet, all considered, "Grotius, while standing among these men" was also "grandly towering above them."[101]

> His coming was like the rising of the sun out of the primeval abyss: his work was both creative and illuminative. We may reverently insist that in the domain of International Law, Grotius said "Let there be light," and there was light.[102]

White closed the speech by recalling the courage of Grotius in standing for peace and the humanization of hostilities amidst the chaos of the Thirty Years' War. The spirit of the man in the tomb they were looking at was calling the members of the Hague Conference to do the same then and pursue their civilizing goals beyond all

[97] Van Ittersum, "Grotius: The Making of a Founder," p. 91.
[98] *Proceedings at the Laying of a Wreath on the Tomb of Hugo Grotius*, p. 16.
[99] Ibid., p. 25.
[100] In those passages of the speech (see ibid., pp. 15–16) White was clearly overestimating the role of international law in US academic institutions and especially law schools at the time: see Chapter 3.
[101] *Proceedings at the Laying of a Wreath on the Tomb of Hugo Grotius*, p. 19.
[102] Ibid., p. 20.

obstacles and oppositions. White then laid the silver wreath on Grotius' funerary monument. It is still there today. Later, the gathering left the church while "The Star-Spangled Banner" played.

Martine Van Ittersum has recently published a piece on the "Dutch-American party." She is one of the main scholars engaged in complicating and fully contextualizing Grotius' figure, in order to go beyond the too often hagiographic accounts of his life and historical significance.[103] As part of that enterprise, she has dug deeper into the meaning of the 1899 celebration. What did it mean to the US delegation? To start with, the event needs be considered in the context of the "Holland Mania"[104] that was sweeping the United States at the time and found its way into White's speech. The aesthetics of the Dutch Golden Age became the taste for the wealthy in the United States of the Gilded Age. However, it was more than about collecting art, purchasing furniture and clothing, or choosing the Netherlands as the ideal tourist destination. The culture went hand in hand with political ideas. New historical research, spearheaded by John Lothrop Motley's work in the mid-nineteenth century, allowed Americans to draw parallels between the birth of the United States and the Dutch Republic, which in 1581 arose out of the successful rejection of Spanish rule. The Dutch Revolt began to be called a "war of independence." The United Provinces defeating royal tyranny, creating a Protestant republic based on religious toleration, and building a commercial empire, became the model taken to the East coast by the Pilgrim and developed into the modern United States. The idea of Grotius as the initiator of the international legal project rising in those years could not but fit right into that narrative.[105]

Yet, in another sense, the narrative behind the 1899 celebration was already out of place. Indeed, as we have seen in Part I, these were the years in which the United States, after winning the Spanish-American War, was becoming conscious of its role as a leading global power and would use international law to mark its difference from European empires. The playing out of those trends, and the towering role the United States had acquired in international politics since, had created the conditions for Grotius to be dethroned. The focus on Grotius of 1899, echoing Scott in his Sunset Club speech a few years earlier, was the appropriation of a European pedigree. This was fitting for an emerging country; much less would it be for the main superpower on the world scene.

In other words, in celebrating Grotius as the founder of international law, the US delegation spun a narrative reflecting their country still busy claiming its seat at the table of the European powers, as it indeed then was. However, when Scott gave the title to Vitoria, his account reflected the American continent and, by

[103] See, for instance, Martine Van Ittersum, *Profit and Principle: Hugo Grotius, Natural Rights Theories and the Rise of Dutch Power in the East Indies, 1595–1615*, Leiden: Brill, 2006.

[104] See Annette Stott, *Holland Mania: The Unknown Dutch Period in American Art & Culture*, Woodstock: Overlook Press, 1998.

[105] See Van Ittersum, "Grotius: The Making of a Founder," pp. 89–90 and 94.

reduction, the United States as the movers of history, conscious of their power to set the international agenda. This way, the key event in the inception of the modern law of nations became the discovery of America, not the European wars of religion. Therefore, the appearance of America on the global stage had inaugurated the new course of progress in itself and not simply because of European cultural roots.

Scott had been heavily involved in the Grotius celebrations of 1925. As a member and an officer of ASIL and the *Institut* he participated in the commemorations by both institutions. Moreover, Scott used the occasion to finally complete the third issue of the Classics of International Law series. Its first volume, featuring the original Latin text of *De jure belli ac pacis*, had already come out in 1913.[106] The second volume with the translated text[107] was delayed by the war and, according to Finch, by the difficulty of assembling an adequately specialized group of translators.[108] In any case, to publish it in 1925, on the occasion of the third centenary of its first appearance was only fitting, as explicitly noted in the volume itself.[109]

Scott contributed a long introduction to the publication. The text is highly celebratory. It focuses on underlining the importance of Grotius and his work both in his own time and over history since. For instance, Scott drew a connection between Grotius and another of his favorite heroes, John Jay (1745–1829), Founding Father and first Chief Justice of the US Supreme Court. Scott wrote of how Jay, at the beginning of his legal career, "spent a full year" on the "treatise of Grotius," seeing it "as the best introduction to the study and, eventually, to the practice of law."[110] For Scott, this was a clear sign of Grotius' influence on what he considered to be Jay's crowning achievement. Jay was the chief US negotiator of the 1794 treaty with Great Britain that closed the War of Independence. Often called the Jay treaty, it provided that certain debt and boundary issues would be solved through arbitration. For Scott and many others, before and after him, this was the birth of modern international arbitration. The work of Grotius had kept determining the impressive progress in the settlement of international disputes up to 1925, when a court for States was finally in operation:

> The nations are co-operating in the common task of civilization and they are submitting their individual wills to the rules of one law of nations. Hugo Grotius, a Dutchman exiled from his own country has become a citizen of the world and an international legislator, and from The Hague he causes judgement [sic] to be passed on the nations through the Permanent Court of International Justice.

106 Hugo Grotius, *De jure belli ac pacis libri tres*, vol. I, Washington, D.C.: Carnegie Institution, 1913. It should be noted that the edition reproduced in the Classics series is not the first one of 1625, but the one of 1646, the last revised by Grotius before his death.

107 Hugo Grotius, *De jure belli ac pacis libri tres*, English translation by Francis W. Kelsey et al., vol. II, Oxford: Oxford University Press, 1925.

108 See Finch, *History of the Carnegie Endowment*, p. 366.

109 See "Translators' Prefatory Note," in Grotius, *De jure belli ac pacis libri tres* (1925), p. xlv.

110 James Brown Scott, "Introduction," ibid., p. xxxix>

Scott could only wish for the sake of the future of mankind, that "the youth of 1925" would "devote themselves to the study of the treatises of Grotius, and among them be found another John Jay."[111]

Somehow unexpectedly, within this thirty-four pages long text devoted to honoring the greatness of Grotius, there are also the first few paragraphs in which Scott developed an argument for other scholars as the initiators of international law.[112] Scott felt he had to address the point because "[t]here [we]re some prone to forget that there were great men before [the] two [Protestant] masters," Gentili and Grotius. "Enough time ha[d] passed . . . since the Reformation to be just to their [Catholic] predecessors."

Scott went on to explain the relationship as he saw it. The "great Spanish trinity," formed by Vitoria, Suárez, and Ayala, had completed the fusion of "two [universal] systems of law[,] Roman law [and] canon law, as universal as the Church from which it emanates." In so doing they had "laid the foundations of the universal law . . . of nations." Indeed, it was "quite natural," Scott thought, that the founding would be the doing of "the faithful of the Church universal[.] International law" was not only of Spanish, but also "of Catholic origin." Where did that leave Grotius? Clearly, "[i]nternational law existed before the publication of the first systematic treatise [by] Grotius." The work of the Spaniards was there for taking; it "would perhaps have enabled another than Grotius to combine [it] systematically." In other words, the "Hollander" had merely "stretched [his hand] to gather the ripened fruit."[113]

## Diverging Formulations of Postwar International Law: Scott's Declining Position in the US Professional Community

It is difficult to point to a smoking gun, to a precise trigger in order to explain why James Brown Scott, in the mid-1920s, decided to dedicate the rest of his career to the theory of the Spanish foundation of international law. Certainly, it is possible to recognize several circumstances and contextual factors that might have favored his choice.

First of all, one could point to Scott's declining position in the US academic international legal community. As I argued at the closing of Chapter 3, the rise of the

111 Ibid., p. xl.

112 As we have seen earlier in this chapter, Scott had already called Vitoria the founder of international law in a published text in 1917. Yet, he did so without developing an argument as to the why, merely pointing to the self-evidence of the assertion in the content of the *Relectiones*.

113 Ibid., p. xiv. This was the first time Scott used the "ripe fruit" metaphor to characterize Grotius' role in the development of international law. He would use it often after that until his retirement. Scott, as he duly reported in the text, had taken it from a book published earlier that year by Jan Kosters, who had been a member of the pre-war Dutch committee to promote the Hague Academy: see Jan Kosters, *Les Fondements du Droit des Gens*, in *Bibliotheca Visseriana*, vol. VI, Leiden: Brill, 1925, p. 32.

League to Enforce Peace since 1915 and the attacks Scott had received at the 1917 ASIL annual meeting were early signs that his judicialist brand of internationalism was becoming obsolete. By the early postwar years, it was clear that the momentum had shifted toward a younger generation, more interested in policy than rules, in political processes of international organization rather than adjudication. The generational conflict had remained dormant between 1918 and 1920, when annual meetings were suspended because of the war and the Society was managed through the executive council, where Scott and Root were unopposed. When meetings resumed in 1921, the two camps' division became patent.[114] The old guard was for continuing with their usual focus, as Root's opening address made clear: the best tools for the advancement of international law were the Hague system of conferences for the codification of rules and the now established Permanent Court of International Justice to adjudicate on them.[115] As soon as the program was made public, one month before the meeting, criticism poured in. At the meeting itself, many took the floor to point out the shortcomings in the approach Scott had championed. Fenwick, who had spoken for collective security at the 1917 meeting, would summarize the issue. Too many of the presentations were focused on reform of the laws of war, just like the pre-war Hague conferences had been. That was a failed project and a relic of an old world that no longer existed. The focus should have been on the law of peace and international organization, which had not been discussed at all. That was the way forward, also because progress merely by judicial decision was welcome but too slow to be a priority. As one member wrote to Scott, this state of affairs, many felt, was because "the Society [wa]s too personally conducted."[116]

At the 1922 meeting Scott was able to set the agenda for the last time amidst growing tension and opposition. By 1923, it was clear that the younger generation had taken charge. Charles Fenwick, Manley O. Hudson, and Edwin Borchard, three of the main younger figures, presented papers at the annual meeting and gave their take on the new directions to be taken by ASIL. The intent of departing from a classic view of the discipline was already manifest through the title of the session in which the three presented: "The existing state of international law, its bases, its scope, and its practical effectiveness, together with constructive suggestions for its extension into new fields."[117] Fenwick, the first to speak, listed his prescriptions for "the formulation of the new international law of peace." First of all, there was need for "[a] clear conception of the collective responsibility of the states for the

[114] On the generational struggle within ASIL in the early 1920s see Hatsue Shinohara, *US International Lawyers in the Interwar Years. A Forgotten Crusade, Cambridge: Cambridge University Press*, 2012, pp. 29–36; Frederick L. Kirgis, *The American Society of International Law's First Century 1906–2006*, Leiden/Boston: Martinus Nijhoff Publishers, 2006, pp. 59–66; Coates, *Legalist Empire*, p. 169.

[115] See Elihu Root, "Opening Address," *Proceedings of the American Society of International Law*, 15, 1921, pp. 1–13.

[116] Albert Bushnell Hart to Scott, March 28, 1922, ASIL Papers, quoted in Shinohara, *US International Lawyers in the Interwar Years*, p. 31.

[117] See *Proceedings of the American Society of International Law*, 17, 1923, p. 47.

maintenance of law and order." That would allow "the international community" to intervene "more prompt[ly] with respect to conflicts of claim which threaten the general peace."[118] Secondly, there was need for an effective international legislature, with an institutional design able to overcome the resistance that had caused much of the work of the Hague Conferences to be wasted. The institution had to be able to produce binding rules of international law or codify them by majority. The ratification of norms approved by the international legislature could be more automatic or dispensed with to simplify further the law-making process. Third, "the domain of international law" needed to expand and regulate "fields" it did not cover yet, "most important[ly] that of international commercial relations." There was a "urgent need of a law covering these subjects, which ha[d] become the chief causes of war in modern times." Notwithstanding the lack of "governmental readiness to act" toward the international regulation of issues such as the distribution of raw materials, Fenwick called for international lawyers to lead the way. After all, "[t]he history of international law in the past show[ed] the gradual widening of its scope to include questions which were at one time regarded as purely political."[119]

Hudson, a future judge of the Permanent Court of International Justice, lauded Fenwick's presentation and built upon it. International law had to be underpinned by a "new philosophy . . . to catch up with what [wa]s going on." There was already "a large body of international legislation" on a growing number of topics that was being ignored. It would be important to study it as material to develop legislation and codification. One of the many examples offered by Hudson was about "international labor conventions [: b]efore the war we had two . . . . Now we have sixteen." Governments were leading the way, not international lawyers as it should have been. This "lag[ging] behind the progress of events" was because the Society was still "in the clutches of" an abstract "natural philosophy."[120] In other words, he was accusing the older generation of missing the practical developments in postwar international law because of a myopic focus on big principles. Their highbrow condescension for concrete and technical legal arrangements was making them underestimate their capacity for innovative international law-making. Scott must have felt that Hudson was referring to him.

Then came the turn of Borchard. While Hudson and Fenwick considered Scott their mentor and would continue to hold him in high esteem, Borchard had been resentful of his leadership in the ASIL for some time. Borchard was close to John Bassett Moore, who had sometimes cooperated with Scott but never went beyond showing him a cold politeness. The two looked down on Scott's scholarship and academic credentials. For them, Scott's greatest ability was in mustering

[118] Charles Fenwick, "An Outline of the Problems Presented in the Further Development of International Law," in ibid., pp. 48–9.
[119] Ibid., pp. 50–1.
[120] Manley O. Hudson, "International Legislation," in ibid., pp. 52–3.

political favor and scheming to obtain powerful positions and their related advantages. His views on international law were made of a simplistic legalism, showing his inability to grasp the complexities of international politics. Indeed, Borchard had been calling for more attention to sociological factors in international legal theory since before the World War. He warned against dismissing too easily the law of war and especially a traditional approach to neutrality, still useful to limit the worst excesses of belligerents. Following that path would mean the return to a "mediaeval doctrine" of just cause, incompatible "with any program for the limitation of armaments." Still, he agreed with Fenwick with regard to the expansion of international law to economic issues. The causes of war lay primarily in "unrestricted, unfair competition between nations for economic advantage," which "escape[d] the control of international law" but had been "painstakingly" regulated "in greatest detail . . . in municipal law." There was need of an "economic conference" to "consider . . . vital . . . subjects" like "the distribution of raw materials and markets, preferential tariffs [and] the internationalization of cables." Only with this new focus on economic competition, "students of international affairs . . . would demonstrate" to be giving attention to "the causes of war and not merely its symptoms, effects and palliatives." That was the most pressing development required for "the resurrection of international law."[121]

A few weeks after the meeting, Root wrote to Scott, sharing his intention to resign his position as president of ASIL. It was time for "a new president, with a new mind and a new experience and a fresh initiative."[122] In 1924, as Root left the presidency, Scott left the position of Editor-in-Chief of the Society's Journal, which he had held since the establishment in 1907. Scott would become himself ASIL president years later, in 1929. He would maintain the position until 1939, the year before his retirement from public life. His role, though, would be mostly symbolic. He would never regain primary responsibility for the academic direction of the Society.

## Vitoria at Georgetown: Scott's 1926 Course on the Founders of International Law

This and other defeats of his classic approach to international law in the early 1920s[123] did not dishearten Scott. Neither did they lead him to fundamentally change his ideas and theories to catch up with the new sensibility in the profession. Instead, like during the World War, he felt he had to make the deeper foundations

[121] Edwin Borchard, "The Resurrection of International Law," in ibid., pp. 69–70.

[122] Elihu Root to Scott, May 11, 1923, ASIL Papers, quoted in Shinohara, *US International Lawyers in the Interwar Years*, p. 31.

[123] One such defeat was, for instance, the refusal of the *Institut de Droit International* to adopt Scott's Declaration of the Rights and Duties of Nations: see Coates, *Legalist Empire*, pp. 167–8.

of his international law more explicit through his scholarship. The 1925 Grotius celebrations offered a favorable environment for the enterprise. They bred a renewed interest in history among international lawyers, resulting in a number of publications on the early modern pioneers. Scott, as we have seen, contributed to the Grotius revival. He marked his introduction to *De iure belli ac pacis* with the place and date "The Hague, 5 August 1925." Around that time, Scott was there to attend both the *Institut* meeting and the third session of the Hague Academy of International Law, at the height of the events through which the profession recognized the "Miracle of Holland" as its founder. Seizing on the circumstance, Scott immediately put himself to work to keep the focus on the early modern foundations of international law but provide his colleagues with a more complete narrative, one that would contemplate the key role of the Salamancans. His first fuller articulation of the case for the Spanish origin of international law would be a course he taught at the School of Foreign Service of Georgetown University in the early months of 1926. Founded in 1789, Georgetown is the oldest Catholic and Jesuit institution of higher education in the United States. Its School of Foreign Service was the brainchild of Father Edmund A. Walsh.[124] Walsh was ordained in 1916 and had become dean of Georgetown College the following year. His tenure, though, was extremely short. When the United States entered the war, he consulted with the War Department to design study programs for government personnel in connection to the management of hostilities. Working in that capacity, he realized how inadequate diplomatic education was in the United States. To obviate the situation, in 1919 he would found the School of Foreign Service and become its first dean. Soon, he would call on Scott to teach there. Starting with a few lectures in the academic year 1920/21,[125] Scott's relationship with Georgetown rapidly grew.[126] Along with a professorship in international law and foreign relations of the United States at the School of Foreign Service, Scott was also professor of international law, Roman law, and jurisprudence at the Georgetown Law School. He kept both positions until his retirement in the summer of 1940.[127]

Scott delivered his course titled "Founders of International Law"[128] in eight lectures, which took place between March 4 and May 6, 1926.[129] The course is relevant to this study for an array of reasons. First of all, it was the first time that Scott developed an articulated account of the theory of the Spanish origin of international law. Secondly, because of the nature of the lecture notes, intended for a student-only

[124] For a biography of Walsh, see Patrick McNamara, *A Catholic Cold War: Edmund A. Walsh, S. J., and the Politics of American Catholic Anticommunism*, New York: Fordham University Press, 2005.

[125] See Constantine E. Maguire to Scott, September 18, 1920, September 22, 1920, October 9, 1920, Folder 1, Box 53, JBS Papers.

[126] See James Brown Scott to Father Edmund A. Walsh, July 14, 1921, Folder 1, Box 53, JBS Papers.

[127] See James Brown Scott to Father Arthur A. O'Leary, August 16, 1940, Folder 6, Box 53, JBS Papers.

[128] See "Notice to Students re: Founders of International Law," January 28, 1926, Folder 3 Box 53, JBS Papers.

[129] The final versions of Scott's lecture notes, along with earlier drafts are in Box 64, JBS Papers.

audience and without a publication in view, Scott could operate without immediate goals in mind. By that I mean that the course represented an early version of his narrative, written relatively in the abstract and not to suit one of the specific political projects he later pursued through the authority of Vitoria and Suárez.

There is a third point, connected to the previous points. The audience of Scott's course was made of students heading for the diplomatic service, not law students. This resulted in a rather different style in respect to the one Scott would employ in his main publications on the Salamanca School. In the lectures, Scott did not go deeply into the legal issues faced by the early modern thinkers; later he would, drawing constant parallels with questions in the international law of his day. The texts of the lectures could rather be classified as pieces in political theory or history of philosophy rather than legal history or simply international law like the later ones. Notwithstanding these differences, all the larger points of relevance for twentieth-century issues in the work of Vitoria and Suárez that Scott would identify in 1928 in his first book on them,[130] he had already noted in the Georgetown course.

That said, if one looks at the structure of the course, it is clear how it was, to a certain extent, still linked to the celebrations for Grotius' third centenary. Four lectures out of eight are dedicated directly to the Dutch, only two to the Spanish predecessors. However, in the lectures on Grotius and in the one on Alberico Gentili, Scott was very careful to underline what the two Protestants owed to Suárez and, especially, Vitoria in terms of method, doctrines, and theory of law, both natural and of nations. At least in every other page of those lecture notes, if not more, Scott mentioned some debt toward the theologians of the Salamanca School; he also underlined that these debts were sometimes recognized with citations by Gentili and Grotius, but very often they were not and Spanish doctrines were just taken without reference.

Scott dedicated most of the introductory lecture to a basic history of Europe between 1492, when Colombo set foot in America, and 1625, the year of the publication of Grotius' *De iure belli ac pacis*. Yet, the rest of the lecture is on the origins of international law: Scott elaborated on and clarified the few paragraphs he wrote on the issue in the introduction to *De iure belli ac pacis* of the previous year. Grotius, Scott told his students, was "called the Father of International Law, and so complete is his victory in the minds of many that he overshadowed his predecessors to such a degree that they are lost . . . in the darkness." Grotius "was not" international law's "founder; [h]e was, however, its systematizer." What did this entail? "[H]e found [the labors of others] at hand and he fitted them into the structure which he himself builded [sic]." To illustrate this relationship Scott borrowed once

[130] James Brown Scott, *The Spanish Origin of International Law: Lectures on Francisco de Vitoria (1480–1546) and Francisco Suarez (1548–1617)*, Washington, D.C.: Georgetown University Press, 1928.

again Kosters' metaphor: "the fruit was ripe" thanks to the work of the Spaniards and Grotius' was the "hand to pluck it." But why, Scott wondered, had the predecessors fall into obscurity? One reason was surely the stylistic form, the "structure" in which Grotius had combined their doctrines, a "structure [that], unlike [theirs], had endured." But that was not all. "Grotius ha[d] benefited by the great intolerance which had marked the last few centuries of th[e] Christian world." Because of the common religion, "Protestants have looked upon him as . . . the founder . . . of international law, to the neglect of his predecessors of the older Faith." Yet, if one "examine[d] the authorities which Grotius cited and upon whose writings he completed his system . . . impartially and without religious fervor," the result "would at once be evident." The scholars on whom Grotius relied "were Catholic theologians . . . of Spain." Scott believed that "the point of departure in the development . . . beg[a]n with Victoria[. T]rough Victoria" it went "through Ayala, and through Gentilis, and through Suárez, until it reache[d] Grotius who summed up the learning of the past, elaborated his system, and delivered it to the outer world."[131]

How then had Vitoria founded international law? According to Scott, by going beyond the scholastic method. Rather than discussing law in the abstract as his predecessors and colleagues had done, with *De Indis* and *De iure belli* Vitoria had brought *ius gentium* to bear explicitly on questions of primary importance to his ruler. The rights of the American natives had to be respected. Moral and legal principles, not mere Machiavellian reason of state, had to be the guide of a Christian prince. Yet, if Vitoria could give a new direction to the law of nations, it was because of the momentous changes that were shaking Europe, primarily the discovery of the New World. Keeping in mind the topic spurring the Dominican's work, one "could see at once," Scott argued, "that international law . . . was not mere speculation, but was the result of new conditions, requiring a new solution, which it received at the hands of those most competent in such matters."[132]

To leave no doubt, at the closing of the third lecture, Scott summarized the main claim of the course:

> [T]he thesis I am to maintain is that the modern international law is the result of the discovery of America and the necessity of Spain to frame a new law to meet new conditions; that the new law was created by Franciscus of Victoria, whose little tractate written on the Indians and on War, today form a summary of the modern law of nations, which his successors, and especially Grotius, put in the form of an elaborate treatise.[133]

[131] "Introductory Lecture in Dr. Scott's Course," Folder 5, Box 64, JBS Papers, pp. 2–4.
[132] Ibid., p. 4.
[133] "Third Lecture on Hugo Grotius delivered by Mr. James Brown Scott," Folder 5, Box 64, JBS Papers, p. 15.

The lectures devoted to the Spanish school were the fourth and fifth. In the fourth lecture, Scott reviewed Vitoria's *De Indis* and *De iure belli*, focusing on the modernity of the Dominican's ideas. On one hand, he commended him for recognizing the rights of the American natives and their communities as perfect, a concept Scott considered equivalent with that of the independent State. On the other, he praised the humanizing restraint Vitoria infused in his law of war, well combined with its focus on justice. The fifth lecture took on the development of Vitoria's work in terms of theory and practice. The former aspect was embodied in the work of Suárez, the latter in that of Balthazar Ayala.

Suárez, according to Scott, had the merit of fleshing out Vitoria's concepts of *ius inter gentes* and *perfecta communitas* and producing a universal legal philosophy out of them. Suárez had woven these concepts, conceiving States as equal in their independence and interdependence, forming an international community with its own law.

> In the opinion of Suárez, as in the opinion of Victoria, the large States of his day were independent—England, France, Spain—of the Empire. They were separate entities if looked at separately, but if looked at largely they were but members of a larger community—the community of Christian States, then coterminous and synonymous with Christianity. When you admit these conceptions, you have a community of nations making its law from day to day; you have the basis of international organization; and every form of organization is the result of this conception promulgated with finality by Suárez in his work [*De legibus as Deo legislatore*].[134]

While Suárez had turned scattered doctrines by Vitoria into a full-fledged legal theory, Balthazar Ayala, legal advisor of the Spanish Armies in the rebellious Netherlands, had instead the merit of testing Vitoria's approach to the law of war on the battlefield. Ayala, indeed, wanted to prove that law had application in the actual behavior of armies and not just in the speculations of theologians and philosophers. Here was another application of Vitoria's doctrine of the State as *perfecta communitas*, which, in Ayala's work, developed into something akin to the modern distinction between international and internal armed conflict. Indeed, according to Scott, Ayala had turned the "principles laid down by Vitoria" into rules and "humane standards" for the "conduct of hostilities." But a war, to be just, did not only need to be motivated by a just cause; it also had to be waged by the right authority, an authority that only perfect communities had. In other words, "[w]ar was an armed contest between States." It followed that the

[134] "Fifth Lecture delivered by Mr. James Brown Scott," Folder 8, Box 64, JBS Papers, p. 6.

law of war "did not apply to rebels within States[.] In the eyes of Ayala, rebels," like the ones he was facing with the Spanish army in the Netherlands, "were like robbers . . . because they had no authority of a supreme power to justify their acts."[135]

After finishing his review of the work of the founders of international law, Scott used most of the last lecture to draw conclusions and lay the moral of the story before his students. The founders' collective legacy was in the formulation of a law of nature so innovative and well organized that it gave birth to international law, a new branch of jurisprudence of universal application. Reflecting on the history of the discipline in these terms would bring new life to "the theory of natural right, which jurists" of Scott's time considered "discarded." The key of the matter was once again in reading the strides of progress through the political culture of the New World and, especially, the United States.

Indeed, natural law among the founders was essentially a belief in a culture of rights. "[T]he good and the wise, and the best" held "that the things they ventured to call natural, as distinct from artificial law, were the rights which every human being should have, because he was a human being."[136] Of course, Scott continued, this was the same philosophy of inherent rights that underpinned the US Declaration of Independence and the country's constitutional culture. The legacy of the founders was, somehow surprisingly, still embedded in the way the United States handled its role as a leading global power in the context of the World War. Looking at "the addresses . . . by President Wilson on the eve of [the] entry [of the US] into the War," Scott "wondered at the time where [he] had drawn his authority." Indeed, being Wilson "a staunch Presbyterian and an Elder of that branch of the Church, he was not likely to have spent . . . time . . . in thumbing the . . . writings of theologican [sic] writers of the 16th Century, for which, generally, Protestants have had not respect."[137] Remarkably though, Scott noted, "the fine phrases and high principles set forth by Mr. Wilson concerning a war of justice, and peace of justice, [we]re to be found"[138] in the works of the Salamanca School and, later, Grotius.

That Wilson, unknowingly, had recovered the wisdom and the morality of just war theology was, for Scott, reason for both hope and concern. Hope, because this sense for war as a matter of justice and not mere power could resurface and had reappeared in his time. Concern, because his contemporaries, even when they

[135] Ibid., p. 9.

[136] "Eighth Lecture of Mr. James Brown Scott," Folder 8, Box 64, JBS Papers, p. 13.

[137] On Wilson's anti-Catholicism and difficult relationship with the Vatican see Luca Castagna, *A Bridge across the Ocean: The United States and the Holy See between the Two World Wars*, Washington, D.C.: The Catholic University of America Press, 2014, *passim*.

[138] "Eighth Lecture of Mr. James Brown Scott", p. 12a.

were right, were unwilling to accept to learn from the past, too proud to look in what they perceived as dark ages. For Scott, such disdain for past knowledge could not be leading to true progress, as it discarded advancements already achieved by mankind. Among those achievements to "return to" were "the great traditions of the 16th Century" owed "to those philosophers of Spain who, in the rustle and bustle of a busy world, have been overlooked in order that we may prostrate ourselves . . . before false gods."[139]

In these observations, there was Scott's recipe for a more effective international law and a better future for mankind. It clearly related to and distinguished itself from the proposals of his younger colleagues made at the 1923 ASIL meeting and elsewhere. Scott agreed on the importance of understanding and studying the causes of war. But there were no quick fixes. Acting without regard for past experience and human nature, simply on the basis of cold political speculation, could not improve global relations and prosperity in the long run. For Scott, it would likely lead to action based on ideas that history had already proven catastrophic. One obvious example in Scott's mind was collective security, a mechanism that so simplified and generalized the relation between justice and the use of force as to make it meaningless.[140] That was why the natural philosophy Hudson had denigrated was still and would always be needed as the basis of international law. Real innovation and progress came when great men were ready, with humility and moderation, to combine reason and experience, taking into account human nature and dignity. Indeed, attention for history and tradition and a belief in natural law were the necessary basis of the science of international law, in Scott's time as it had been for its founders. With that attitude, one could sensibly face world-changing conditions, like Vitoria and his disciples had done following the discovery of the American continent. And, indeed, with his passionate defense of history and natural law in the present, the reasoning of Scott's course had come full circle: explaining the foundation of the discipline was also explaining the discipline itself and, most crucially, its future. So he could "end" the course "as [he] began," celebrating "the Spanish . . . theologians [who] laid the foundations in touch with the events of international life, and . . . supplied the materials from which Grotius was able to rear . . . a temple of justice which has stood . . . the weathers of time." It was then left to the people "of the new world to justify its discovery and to perfect the new law for the new world."[141]

139 Ibid., p. 12b.
140 See Chapter 3.
141 "Eighth Lecture of Mr. James Brown Scott, p. 16.

## 3. The Lessons of the Spanish Origin: Vitoria, Suárez, and the International Law of the Twentieth Century

### "Spain, for me the Holy Land of International Law": Scott's 1927 First Visit to Salamanca

Following the course, Scott spent the summer in Europe, as he usually did. In The Hague, he met Henri Van der Mandere, the secretary of the Dutch committee that had visited Spain the previous spring. Scott had seen the coverage of the visit by a Canadian newspaper in June[142] and had already exchanged letters on the subjects with Minister Yanguas Messia[143] but wanted to know more. He asked Van der Mandere to provide him with all the documents and information he could muster. The quest was successful; Scott even managed to score one of the Grotius medals in the process.[144] Among the wealth of material Van der Mandere gave to Scott were the issues of *El Adelanto* with the lectures on Vitoria by Barcia Trelles. Scott was impressed.

Barcia Trelles had tried to initiate cooperation with Scott and the CEIP already in 1924. However, his letter to Scott would receive only a rather perfunctory reply from a clerk, offering to send CEIP publications for the library of his university.[145] After reading Barcia's lectures, Scott would be the one to contact him by letter on September 9.[146] He praised highly Barcia Trelles' account of Vitoria's relevance for the inception of modern international law and told him how they shared similar ideas: he had just dedicated an entire course at Georgetown to the founders. After the pleasantries, Scott moved on to talk business. First of all, he informed Barcia Trelles of his plans, hatched with Bustamante, to start a new Vitoria association, with the purpose of spreading further the works of the Salamanca scholars and the idea of the discovery of America as a key inspiration for their doctrines. Praising the Spanish colleagues for having already started a similar organization, Scott asked Barcia Trelles to send him all related documents to enable him to follow in their steps. Secondly, he offered Barcia Trelles a professional opportunity. Reminding him that he was a member of the Curatorium, he informed him that he would receive an invitation to give a course on Vitoria at the Hague Academy of International Law in the summer of 1927.[147]

[142] See James Brown Scott to Camilo Barcia Trelles, September 9, 1926, Folder 5, Box 1, JBS Papers.

[143] See José de Yanguas Messia to Scott, July 5, 1926, Folder 7, Box 9, JBS Papers.

[144] See Henri Van der Mandere to Scott, September 20, 1926; Scott to Van der Mandere, September 30, 1926; Van der Mandere to Scott, October 6, 1926, Folder 7, Box 8, JBS Papers.

[145] See Camilo Barcia Trelles to James Brown Scott, August 19, 1924, and Henry G. Crocker to Camilo Barcia Trelles, December 15, 1924.

[146] See Scott to Barcia Trelles, September 9, 1926.

[147] Barcia Trelles would deliver the course under the title "Francisco de Vitoria et l'École moderne du Droit international," published in *Recueil des cours de l'Académie de droit international de La Haye*, 17, 1927, pp. 133–337.

This letter gives an idea of how Scott was planning to proceed in his campaign to make Vitoria the recognized founder of international law and which political buttons he wanted to push. Working with Bustamante indicated that he planned to connect Vitoria with the same Pan-American sentiment he aimed to inspire through the American Institute of International Law. Involving Barcia Trelles was also part of a European strategy. The Spanish, as the Dutch visit proved, were more than happy, thanks to national and Catholic pride, to claim the foundation of international law through their Dominican countryman. Spain could be a stronghold. From there, the Spanish origin idea could be reinforced both in Latin America, through the still strong cultural ties with the region, and in the rest of continental Europe. Barcia Trelles was the perfect poster-boy, especially for this latter task and not only because of his nationality or religion. His political positions, to the left of the generally conservative Spanish legal mainstream, would curry him favor more easily with the average member of the international legal profession in the rest of Western Europe. This was especially true if one considers the tensions of the period between 1926 and 1928: the nationalist dictatorship led by Primo de Rivera governing Spain came very close to retire the country from the League of Nations.[148] In such a context, insisting on the glories of the Spanish past was a way to promote internationalism that would sit well with the nationalists in power. Indeed, it was in 1926 that Barcia Trelles had started a campaign for a revival of the Salamanca School in light of its contributions to international law from the columns of the Madrid-based progressive newspaper *La Libertad*, close to the workers' cause.[149]

Scott's plan was supported by Nicholas Murray Butler, President of CEIP since Root's age-motivated resignation in 1925, and fit well into the US government's diplomatic agenda. This was made explicit by a letter sent to Butler by Secretary of State Frank Kellogg on November 15, 1926. Kellogg was "anxious" to meet Butler to discuss "extending the activity of universities in the exchange of students and professors between the United States and the countries of Central and South America." There were reasons to seek a reinforcement and improvement of cultural relations beyond the "rapidly increasing . . . investment of American capital . . . in these countries." First, there was a need to match rival efforts in the region: "no effort is being spared by the League of Nations and by certain European countries to establish the closest possible cultural ties with Latin America and to develop therein an asset of goodwill." Secondly, the image of the United States itself needed to be restored. Kellogg sought to counteract the "wide-spread feeling that

[148] See Yolanda Gamarra Chopo, "La ilusión española de la Sociedad de Naciones," in Yolanda Gamarra Chopo and Carlos Fernández Liesa (eds.), *Los orígenes del Derecho internacional contempóraneo. Estudios conmemorativos del Centenario de la Primera Guerra Mundial*, Zaragoza: Institución Fernando el Católico, 2015, pp. 289–96.

[149] One of the founders of the newspaper in 1919 had been Barcia Trelles' brother, Augusto, several times Minister in the government of the Second Spanish Republic. Because of his brother's prominence in the Republic, Camilo would come under scrutiny and his career impeded in the early years of the Franco regime.

we are a purely materialistic people," taking into account the "disquieting fact that the most pronounced anti-American sentiment is to be found in the universities of Latin America."[150] Kellogg suggested that the CEIP should take action in the matter. Butler replied, listing with pride all the achievements of the Endowment in the region, including the publication of a series of books in Spanish on American history and literature, "going steadily into use in Latin-American schools and colleges."[151] Moreover, Butler informed the Secretary of State, there were already plans to create a more stable program of exchange professorships, based on longer stays of at least a few months. Indeed, James Brown Scott would soon be named the first Carnegie Exchange Professor to Latin America, leaving in January 1927 for a tour that would touch several countries.[152] He first sailed to Cuba[153] and then visited the countries on the Western coast of South America. Crossing the Andes, he reached Buenos Aires before the two final official stages of the trip. First, he would preside over a meeting of the American Institute of International Law in Montevideo. Later, he would go Rio de Janeiro where he represented the United States at the International Commission of Jurists tasked with the codification of American international law.[154] He would not return to the United States until June. In his various speeches and lectures across the region, Scott echoed the message of the tours by Root in 1906 and Bacon in 1913. In line also with his previous statements, he focused on Pan-American sameness and the common political culture, encompassing a progressive international law, in the continent.[155] The only novel theme he introduced was the Spanish origin of international law.[156] On May 24, on his way back to the United States, he stopped in Montevideo. In a lecture at the local university, he would state, in no uncertain terms, that the foundation of the discipline was due to the discovery of the American continent and the doctrines to which it led Vitoria.[157]

The revival of American international law and its underlying Pan-American exceptionalism concerned European international lawyers, as it had done before the

[150] Frank B. Kellogg to Nicholas Murray Butler, November 15, 1926, Box 37, CEIP Papers. About other attempts by James Brown Scott to improve US relations with Latin America in the mid- and late 1920s see Chapter 2.

[151] Nicholas Murray Butler to Frank B. Kellogg, November 18, 1926, Box 37, CEIP Papers.

[152] On the itinerary see James Brown Scott to Henry S. Haskell, July 2, 1927, Folder 5, Box 60, CEIP Papers.

[153] On Scott's early plans for the tour and the arrangements for his lectures in Cuba see James Brown Scott to Antonio de Bustamante, December 7, 1926, volume 305, CEIP Papers.

[154] On the codification of international law in the Americas from the 1920s until the 1933 conference of Montevideo and the related political stakes see Arnulf Becker Lorca, *Mestizo International Law. A Global Intellectual History 1842–1933*, Cambridge: Cambridge University Press, 2014, pp. 337–52.

[155] The texts of some of Scott's standard speeches for the tour, with the titles such as "A Glimpse of Latin America" or "Inter-American Intellectual Relations," can be found in Folder 5, Box 60, CEIP Papers. See also CEIP Yearbook, 17, 1928, pp. 109ff.

[156] On Scott's intention to champion the Spanish origin theory during the Latin American tour see James Brown Scott to Antonio de Bustamante, October 20, 1926, Folder 34, Box 11, JBS Papers.

[157] See CEIP Yearbook, 17, 1928, p. 109.

World War. Scott used Vitoria also to dispel such worries and to deny any challenge to the unity of the international legal system. His presidential address at the Lausanne meeting of the *Institut de Droit International*, delivered on August 24, 1927, was indeed titled "*L'universalité du droit des gens*."[158] Here Vitoria figured as the prophet of universal equality through its recognition to American natives, rather than a thinker pushed to come up with a new branch of jurisprudence by the discovery of America. This shift of emphasis was obviously a matter of nuance and rhetoric rather than substance. Yet, it has relevance because it shows Scott already skillfully emphasizing different perspectives of Vitoria's legacy and the Spanish origin theory according to the audience and the point to be made.

News of Scott's statements on the Spanish origin in South America[159] and Lausanne[160] reached Spain. They helped to forge a stronger relationship with the *Asociación Francisco de Vitoria* and led to an invitation to Salamanca. The invitation, in any case, was a long time coming and it was due to several connections coming together. For instance, that letter of September 1926 from Scott to Barcia Trelles had started a collaboration and an intense epistolary exchange that would continue until the end of the former's career. They both felt they had found a kindred spirit. Replying to Scott's first letter, Barcia Trelles wrote that he was "moved by" Scott's "opinions of Vitoria" whose "figure, at the end of the day did not belong to Spain; he belonged to the great moral unity we form with the New World."[161] For Scott, it was "a great pleasure to see that we agree on the true origin of international law, as on this matter I am more orthodox than the Pope, if a protestant is allowed to use that expression."[162] Barcia Trelles immediately pulled strings to get Scott into the Vitoria Association, bringing him to the attention of the Minister of Education Eduardo Callejo de la Cuesta.[163] Soon, Scott was named the Association's first honorary member.[164] As such, Scott received a rather vague invitation by Yanguas, in the beginning of September 1927, while they were still both in Lausanne for the *Institut* meeting. Yanguas informed Scott that the association was planning a course on Vitoria's contribution to international law to be held at some point between the coming November and the following May; he hoped that Scott would be able to join them in Spain and to lecture.[165] Even if that was a particularly busy year, Scott did not let the occasion go. Once they knew he would be joining them, the

[158] See Discours de M. James Brown Scott, Président de l'Institut," *Annuaire de l'Institut de Droit International*, Paris: A. Pedone Editeur, vol. III, 1927, pp. 34–65.

[159] See José de Yanguas Messia to James Brown Scott, April 25, 1927, Folder 7, Box 9, JBS Papers.

[160] See Camilo Barcia Trelles to Scott, September 12, 1927, Folder 5, Box 1, JBS Papers.

[161] Camilo Barcia Trelles to Scott, September 16, 1926, Folder 5, Box 1, JBS Papers, my translation from Spanish.

[162] James Brown Scott to Camilo Barcia Trelles, September 28, 1926, Folder 5, Box 1, JBS Papers, my translation from French.

[163] See Eduardo Callejo de la Cuesta to Camilo Barcia Trelles, October 7, 1926, Folder 5, Box 1, JBS Papers.

[164] Camilo Barcia Trelles to Scott, November 19, 1926, Folder 5, Box 1, JBS Papers.

[165] José de Yanguas Messia to Scott, September 2, 1927, Folder 7, Box 9, JBS Papers.

Spanish colleagues turned the event into something bigger and more formal than initially planned.

Scott was due to participate as a delegate to the Sixth Pan-American Convention, opening in Havana on January 16, 1928, where the codification projects approved by the Commission of Jurists in Rio would be discussed.[166] That meant that he could go to Spain only at the earliest possible time in November. At the end of September, on his return to Washington, he received Nicholas Murray Butler's opinion on his plans. It was a good idea to go "preaching our gospel in countries that we have not yet done much to reach, Spain or Portugal, for example." Butler noted also that it had been "a long time since any one of us" of the Endowment "has been on the Continent during the winter season when universities are in full blast and every one is at home."[167] Scott immediately informed Yanguas and Barcia of his visit. So, after less than a month in Washington, D.C., Scott was crossing the Atlantic again to spend just three weeks in Europe before sailing back. Indeed, according to many who knew him, Scott often used to say that he had crossed the ocean more times than the Dominican missionary Bartolomé de las Casas.[168]

By the time Scott reached Spain, more and more had been added to conjure up a grandiose celebration. Barcia Trelles had convinced the University of Salamanca to bestow on him a doctorate *honoris causa* for his promotion of the Spanish School,[169] while Yanguas had arranged a further stage of the visit in Madrid.[170] From the correspondence, it is clear that Scott was notably excited about the upcoming visit. He wrote to Barcia Trelles how honored he was "to become formally attached to the University of Salamanca . . . where from his chair, Francisco de Vitoria has professed the modern international law of which we all benefit."[171] In the same letter, Scott went so far as to say that he had started the Classics of International Law in order to demonstrate and promote the Spanish origin theory, which, as we have seen, seems to be an overstatement at best, considering the evidence available.

Scott reached Salamanca on November 9, together with his wife Adele.[172] In the evening, Scott and Barcia Trelles met in person for the first time. The next day, the

[166] President Coolidge would take the occasion of the Conference to visit Cuba in a clear attempt to garner goodwill among growing Latin American criticism of the United States' hegemonic policies. It was the last time that a US president visited Cuba until the recent trip of President Obama in March 2016. For an historical account by Scott of the codification of international law in America up to the results of the 1928 Havana Conference see CEIP Yearbook, 18, 1929, pp. 137–40.

[167] Nicholas Murray Butler to Scott, September 27, 1927, Folder 5, Box 60, CEIP Papers.

[168] See, for instance, Camilo Barcia Trelles, "James Brown Scott y Francisco de Vitoria," *ABC*, August 5, 1955.

[169] Camilo Barcia Trelles to Scott, October 19, 1927, Volume 309, CEIP Papers.

[170] José de Yanguas Messia, November 3, 1927, Folder 9, Box 7, JBS Papers.

[171] James Brown Scott to Camilo Barcia Trelles, October 29, 1927, Folder 1, Box 12, JBS Papers, my translation from French.

[172] Scott's visit to Salamanca was first announced and then reported in detail on *El Adelanto*, issues of November 2, 3, 6, 8, 9, 10, 11, 12, 13, and 15, 1927. His trip to Spain received attention also by the press in the United States, especially by the Spanish-language New York-based newspaper *La Prensa*. Short

Salamancan leg of Scott's trip entered its *clou*. The main auditorium of the university was packed with local and national authorities, diplomats, mostly from South America, and students. Scott and Benjamin Fernandez Medina, the Uruguayan Minister to Spain, who was also receiving an honorary degree, entered wearing Spanish doctoral robes. The Minister of Education Callejo started the proceedings by uncovering a memorial stone, inscribed to Vitoria for his contributions to the law of nations on the day of the inauguration of the Chair dedicated to him. Then Rector Enrique Esperabé de Arteaga took the floor. He declared his satisfaction in giving recognition to Scott and Fernández Medina and, through them, to the Vitoria Association. They had the merit of teaching the world the relevance, in his own time and in the present, of the foremost thinker of the University of Salamanca. In so doing, they were giving the younger generations the chance to learn and pass on the egalitarian doctrines and values of peace and justice of "the Spanish Socrates,"[173] as Arteaga called Vitoria in the speech. Callejo then proceeded to bestow the doctoral hat and medal on Scott and Fernández Medina. In that moment, Scott said in *castellano*: "Now I feel Spanish with all my heart."[174]

The next day, Scott participated to the meeting of the *Asociación Francisco de Vitoria* in the morning and to the naming of a street of the city after Vitoria in the afternoon. In between those two events, Scott delivered his first lecture on the Dominican. To the pleasure of the audience, he spoke in Spanish. The points he made should, by now, be familiar. The discovery of America was a starting point of a new law to face new conditions. Indeed, he remarked, it was fitting that he and Fernández Medina, one American of the North and one of the South, were there to honor the master that day. Vitoria, teaching in Spain, then the intellectual center of Europe, had provided the key doctrines of the new law for the new world. The *relectiones de Indis* and *De iure belli*, dictated in that same university almost four centuries before, had marked the beginning of modern international law. On the twelfth, the last day of the Salamancan celebrations, Scott gave a second lecture. To prove the points he had made in his previous lecture, he explained the content of the *Relectio de Indis*. His conclusion, reflecting on the text, was that, without a doubt, Grotius learned from those doctrines. The correct way to characterize the relationship was to define the Dutch as a successor of Vitoria, the true founder of international law.

By the thirteenth, Scott was in Madrid as a guest of Yanguas, now president of the newly created *Asamblea Nacional*. Prime Minister Primo de Rivera received him and hosted a banquet in his honor the next day at the Ministry of State. Before

articles were also published in the *New York Times* and the *Washington Evening Star*, among others. See also CEIP Yearbook, 17, 1928, pp. 120–1.

[173] See *El Adelanto*, November 11, 1927, p. 1.

[174] See *La Prensa*, November 11, 1927, my translation from Spanish.

the banquet, Scott was received by King Alfonso XIII. Leaving the Royal Palace, Scott told the press that he had found the king interested in the events of Salamanca and the activities of the Vitoria Association.[175] In the evening, he gave a lecture on Vitoria's law of war at the Academy of Jurisprudence. Then, he was ready to end his pilgrimage and leave "Spain, which remain[ed . . . ] for [him] the holy land of international law."[176]

## Putting the Argument on Paper: Scott's First Book on the Spanish Origin

Scott, thankful for the treatment and the honors received, was quick to reciprocate by publicly praising the Spanish government once he was back in the United States. On November 27, the *New York Times* published an interview with him where he praised the Primo de Rivera regime, which, let's not forget, had been installed by a military coup. Ascending to power in 1923, Primo de Rivera had suspended the Constitution and maintained dictatorial powers until he was toppled in 1930. In commenting on the Spanish political situation, Scott seemed to turn his back to the universal value of democracy or, at least, to imply that Spain was not ready for it and Primo de Rivera was correctly operating under that assumption.

> The real difficulty in Spain today, as in France and other countries attempting to progress with the parliamentary government, is that this form is not suited to them. The parliamentary system was developed in England after long training. . . . Since 1815 Spain's troubles have been due mainly to the attempt to introduce the English parliamentary system there; but Spain is a different country, and the system could not be successful. . . . What Primo de Rivera is attempting to do is to have a system of government worked out that is acceptable to Spain and in line with her traditions[.][177]

Scott went on to explain that Spain currently was reflecting the significance of its past: "[t]he Spain of today is the Spain of the great ages of that country, the fertile mother of a mighty race, immortal in her own right and in the lives of the eighteen Spanish-speaking republics of the Western world." Concluding, Scott "expressed" to the *Times* "confidence that Spain will solve her problems peacefully."[178]

Scott's successful visit went beyond establishing his own relations with the Spanish government and academia. It sparked up correspondence and projects of

[175] See *La Prensa*, November 16, 1927.
[176] James Brown Scott to Camilo Barcia Trelles, December 14, 1927, vol. 309, CEIP Papers, my translation from French.
[177] "Says Spain gains under de Rivera," *New York Times*, November 27, 1927.
[178] Ibid.

cooperation involving several members of the establishment and institutions, both public and private, in Spain and the United States. One such project, which immediately came to fruition, involved the Endowment. The Spanish made known, through several informal channels, that they would be pleased if the CEIP offered fellowships to Spanish students and scholars to study in the United States and for Americans of the North and the South to spend time at the University of Salamanca. Yanguas and the Duke of Alba, President of the Ibero-American Association, expressed the idea in letters to the US ambassador to Spain as Scott was leaving the country. The ambassador immediately forwarded them to Scott.[179] Scott later informed Nicholas Murray Butler that the king himself was highly interested in educational issues and had "the ambition to restore [Salamanca's] prestige, so that it should become, as in the Middle Ages, the great intellectual city of Spain." This, Scott argued, was within the Endowment's mission, as raising the profile of "the cradle of international law" would go a long way to promoting the peaceful settlement of disputes. But it also had a more immediate political angle to which Scott knew Butler would more receptive. "Anything we could do, even in a modest way, to bring Salamanca to the front again, would not be merely in the interest of Spain, but would be, I venture to believe, especially pleasing to the eighteen Spanish-American republics."[180]

Scott's arguments had enough purchase within CEIP to guarantee almost immediately the funding for one fellowship that was close to his heart. By December 16, he could inform Barcia Trelles that the scholarship he had planned for him was officially approved.[181] Barcia Trelles would move to Washington to research and work with Scott at the Division of International Law of CEIP through 1928 and 1929. With the close support of a like-minded scholar and the work of promotion previously done, Scott would use 1928 to give the Spanish origin theory a more developed form and explicitly draw the lessons the Salamanca theologians could teach for the practice of international law in his day. This was the year in which he published his first book, both in Spanish and in English, on Vitoria and Suárez.

Indeed, it was a momentous occasion to push on, as Scott explained to Barcia Trelles in that December of 1927. "We are at the decisive moment of the history of international law. If internationalists accept the thesis that Vitoria, Suárez and their great countrymen of the golden age have created international law, . . . we would make them give to the Latin race and the Catholic Church the honor of having given birth to international justice." This pedigree had the potential to join in its ownership Spain and the Latin American republics. Through this powerful ideological tool "we will encourage the Spaniards of the peninsula and of America

[179] See José de Yanguas Messia to Ogden H. Hammond, November 16, 1927; Jacobo Fitz-James Stuart to Ogden H. Hammond, November 19, 1927; and Ogden H. Hammond to Scott, November 21, 1927; all in Folder 5, Box 60, CEIP Papers.

[180] James Brown Scott to Nicholas Murray Butler, December 5, 1927, Folder 5, Box 60, CEIP Papers.

[181] See James Brown Scott to Camilo Barcia Trelles, December 16, 1927, vol. 309, CEIP Papers.

to continue their great common traditions to develop international law so that it takes into account the exigencies of the present, as well as of the future."[182] In other words, Scott was reiterating the key value of history in very pragmatic terms. If he could get Spanish-speaking countries to own the champions of the law of nations of the *siglo de oro*, then they would be ready to accept the corollaries of the principles they formulated in the present. This, of course, had particular value in the context of the codification of American international law through Pan-American institutions, where almost all the States represented were Spanish-speaking.

Scott and Barcia Trelles immediately put themselves to work. Between January and February, Scott used the opportunity of the Pan-American Conference in Cuba. As preparation for the meeting, he made sure that his editorial comment titled "*Asociación Francisco de Vitoria*" would be published in the January issue of AJIL. It is important to note that the AJIL reached primarily North American international lawyers and foreign policy officials but had a wide circulation in Latin America, even if its direct translation into Spanish had been discontinued in 1921.[183] In his five-page piece, Scott told the story of the 1925 celebrations of Grotius organized by the *Institut de droit international* and how they led to the 1926 Dutch visit to Salamanca and the foundation of the Vitoria Association. Then, he gave a short account of the main event organized by the Association to date: the establishment of the Francisco de Vitoria Chair in which he had participated the previous November. In view of the persuasiveness of "attributing to Francisco de Vitoria the paternity of international law," Scott explained, "[i]nternationalists in all parts of the world must wish the association well."[184]

Once in Cuba, Scott revived the idea of sister national Vitoria associations, to be created in each State of the Americas, and of an umbrella continental association, with the goal of cooperating with the *Asociación Francisco de Vitoria*.[185] Approaching informally delegates and dignitaries, he explained to them the importance of having new and better editions with translations of the works of the authors of Salamanca schools, something the Spanish Vitoria Association and, especially, Barcia Trelles were already working on. Notwithstanding the busy schedule of the Conference, Scott managed to ensure many of the participants attended a key academic event. Speaking at the *Institución Hispanocubana de*

[182] James Brown Scott to Camilo Barcia Trelles, December 14, 1927, vol. 309, CEIP Papers, my translation from French.

[183] The AJIL was translated into Spanish between 1912 and 1921, when Scott and Bustamante agreed that it would be more effective to have a more targeted, independent publication where Latin Americans would be able to publish more easily. Then, from 1922, Bustamante directed, under the aegis of the AIIL, the *Revista americana de derecho internacional*, edited and printed in Cuba. See also Juan Pablo Scarfi, *El imperio de la ley*, Buenos Aires: Fondo de Cultura Económica, 2014, pp. 153–62.

[184] James Brown Scott, "Asociación Francisco de Vitoria," *American Journal of International Law*, 22, 1928, pp. 137–8.

[185] See James Brown Scott to Camilo Barcia Trelles, December 5, 1927, vol. 309; James Brown Scott to Camilo Barcia Trelles, January 6, 1928, vol. 311, CEIP Papers.

*Cultura*, he delivered his lecture on Vitoria's *relectiones* as the foundation of international law, by now his signature piece.

Scott hoped to distribute at the Conference the book on the Spanish School and international law that he had been working toward at least since 1925. However, neither edition, one in Spanish and the other in English, was ready in time. The Spanish edition would come out soon after his return to the United States. Barcia Trelles had been working since November to revise and improve the Spanish text of the lectures on Vitoria delivered by Scott in Salamanca. In the meantime, Scott had sent the English text of lectures on Ayala and Suárez to Paris. There, José Matos Pacheco, ambassador of Guatemala to France and Scott's collaborator in Pan-American ventures, would translate them and send them on to Barcia.[186] Scott maintained a hands-on approach toward the edition, adjusting the content and tailoring it toward a Spanish-speaking audience. That was also one of the main functions of Barcia Trelles' introduction to the book: explaining the reasons for a Spanish edition.[187] Scott's idea was to gift a copy to each delegate in Cuba,[188] but he received the proofs just as he was leaving to catch the ship in Miami. There he met his sister Jeannette and left the final proofs with her, revised and accepted, to take back to Washington in what would be a failed last-ditch attempt to have the book sent to Cuba before the adjournment of the Pan-American Conference. In any case, the book was ready in the beginning of April,[189] under the title *El origen español del derecho internacional moderno*.[190]

The English edition, *The Spanish Origin of International Law*,[191] would come out slightly later. In this case, he decided to seek the collaboration of the Jesuit leaders of his university, Georgetown.[192] Published with the university press, the book bore an introduction by Father Walsh, where he underlined the connection of the content with the course on founders given by Scott at the School of Foreign Service in 1926.

The two books bore the same title, save one word,[193] and were indeed very similar. But they were not identical, and their differences partly reflected Scott's evolving thought. As I noted, some differences were mostly formal, aimed at increasing appeal for their respective audiences. For instance, Scott made sure that the Spanish version was lighter on examples from US history, mostly by removing a few paragraphs here and there. The appeal to different audiences was reflected also

[186] See Camilo Barcia Trelles to Scott, November 28, 1927, vol. 309, CEIP Papers.
[187] See James Brown Scott to Camilo Barcia Trelles, December 5, 1927, vol. 309, CEIP Papers.
[188] Ibid.
[189] Camilo Barcia Trelles to James Brown Scott, April 7, 1928, vol. 311, CEIP Papers.
[190] James Brown Scott, *El origen español del derecho internacional moderno*, Publications of the *Sección de estudios americanistas—Universidad de Valladolid*, Valladolid: Talleres tipográficos Cuesta, 1928.
[191] Scott, *The Spanish Origin of International Law*.
[192] See James Brown Scott to Thomas H. Healy, January 23, 1928, Folder 4, Box 53, JBS Papers.
[193] The Spanish title added the adjective "modern" to international law.

by the choice of publishers and authors for the introduction. Barcia Trelles and the University of Valladolid played up the connection of the *siglo de oro* authors with Spain and South America. That the cultural milieu evoked was as well a Catholic one was an obvious aspect that did not need to be underlined in that instance. This was not the case, however, with the United States and, more generally, English-speaking audiences. Having the book published by Georgetown University Press and introduced by a well-respected Catholic priest, educator, and government consultant carried the point effectively. At the same time, to claim objectivity on the subject, Scott would very often remind his audience of his being a Protestant while speaking or writing about the Spanish origin.

The two books, though, had some more substantial differences in terms of content and structure. The Spanish edition was divided in three main sections, each dedicated to one author. The number of pages dedicated to Vitoria was more or less equivalent to the ones treating the work of the other two authors—Balthazar Ayala and Francisco Suárez—combined. The English edition, instead, reflected its subtitle: "Lectures on Francisco de Vitoria (1480–1546) and Francisco Suárez (1548–1617)." There was no separate treatment of the work of Ayala; while the lectures on Vitoria still occupied most of the book's pages, the part on Suárez was only slightly shorter. To make sense of this divergence in the two editions, one could reflect on the more accentuated Catholic characterization given to the *siglo de oro* tradition by Scott in the English-language one. Ayala was a Catholic, but a layman and a legal advisor embedded with an army; the other two were renowned members of the clergy and theologians, with a direct connection to the Church and two powerful monastic orders still operating and influential in Scott's time. Beyond formal attachments, the different context of the work of these thinkers mattered. Indeed, while Ayala's law of war doctrines were in line with Vitoria's, his being engaged in the attempted crushing of a rebellion led him to focus on the lack of legitimate authority to wage war on his foes. That meant, as it would have for Vitoria, that the Dutch were to be considered common criminals, outside the protection of the law of war. Now, this, as Scott was painfully aware, was still a very contentious topic in his time; it would also be one later and up to the present—just think of international legal debates on wars of national liberation in the context of decolonization or on civil war and intervention in the last couple of decades. Wherever Scott's sympathies stood he knew that Ayala's radical approach, "colored . . . by religious feeling and resentment,"[194] was not tenable anymore. As he had himself noted in the course on the founders, it had become "the practice of our day" to recognize some limited rights of belligerency to "an insurgent community."[195] While also Vitoria vested the legitimate authority to wage war on perfect communities, his main application of the norm could be explained through a positive example: the

194 Scott, *The Spanish Origin of International Law*, p. 74.
195 "Fifth Lecture delivered by Mr. James Brown Scott," Folder 8, Box 64, JBS Papers, p. 10.

recognition of that status and the consequent applicability of the rules of just war to the native communities of America. Scott tended to focus on the elements of potential inclusiveness of an ancient theory; then proceeded to simplify the reasoning sustaining it to adapt it more easily to contemporary sentiment and issues. These were key techniques behind Scott's narrative of the Spanish origin—as well as of his earlier historical work. In other words, Vitoria was easier to portray as a humanitarian and the champion of a progressive international law than Ayala was. That might be why Ayala was dropped.

Whatever the initial reasons, from the English edition of the 1928 book onward, Scott's narrative of the Spanish origin would focus almost exclusively on Vitoria and Suárez. As we have seen, Scott had already assigned them their respective roles as protagonists in the inception of international law years before: Vitoria was the founder who had brilliantly found legal solutions to unexplored and unexpected issues; Suárez was the theorist who had worked out the implications of Vitoria's advancements into a philosophy of law. The novelty of the book was not in that. It was in the confidence and frequency with which Scott drew direct and bold connections between their work and contemporary international legal issues. The same style would characterize Scott's later publications on the School of Salamanca, including his best known work on the subject: the two books published in 1934, titled *The Catholic Conception of International Law* and *The Spanish Origin of International Law: Francisco de Vitoria and his Law of Nations*. In light of this, one could arguably call the 1928 book the first mature formulation of Scott's narrative of the Spanish origin.

## Vitoria and the Modern International Law

Scott started the book with an introductory section, based on the first lecture delivered in Salamanca in November 1927, contextualizing Vitoria by remarking on the importance of the discovery of the American continent and describing the sixteenth century as an era of epochal change. The next two sections, based on the second lecture in Salamanca and on the one in Madrid, treat respectively *De Indis* and *De iure belli*. They are made up of summaries of the two *relectiones* to which Scott added comments on the applicability of certain doctrines to the present when he encountered them in the narration. Indeed, the recognition of *dominium* to the natives turned seamlessly into a recognition of statehood: "they were States of the New World to which he would attribute the rights of States in the Old World."[196] Continuing on *De Indis*, Scott remarked how this meant also a universal equality of individual rights, putting Spaniards and American natives on the same foot.

[196] Scott, *The Spanish Origin of International Law*, p. 25.

Adopting once again an ultra-formalistic strain of rights discourse, he argued that Vitoria "was careful to accord to his fellow-countrymen only rights and privileges which the aborigines of America would have, had they made up their minds to visit Spain, to reside there, to engage in industry and commerce, and to preach the doctrine of a higher life."[197]

It was not simply a question of natives making up their minds, though. The consideration that these were rights that the American natives were not in a position to exercise never transpired in Scott's analysis. Neither did the fact that the rights accorded by the Dominican on the matter, very useful for the Spanish activities in America, were criticized as too extensive even by other authors in the Salamanca tradition.

Vitoria had included these actions in *De Indis* under "the *ius communicandi*, the right of inter-human communication or sharing[,] the first and most controversial" among "a series of" potentially "just titles of conquest based on an Indian violation of the *jus gentium*."[198] This right kept at a certain level of unity a mankind otherwise divided in separate communities. It covered a staggering variety of human behaviors, including traveling and living in a foreign land and, crucially, the right to trade among foreigners. The Spanish also had the right to spread the Gospel and the Christian religion and protect the converts. If the natives had prevented the Spanish from exercising those rights, a just cause of war would be triggered, which would open an avenue for legitimate Spanish rule.

It is not surprising that the *ius communicandi* as construed by Vitoria has been considered controversial not only by later commentators but also by theologians in the Salamanca School: no European ruler would have allowed such unfettered freedom of movement to large scores of outsiders, let alone if equipped for war, as was the case. Bypassing the difficulties connected to Vitoria's *ius communicandi*, Scott finally translated it into a modern-day and simplified conception of the right to free trade. As a first step, he equated *ius communicandi* to the global interaction of peoples and connected it to Vitoria's "first adequate definition of international law." Indeed, by defining *ius gentium* as a law determined by natural reason *inter omnes gentes*, among all peoples, and not simply among all men, Vitoria, Scott argued, had created singlehandedly a new legal system: a legal regulation "of the interdependence of States, of their rights and of their reciprocal duties. . . . This law is a real law, which is based upon association, for there is a natural society, there is a mutual intercourse, a communion and a bond among peoples."[199] However, at the end of the day, in explaining the concrete applications of *ius communicandi*,

[197] Ibid., p. 31.

[198] Annabel Brett, "Francisco de Vitoria and Francisco Suárez," in *Oxford Handbook of the History of International Law*, Anne Peters and Bardo Fassbender (eds.), Oxford: Oxford University Press, 2012, p. 1089. See Vitoria, "On the American Indians," Question 3, pp. 277–91.

[199] Scott, *The Spanish Origin of International Law*, pp. 32–33.

Scott reduced this large concept into the need for unencumbered global commercial relations.

Scott found the origin of many more contemporary legal principles prefigured within the passages of *De Indis* to link with his idea of Vitoria as a prophet of modern international equality. One he would insist particularly on in later years was "citizenship *ex jure soli*."[200] Scott deduced it from Vitoria's assertion that "children born in the Indies of a Spanish father . . . cannot be barred from citizenship or from the advantages enjoyed by the native citizens born of parents domiciled in that community."[201] Along with this one, other passages led Scott to find expressed, ahead of their time, "the doctrine of naturalization" and "the doctrine of immigration in what modern practice would consider an exaggerated form." This prompted him to conclude that, "[i]f the term were permissible, we might indeed call these the advance guard of American international law."[202]

The connection between Vitoria's equality and modern America did not stop there. "In branding as illegitimate the title to territory by discovery" to the Spaniards, "as it was held in lawful possession by the Indians and could not, therefore, be *res nullius*," Vitoria had protected America from an illegitimate European seizure. Scott depicted this opinion as "an anticipation of the Monroe Doctrine."[203] To this effect, he quoted the lecture of Barcia Trelles during the 1926 Dutch visit to Salamanca:

> Three centuries later, what Vitoria had wholesouledly defended was maintained by President Monroe in his famous message of 1823, in which he declared that the New World was not susceptible of colonization. The Monroe Doctrine—a sort of gospel, which inspired America's international policy—was defended three centuries earlier by a Spaniard, who proclaimed the principle even more courageously than Monroe.[204]

Scott's explicit goal was "to show Vitoria's foresight, and what may properly be called his prophetic vision. . . . Vitoria must have seemed to those who heard him from his chair in the University of Salamanca, to be far ahead of his time, when to us he seems modern and, in some respects, in advance of our practice if not our thought."[205]

Yet, for all his focus on the equality bestowed by Vitoria on the natives and the prophetic modernity he accorded to the Dominican's thinking, Scott also showed a lot of interest on aspects that could point, arguably, toward a less benevolent

200 On Scott's activism about nationality issues see Chapter 6.
201 Vitoria, *Political Writings*, p. 281.
202 Scott, *The Spanish Origin of International Law*, p. 40.
203 Ibid., p. 39.
204 Camilo Barcia Trelles, Address at the University of Salamanca, April 21, 1926, quoted ibid.
205 Ibid., pp. 39–40.

treatment of the natives. The standard of civilization, a staple of international law between the late nineteenth century and the early twentieth, requiring different rules for less civilized people, seeped in through the cracks of the superficially monolithic depiction of equality Scott made. Vitoria allowed for the theoretical possibility that the Spanish might assume rule over the natives in their interests, by reason of their potential unfitness for a proper government of their community. Scott equated the idea in this passage with the mandate system established by the League of Nations, to which he recognized a humanitarian function.

> We are today, since the World War, wrestling with this problem, and, without acknowledging in any power the right to enter the territory and to take possession of backward peoples, some of the enlightened powers are being entrusted with mandates, on behalf of the nations at large, to assume control of these people in order that, through just laws and their faithful administration, our less fortunate brothers may be fitted for self-government, according to the higher standards than they have known, and for independent existence.[206]

Another humanitarian burden on the community of civilized States in the present Scott found prefigured in *De Indis* was the one of intervention. Vitoria considered it legitimate if it was motivated with the "preserv[ation of] the aborigines of America from tyrannical laws, like those which sacrifice innocent people[.] We who have made a shibboleth of the 'white man's burden' may not condemn the churchman who believed that he was his brother's keeper."[207] More generally, Vitoria in *De Indis* had made the point that a potential legitimate title for Spanish rule over the natives would have been as the result of a just war. And for the Dominican the only just cause of war was the violation of a right, for instance if the natives had forbidden the Spanish to exercise the *ius communicandi*, travel to their lands and trade among them. This consideration led Vitoria to elaborate in another *relectio, De iure belli*.

The following section of the book is dedicated to the comment of the *relectio de iure belli*. Scott had already underlined in the course on the founders that a just war required not only a just cause but also a just authority. Vitoria identified a just authority in the concept of *perfecta communitas*. This concept is, for Scott, identical to that of the sovereign State, *superiorem non recognoscens*, under international law. So, to recapitulate, Vitoria's contribution to the inception of modern international law was chiefly in the elements of the following definition: it was the law "existing between States, which States are obliged to obey, and the rights under this system of law are to be enforced by an appeal to arms if necessary by States against States."[208]

[206] Ibid., p. 39.
[207] Ibid., p. 37. Note that "to be one's brother's keeper" is the biblical expression Scott had already used to characterize the deep motivation behind the US intervention in Cuba in 1898 (see Chapter 2).
[208] Ibid., p. 41.

Starting from this formulation, Scott argued that his belief in international judicial institutions as the most effective tool for peace was a direct corollary of Vitoria's just war theory.

Scott opened his argument by describing "States in the Franciscan system of international law," that is, perfect communities. They were not part of another community and had their own system of government and laws. "[B]eing independent of one another, . . . they are equal as well[.] But while each is self-sufficient as regards the other, this does not exclude interdependence as respects the States taken as a whole. There was such a thing as an international community in [Vitoria's] conception of things."[209]

In the case of monarchies the authority of the community was vested in and exercised by its prince. Therefore, the prince held the just authority to wage war but he could exercise it legitimately only on behalf of the commonwealth and not for private gain or personal glory. Indeed, Scott believed that Vitoria considered "war" as "a law-suit" between States "prosecuted by force in the absence of a court of a superior to which disputes could be submitted."[210] Yet, the absence of a judge meant that the prince himself should perform that role, acting in war and victory with justice and moderation, after carefully considering the advice of wise men. As Scott correctly pointed out, "[t]his idea of the prince as judge permeates the entire Reading."[211] He found it best summed up in the third rule of the last paragraph of *De jure belli*, the one he had used in the 1918 CEIP Yearbook to describe the US attitude in the World War:

> THIRD CANON: once the war has been fought and victory won, he must use his victory with moderation and Christian humility. The victor must think of himself as a judge sitting in judgment between two commonwealths, one the injured party and the other the offender; he must not pass the sentence as a prosecutor but as a judge. He must give satisfaction to the injured, but as far as possible without causing the utter ruination of the guilty commonwealth.[212]

Scott used the "prince as judge" metaphor to push the parallels between a just war and a lawsuit to the maximum extent. To do so more convincingly, he decided to bypass "the question discussed by Francisco whether war can be just on both sides"[213] and offer instead his own more clean-cut solution. Indeed, while Vitoria did not explicitly argue that war could be just on both sides, he and later authors of the Salamanca School are often credited with starting the transition from *justa causa belli* to *justus hostis*, moving the focus from the motivation of the war to the

[209] Ibid., p. 46.
[210] Ibid., pp. 47–8.
[211] Ibid., p. 49.
[212] Vitoria, *Political Writings*, p. 327.
[213] Scott, *The Spanish Origin of International Law*, p. 52.

legitimacy of the belligerents. This, in the case of Vitoria, might be because of his detailed discussion on subjective just intention, describing the moral positions of various actors in a war, starting from the prince down until the common soldiers. Such an interest on the subjective element, fitting for a theologian, rather than on the objective idea of justice, would point to the possibility of a war just on both sides. Scott scrapped this complexity, putting in its place a simplified objectivist legalism. "As the war is a law-suit prosecuted by force, the prince must be sure that the wrong which the State has suffered would justify a cause of action at law. . . . If belief were sufficient, then war would be just on both sides which cannot be if war is in the nature of a law-suit."[214] In a letter to Butler of that same year, Scott summarized the general point in a more explicit way:

> [T]he Scholastic School only allowed of war for a violation of right because there was no court "of the superior" between nations—the implication being that the existence of such a Court would render war unjustifiable. The creation of the Permanent Court of International Justice, with the obligation to resort to pacific methods for settling international disputes, deprives war of its justification; . . . this . . . is the culmination of the philosophy of the Church Universal through the centuries.[215]

After discussing *De iure belli*, Scott concluded the part of the book dedicated to Vitoria with a short section titled "General Observations." There Scott summed up for maximum effect the main intellectual contributions of Vitoria and directly translated them into fundamental principles of modern international law. First, with "[t]he rejection of the claim of the emperor to overlordship and . . . claim to theoretical supremacy,"[216] Vitoria had conceived the principle of equality of States. Secondly, his "[r]ejection of the universal temporal sovereignty of the Pope,"[217] while still considering Christianity as a unity, prefigured the interdependence of States, forming an international community. Nevertheless, Scott argued, "the international community, in the conception of this great and good man, exceeds the limits of Christianity, inasmuch as the outlying principalities of America were regarded as States."[218]

This led to the final point: the achievements of Vitoria would have been unthinkable without the discovery of America. Quoting the Spanish legal historian Eduardo de Hinojosa, Scott explained that the "[q]uestions relating to the conduct of the Spaniards toward the Indians" led Vitoria "to consider and to solve such problems; to recognize the insufficiency of the prevailing theories of international relations, in order to give them a complete solution; to enlarge the scope of its

[214] Ibid., p. 50.
[215] Scott to Nicholas Murray Butler, September 21, 1928, vol. 468, CEIP Papers.
[216] Scott, *The Spanish Origin of International Law*, pp. 59–60. In italics in the original.
[217] Ibid., p. 60. In italics in the original.
[218] Ibid., p. 61.

investigations, extending them to entirely new questions, and by this touchstone, to test the value of ancient theories."[219] Through this process, Scott concluded, "Vitoria . . . created, as I believe, the modern school of international law."[220]

## Suárez and the Philosophy of International Law

Scott began his treatment of Suárez by distinguishing his contribution to international law from Vitoria's. Once again he simplified, possibly to excess, the complexity of scholastic thought: "the fundamental contribution . . . is . . . that the two systems of law, the natural and the law of nations, are two separate systems although it is true they have certain points in common."[221]

For Scott, the intricate scholastic distinctions of Suárez to explain the workings and the spirit of natural law, on one hand, and the law of nations, on the other, boiled down to one main consideration: they were obviously different, the first being a law of necessity, derived from the nature of things, and the latter positive, man-made but their universality and closeness in content accounted for the why they could be easily confused with one another. This characterization related to Scott's recipe for international law in his day. To be sure, he wanted international law to become more like municipal law, finally defeating the Austinian challenge—a positive law, adjudicated by an independent and authoritative judicial system. But this could never happen by just putting wishful thinking on paper. It had to be done according to the wisdom of centuries, embodied in the moral principles developed first by the Spanish theologians. That is what made awareness of both the differentiation and close connection of natural law and international law, conceived by Suárez, so crucial for global progress in Scott's mind.

Scott regretted that in his work "as a theologian, philosopher and logician," Suárez had uttered only "scattered and incidental observations upon the origin and nature of international law." Yet, he found those "fundamental in substance and classic in form."[222] In the 1928 book, Scott focused on two extracts. In one, the thirteenth *disputatio* of the third book on charity of the posthumously appeared *De triplici virtute theologica* (1621), Suárez gave his take on the law of war. In the other, in Chapters 17 to 20 of the second book, *De legibus ac Deo legislatore* (1612), he treated the topics briefly noted at the beginning of this paragraph: the definition of the law of nations and its relationship with other legal systems, both human and divine.

[219] Eduardo de Hinojosa, *Discursos*, pp. 39–40, quoted in ibid., pp. 64–5.
[220] Ibid., p. 65.
[221] Ibid., p. 72.
[222] Ibid., p. 73.

Starting from the former text, Scott praised it for its "scientific" approach, in line with his account of Suárez as the systematic theorist who gave full and final form to the wisdom of the Scholastic tradition. In particular his *disputatio* on war, Scott believed, was the sum of the knowledge of the Spaniards on the subject, on which Grotius would base his own treatise. "Suárez' tractate on war may be taken as the dispassionate treatment of . . . the causes of war, its aim and purposes, and the purposes, and the methods by which it should be conducted. It is the culmination of the Spanish school . . . with no thesis to maintain other than the sacred cause of justice and charity."[223] Now, one could surely agree with Scott, from the point of view that the *disputatio* is definitely not Suárez' most original work. It is indeed, for the most part, an illustration of earlier doctrines. Most importantly here, Suárez agreed with Vitoria on bestowing just authority to wage war on perfect communities and a form of jurisdictional power on the justly warring prince. Scott, then, used the text primarily as a springboard for further elaborations on the relation of war and the international political system along the same lines of his comment to *De jure belli*.

Scott started by repeating his conclusions on legitimate authority. In the same way as Vitoria and Suárez had given such authority to perfect communities, in Scott's age war was an armed confrontation between equal and independent States. The twist Scott found in Suárez' discussion of legitimate authority was in the relationship between the community and its prince. While Vitoria had simply stated that sovereign power was in the community and only conferred on the ruler, Suárez had drawn consequences from it. The Jesuit had been the champion of the Papacy against the theory of the divine rights of kings.[224] That brought him to admit the potential justice of a popular revolt against a tyrannical ruler. This, Scott believed, was another crucial step forward toward the progressive international law of the Americas, the one of republican States: "Suárez is . . . intent on having a monarchy subjected to the people, he is such an advocate of popular sovereignty, which served the end of the Church as well as that of the people of the State." Here we have Scott's first basic element of the international legal system of his present and the future. In the scholastic discussion of legitimate authority one finds a system of independent and equal states, which, being construed on popular sovereignty and justice administered by courts, would eventually guarantee individual equality to their citizens as well.

Once Scott conceived the subjects of the international system in this way, he moved on to describe the law regulating their interactions in case of disputes. The starting point on this issue with Suárez is the same as with Vitoria: the prince having to adopt the role of a judge for lack of a court superior to nations which

[223] Ibid., p. 74.

[224] Suárez' most important work on the topic was *Defensio catholicae fidei contra anglicanae sectae errores* (1613).

could dispense justice between them. Catholic princes had the option of involving the Pope as an arbitrator, but Suárez noted how Popes had very rarely intervened in such fashion, properly exercising caution. Scott was quick to pick on this remark by Suárez to add that "many good people in many parts of the world . . . are still of the opinion that a more frequent intervention of the Pope, through good offices, would be in the interest of peace and good understanding."[225] This included Scott himself, who believed in the positive influence of the Pope on international relations: he personally lobbied the Holy See to come out explicitly in support of the international legal system.[226]

After this digression, Scott followed Suárez back to the main topic: the content of the restorative justice entrusted to the prince-judge. For instance, as the Jesuit asked himself, could a prince, whose community had not directly suffered injustice, "intervene on behalf of others?" In Scott's usual biblical words, "[m]ay he be his brother's keeper?" Suárez denied that a ruler might have the right of avenging wrongs anywhere in the world, without being affected by the injury. Neither God had given this power nor could it be deduced through reason. This generalized power to restore justice would violate the equality of States and engender chaos in international relations, Scott added with a thinly veiled criticism of supporters of collective security in his time. Then, how could intervention be legitimate? To explain the point, Suárez adopted Aristotle's quote: "a friend is another self." A relation of bilateral friendship or alliance with the community wronged made the interest in restoration shared. "[T]he desire, expressed or implied, of the friend and . . . the justice of the cause of war" were the elements of a legitimate intervention. Once again, Scott had an example. It is not a wild speculation to say that he was rehashing his arguments in favor of the intervention of the United States in Cuba in the context of the 1898 Spanish-American War.

Then, the main rule, in this tradition of just war thinking, was that the prince should be somehow directly affected by the wrongdoing to have cause. This, generally, put the prince in the conflicting position of "be[ing] accuser and judge in his own behalf and on behalf of the State or its people."[227] Suárez admitted that this situation was problematic and not according with natural law. Yet, "this act of punitive justice has been indispensable to mankind, and . . . no more fitting method for its performance could, in the order of nature and humanly speaking, be found."[228] Scott once again remarked how the situation had changed from the days of Suárez:

> "[N]ations, . . . because of wars on such a large scale as to threaten the very existence of civilization, have themselves through treaty, constituted a superior, . . . a

[225] Scott, *The Spanish Origin of International Law*, p. 80.
[226] See Chapter 5.
[227] Ibid., pp. 80–1.
[228] Suárez, "Disputation XIII: On Charity," in *Selections from Three Works*, vol. II, p. 819.

> Permanent Court of International Justice . . . , where all disputes of a nature to be settled by a just judge may be decided in advance, not after the resort to arms, by argument of counsel and the application of the principles of international law to which the nations have already give their assent.[229]

Suárez had provided one important step in this long process toward the peaceful settlement of international disputes. Vitoria had prescribed that the prince pondering the justice of his cause of war should rely on the advice of wise men. Suárez went further, suggesting that, when in doubt, the prince could be bound to leave the decision of the dispute with such reputable figures in order to avoid the consequences of a doubtful war. Unfortunately, considering the highly subjective nature of determinations of right intentions, the prince could not be bound by the decision of men he had not himself appointed to such end. Therefore, in practice, given the usual distrust princes had for decisions of foreigners, this procedure rarely produced a solution shared by both parties of a dispute. In any case, Scott argued, this "timid" suggestion of Suárez would gradually turn into modern arbitration.

Then, Scott turned his attention to the chapters in *De legibus* treating matters relevant to modern international law. I have described, at the beginning of this subsection, how, in that work, Suárez clarified both the distinction between natural law and *jus gentium*, and their connection. This, in Scott's view, was a philosophy of the law of nations and a theory of its sources. In the *disputatio* on war, he had found a discussion of subjectivity and dispute resolution under the law of nations. In *De legibus* he also found a theorization of the community of nations, expressed by Suárez in one single section.[230]

Scott's close reading of the passage is divided into four headings. First, Suárez explained that "[t]he rational basis" of *jus gentium* is in the "unity, not only as a species, but also . . . moral and political" of the human kind, notwithstanding its division in communities. This was because of "the natural precept of mutual love and mercy; a precept which applies to all, even to strangers of every nation."[231] This, for Scott, implied "[t]he necessity for an association of States."

Scott's second heading pointed to "[t]he necessity of law for the Association of States."[232] This he derived from Suárez' recognition of a "fact . . . made manifest by actual usage." Even perfect communities "are never" completely "self-sufficient[. T]hey require some mutual assistance, association, and intercourse, at times for their own greater welfare and advantage, but at other times because also of some moral

[229] Scott, *The Spanish Origin of International Law*, p. 82.
[230] Suárez, "A Treatise on Laws and God the Lawgiver," Section 9, Chapter XIX, Book II, in *Selections from Three Works*, vol. II, pp. 348–9.
[231] Ibid., p. 348.
[232] Scott, *The Spanish Origin of International Law*, pp. 90–1. In italics in the original.

necessity."[233] Therefore, Suárez saw the need for a legal system to regulate these interactions among communities.

Suárez' description of "[t]he law of the Association of States"[234] was under Scott's third heading. The Jesuit argued that "although . . . guidance" on this associative aspect of international human relations was "in large measure provided by natural reason," it was "not . . . in sufficient measure and a direct manner with respect to all matters;" it followed that "special rules of law" could "be introduced through the practice . . . of nations."[235] As there was customary law at local or State level, there was a customary law of mankind based on the behavior of nations.

With this point, we have come full circle, back to where we started: the law of the association of nations, according to Suárez, could be fully understood only in the complexity of its relation with natural law. And, indeed, the closing of Suárez' passage is treated by Scott under the following heading: "[t]he law is similar to but not an evident or necessary deduction from natural law."[236] And yet, Suárez concluded, the law of nations, "not . . . absolutely required for moral rectitude," remained "nevertheless quite in accord with nature, and universally acceptable for its own sake."[237]

Scott went on to describe further characteristics of the community of nations he saw in Suárez' conception. Unsurprisingly, they coincided with what Scott had advocated since the earliest steps of his career. In conceiving mankind as united, Scott argued, Suárez had not foreseen an overcoming "of the States nor . . . question[ed] their independence of one another," far from it. His association of nations and its customs were the legal reflection of the moral bond among all human beings, not a call for federation and replacement of the institutions ruling the single communities. An association of nations, not a league, one could say.

As we have seen, Scott had often argued that international law would still be there if, for any reason, all treaties suddenly disappeared. This was because, as Suárez had explained, the main principles and rules of international law derived from human unity rather than passing agreements and institutions, which could at best declare and specify what was already there. But what were the basic rules deriving from the moral bond of humanity? The ones that permitted the interaction between peoples in the first place, Scott and Suárez responded in unison: for instance, immunity for ambassadors and, crucially, freedom of commerce with foreigners. Scott added, through a quote by Suárez, that the prohibition of commerce would be a violation of *jus gentium*. What he did not add was the corollary: Suárez explicitly wrote that such a disruption of trade constituted a just cause of war. Scott had tried to emphasize the cooperative spirit of the law of nations embodied in trade, in an attempt

233 Suárez, "A Treatise on Laws," p. 349.
234 Scott, *The Spanish Origin of International Law*, p. 91. In italics in the original.
235 Suárez, "A Treatise on Laws," p. 349.
236 Scott, *The Spanish Origin of International Law*, p. 91. In italics in the original.
237 Suárez, "A Treatise on Laws," p. 349.

to unite the Americas in a common endeavor of global progress. Yet, the aggressive face of commercial imperialism was hidden just under the surface. And Latin Americans had seen the United States enforce the commercial rights of its citizens with warships too many times in the previous decades not to be alert to the dark sides of the argument.

## "The Ripened Fruit": The Spanish Origin Campaign Looking Forward

The concluding chapter of Scott's book was dedicated to the argument on the foundation of international law we are familiar with by now. He explained why the School of Salamanca had been overlooked in favor of Grotius, primarily for reasons of writing style and religious prejudice; he listed authorities of various national and religious backgrounds that had gone against the current and argued for the Spanish origin of international law before him; finally, he asserted that the time had come to re-establish a more truthful account of the past of the discipline. Adopting again Kosters' metaphor, Scott reminded his readers that Grotius' "hand" had to "pluck the ripened fruit" of Scholastic thought to make him able to give the law of nations a systematic treatment. Now, another fruit was ripe and ready to leave the tree: the awareness of international lawyers, beyond blind spots, of the proper place of Vitoria and Suárez in the inception of their professional subject.

With all the limitations in Scott's approach considered, the book was still an important achievement. His constant parallels between Scholastic doctrines and the international law of the twentieth century, while simplifying and anachronistic, were effective. This was because of Scott's habitual writing techniques that I have already noted in the Prologue about his 1896 speech. His matter-of-fact language aimed at making his assertions self-evident; he presented his simplifications of complex issues as just simple matters after all: what clouded them had been the evolution of language and argumentation over the centuries. This argument could be persuasive with an audience of international lawyers and political operators, often not well versed in the fine points of the history of political thought. Moreover, Scott made himself credible as a translator of that past into the present through humility. His language was flowery, even pompous at times, but always aimed at praising great ideas, political cultures, and men of authority, never himself or his own achievements. In other texts, when he referred to his governmental activity or academic writings, he would always add some formula of modesty, undervaluing his role. This way, putting himself in the background, he allowed his projects to shine more, carried by a claim of self-evidence and the authority of others.

Persuasive or not, with the 1928 book, Scott had achieved a goal close to his heart. He had finally published a text containing several points crucial to his Spanish origin campaign. First, he had established that the foundation of modern international law rested with the theologians of the Salamanca School and the Catholic Church. Second, he had established the connection of that foundation with the discovery of the American continent and made the further link with the continent's egalitarian political culture. For instance, he had introduced freedom of commerce as a crucial feature in the thought of the Salamanca theologians as well as of the progressive international law practiced in the Americas. In a similar fashion, he had employed their just war theory in support of an international judiciary. Third, by depicting differences in the thought of Vitoria and Suárez as limited but crucial steps toward the fundamental principles of the international law of his present, Scott had shown in operation the key elements of his legal philosophy: gradual progress based on moral tradition.

With this intellectual framework in place, along with the institutional and academic alliances he had built in support of the Spanish origin, Scott would set out, in the following years, to employ the authority of Vitoria and Suárez toward concrete political goals. In the remaining chapters of the book I offer an account of two such projects. Chapter 5 details Scott's attempt to forge an alliance with the highest echelons of the Catholic Church. Supported by Father Walsh and Nicholas Murray Butler, Scott would cooperate with several key figures in religious orders and at the Holy See. On countless occasions, Scott explained to the Catholic hierarchy, reaching up to Pope Pius XI, that international law was far from being a secular enterprise. His work was there to show that Catholic clergymen had conceived it in its modern form and, therefore, the Church should own it. The goal was to obtain a full endorsement by the Church of international law as a tool for peace.

Chapter 6, instead, strikes a very different note, at least on the surface. It tells the story of Scott's cooperation with feminist leaders Doris Stevens and Alice Paul. Their common goal was to bring governments to sign the first treaties on women's rights. They achieved this at the 1933 Montevideo Pan-American Conference. Scott's feminist campaign may seem out of character. For him, it meant taking a controversial stand that found a strong resistance even within the Carnegie Endowment. Until then, Scott had methodically avoided controversy during his career. Reading the testimony of people close to him, I have formed the idea that this was not only a political tactic but also a trait of his personality, cherishing respect for tradition, authority, and the powers that be. An example of this usual behavior was his public stance toward the policies of Woodrow Wilson, always supportive even when he was, implicitly or behind the scenes, fighting hard against the president's plans for the postwar global order.[238] Yet, he put himself on the frontline in the fight of women for equal rights, facing criticism in his professional milieu. In this fight, he depicted Vitoria and Suárez as the champions of progress and equality for all human beings, while to the Catholic hierarchy he portrayed them as the symbols of

[238] See Chapter 3.

the moral tradition and authority of the Church. Yet, Scott had not suddenly gone radical. His feminist work started in the late 1920s, when suffrage for women had been already achieved in the United States and the controversy around feminism had subsided to a certain extent. Moreover his activity needs to be understood according to the complexity of the feminist movement in those years, far from being a monolith. Scott's allies were white, liberal, middle- and upper-class women striving for equal rights. After the successful fight for suffrage they had broken off relations with black and working-class feminist groups. In turn, these groups criticized equal-rights feminists for being hypocritically blind to discrimination based on race and class. With this I mean that, while Stevens and Paul had been to jail during the campaign for suffrage and were vocal opponents of the status quo, they were also well-educated insiders of the ruling class. At the end of the day, their political beliefs and views on society were not so far from Scott's own.

Concluding, a key objective of describing these two concrete political uses is to give a sense of the versatility of Scott's narrative of the Spanish origin of international law. The narrative has maintained versatility to this day: Vitoria is still widely portrayed in international legal discourse as a relevant authority, within a striking array of approaches to the discipline and to make extremely diverse types of arguments.

# 5
# The Catholic Conception of International Law

## 1. Early Approaches: Scott and the Catholic Church before the Great War

### American Catholicism at the Turn of the Twentieth Century

James Brown Scott's fascination with the Catholic Church manifested itself early on. It was there much before the beginning of his professional affiliation with Georgetown University in 1920 or his attempts to start a cooperation in the early days of the Carnegie Endowment for International Peace (CEIP) in 1911. In the 1896 speech, he described the important role the Pope had played and could still play as arbitrator of international disputes. In a few paragraphs, Scott gave a historical account spanning centuries, to show the kind of stabilizing power the Church exercised over European nations. The moment that changed the quality of Papal power, according to Scott, was the donation by Pepin the Short of the Franks; in the middle of the eighth century Pepin had conferred to the Pope a strip of territory he had conquered from the Lombards, providing the legal basis for the eventual establishment of the Papal States. "This was a modest beginning no doubt," Scott continued, "but it laid the foundations of that vast temporal power which lasted more than a thousand years and which has fallen only in our day." The "Bishop of Rome," in addition of being "the Spiritual head of the Church," began "to be regarded as the Viceregent of Christ on Earth." As "Christianity [became] an organized power," through this peculiar union of spiritual universal authority and temporal rule, "mankind began to find themselves drawn into a closer union than they had ever known"; it was a move beyond "the power of a single race or nation."[1]

In the growing authority of the Pope over temporal rulers, Scott saw the possibility of the moral enforcement of international justice. In the Middle Ages the Pope had been able to decide the fate of thrones and excommunicate kings and Holy Roman Emperors. "[A] singular" example of "recognition of this universal supremacy" would have an enormous impact on the history of the Americas. It was "in the appeal

[1] James Brown Scott, "International Arbitration: Address of Mr. James Brown Scott before the Sunset Club, Los Angeles, California,1897," MS 1207, Harvard Law School Library Special Collections pp. 16–17.

*Rewriting the History of the Law of Nations: How James Brown Scott Made Francisco de Vitoria the Founder of International Law*. Paolo Amorosa, Oxford University Press (2019). © Paolo Amorosa
DOI: 10.1093/oso/9780198849377.001.0001

of Spain and Portugal to the Pope as Arbiter" following the discovery. Scott attributed to Pope Alexander VI the settling of their claims and the division of "the New World . . . between . . . these two countries." At the point of "highest authority of the Papacy," at the beginning of fourteenth century, "Boniface the 8th" could claim to be the "Arbiter of the World." This "was no idle boast," Scott argued. Indeed, the development of Papal authority could have led international organization in a different direction if "the disputes of opposing religions" had not "interrupted . . . the civilizing and harmonizing work of the Renaissance." If the Reformation "[h]ad not broken from within . . . the power of the Church[,] it is not improbable that the Ecumenical Council of Rome would today constitute a Supreme Court of International Arbitration," Scott affirmed. Once the unity of Christianity was lost and "Europe" was "in the throes of a religious war," "[d]reams of a universal peace"[2] became impossible.

These passages uttered by a young Scott suggest that his long-held convictions on the positive role of the Papacy in international politics went beyond pragmatic alliances or professional connections. These ideas, probably fueled by his studies in legal history in Germany in the first half of that decade, had a strong relation to his mindset and education. On one hand, there was the piety instilled in him since childhood by his Presbyterian family. On the other, there was his legal education and his will to combine Langdell's theory of equality through judicial development and international law. In his mind, this boiled down to clear conclusions. The tradition of Christian morality was the pillar that could sustain adjudication on a universal basis without a coercive mechanism of enforcement; the authority securing and nurturing that moral tradition on a universal scale, and therefore able to interpret it into rules of justice, was the Papacy. It was not to be a marriage of convenience. For Scott, he and the Church of Rome were natural allies.

These were not easy positions for a Protestant to take in the United States in those years, though. That same peculiar form of power enjoyed by the Pope, mixing universal spiritual authority and temporal sovereignty, fueled arguments against Catholicism: it was an extraneous object to the American democratic society; Catholics were a potential fifth column. This was because "of the belief that the Church's hierarchical, authoritarian, and dogmatic structure stood opposed to American political values of freedom and individuality."[3] Moreover, the sovereign nature of Papal power led to a question of conflicting loyalties. Catholics could not be faithful to US institutions, the argument went, because they were already subjects of the Church of Rome. Those arguments were commonly in use since the early days of the republic and would remain popular in similar guises for decades

2 Ibid., pp. 18–19.

3 Zachary Calo, "'The Indispensable Basis of Democracy': American Catholicism, the Church-State Debate, and the Soul of American Liberalism, 1920–1929," *Virginia Law Review*, 91, 2005, p. 1038. For a general account of the peculiarities of the Catholic minority in the United States at the turn of the twentieth century and their implications see Frank T. Reuter, *Catholic Influence on American Colonial Policies, 1898–1904*, Austin: University of Texas Press, 1967, pp. 20–35.

to come. To give but one example, they were the main objections aimed at the presidential bid by the Catholic John F. Kennedy, still in 1960. Electing a Catholic president could mean that the US government would take orders from Rome.

The traditional Protestant hostility to the Catholic Church had turned into an internal problem only in the 1840s. Until then, Catholics had been a very small minority in the United States. The situation changed with the acquisition of Southern territories in consequence of the Mexican-American War (1846–48) and the immigration caused by the Irish Potato Famine (1845–52). "[L]arge numbers of Catholics suddenly became part of the population. The result was to reinvigorate long-standing Protestant hostility to 'Popery' and further reinforce the identification of liberty with the nation's putative Anglo-Saxon heritage."[4]

By the end of the nineteenth century, the anti-Catholic sentiment had grown. The number of immigrants from Ireland and other Catholic countries had risen vertiginously. It had become common to direct at Catholics the stereotypes already rehearsed toward the population of African descent: they were childlike, with little or no self-control. This made them unable to take the responsibility of participating meaningfully in democratic institutions. Instead, they remained completely submissive to the Catholic Church to which they left the full direction of their lives. Several activist groups and legislative campaigns in the late nineteenth century, including the immigration restriction movement and attempts to close parochial schools, had the main goal of curbing the increasing political clout of Catholics. One paradigmatic example of this trend was the widespread support for the Blaine Amendment. In 1875, James G. Blaine, a Republican Congressman from Maine who would later become Secretary of State, proposed a constitutional amendment to forbid government funding of religious schools.[5] The argument was that the Amendment would better ensure the separation of Church and State, already enshrined in the Constitution by the Establishment Clause of the First Amendment. It was also seen as a step toward the establishment of an effective system of public education, free from dogma. The Blaine Amendment was approved by an overwhelming majority in the House, but failed to reach the required two-thirds majority in the Senate by only four votes. Even though it did not make it to the federal Constitution, the text of the Amendment or modified versions of it were introduced in State legislatures. In the course of the next few years, the vast majority of State Constitutions would introduce their Blaine Amendment. They are still in force in over thirty States today. Blaine did not adopt direct anti-Catholic rhetoric during the campaign. Yet, it was obvious to most that the Amendment was an attempt, which turned out to be very successful, to capitalize on anti-Catholic sentiment and muster Protestant support around the Republican Party.

[4] Eric Foner, *The Story of American Freedom*, New York: W. W. Norton, p. 77.

[5] On the history of the amendment and its political implications see Steven K. Green, "The Blaine Amendment Reconsidered," *American Journal of Legal History*, 36, 1992, pp. 38–69.

The 1898 Spanish-American War complicated the situation further. The confrontation with a major Catholic power, motivated by the massive atrocities perpetrated by Spain on the Cuban population, could not but reinforce sentiments of Protestant exceptionalism and their natural complement, assertions of Catholic inferiority and backwardness.[6] The quick and effortless victory of the United States made it easier to attribute the country's rise to Protestantism, while Spain's decadence was linked to its Catholic religion.

Nevertheless, Catholics in the United States saw the war as an opportunity to make a show of patriotism and integrate better in the country. Their unexpected support for the war came out of an analysis of religious loyalties that was necessarily less straightforward than the one made by Protestants. True, Spain was a country of Catholic heritage, trying to maintain "control of a traditional hub of New World Catholicism. But the people being oppressed by Spanish colonialism—not only Cubans, but Puerto Ricans and Filipinos as well—were also mostly Catholic. Thus any war would be a campaign *against* Catholics *for* Catholics."[7]

To better grasp the context, one should also consider the changes that Catholicism was undergoing in the United States in those years. Made up of diverse national communities, living in widely different socio-cultural conditions within the United States, American Catholics were finding their own identity under the leadership of Americanist clergymen like John Ireland, Archbishop of Saint Paul, Minnesota. This shaping identity was modeled around US national values, along more individualist and liberal lines than Catholicism at its traditional geographic core, at least in social and political if not in church matters. This trend found opposition among US Catholics[8] but especially in Rome:[9] the tension between the Papacy and the American branch would be managed but the divergence of approaches would remain. In any case, American Catholic leadership placed itself firmly within Church orthodoxy and denied any link to modernism.[10] Human progress, patriotism, and democracy co-existed harmoniously with submission to the Pope's dogmatic authority in the belief-system of the American Catholics and their Church, John Ireland argued. "Liberty and authority are one." They both had divine origin and guaranteed each other. Catholic tradition recognized the people's right to decide the form of government, and the duty to respect it once it was constituted: "[a]uthority is from God, and civil governments rule by right divine."

[6] See Matthew McCullough, *The Cross of War: Christian Nationalism and U.S. Expansion in the Spanish-American War*, Madison: The University of Wisconsin Press, 2014 , pp. 46–52.

[7] Andrew Preston, *Sword of the Spirit, Shield of Faith: Religion in American War and Diplomacy*, New York: Alfred A. Knopf, 2012, p. 217. Italics in the original.

[8] On the debate between Americanists and conservatives, focused on how American Catholicism should relate to the modern age see McCullough, *The Cross of War*, pp. 52–4.

[9] In this respect see Leo XIII's encyclicals *Longinqua* (1895) and *Testem Benevolentiae Nostrae* (1899), both specifically directed at the Church in the United States.

[10] See, for instance, John Ireland, "The Dogmatic Authority of the Papacy: The Encyclical on Modernism," *The North American Review*, 187, 1908, pp. 486–97.

Therefore, "[t]he charge . . . against the Catholic Church that she interfere[d] with the duties of citizenship by dividing the allegiance of subjects" was "without foundation." Jesus himself had marked the boundary between spiritual and temporal power, leaving the latter to Caesar. "It [wa]s, consequently, Catholic doctrine that in America loyalty to the Republic is a divine precept, and that resistance to law is a sin crying to heaven for vengeance." Ireland closed the 1884 speech containing these quotes with a pledge:

> Republic of America, [. . . b]elieve me, no hearts love thee more ardently than Catholic hearts, no tongues speak more honestly thy praises than Catholic tongues, and no hands will be lifted up stronger and more willing to defend, in war and in peace, thy laws and thy institutions than Catholic hands. [11]

US Catholics kept Ireland's promise. "Catholics joined [military service] in disproportionate numbers; indeed well over half of the *Maine*'s casualties were Roman Catholic."[12] The approaching war prompted a show of unity. Both Americanist and conservative Catholics fully supported the government. On March 19, after the sinking of the *Maine* but before the beginning of the war, Ireland ensured in an interview that "[n]o true American Catholic . . . w[ould] think of espousing the cause of Spain against that of this country because the former is a Catholic nation."[13]

Once war broke out, the Catholic response went beyond patriotism and direct participation in the military effort. Catholic leaders inscribed the confrontation between the United States and Spain in the same larger historical and providential framework as Protestant ministers. Also for them, the United States was the chosen nation fighting on behalf of humanity against a nation representing brutality and moral corruption. The only difference in the Catholic account, not surprisingly, was that they strongly denied that Spain's religion had anything to do with its fall. Even the staunchest Catholic conservative, when speaking in connection with the war, could sound like "the most radical Americanist or Catholic-hating Protestant."[14] Take the example of the juxtaposition of America and Europe given in May 1898 by Bishop Bernard McQuaid of Rochester, who had denounced Ireland's Americanism from the pulpit in that same year:

> When we find that the principles underlying our government are those which make people great and noble, have we not cause to be proud of this country of ours. The nations of Europe have again and again pointed at us the finger of scorn, and have taken pains to blazon our failings to the world. But we are not

[11] John Ireland, "The Catholic Church and Civil Society," in *The Church and Modern Society: Lectures and Addresses*, New York: D.H. McBride & Co., 1903, pp. 41, 43, 52, 61, and 65.

[12] Preston, *Sword of the Spirit, Shield of Faith*, p. 217.

[13] Quoted in McCullough, *The Cross of War*, p. 54.

[14] Ibid., p. 58.

looking for lessons from Europe. We want a country unshackled by the chains of European customs.[15]

When looking at their reaction to the Spanish-American War, it is easier to understand the mindset that would bring US Catholic leaders and James Brown Scott closer. It went beyond the aspects I underlined in the 1896 speech at the beginning of this section, the historical role and the universal authority of the Papacy over the Christian moral tradition. They shared an understanding of the place of the United States in God's design to civilize mankind. US Catholics too were ardent believers in a providentially sanctioned American exceptionalism.

## CEIP and the Pontifical Letter of 1911

Like Scott, the US Catholic clergy considered the Spanish-American War a war for justice. Traditional authorities like Vitoria and Suárez had affirmed that war was not sinful or to be condemned in itself: the yardstick against which the faithful should measure it was the justice of its cause. This mindset, ingrained in Catholic doctrine for centuries, was very much alive at the turn of the twentieth century. Accordingly, US Catholic leaders were suspicious of everything that sounded like militant pacifism. "A few, like Archbishop John Ireland frankly glorified war and gave the peace movement no sympathy whatsoever."[16] Most, instead, took a pragmatic approach. They praised the work of peace organizations when they were at the peak of their popularity with the political establishment; they were quick to disassociate themselves when the deteriorating international situation caused the peace movement to be less appealing. Prominent among the pragmatists was Cardinal James Gibbons of Baltimore. Only the second American to be created Cardinal in 1886, he was the first to attend a Conclave, the one which saw the election of Giuseppe Melchiorre Sarto as Pope Pius X in 1903.

In 1911, when the movements for peace and international adjudication enjoyed extensive support, Gibbons and James Brown Scott found common ground to cooperate. In the May of that year Gibbons was among the speakers at the American Peace Conference, together with US President William Howard Taft and James Brown Scott. The conference had been organized by Theodore Marburg and Hamilton Holt, still close allies of Scott and not yet supporters of collective security. It was held in Baltimore, the see of Gibbons' Archdiocese and Marburg's hometown. The main topic discussed at the conference was arbitration established by bilateral treaties, a topic President Taft had put back on the political agenda

[15] Quoted in ibid.

[16] C. Roland Marchand, *The American Peace Movement and Social Reform, 1889–1918*, Princeton: Princeton University Press, 2015 [1973], p. 334.

the previous year. In a speech of March 1910, he had proposed arbitration treaties covering international disputes of all natures, beyond the usual exclusion of vital interests or questions of national honor. Taft admitted to his aide that the speech's goal was to soothe "the opposition of 'Carnegie and other peace cranks' to the four new battleships provided in the Naval Appropriations Bill."[17] Nevertheless, international arbitration quickly and genuinely grew on him until it became one of his favorite causes.[18]

Gibbons opened the Baltimore Conference with a short speech entitled "A Prayer for Peace." The possibility of a general arbitration treaty between the United States and Great Britain, prompted Gibbons to reflect on the common providential role of the Anglo-Saxon race. "England and the United States," he said rehearsing a familiar argument, "have been more happy in reconciling and in adjusting legitimate authority with personal individual liberty than any other nations on the face of the earth." After the flood, God had renewed the covenant with mankind through Noah and marked the event by causing "a rainbow to appear in the Heavens." In the same way, the "outstretched arms" of "Britannia and Columbia[,] join[ed . . . ] across the Atlantic [would] proclaim to mankind that with God's help never more again shall this earth of ours be deluged with bloodshed, fratricide or war." Gibbons concluded by praying for the audience of the Conference, hoping that they would "deserve . . . that title bestowed upon the friends of peace by the Prince of Peace, 'blessed are the peacemakers, for they shall be called the children of God.'"[19]

Unsurprisingly, Scott highly appreciated Gibbons' speech. He immediately wrote to Nicholas Murray Butler recommending the publication of the speech under the aegis of the Carnegie Endowment.[20] In the same letter, Scott informed Butler that he had met Gibbons to discuss a collaboration. During "the course of the conversation [Scott] learned that the Church in America look[ed] after the school books used in th[e] country in [Catholic] schools, colleges and universities." In other words, Gibbons "could have histories prepared along" the Endowment's "lines and introduced into Catholic Institutions, if he [had been] convinced of the advisability of [the] project." The Cardinal agreed with Scott that history books should focus more "upon the peaceful development of the United States and that he would recommend that wars, campaigns and the details of battles should play a

[17] John P. Campbell, "Taft, Roosevelt, and the Arbitration Treaties of 1911," *The Journal of American History*, 53, 1966, p. 279.

[18] For an account of the development of and the opposition to Taft's arbitration treaties see E. James Hindman, "The General Arbitration Treaties of William Howard Taft," *The Historian*, 36, 1973, pp. 52–65.

[19] *Proceedings of the Third American Peace Congress held in Baltimore, Maryland, May 3 to 6, 1911*, edited by Eugene Noble, Baltimore: William & Wilkins Company, 1911, pp. 2–4.

[20] Eventually the speech was published in *International Conciliation*, the organ of the homonymous association led by Butler (vol. I, 1907–11, pp. 733–5), and in the periodical of the American Peace Society (*Advocate of Peace*, 73, 1911, pp. 277–8).

less important role than heretofore." Scott "saw [Gibbons] smile at the moral leadership which" the introduction of "improved school books . . . would give to his Church." Now, this was the very interesting chance of collaboration that had come out of the meeting. But Scott had gone in with something larger in mind. The goal was to reach the Curia in Rome and, eventually, bring the Pope himself over to the cause of peace through international justice. But, given the success of the meeting, Scott "made no mention of interesting Rome in the matter," as things seemed already heading in the right direction.

> [I]f we succeed in having proper histories prepared and used in the Catholic schools of America we would be doing all that we now have in mind and a concrete example and the approval it would elicit would probably be more persuasive with the Vatican than any and all theoretical arguments we might lay before [Cardinal Secretary of State] Merry del Val or others of authority.[21]

Scott's cautious approach in reaching the Catholic hierarchy in Rome lasted only a couple of weeks. By the beginning of June, he was able "to report considerable progress in . . . interesting the Catholic Church in the educational aspect of the peace movement." Scott was not simply speaking of history schoolbooks in one nation this time. At that year's Mohonk Conference, he had met Archbishop Diomede Falconio, the Apostolic Delegate to the United States. Scott "was delighted to inform" Butler that Falconio had "written a long and careful report, upon his own initiative, to Rome." The goal of the communication was to suggest "to the Pope that an encyclical be issued, proprio motu, and addressed to the Catholic hierarchy throughout the world requiring that emphasis be laid in all the Catholic schools upon . . . the advantage of the pacific settlement of international conflicts . . . and . . . the spiritual, moral and peaceful development of the peoples forming the family of nations."

Scott affirmed "to have taken the greatest care not to appear in the movement, because the chances of success are greater if the initiative seems to be taken by the Church instead of upon the suggestion of an outsider."[22] Yet, the style and the wording of the letter Falconio sent to Rome suggest at least some inspiration by him. In any case, the text brought "to the notice of his Holiness, the Pope, the universal movement making for peace among nations." However, the universality of the movement did not transpire from the letter, which mentioned specifically only US efforts: the work of President Taft on international arbitration and the commitment to the cause of "[p]olitical and philanthropical bodies" and the public opinion. It was only fitting and coherent with "the role [the Holy See] had played

[21] Scott to Nicholas Murray Butler, May 15, 1911, Folder 7, Box 10, JBS Papers.

[22] Scott to Nicholas Murray Butler, June 1, 1911, Folder 8, Box 10, JBS Papers. Underlining in the original.

in the past . . . to secure peace . . . that the Vicar of the Prince of Peace" would use "the august word . . . among the distracted nations of the earth [and] give the movement . . . the impulse necessary to achieve its success."[23]

Scott's excitement at the idea of an encyclical on peace was evident. He was preaching caution in a passage of the letter, just to get ahead of himself in the next, planning the next moves as if the encyclical had already been issued: one third of the letter to Butler is dedicated to explaining how to "secure intelligent compliance with it" by the "ninety dioceses in the United States."[24] The encyclical never came, though. Pius X gave an official response to Falconio's request, but not with an encyclical, the highest form a Papal pronunciation on Catholic doctrine could take. The Pope would send Falconio a Pontifical letter, but Scott was not disheartened. Rather, he set out to explain to his colleagues how big a success this was and made arrangements to give the letter as much public resonance as possible. After all, "the Pontifical letter" was "the highest of all documents except the encyclical,"[25] as he was quick to remark. Before its arrival, he informed Butler that it would "appear in the Acta Sanctae Sedis, . . . the official journal of the Holy See, . . . sent to the officers of the Church in all parts of the world. [ . . . I]t [wa]s not merely a letter but . . . a solemn pronouncement of the Church," that would be declared in "sermons from the pulpit" so that Catholic believers could "live up to its recommendations."[26]

The letter was expected by the first or the second day of July.[27] Not seeing it on the third, Scott was already panicking: "What if it should get lost—and we should never see it? Such a thought, with due apologies to your Church," he wrote to his friend Father Maguire, "is as a Purgatory to me."[28] When the letter reached him two days later, Scott immediately forwarded it to Butler,[29] Root,[30] and Carnegie.[31] He had also already made arrangements for Falconio to send it through official channels to President Taft, warning the White House to be ready with an appropriate reply to the Pope on behalf of the American people.[32] Moreover, he shared with his colleagues the editorial comment he had already written for the next issue of the *American Journal of International Law* (AJIL). He had even held up the final editing and printing so that the Journal could mention the event.[33] In the short editorial, Scott sought to give the letter the widest significance possible. With it,

23 "Contents of the letter addressed to the Holy See, on May 30th, 1911," Folder 8, Box 52, JBS Papers.
24 Scott to Butler, June 1, 1911.
25 Scott to Nicholas Murray Butler, July 6, 1911, Folder 9, Box 10, JBS Papers.
26 Scott to Nicholas Murray Butler, June 24, 1911, Folder 8, Box 10, JBS Papers.
27 See Scott to Nicholas Murray Butler, June 27, 1911, Folder 8, Box 10, JBS Papers.
28 Scott to John D. Maguire, July 3, 1911, Folder 9, Box 10, JBS Papers. Father Maguire, a priest from Philadelphia who taught Latin at the Catholic University of America, had been the insider helping Scott with his approaches to the clergy leaders. Scott would involve Maguire also in the edition of the early issues of the Classics of International Law.
29 See Scott to Nicholas Murray Butler, July 5, 1911, Folder 9, Box 10, JBS Papers.
30 See Scott to Elihu Root, July 5, 1911, Folder 9, Box 10, JBS Papers.
31 See Scott to Andrew Carnegie, July 8, 1911, Folder 9, Box 10, JBS Papers.
32 See Scott to John D. Maguire, June 27, 1911, Folder 8, Box 10, JBS Papers.
33 See ibid.

Pius X had "assumed the moral leadership of the world." Comparing the current Pope to his predecessor Gregory VII, who had Holy Roman Emperor Henry IV on his knees at Canossa in 1077, Scott saw "the world bow[ing] before the Pontiff true to his mission, armed only with the sword of Spirit and the breast-plate of righteousness."[34]

Beyond Scott's lyricism, the Pontifical letter was a source of satisfaction for the CEIP leadership with good reason. Not only had Pius X touched on many of their favorite themes, but he also gave them credit for their work, in an indirect yet unmistakable way. The Pope opened the letter by acknowledging "that in the United States . . . the more judicious members of the community are fervently desirous of maintaining the advantages of international peace." This was possible because of "the leadership of men enjoying the highest authority with the people." The prominence given to the letter in the publications of organizations led by Scott and his closest colleagues[35] was also meant to underline that those leading men praised by Pius X were none other than them, if there was any doubt.[36] The Pope shared their diagnosis of the current state of world affairs: "vast armies, instrumentalities most destructive of human life, and the advanced state of military science portend wars which must be a source of fear even to the most powerful rulers." Therefore, the Pontiff crucially underlined, peace activism was not necessarily an expression of subversive politics, quite the contrary. It had the power to strengthen order and national institutions:

> To compose differences, to restrain the outbreak of hostilities, to prevent the dangers of war, to remove even the anxieties of the so-called armed peace, is, indeed, most praiseworthy, and any effort in this cause . . . manifests . . . a zeal which cannot but redound to the credit of its authors and be of benefit to the state. . . . For, inasmuch as peace consists in order, who will vainly think that it can be established unless he strives with all the force within him that due respect be everywhere given to those virtues [of justice and charity] which are the principles of order and its firmest foundation?

Pius X pointed out how peacemaking had been a traditional cause for the Church, citing "the example of so many of [his] illustrious predecessors." Concluding, he "most earnestly pray[ed] God . . . that He may . . . grant to the nations which with united purpose are laboring to this end that the destruction of war and its disasters

[34] "The Pontifical letter of June 11, 1911 on International Peace," *American Journal of International Law*, 5, 1911, p. 708.

[35] For instance, beyond Scott's editorial in AJIL, the text of letter was published, like Gibbons' speech, in Butler's *International Conciliation* (vol. I, 1907–11, Document No. 46, September 1911, pp. 799–804).

[36] "Personally, I am proud of this mark of appreciation, but I appreciate it even more from a practical standpoint because it will show who originated the project, and it will perhaps go far to convince the doubting Thomases of what the future has in store" (Scott to Butler, July 6, 1911).

being averted, they may at length find repose in the beauty of peace."[37] Scott found "the Papal utterance" so "[a]dmirable" and encouraging that he "look[ed] upon it as a first step, as a prelude to an encyclical on peace." He was convinced that the Pope would come to fully espouse his views "and prescribe the means, particularly educational, by which the coming generation can be impressed with the advantage of peaceful settlement, and history taught as the hand-maid of justice and progress."[38]

With this goal in sight, Scott abandoned all earlier caution about addressing the Vatican directly. By the end of September he was in Rome, making his case in a private audience with Cardinal Secretary of State Rafael Merry del Val, the Pope's right-hand man. After "listen[ing] attentively to" Scott's "rather lengthy monologue . . . detail[ing] the project," the Cardinal exposed his doubts, the usual ones the Catholic Church harbored toward peace activism. "He seemed to think that I wished war as such condemned," Scott wrote to one of his insider allies, British Benedictine Abbot Francis Aidan Gasquet. Unsurprisingly, Merry del Val reasserted the basic tenet of just war theory: "it was impossible to condemn it absolutely and he stated that the use of force was often necessary to secure justice." Scott explained that he did not take issue with that and his "chief desire was to remove the causes of war and to call into being an enlightened public opinion which would insist upon justice being done." As Scott affirmed many times in those years, it was a "process of education."[39] The title of the memorandum Scott had provided Merry del Val with in view of their meeting also made that clear: "Educational Opportunity of the Church to Further Universal Peace."[40] The memorandum treated familiar themes and goals: disarmament, arbitration, and judicial settlement.

But Cardinal Merry del Val had further doubts. He objected that the "proposals dealt with the material aspects of the case whereas the Church if it should undertake the project would approach it from the moral and spiritual standpoint." In reply, Scott "assured him that the brief memorandum purposely excluded this phase of the subject as wholly within the province of the Church." His intention had been "merely to aid any action the Church might care to take by calling attention to matters of a kind calculated to supplement spiritual measures."

After the rocky start of the meeting, the conversation finally moved to the matter of the letter and its possible follow-up by an encyclical. The Cardinal informed Scott that an encyclical had been already considered when the Pope had issued the letter in June. The fact that the letter had been received positively within the Church and the general public opinion had left the Holy See open to the possibility of a

[37] The official version of the letter is published in the Latin original in *Acta Apostolicae Sedis,* vol. III, 1911, 473–4. Both the Latin text and its official English translation, which I have been quoting, are available as *International Conciliation*'s Document No. 46, September 1911, pp. 799–804.

[38] Scott to Butler, July 5, 1911.

[39] Scott to Francis Aidan Gasquet, October 8, 1911, Folder 11, Box 10, JBS Papers. Underlining in the original.

[40] Folder 13, Box 52, JBS Papers.

further pronouncement on the subject of peace. Merry del Val was non-committal but Scott, characteristically, decided to see the glass half-full. For instance, he decided to consider positively that the Cardinal did not invite him to meet the Pope, as that could have been simply "a diplomatic way of ending matters."[41]

However, writing his account of the meeting in early October, Scott was able to mention the main obstacle to his quest for an encyclical. Two days after his conversation with Merry del Val, on September 29, 1911, Italy had declared war over Libya to the Ottoman Empire. Scott perfectly understood that the Church would not come out with an official document on peace until the war was over.[42] But he did not worry much about it, as the general conviction was that Italy would win easily and quickly. Scott remained confident that the encyclical was forthcoming through the autumn and the winter,[43] notwithstanding the prolonging of the Libyan war. He spent that time continuing his work of bringing Catholics and peace activism closer together: in the early months of 1912 he delivered a course titled "The Constructive Peace Movement" at the Catholic University of America.[44]

By the end of the course in May, with the Italian army still struggling to gain any stable control of the Libyan interior, Scott finally realized that his goal would not be fulfilled anytime soon.[45] The Italo-Turkish war would continue until October 1912. Notwithstanding the unexpected Ottoman resistance in Libya, the war had given a practical demonstration of the known weakness of the Empire. Balkan States sought to exploit it for territorial gains. Serbia, Bulgaria, Greece, and Montenegro attacked the Ottoman Empire, starting that series of conflicts known as the Balkan wars, which lasted until August 1913. At least by October 1913, Scott was already back at work, recruiting new Catholic allies for a further attempt to bring the Vatican around.[46] It was in this period that Alfred Vanderpol, the Frenchman who shared Scott's passion for Scholastic theology,[47] explained to him why he had founded the *Ligue des catholiques français pour la Paix*. His goal had been to show how much Christian doctrine had traditionally favored peace over war and that just war theory had been much more rigorous in its evaluation of legitimate use of force in earlier centuries. Looking toward the past was not a mere cultural fancy but a strategy aimed at "effect on public education and

[41] Scott to Gasquet, October 8, 1911.

[42] Confirming Scott's thinking, Merry del Val would say to the Canadian priest Alfred Edward Burke, also enquiring about a peace encyclical, "that with the drums beating and the cannons belching, and the rumours of wars throughout the world at the moment, it were better to seek a more opportune time for the lancing of any such document, so that it might have more effect and not be misconstrued by any power actually engaged in militant operations" (Alfred Edward Burke to Charles Fitzpatrick, January 20, 1912, Folder 6, Box 1, JBS Papers).

[43] See Scott to Charles Fitzpatrick, November 20, 1911, Folder 11, and February 13, 1912, Folder 12, Box 10, JBS Papers.

[44] An extended draft of the first lecture titled *The Pontifical Brief and the Peace Movement* is in Folder 5, Box 55, JBS Papers.

[45] See Scott to Charles Fitzpatrick, May 26, 1912, Folder 14, Box 10, JBS Papers.

[46] See Scott to Alfred Vanderpol, October 31, 1913, Box 562, CEIP Papers.

[47] See Chapter 4 section 1.

opinion." This made sense especially if one took "into account the influence that [could] be exerted on Catholics—that is to say, the members of a religion based on authority and tradition—by showing what this tradition is."[48] If Scott had not considered the power of the Scholastic tradition with Catholics in this light before, he surely would in the following years thanks to Vanderpol. Indeed, Scott praised his colleague's publications on the early Christian doctrine on war because, with them, he "ha[d] rendered not merely a service to international law[,] but he ha[d] shown that sincere and devout Catholics can very properly accept the views of the partisans of international peace." His historical work proved that "the most accredited theologians and canonists of the Catholic Church have pronounced themselves squarely in favor of restrictions and limitations upon the right of war, which, if they were observed in the present day, would go far to maintain international peace. If the Catholic Church . . . would insist upon the views of its greatest theologians[,] a great impetus would be given to our movement,"[49] Scott argued.

He would not be able to use this insight right away, because of the outbreak of the Great War in the summer of 1914. Shortly after, Pope Pius X, already in poor health, would die of a heart attack. Writing in 1915 to his colleague Hans Wehberg, Scott told of his efforts and regretted that "[t]here was really no opportunity during the lifetime of the late Pope for him to issue the Encyclical in times of profound peace." Nevertheless, the project of engaging the Vatican was worth it and Scott vowed to "take the matter up again when peace [would be] restored." After all, "in [his] opinion, the Papacy [wa]s the one great agency which c[ould] do most for the cause of peace, if it [wa]s only so inclined."

> The great thing is to create public opinion, and I have no better way than to begin with the children in the schools. We Protestants, divided as we are into a thousand and one jarring sects, cannot take, it would seem, concerted action, whereas at a nod from the Pope the whole system of education can be changed in Catholic schools, and, if that were done, the Protestants would have to follow.[50]

In short, Scott would keep "[b]elieving . . . that the Papacy ha[d] more power for good than any single other organization"[51] and trying to explain the Catholic hierarchy how to wield that power toward the goal of global peace. Further attempts to sway the Vatican to international law by CEIP would have to wait until the mid- and late 1920s, a time of renewed anti-Catholicism in the United States. Scott would make his improved case even later, in the mid-1930s. This time, he

48 Alfred Vanderpol to Scott, December 3, 1913, Box 562, CEIP Papers.
49 Scott to Jules Prudhommeaux, January 17, 1913, Box 562, CEIP Papers.
50 Scott to Hans Wehberg, June 8, 1915, Box 566, CEIP Papers.
51 Scott to Hans Wehberg, September 15, 1915, Folder 5, Box 11, JBS Papers.

would employ the theological tradition of Salamanca as the common language he shared with the Catholic Church.

## 2. The Background of the Catholic Conception

### Neo-Scholasticism and US Democracy

Throughout the 1920s, a series of disparate developments brought Scott closer to the Catholic Church and facilitated his renewed quest for a Papal endorsement of international law. As we saw in the previous chapter, Scott had been working for a prominent Catholic academic institution, Georgetown University, since the start of the decade. In addition, he could count on a direct relationship between the Holy See and the CEIP, which, starting in 1926, provided funding and expertise for a major reorganization of the Vatican Library. Yet, the intellectual fodder for a more articulated case for international law to present to Rome came from a rethinking internal to US Catholicism. During the 1920s, the uncertain place of Catholicism in the country led to a productive reflection on the larger issue of the role of religion in a liberal society, whereby Catholics claimed a role as the foremost defenders of American democracy. Part of this intellectual process was a recovery of the rationalist tradition within Catholic political and moral thought. This Neo-Scholasticism relied not only on the authority of Thomas Aquinas and the Salamanca School, but also on later Jesuit thinking.

This reflection had developed out of the realization that Protestant America still harshly rejected Catholicism. As with the Spanish-American War, US Catholics had seen in the First World War, an opportunity to prove their patriotism and loyalty to democratic institutions.[52] Once again, they delivered an impressive contribution to the war effort.

> A sense of expectation, even entitlement, pervaded the Catholic community in the early 1920s as wartime enthusiasm transformed into postwar optimism and the belief that anti-Catholicism was finally withering. . . . In spite of such confidence, the anticipated embrace from non-Catholic America never materialized.[53]

Indeed, the postwar years saw a revival of the Ku Klux Klan, the restriction of immigration from Catholic countries, and further institutional action, especially at the State level, against the Catholic school system. These were "incarnation[s] of the nativism that had targeted Catholics in the past. But what

[52] On the Catholic response to the First World War in the United States see Preston, *Sword of the Spirit, Shield of Faith*, pp. 268–71 and Calo, "'The Indispensable Basis of Democracy,'" pp. 1043–4.
[53] Calo, "'The Indispensable Basis of Democracy,'" p. 1044.

distinguished anti-Catholicism in the 1920s was the participation of more respectable Americans"[54] who kept insisting on the issue of divided loyalties. Obedience to Rome prevented full commitment to the US Constitution. Protestant fears of a US president directed from the Vatican became more concrete as the popularity of Alfred Smith, the Catholic governor of New York, was rising.[55] A Catholic president, the argument proceeded, would act to undermine the constitutionally sanctioned separation of church and State, allowing the Catholic Church to take over governmental institutions and destroy democracy itself.

Catholics reacted in immediate, visible ways, finally showing a relatively united front beyond their ethnic divisions.[56] The most remarkable public demonstration came on September 21, 1924 when a reported 100,000 members of the Society of the Holy Name,[57] gathered in Washington, D.C. to protest anti-Catholicism and reaffirm loyalty to the nation, and were addressed by President Coolidge. The intellectual response to anti-Catholicism I have referred to came, naturally, more slowly and less noticeably. The main figure in this enterprise was John A. Ryan (1869–1945),[58] professor of moral theology at the Catholic University of America. Ordained priest by Archbishop Ireland in 1898, since the early years of the twentieth century Ryan had become known as a leading Catholic advocate of economic reform,[59] employing theological insights to deal with social and political issues. During the 1920s, Ryan sought to explain how US Catholics could consistently support the separation of Church and State, in apparent opposition to the official doctrine set in Rome. The Papacy had not condemned liberalism as such, rather the virulent anti-clericalism and opposition to religion of its European form. Liberalism in the United States, in its turn, had produced separatism in order to protect and promote a generalized freedom of religion. Under the American pro-religion brand of liberalism separation was a satisfactory arrangement under actual social conditions for Catholics. It was compatible with the Papal teachings which pointed to Church–State union only as an ideal state of things. Through the ideal-actual distinction, Ryan had created a space for US Catholics to respect Rome's

[54] Ibid., p. 1045.

[55] Rebuffed by his own party for his religious affiliation in 1924, Smith would obtain the Democratic nomination for the Presidential elections of 1928, only to lose to the Republican candidate Herbert Hoover.

[56] See generally, Lynn Dumenil, "The Tribal Twenties: 'Assimilated' Catholics' Response to Anti-Catholicism in the 1920s," *Journal of American Ethnic History*, 11, 1991, pp. 21–49.

[57] See ibid., p. 21.

[58] For a detailed account and analysis of Ryan's thought on the matters at hand and its relationship to Papal pronouncements see Calo, "'The Indispensable Basis of Democracy,'" on which I also primarily rely.

[59] The work that established Ryan as a public intellectual was John A. Ryan, *A Living Wage: Its Ethical and Economic Aspects*, New York: The MacMillan Company, 1906, in which he argued for the right of workers to an adequate income. Ten years later he expanded his analysis of economic inequality with the book *Distributive Justice: The Right and Wrong of our Present Distribution of Wealth*, New York: The MacMillan Company, 1916.

line on spiritual matters, on one hand, and fully commit to the American political system on the other.

Ryan had developed a series of nuanced arguments asserting that US democracy and Catholic teachings were compatible, but he did not stop there. To find even deeper connections between Catholic and American values, he and other Catholic intellectuals looked back at earlier periods in their Church's political thought. That entailed bypassing the harsh condemnations of liberalism that had characterized Papal doctrine in the nineteenth century; interestingly, though, this historical project originated within a trend spurred by one of those Popes highly concerned with the modernist threat in politics. In the 1879 encyclical *Aeterni Patris*, Leo XIII had pointed to the work of Thomas Aquinas as a compass for philosophical inquiry in those uncertain times giving birth to dangerous theories and political doctrines. As Aquinas had explained the harmonious relation of faith with reason in a way that could not be surpassed or even matched,[60] his formulations were the necessary basis for any meaningful—and orthodox—theoretical reflection. Therefore, the Pope "exhorted . . . to spread . . . Saint Thomas' wisdom . . . for the protection and glory of the Catholic faith, the good of society, and the advancement of all sciences."[61]

Leo XIII's encyclical favored the spreading of a trend that had already manifested in Italy: the revival of Thomist and, more in general, Scholastic thought with the purpose of counteracting modernism.[62]

> By the early twentieth century, Thomism dominated American Catholic intellectual life.[63] New journals such as *The Modern Schoolman* (1925) and *The New Scholasticism* (1927) were established to promote Scholastic philosophy, Catholic universities were organized along a Scholastic model, and several centers for Thomistic and medieval studies were established. The fields of politics, law, sociology, and economics all came to be organized around natural law philosophy.[64]

In the midst of this revival, Scholastic thought would be employed to affirm that, in that time and age, Catholicism was the best guarantee that liberalism would keep prospering in the United States. The starting point was a common argument

[60] See *Acta Sanctae Sedis*, vol. XII, 1879, pp. 109–10.

[61] Ibid., p. 114, my translation from Latin. In 1923, Pius XI would repeat and reinforce the message with an encyclical wholly dedicated to Aquinas, *Studiorum Ducem*.

[62] For a reflection on the ideological purpose and value of Neo-Scholasticism see Philip Gleason, "Neo-Scholasticism as Intellectual Ideology," *U.S. Catholic Historian*, 7, 1988, pp. 401–11. For a general account of Catholic thinking in relationship to modernity throughout the twentieth century see Phillip M. Thompson, *Between Science and Religion. The Engagement of Catholic Intellectuals with Science and Technology in the Twentieth Century*, Lanham: Lexington Books, 2009.

[63] On early Neo-Scholastic initiatives in American Catholic academic institutions at the turn of the century see Francis Aveling, "The Neo-Scholastic Movement: A Retrospect and a Prospect," *American Catholic Quarterly Review*, XXXI, 1906, pp. 25–6.

[64] Calo, " 'The Indispensable Basis of Democracy,' " p. 1060.

we have already encountered. It connected faith with respect to civil rule and, in these later incarnations, explicitly with democratic and popular legitimacy. As all authority came from God, the people's role was to transfer it through its consent to the rightful institutions and then respect their divine mandate.[65]

Scott had rehearsed this argument through Suárez in his 1928 book, as we saw at the end of the previous chapter. His use was in the context of international legal discourse, as Scott sought to provide with a Salamancan pedigree the deep connection he saw between progressive international law and democratic and egalitarian principles. But we have also already encountered a use by a Catholic in the context of US politics. At the beginning of this chapter, we saw Archbishop Ireland employ the argument defensively in 1884, purely to ensure the loyalty of Catholics to the nation. When John Ryan picked it up again in the late 1920s—at the same time as Scott—he would use it to go on the offensive. Beyond loyalty, the consistency of that conception of civil rule within Catholic thought entailed a harmony of sound religious ethics and freedom. Without religious morality as its foundation and restraint, democracy was no different from autocracy. Ryan would find an obvious expression of this belief in the nature of political rights. Rights found a meaningful justification only in the realization that all human beings were created in God's image. From creation derived the equality and the human dignity that represented inviolable limits to the authority of the State. "Were it not for this doctrine of the essential equality of human beings," Ryan argued, "the intrinsic worth of . . . every human person in the eyes of God, we should [not] have today . . . political democracy."[66]

> In other words, only a view of rights rooted in religion could effectively counter the claim that "all individual rights, personal, political, religious and economic, are created by the State and can be modified or taken away by the State."[67]

Religion, then, was the "vindicat[ion of] democratic beliefs by conclusive reasoning[,] the indispensable basis of democracy":[68] a basis that only Catholicism was fit to provide.

Indeed, if Protestantism had been able to sustain the ethical development of democratic institutions and rights discourse in the United States in the past, this was

[65] The seminal formulation of this argument is generally considered to be Vitoria's *relectio* of 1528, *De Potestate Civili* (*On Civil Power*). For Scott's reading of the *relectio* as the articulation of Vitoria's theory of the international community see below.

[66] John A. Ryan, *Address at the Third Triennial Convention of the Brotherhood of Locomotive Engineers*, May 15, 1921, Box 11/24, Ryan Papers, Department of Manuscripts, Catholic University of America, quoted in Calo, " 'The Indispensable Basis of Democracy,' " p. 1063.

[67] Calo, " 'The Indispensable Basis of Democracy,' " pp. 1063–4, quoting John A. Ryan, *Religion as the Basis of the Postulates of Freedom*, January 30, 1940, Box 11/28, Ryan Papers.

[68] John A. Ryan, *Religion, the Indispensable Basis of Democracy*, Address at the University of Virginia, July 13, 1939, Box 11/24, Ryan Papers, quoted in Calo, " 'The Indispensable Basis of Democracy,' " p. 1064.

clearly not the case anymore, according to Neo-Thomists. By definition weaker than Catholicism in its church structure, Protestantism had entered the twentieth century further marred in its theological foundations by Biblical criticism. In political and social life, it had mistaken extreme individualism for genuine freedom, the Catholic argument proceeded. How could Protestantism protect American democracy from the dangers of radical political doctrines when it had turned into some form of materialistic nihilism itself? It simply could not, argued Lawrence Flick, renowned physician and co-founder of the American Catholic Historical Association. The inherent radicalism ingrained in Protestantism had allowed "[s]uch monstrosities as Know-Nothing-ism, Native Americanism and Ku Kluxism," which had "never sprung up in any part of the country [where] the Catholic exist[ed] in large enough numbers." It was obvious that "[i]f America [wa]s to remain Christian it w[ould] have to be through the Catholic."[69]

Of course, Scott did not and never would have subscribed to such a harsh criticism of Protestantism. Except for that aspect, it is easy to see how he could feel perfectly comfortable in the intellectual milieu of the Catholic academia of the interwar years. The inextricable relation of Christian morality and the US political egalitarian culture, asserted with renewed strength by Catholic intellectuals in those years, had been the cornerstone of Scott's scholarship since the beginning of his career. A more specific point of contact was the reliance on the natural rights tradition of the Scholastics, reinterpreted to make sense of the political challenges of twentieth-century democracy.

Now, as we saw in the previous chapter, Scott's interest in the Salamanca School and focus on rights discourse predated his closer relation with Catholic environments and his affiliation with Georgetown University. Yet, Scott did not simply bring his long-held ideas when joining a seat of Neo-Scholastic culture: he was influenced too. This made him able to develop a richer account of the Catholic conception of international law, even more in line with the thought and the internal discourse of the Church. One clear example would be his adoption of the so-called Bellarmine argument.[70] One of the tropes of Catholic historical projects of the 1920s was the recovery of a supposed connection between the principles of the Declaration of Independence and the work of Church authorities such as the Italian Jesuit Cardinal, Robert Bellarmine (1542–1621). This connection of Catholic thought and US founding principles, argued as unmistakable to the objective student of the sources,[71] could no longer be denied on the basis of Protestant prejudice. It was the key proof that

[69] Lawrence F. Flick, "What the American has got out of the Melting Pot from the Catholic," *The Catholic Historical Review*, 11, 1925, p. 429.

[70] See Calo, "'The Indispensable Basis of Democracy'," p. 1057. For an early articulation of the argument, tracing the literary connections between Bellarmine and the Founding Fathers see Gaillard Hunt, "The Virginia Declaration of Rights and Cardinal Bellarmine," *The Catholic Historical Review*, 3, 1917, pp. 276–89.

[71] For instance, according to the Archbishop of New York Patrick Hayes, "the principles, almost the very language of our Declaration of Independence, were written by the Venerable Bellarmine" ("The

Catholicism was not an extraneous object to American democracy. On the contrary, it had been its moral and intellectual foundation since the beginning.

While Scott's focus would remain on Vitoria and Suárez, he would begin to enlarge his narrative of the Catholic foundations of international law. He also came to endorse "the Catholic conception of our Declaration of Independence": the equality of rights based on creation, which was the backbone of US democracy as well as of the modern international law, had been affirmed by "the words . . . of Robert Bellarmine before Jefferson's."[72]

When Scott approached the Papacy again with the purpose of soliciting an encyclical on peace, he would do it better prepared and with a much stronger case than in the earliest years of the CEIP. Embedded within an American Catholic academia redeploying the Church's tradition in politically creative ways, Scott was inspired to add new layers—Bellarmine being just one example—to the Salamancan core of his narrative. Working closely with Father Edmund Walsh, he would return to the Vatican, over two decades after his first attempt, ready to complete the mission he had given himself while the World War was raging. As planned he had "beg[u]n at the beginning and buil[t] up" in order to "show the Mother Church that its time-honored doctrine not merely favored the peace movement, but was in reality the foundation upon which the peace movement rests."[73]

## CEIP and the Reorganization of the Vatican Library

During the second half of the 1920s and the early 1930s, Scott was focusing on working out his narrative of the Spanish origin of international law and then expanding it into a larger Catholic conception of the discipline. In this phase, his contribution to the approaches to the Vatican was essentially intellectual. His colleagues at CEIP, however, were starting a major project of material cooperation with the Holy See.

It all started with a tip Butler received from a friend. William Barclay Parsons, a successful civil engineer promoted General in the US Army during the First World War, had dedicated himself to literary pursuits in his later years. To research for his *magnum opus*, titled *Engineers and Engineering in the Renaissance*,[74] he had

Champion of Liberty," *Catholic Bulletin*, November 5, 1927, quoted in Calo, "'The Indispensable Basis of Democracy'").

[72] James Brown Scott, *The Catholic Conception of the State and of the Law of Nations*, Address delivered at the Seventy-fifth Anniversary of Boston College, February 21, 1938, Folder 4, Box 55, JBS Papers. See also James Brown Scott, "St. Robert Bellarmine and our Political Heritage," *Georgetown College Journal*, LX, 1931, pp. 19–31.

[73] James Brown Scott to Jules Prudhommeaux, dateable to summer 1915, Box 566, CEIP Papers.

[74] Parsons' book would be published posthumously in 1939 (Baltimore: The Williams and Wilkins Company).

visited the main libraries of the world, including the Vatican Library. Parsons was impressed by the vastness of its archives and the rarity of its holdings. The Library represented a "rich mine of material" collected by the Church since the fifteenth century at least. However, it "was almost inaccessible . . . through lack of a catalogue and of modern library classification and arrangement." That was why "relatively few scholars went to it . . . despite the treasures which it was known to contain."[75] In 1925 Parsons suggested to Butler that the CEIP could help to bring the organization of the Library up to date.

Butler followed up by dispatching to Rome the former President of MIT Henry S. Pritchett, one of the original trustees of CEIP. Pope Pius XI and the library officials appreciated the offer of support and agreed to welcome an American specialist tasked with devising a plan of action.[76] Pritchett, in turn, produced a report on his visit in order to start the appropriate procedures with CEIP's official organs. In this early phase, the Endowment's Board of Trustees was only informed of vague plans. Nevertheless, on December 30, 1926, the Executive Committee, steered by Butler and Scott, allotted 30,000 dollars to the project, even before the specialist inquiry from the United States could be sent to Rome.

By then, though, Butler had already selected the two men for the mission. The only actual specialist would be William Warner Bishop,[77] the chief librarian of the University of Michigan. To accompany him, Butler had chosen the British diplomat Robert Wilberforce,[78] who had served at the Legation to the Holy See and was well acquainted with the Vatican's main players.

On March 9, 1927, the CEIP duo began their visit, greeted by Francis Aidan Gasquet, the British Benedictine who had helped Scott in his pre-war approaches to the Holy See. By now Gasquet was the Cardinal Librarian of the Vatican. He decided to entrust the visitors to the care of Monsignor Eugène Tisserant, the Vice-Prefect of the Library, who provided Bishop with "every facility for a careful and most thorough study" and "courteous[ly] replie[d] to all [his] questions."[79] By the end of March, Bishop was ready to send back to Butler an extensive and thorough report. Bishop cared to remark on the difficulties involved in the project of reorganization, intrinsic to the exceptional nature of the Vatican Library. Operating in the same spaces since the Renaissance, the Library housed over three hundred

[75] Nicholas Murray Butler, *Across the Busy Years*, vol. II, New York: Scribner's Sons, 1940, pp. 180–1.

[76] See Nicholas Murray Butler to Francis Aidan Gasquet, May 26, 1926; Francis Aidan Gasquet to Nicholas Murray Butler, June 19, 1926, Box 325, CEIP Papers.

[77] See Nicholas Murray Butler to Henry S. Pritchett, December 16, 1926, Box 325; Nicholas Murray Butler to William Warner Bishop, December 17, 1926; William Warner Bishop to Nicholas Murray Butler, December 21, 1926; Nicholas Murray Butler to William Warner Bishop, December 24, 1926, Box 6, CEIP Papers.

[78] See Nicholas Murray Butler to Robert Wilberforce, December 14, 1926, Box 325; Robert Wilberforce to Nicholas Murray Butler, December 20, 1926, Box 37, CEIP Papers.

[79] William Warner Bishop, *Report to the President of the Carnegie Endowment for International Peace of a Study of the Vatican Library with some suggestions for its future development*, March 29 1927, Box 104, CEIP Papers, p. 2.

thousand printed books,[80] including 6,500 rare incunabula.[81] The manuscript collection, equalled by "no other library . . . either in number or in importance,"[82] was made of over 51,000 pieces and constantly growing through donations or acquisitions. Considering the difficult working conditions, Bishop lauded the level of functionality maintained by the relatively small staff of the Library. But he had no doubt that more could be done in order "to make this wonderful Library an effective and indeed unsurpassed instrument of research."[83]

When the matter finally came back before CEIP's Board of Trustees on April 29, there was one preliminary issue to solve before discussing Bishop's plans of cooperation. It was Robert Lansing, the former Secretary of State, who raised a rather obvious and legitimate doubt: what did the cataloguing and reorganizing of the Vatican Library have to do with CEIP's mission? Lansing "regarded the project as of a purely educational nature and not one for the advancement of peace for which the funds of the Endowment could be properly used."[84]

Notwithstanding Lansing's position, the Trustees approved an additional allotment of 40,000 dollars. The CEIP vowed to embark on a series of expensive and complex endeavors suggested by Bishop, ranging from the training of Vatican staff "in the modern spirit of library service"[85] in the United States to the production of a summary inventory by author of the manuscripts and an index of the incunabula. Butler would explain the reasoning behind the decision in the CEIP Yearbook:

> It was felt by the Trustees of the Endowment that such an undertaking would be a manifestation of friendship and goodwill towards an organization of worldwide importance and influence, and that its effective working out would make available to scholars from every land the priceless treasures not only of the known but of the unknown manuscripts that are believed to be hidden there, forgotten or overlooked in the course of centuries, and so promote new and most helpful forms of international intellectual cooperation.[86]

Leaving aside the intrinsic cultural value of the project and the unpersuasive argument by Butler connecting it to international peace, there is evidence that the president of CEIP had ulterior hidden motives. Indeed, from correspondence it emerges clearly how Wilberforce's participation to the inquiry mission had two

[80] Ibid., pp. 20ff.
[81] Ibid., pp. 32ff.
[82] Ibid., p. 12.
[83] Ibid., p. 42.
[84] George A. Finch, *History of the Carnegie Endowment for International Peace, 1910–1946*, unpublished manuscript, Folder 3, Box 67, JBS Papers, p. 590.
[85] Bishop, *Report*, March 29, 1927, p. 42.
[86] CEIP Yearbook, 17, 1928, p. 81. Since then the funds granted for this project would be marked in the CEIP budgets with the following motivation: "For the purpose of increasing the effectiveness of the Vatican Library as an international influence."

functions, one open and the other covert. "The first duty I had to perform for you," Wilberforce wrote to Butler, "was to act as liaison officer between Dr. Bishop and the Vatican Library authorities. . . . The second and more difficult part of my mission was to ascertain for you what chances there were of the Vatican making a pronouncement on international arbitration." Butler had authorized Wilberforce to go as far as "to persuade certain of the Cardinals in Curia to use their influence in hastening" the pronouncement's "publication."[87]

This proves that the Library cooperation project was conceived by the CEIP leadership as a continuation of their approaches to the Vatican between 1911 and 1914. As they gained credit and forged relationships with members of the Curia through their help with the Library, Butler and Scott would continue lobbying for the explicit Papal endorsement of international law and adjudication they had wanted all along.

Indeed, the cooperation would turn out to be long lasting and highly fruitful. It would last two decades, until CEIP's last instalment of funds for the cataloguing work in 1947, enduring through many difficulties. The funding continued through the 1930s, while CEIP was ending their support for many other projects because of income lost as a consequence of the Depression and the falling value of the dollar.[88] Later, during the Second World War, the Library remained closed while Rome was under German occupation, but the cataloguing work never stopped.

The results came quickly, notwithstanding the partial collapse of the roof of one of the reading rooms of the Library in December 1931, which caused the death of four people and delayed operations.[89] Beyond the indexing of the collections, Bishop had insisted at the outset on the importance of modernizing the infrastructure. Following his advice, the Pope funded the establishment of a new reading room and the construction of a new entrance to the Library. Moreover, "[t]he stack rooms were lined with American-made steel shelving to accommodate 750000 volumes, equipped with electrically operated stack elevators and booklifts."[90] CEIP provided a ventilating system and the machinery for the photographic reproduction of manuscripts.

Already in 1934, following the last of his annual visits to Rome, Bishop could report with pride on the achievements of the cooperation between CEIP and the Vatican till then.

> In place of room after room crowded even beyond belief with dusty books . . . most inconveniently disposed for service, there are now six floors of American

87 Robert Wilberforce to Nicholas Murray Butler, October 19, 1927, Box 37, CEIP Papers.

88 See, for instance, James Brown Scott to Nicholas Murray Butler, December 22, 1933; Nicholas Murray Butler to James Brown Scott, December 26, 1933, Folder 2, Box 61; Henry S. Haskell to William Warner Bishop, February 24, 1934, Folder 1, Box 7, CEIP Papers; "Drop in Dollar Hits Peace Group. Carnegie Endowment Draws on Reserves to Carry on Work," *Washington Evening Star*, April 30, 1934.

89 See, for instance, the account of Tisserant in a letter to Bishop, January 14, 1932, Box 6, CEIP Papers.

90 Finch, *History of the Carnegie Endowment*, p. 592.

> steel stacks, . . . permitting rapid and efficient service of printed books. . . . In place of eleven different card catalogs of the printed books, there are now but two, . . . housed in steel cabinets of the most modern style and open freely to consultation by readers with a maximum of convenience. Instead of a badly lighted . . . reading room . . . there is now a beautiful, convenient, well-lighted reference room, . . . equipped with the best reference collection known to me[.] The Library has published two sets of rules for its catalogers. . . . They make a long step forward in international cataloging both of books and of manuscripts. . . . The work on scientific cataloging of the manuscripts has made considerable progress, in part through subventions from the Endowment. Altogether the scholar visiting the Vatican Library has an entirely different place in which to work. He is sure of every facility and his needs are satisfied speedily . . . I know of no better place for a scholar to work.[91]

Alongside the Library cooperation, there was the lobbying for international law. Butler pursued his efforts along the older lines, rather than developing a new approach, as Scott would later do. Butler kept cultivating institutional links and personal relationships, hoping it would be enough to get the Holy See to come out in favor not just of peace but of peace through law and adjudication.

As we have seen, Butler directed Wilberforce's approaches to various Cardinals since the beginning of 1927. The British diplomat could "confidently report that the Vatican ha[d] a pronouncement on international arbitration in mind."[92] In the summer of that same year Butler would have his first audience with Pius XI,[93] in which the two officially sealed the agreement on the Library cooperation between their institutions. After that meeting Butler appeared even more assured that the Holy See would come out with an endorsement of international law soon.

Nothing came in the following two years, though, but by the closing months of 1929 Butler believed the time was ripe and decided to apply more pressure. In the first place, Butler was convinced that the resolution of the Roman Question had given the Vatican more space to maneuver in international politics. Since 1870, with the final demise of the Papal States in the context of the Italian process of unification, Rome had become the capital city of Italy and the Holy See had remained without a sovereign territory. The tense relations with the Italian government slowly improved until a solution was agreed upon with the leader of the Fascist regime Benito Mussolini, who had been ruling Italy since 1922. On February 11,

[91] CEIP Yearbook, 24, 1935, p. 65. Updates on the progress of the Vatican Library cooperation can be found in the CEIP Yearbooks of the two decades of its implementation, within the reports of the Division of Intercourse and Education. More detailed and extensive reports by Bishop to the CEIP leadership, covering the years between 1927 and 1934 can be found in the CEIP Papers.

[92] Wilberforce to Butler, October 19, 1927.

[93] Pope Pius would receive Butler two more times, in 1930 and in 1934. For Butler's account of the meetings see *Across the Busy Years*, vol. II, pp. 159–63. See also Finch, *History of the Carnegie Endowment*, pp. 609–10.

1929, the Kingdom of Italy and the Holy See signed the Lateran Treaty, which recognized the independence of the Vatican City State.[94] Now that the Holy See had finally resolved this fundamental issue, Butler was sure that "the immediate aid of his Holiness" on the issue of peace would not be further "delayed."[95]

Secondly, now there was a concrete issue to rally around and have the Vatican express an opinion on. In 1928 there had been the signing of the Pact of Paris, also known as the Kellogg-Briand Pact, a multilateral treaty by which the State parties renounced "war as an instrument of national policy."[96] This time, not only was the United States a party, it was, in fact, the initiator of the treaty, together with the French government. The CEIP leadership had been instrumental in bringing the US government around both by campaigning in favor of the Pact, in line with public opinion, and exploiting their closeness to Secretary of State Frank Kellogg. The CEIP counted the Pact of Paris as a major success for internationalism but they willingly overlooked a fact: their initiative was successful in the United States primarily because it was perceived as a sign of disengagement from European tensions. Instead, all their plans seen as creating entanglements, like a possible US membership in the Permanent Court of International Justice, were ultimately rejected because of the isolationist mood of the country and the Congress in the interwar years.

In any case, Butler took the Pact as a win for CEIP and sought to obtain "some public outgiving . . . of . . . the Pope . . . in support of" it.[97] On Wilberforce's suggestion, he sent confidential letters to high-level foreign policy officials of countries enjoying diplomatic relations with the Vatican.[98] In the standard text he sent to top diplomats of Poland, Great Britain, Belgium, Czechoslovakia, and Germany he suggested having "diplomatic representative[s . . . ] discuss the matter with his Holiness." This would pave "the way . . . for a very important utterance that would exert world-wide influence on behalf of the now almost irresistible movement to abolish war."[99]

The responses were not encouraging, sympathetic but substantially refusing any action. Only Paul Hymans, the Belgian Minister of Foreign Affairs, interested the Ambassador of his country to the Holy See in the issue. Hymans informed Butler that Ambassador van Ypersele had a different sense of the situation: the Vatican

[94] The whole settlement was made of three agreements, collectively known as the Lateran Pacts. The Pacts included, alongside the treaty dealing with international legal matters, a Concordat regulating the religious and civil relations between the Catholic Church and the Italian State, and a financial convention.

[95] Nicholas Murray Butler to Paul Hymans, October 28, 1929, Box 37, CEIP Papers.

[96] See *League of Nations—Treaty Series*, vol. XCIV, 1929, pp. 57–64.

[97] Butler to Hymans, October 28, 1929.

[98] The United States would establish diplomatic relations with the Vatican only in 1984. The previous attempts by US presidents toward that goal were all met by overwhelming Protestant opposition. For an historical account of US-Vatican relations since the former's independence up to the outbreak of the Second World War, with special focus on the interwar years see Luca Castagna, *A Bridge across the Ocean: The United States and the Holy See between the Two World Wars*, Washington, D.C.: The Catholic University of America Press, 2014.

[99] The letters are all dated October 28, 1929 and can be found in Box 37, CEIP Papers.

regarded the possible endorsement of the Pact of Paris as an intrusion in an international political matter, which could undermine the universal spiritual authority of the Papacy.[100]

Butler did not accept this position: "[c]ertainly a declaration in favor of international peace and the renunciation of war must be looked upon as far removed from anything that can properly be called political, particularly since the whole civilized world is united in making the declaration." He asked Wilberforce "to meet this objection, if objection it be,"[101] before his arrival in Rome in the end of March and take every necessary step to prepare the ground for his audience with the Pope. Wilberforce made sure the key Vatican authorities would be duly informed and that Pius XI would receive a memorandum with Butler's suggestions.

When he met the Pope on March 29, 1930, Butler would ask for an "*Encyclique sur la question de l'Ethique Internationale*,"[102] as he and his CEIP allies had done almost two decades before. The case had a similar argumentation too: the Pact of Paris was the legal incarnation of the moral principles developed by the Catholic Church; the appeals to peace of successive Popes had been taken up by the peace movement. Basically the Papacy had already given its blessing and direction, Butler argued in the memo. A new "encyclical . . . would" only "bring together, re-constitute and emphasize the historic pronouncement and position of the Church on the subject of international peace, fitting the language to the conditions of the moment." Yet, while not adding anything new, it would be "a long step forward."[103] "*La force morale qu'une telle déclaration apporterait à la cause de la Paix Internationale serait incalculable*,"[104] read the memo. Among the examples of positive effects of an encyclical, Butler mentioned the higher authority that the judgments of the Permanent Court of International Justice would carry and the encouragement the public opinion would receive toward swaying governments away from belligerent plans.

Butler's quest for an encyclical was again unsuccessful. The Pope, in December, would issue an allocution, a formal speech, titled "Peace on Earth,"[105] for which Butler took credit in his autobiography.[106] Yet, it was again a very short and vague appeal to peace, nothing like the momentous restatement of the Church's moral doctrine on international relations Butler had sought from the Pope. Arbitration, the Pact of Paris, and international law were not even mentioned, let alone endorsed.

Butler could count on the gratitude and esteem he had gained in the Vatican thanks to the Library project. But otherwise, notwithstanding the advice and

[100] See Paul Hymans to Nicholas Murray Butler, January 14, 1930, Box 37, CEIP Papers.

[101] Nicholas Murray Butler to Robert Wilberforce, January 18, 1930, Box 37, CEIP Papers.

[102] *Résumé des Arguments en faveur d'une Encyclique pro Paix Internationale, présentée le 29 Mars 1930 à Sa Sainteté le Pape Pius XI*, Box 37, CEIP Papers.

[103] Nicholas Murray Butler to Robert Wilberforce, February 20, 1930, Box 37, CEIP Papers.

[104] *Memoire*, Box 37, CEIP Papers.

[105] Pope Pius XI, "Peace on Earth," *International Conciliation*, 14, 1931, pp. 81–2.

[106] See Butler, *Across the Busy Years*, vol. II, p. 163.

warnings he received from Wilberforce, he spent little effort harnessing support within the Curia and the religious orders and explaining them why an encyclical on peace was needed from the Church's point of view. In part, this failure to adapt his message reflected Butler's style and personality. True, his memorandum contained a passing reference—most likely suggested by Scott—to the "*théologiens catholiques définissant les principes fondamentaux de la Morale chrétienne en ce qui concerne les droits et les responsabilités que les Etats Souverains ont les uns vis-à-vis des autres.*"[107] Yet, the text mainly read like a policy paper of internationalist advocacy. Most of its few pages were dedicated to the impact a Papal endorsement would have on the effectiveness of the Permanent Court of International Justice or the Pact of Paris. That this was in line with the moral doctrine of the Church or within its spiritual domain, Butler had simply assumed or failed to meaningfully consider. As an additional factor, one should keep in mind that Butler was always highly confident in his ability to influence the main figures in global politics, as his autobiography and correspondence make clear. His strategy essentially rested on charming and convincing the Pope during their meeting.

But the most relevant consideration here is that Butler could not present a better case to the Holy See primarily because he lacked the cultural and intellectual background to build it. This was in stark contrast with the following campaign for an encyclical started by Scott in 1934. In the years since his first book on the Salamancans in 1928, Scott would involve more deeply his Georgetown colleagues and other Catholic allies in the promotion of the Spanish origin theory, a promotion he would institutionalize with the foundation of the *Association Internationale Vitoria-Suárez.* In turn, this would lead him to learn even more about the Catholic theological tradition and include it in a new perspective of his historical account. Scott expanded the Spanish origin to develop a case tailored to the Catholic Church, for it to recognize in full the deep connection of its tradition and international law. He would call this tailored narrative the Catholic conception of international law. When Scott tried to bring the Pontiff around again, he would not only prepare a memo: he had explained and expounded the Catholic conception in a ponderous volume that would circulate around the Curia before arriving in the hands of the Pope himself.

## Building the Alliance: The American Committee for the Vitoria Celebrations

As we saw in the previous chapter, the publication of the *Spanish Origin of International Law* in 1928 had represented a milestone in Scott's revival of Vitoria

[107] *Memoire.*

and Suárez. It was his first extensive formulation of two bold scholarly theses: first, the two Scholastic theologians were responsible for the foundation of international law as a branch of jurisprudence; second, their work was still relevant to assess the status and direction of the discipline and global politics.

The next steps Scott took showed once again his intention to deploy his account of the historical and moral foundations of international law in ways that would reach diverse audiences and achieve diverse political goals. His activity in 1929 was geared toward the popularization of Vitoria as a prophet of the New World's political culture within the United States, engaging in the enterprise Catholic educational institutions in the country.

Indeed, in February, Scott would deliver for the first time, at the Catholic University of America, a speech titled *The Discovery of America and its Influence on International Law*. Soon published as a pamphlet,[108] this text was, in Scott's words, "a propagandist article."[109] This became Scott's piece of choice to introduce and illustrate the Spanish origin and its deep connection with the American continent, especially in front of non-expert audiences.[110] He would recite it on several occasions over the following years, with slight modifications and the necessary updates.[111]

In its original version, *The Discovery of America* revolved around "1492, 1532, 1928 and 1932[,] dates which, while seemingly separated and distinct, [we]re," according to Scott, "nevertheless inter-related."

> In 1492 America was discovered; in 1532 new rules of law were proclaimed to meet the new condition of things brought into being by the discovery of the New World; in 1928 the representatives of the twenty-one American Republics assembled in Havana to codify the "new law" for the New World; and the celebration of the four hundredth anniversary of the proclamation of the new rules of 1532 will enable us to take the Spanish law as accepted and formulated in systematic form

[108] James Brown Scott, *The Discovery of America and its Influence on International Law; The Four Hundredth Anniversary of Francisco de Vitoria's Disquisition "De Indis" of 1532—Address of Mr. James Brown Scott Delivered at Catholic University, February 25, 1929*, Washington, D.C., 1929. Scott published a Spanish translation of the text the following year: *El descubrimiento de América y su influjo en el derecho internacional*, Madrid: Tipografía de Archivos, 1930.

[109] See *Minutes American Committee—First Meeting*, pp. 10–11, Folder 3, Box 62, JBS Papers.

[110] He occasionally employed it, in solemn occasions, also in front of expert audiences. For instance he recited it as his presidential address at the 1929 meeting of the *Institut de Droit International* at Briarcliff Lodge, New York (see James Brown Scott, *The Spanish Origin of International Law: Francisco de Vitoria and His Law of Nations*, Oxford: Oxford University Press, 1934, pp. 14ff). As Scott underlined, he pronounced the speech on October 12, Columbus Day. For general information on the meeting, the first to be held outside of Europe since the foundation of the *Institut* in 1873, see James Brown Scott, "Report of the Director of the Division of International Law," in CEIP Yearbook, 19, 1930, pp. 108–10. Hosting the *Institut* in the United States was for Scott "a dream come true" ("*La session de New-York est la réalisation d'un rêve*," James Brown Scott to Albert de Lapradelle, October 26, 1929, Folder 6, Box 12, JBS Papers).

[111] See, for instance, James Brown Scott, *Address at the Summer Session of the University of Michigan, Ann Arbor, Michigan, July 22, 1938*, Folder 1, Box 63, JBS Papers.

> by Grotius and, from 1932, to continue without interruption the classical traditions of the founders, in order that the resultant law may rest upon the traditions of what we are accustomed to call the modern law of nations.[112]

After this introduction, Scott used the first part of his speech focusing on the first two dates. He explained how the Discovery had occasioned the foundation of international law by Vitoria with his *relectiones, De Indis*, and *De jure belli*, with arguments we are already familiar with. The second part, though, had some novelty. As he had said in the introduction, Scott considered 1928 a significant year because of the Sixth Pan-American Conference in Havana. Rather than focusing on the content of the codification treaties approved at the Conference,[113] Scott looked at its symbolic meaning. This effort of codification represented the current forefront of the progress of the law of nations. Meeting in Cuba, the same island where Columbus first set foot in the New World, the "American States no longer barbarous" represented the "triumph . . . of [t]he theory of Vitoria . . . after the lapse of centuries." Now each of them, from the small "Cuba" to "the United States of America," was "a State, a perfect and complete community, the equal of all perfect States, independent of every other State, however powerful." Working on this footing of equality, the "perfect American Republics," by "consciously . . . codify[ing] the new law of nations," were advancing "the international community of Vitoria, which," Scott argued, "is slowly . . . but surely taking place before our very eyes."

"Finally of 1932," the last of the four meaningful dates Scott sought to underline with his speech. As he reminded his audience, speaking in 1929, "the four hundredth anniversary of [the] delivery" of *De Indis* by Vitoria and, therefore, "of the foundation of modern international law [was] but three years removed." Scott had no doubt that "appropriate . . . notice should be taken . . . and arrangements should be made . . . in advance of" such a key "international event." He announced that together with "a number of American gentlemen" he had "form[ed] a Committee" to set up celebratory events in Salamanca and "communicate its ideas to the Spanish government."[114]

Scott proceeded to reveal a series of ambitious and detailed plans for the 1932 celebrations. The main "commemorative ceremony" was to be held on October 12,

[112] Scott, *The Discovery of America*, p. 1. Scott dated the delivery of *De Indis* to 1532, according to the opinion prevalent in his time. Today, experts are in agreement that Vitoria gave the lecture later, in 1539 (see, for instance, Francisco de Vitoria, *Political Writings*, edited by Anthony Pagden and Jeremy Lawrance, Cambridge: Cambridge University Press, 1991, p. 231.)

[113] For Scott's detailed account of the events, legal results, and initiatives of the Conference see James Brown Scott, "The Sixth International Conference of American States, Held at Habana, January 16–February 20, 1928: A Survey," *International Conciliation*, Document no. 242, 12, 1928–29, pp. 277–349.

[114] Scott, *The Discovery of America*, p. 14. On the support of the Spanish government for Scott's plans see "Parece prepárase un homenaje en honor de Francisco Vitoria en Estados Unidos," *La Prensa*, February 13, 1929.

honoring "the discovery of two worlds, a material one by Christopher Columbus, and a moral and juridical one by the Spanish school of the sixteenth century, through their application of ethical rules to international relations."

Scott also proposed to hold in Salamanca, at the same time as the celebration, a meeting of the *Institut de Droit International* and "the founding of a 'Vitoria Institute of International Relations'[,] a spiritual monument to" the Dominican. The latter was a clear follow-up of the plans Scott had made with King Alfonso XIII and officials of the Primo de Rivera regime during his 1927 visit to raise Salamanca's profile as an international cultural center. "The purpose of the . . . Institute," Scott explained, "would consist principally in explaining the fundamental doctrines of international law, inspired by the theories of the Spanish school of the sixteenth and seventeenth centuries." He envisioned the creation of scholarships that would bring students to Salamanca and Valladolid from all over the world to study international law according to "the Spanish conception." He even called for a "petition [to] the Spanish government" to turn the former Monastery of San Gregorio, where Vitoria had lived in Valladolid, into a residence for the students of the Vitoria Institute. As an initial promotion, Scott had in mind to invite the teachers of international law of "[a]ll the universities of the world where [it wa]s taught" to the founding event in "Salamanca in October, 1932—an assemblage without precedent in international relations."[115]

The "American Committee for the appropriate celebration in 1932 of the four hundredth anniversary of the delivery of Francisco de Vitoria's Disquisition De Indis" would meet for the first time in May 1929.[116] Scott was responsible both for its impractical name and its composition. He stuffed the Committee with his usual collaborators: it was clear that the organization of the 1932 celebrations was also an opportunity for Scott to bring together in the Spanish origin campaign allies who operated in different contexts in the United States, as well as giving them a chance to cooperate with his contacts in Spain.

Indeed, Barcia Trelles, still in Washington for the research stay funded by the CEIP, participated as an observer and liaison with the Spanish institutions. The members Scott chose included international lawyers active in Pan-American cooperation like Leo S. Rowe, Director General of the Pan-American Union and Jesse S. Reeves; the dean of Harvard Law School Roscoe Pound; and feminist leader Doris Stevens.[117]

Yet, the most represented group was made of Catholic scholars and academic administrators. For instance, the Catholic University of America was represented by its Vice-President, Reverend Edward A. Pace, co-founder of the journal *The New Scholasticism* in 1927. The lion's share, though, was, unsurprisingly, kept for

115 Scott, *The Discovery of America*, pp. 15–16.
116 On the meeting see the documents in Folder 3, Box 62, JBS Papers.
117 For the collaboration between Doris Stevens and James Brown Scott see Chapter 6.

Georgetown. Reverend William Coleman Nevils, President of the University, acted as chairman of the committee. Thomas H. Healy, a close collaborator of Scott as Assistant Dean of the Georgetown School of Foreign Service, was chosen as treasurer.

The first meeting of the Committee would also be its last. The celebrations of October 1932 would not take place. The Great Depression made sure that the CEIP could not bankroll initiatives as ambitious as the ones Scott had in mind in 1929. In addition, the fall of the De Rivera regime in January 1930 and the continuing volatility of Spanish politics during the Second Republic complicated the cooperation with the local institutions, whose full support had been considered a given over the course of 1929. Nonetheless, the creation of the Committee and its composition prompt two considerations. First, they showed Scott's intention to institutionalize the campaign for the Spanish origin theory and provide platforms for cooperation among its supporters. Indeed, following the inspiration of the Spanish *Asociación Francisco de Vitoria*, he would soon promote the foundation of the *Association internationale Vitoria-Suarez*. Second, even if Scott's effort was ecumenical, involving people of various backgrounds, the make-up of the Committee reflected his conviction that the Catholic Church and its leadership had a key role to play. Indeed, during 1929 Scott continued to focus his attention on the Vatican and reflected on what the settlement of the Roman question could mean for its international standing.[118]

## The Vatican's Universal Sovereignty

Two months after the signing of the Lateran Pacts in February 1929, Scott took the floor at the annual meeting of the ASIL. On the opening day, April 24, he presented a paper titled "The Treaty between Italy and the Vatican."[119] After introducing the settlement in its entirety, Scott, as the title suggests, focused on the Treaty and its significance for "the international functions of the Holy See." The conquest of Rome by Italy in 1870 had "deprived the Pope of a Kingdom of 4,891 square miles, destroyed his territorial power and seriously affected the exercise of his spiritual prerogatives."[120] The Lateran Treaty re-established the Pontiff as "a sovereign in the strictest sense of international law" by recognizing the independence of "the State of the Vatican City" and the "exclusive jurisdiction" of the Holy See within its

[118] Scott would later confess to the Auxiliary Bishop of Baltimore, half-jokingly, that his "Protestant friends consider[ed the] subject . . . to be [his] obsession" (James Brown Scott to John M. McNamara, May 22, 1933, Folder 7, Box 5, JBS Papers).

[119] James Brown Scott, "The Treaty between Italy and the Vatican," *Proceedings of the American Society of International Law*, 23, 1929, pp. 13–23.

[120] Ibid., p. 14.

"territorial limits." But the Treaty went beyond, referring to "a larger sovereignty possessed by the Pope."[121]

Indeed, Article 2 of the Lateran Treaty affirmed that "Italy recognize[d] the sovereignty of the Holy See in the international realm as an attribute inherent to its nature in conformity with its tradition and with the requirements of its mission to the world."[122] For Scott, this formula crystalized the idea that "the sovereignty of the Holy See in international law . . . result[ed] from . . . the [spiritual] mission of the Supreme Pontiff." The territorial sovereignty—or "temporal" as opposed to "spiritual" in Scott's formulation[123]—was an addition to the Holy See's international subjectivity, not its basis. To prove this assertion, Scott pointed to the fact "that in the interval between the annexation of the Papal States, and the year 1928," the Holy See maintained diplomatic relations with "no less than twenty-nine temporal Powers[.] It therefore appear[ed] that in the opinion of [those] Powers, the Holy See, without title to its territory, was nevertheless a sovereign to which diplomatic agents could be sent, and actually were accredited. [ . . . T]he sovereignty of the Holy See, without territorial background or sphere within which to exercise it, is a fact of international life."

To Scott, the affirmation of the Papacy's spiritual sovereignty was relevant even after it had acquired territorial sovereignty over the Vatican City State. It was necessary to explain its peculiar place within the international community. It was a regular member State, before and—all the more so—after the Lateran Treaty. But it was also something more and different because of its religious function.

Indeed, Scott explained, it was Pius XI himself who had requested "in advance of the negotiations that the Vatican City should be so limited in territorial extent that he could not . . . exercise the temporal power of other days." The renewed acquisition of territorial sovereignty did not serve the purpose of re-establishing the figure of the Pope-King as a direct participant in international power politics. It was to guarantee and support the practical exercise of the Pope's spiritual mission: the size of Vatican City reflected that choice. The role claimed by the Pope within the international community was clarified by Article 24 of the Lateran Treaty:

> In regard to the sovereignty appertaining to it also in the international realm, the Holy See declares that it desires to remain and will remain outside of any temporal rivalries between other States and the international congresses called to settle

[121] Ibid., pp. 16–17.

[122] The official English version of the Treaty is available in the section "Laws of Vatican City State" of the website http://www.vaticanstate.va (last accessed February 13, 2019).

[123] "In the case of the Supreme Pontiff there are two kinds of sovereignty: spiritual and temporal. The spiritual, he exercises within a spiritual domain, that is to say, within the community of the Holy Roman Catholic Church, irrespective of territorial lines; and the temporal sovereignty he exercises within the limits of the City of the Vatican. Both are combined within his person, as both are admitted to be necessary to the exercise of the functions spiritual and temporal with which he is vested" (Scott, "The Treaty between Italy and the Vatican," p. 18).

> such matters, unless the contending parties make a mutual appeal to its mission of peace; it reserves to itself in any case the right to exercise its moral and spiritual power. Consequently, Vatican City will always and in any case considered neutral and inviolable territory.

These considerations over the minuscule size of the Vatican territory and its stated motivations prompted Scott to re-launch an idea he had been championing since his 1896 speech: the Pope would represent the ideal arbitrator of international disputes. An "important implication of the treaty [wa]s the prospect it offer[ed] the Powers of a solution of their conflicts upon the basis of law, morality and the imponderables, without an eye to territorial aggrandizement or temporal interests on the part of the mediator."[124]

Scott concluded the speech by drawing a parallel tailored to his American audience. To better explain the peculiar "attributions of the Papacy" under international law, he likened it to the Federal Government in the United States. "[T]he Federal Government [held] title [and] exercises exclusive jurisdiction" only over the small "District of Columbia." When it came to the rest of "the vast territory of the United States, . . . the Federal Government and the States exercis[ed] their respective sovereignties without juridical conflict, because the Federal sphere is distinct from the State sphere." In the same way, "from the City of the Vatican as a center, the spiritual sovereignty of the Pope crosse[d] the artificial boundaries separating the States of the far-flung international community, in order to reach every man, woman and child of the Catholic persuasion." The Federal and the State powers could not clash according to the US constitutional legal theory, Scott continued. Similarly, "the spiritual power of the Pope, separate and distinct from the civil power of each of the States of the international community, [could not], in law, come into conflict with the civil power of any of them."[125]

Scott's short speech aimed at doing more than presenting a recent treaty to an audience of international lawyers. It contained typical themes and arguments of the Neo-Scholastic political discourse championed in those years by US Catholic intellectuals. For instance, the comparison of the separation of powers between States and Federal Government in the US context and the position of the Papacy in the international community pointed to a shared political culture. Not only did the Vatican have no interest in influencing temporal politics, it did so out of a respect of separate spheres that was crucial in its own centuries-old tradition. To show

[124] Ibid., p. 20. Scott would elaborate on the point in his Presidential Address at the ASIL meeting two years later: "[T]he decision [of a] dispute laid before the State of the Vatican . . . is bound to be in conformity with the moral code of the centuries and to be dominated by a spiritual conception of things which temporal judges may sometimes be without" (James Brown Scott, "The Progress of International Law during the last Twenty-Five Years," *Proceedings of the American Society of International Law*, 25, 1931, p. 23).

[125] Ibid., pp. 20–2.

how alike the concept of separation of powers was in Catholic and in US political thinking, Scott resorted to a quote. Only after reciting it, did he reveal its author.

> "Each of them is sovereign . . . within its sphere; each of them is restricted within limits determined and traced in exact conformity with its nature and principle: each of them is thus circumscribed within a sphere where it may move and in virtue of the rights which belong to it." From the language and the precision with which the powers are separated, we would be justified in believing that this is a decision . . . of the Supreme Court of the United States. But it is not. It is a passage from the Encyclical *Immortale Dei* of Leo XIII, in which he draws the line between ecclesiastical powers of the Vatican and the civil powers of the States of the World.[126]

Indeed, the speech showed that Scott had not only internalized the Neo-Scholastic discourse of his Catholic colleagues, but also redeployed it in a new fashion. The assertion of a shared liberal political culture had normally sought to establish the loyalty of US Catholics to the national institutions. Scott enlarged the relevance of the argument to apply also to the realm of international politics. The corollary was that the Pope and the Catholic Church could be valuable allies in spreading globally the progressive values of the modern international law. Indeed, Scott argued that the Lateran treaty "ha[d] liberated the spiritual power of the Pope," now fully free to "exercise [his] functions for the spiritual and moral perfection of mankind without regard to race, nationality, or geographical situation."[127] In other words, the Papacy was a messianic force, acting to make into reality that spirit of equality and justice that moved history forward. As we have seen in previous chapters, Scott had described the United States and its championing of international law in very similar terms on several occasions. The United States and the Papacy shared a mission. And, while Scott did not mention him in this speech, he had made clear elsewhere who he believed the initiator and symbolic figure of this common mission to be. It was Francisco de Vitoria, the apostle of equality and founder of international law. It was with him, Scott thought, that the progressive values of the American continent and the moral tradition of Christianity came together to trace the way forward for mankind.

## The Inception of the Vitoria-Suárez Association between Academic Neo-Scholasticism and Catholic Activism

At the 1929 meeting of the *Institut de droit international* hosted in the United States, Scott had directed the attention of the international legal elite toward Vitoria

126 Ibid., p. 22.
127 Ibid.

and the upcoming 400th anniversary of the delivery of *De Indis*. At the following meeting, which took place in Cambridge in 1931, Scott was joined by members of the *Institut* in the project of creating the *Association internationale Vitoria-Suarez*.[128] According to Scott's choice,[129] as President of the *Comité provisoire* and later of the Association was named the Greek Ambassador to France, international lawyer Nicolas Politis (1872–1942).

When the *Institut* met again in Oslo in 1932, Politis presented draft statutes for the Association, which were readily approved.[130] Article 1 declared the purpose of the Association: "to encourage the scientific study of the doctrines of the theologian pioneers of modern international law, of the historical origins of this law and, in general, of the progress of human thought about the relations between peoples."[131]

The membership,[132] reflecting the one of the *Institut*, was made up mostly of European international lawyers with the addition of some Americans. Beyond Scott, the United States was represented by George Finch and Philip Marshall Brown. Among the Latin Americans were Alejandro Álvarez and Antonio de Bustamante. Some of the members, like Kosters, Verdross, De la Brière, and Barcia Trelles had already worked and published on the relevance of the Salamanca School for the international law of the current day. The three members from Spain—Barcia Trelles, Yanguas Messia, and Aniceto Sela—had all been in the leadership of the *Asociación Francisco de Vitoria*.

Scott controlled the Association as its initiator and the only member who could provide funding for its activities, in any case few and basic. His selection of the leadership was consistent with his usual *modus operandi* and thinking. Politis as president was supposed to be the face of Association. A figure of prestige, Politis was known both as a scholarly international lawyer and an influential diplomat.[133] After being the Greek Minister of Foreign Affairs during the World War and in the immediate postwar years, he had been very active within the League of Nations, also presiding over its Assembly. Yet, I suspect that the decisive factor for Scott was that Politis came originally from a non-Catholic country. This was a way of

[128] See, for instance, *International Association of Francis of Vitoria and Suarez*, Folder 2, Box 63, JBS Papers; James Brown Scott to Walter Schätzel, March 28, 1935, vol. 342, CEIP Papers; "Asociación Internacional Vitoria-Suárez," *El Debate* (Madrid-based newspaper), October 16, 1931.

[129] See Yves de la Brière to James Brown Scott, August 11, 1939, Box 86, CEIP Papers.

[130] Before Oslo, Politis shared his draft with the other members of the *Comité provisoire* (Huber, Verdross, Raestad, and Kosters) and Scott, receiving convinced approval and a just a few minor comments (See *Rapport sur le projet de Statute présenté par N. M. POLITIS*, vol. 342, CEIP Papers.

[131] *Association Internationale Vitoria-Suarez—Statuts approuvés par l'Assemblée Générale constitutive, tenue à Oslo, le 17 août 1932*, vol. 342, CEIP Papers. My translation from French.

[132] See *Liste des membres fondateurs*, vol. 342, CEIP Papers.

[133] For two general accounts of Politis' career see Marilena Papadaki, "Nicolas Politis, une approche biographique," *Monde(s)*, 7, 2015, pp. 45–64 and Marilena Papadaki, "The Government Intellectuals: Nicolas Politis—An Intellectual Portrait," *European Journal of International Law*, 23, 2012, pp. 221–31.

showing that the Association was dedicated to an objective scientific study of the Salamanca theologians as the founders of international law, not moved by confessional interests. Scott had often employed this technique himself: when claiming that the origin of international law rested with Vitoria and Suárez, he routinely submitted his Presbyterianism as proof of his impartial judgment.

However, when it came to the operational direction of the Association, Scott decided to put it in the hands of a devout Catholic, Alfred Verdross (1890–1980), professor of international law and legal philosophy at the University of Vienna, who took the position of Secretary-General. Verdross' Catholic faith influenced both his scholarship and his political action. A pupil of Hans Kelsen, throughout the 1920s Verdross gradually integrated his mentor's pure theory of law with value-oriented fundamental norms of international law.[134] Indeed, his main international legal works of the decade[135] show an increasing reliance on natural law through the doctrines of Vitoria and Suárez.[136] This Neo-Scholastic universalism was reflected in the course Verdross held at the Hague Academy of International Law in 1927, titled *Le fondement du droit international*. The eclectic nature of Verdross' scholarship in this phase can be evinced by the title of the first chapter of the course (*La morale universelle comme base du droit des gens positif*) bringing together the concepts of universal morality and positive law. The chapter opened with an account of the birth of the universal law of nations in the Middle Ages as an outgrowth of the Christian dogma of the unity of mankind;[137] it then followed the law's evolution until the demise of its universalist foundations in the nineteenth century, caused by the rising "*doctrine d'un positivisme absolut*."[138] For Verdross, Vitoria and Suárez were not just the founders of modern international law, but also the saviors of its universalist conception: they had managed to provide it with a strong intellectual description, even if operating in the difficult context of religious division in Europe caused by the Reformation and the rise of the nation State.[139] According to Verdross, the merits of their theories were being vindicated, consciously or not, by the international lawyers of the early decades of the twentieth century. After the absolute positivism of the late nineteenth century, international legal theorists were again assuming the "*existence préalable d'une loi morale supérieure à l'État et qui lui*

[134] See, for instance, Jochen Von Bernstorff, "Georg Jellinek and the Origins of Liberal Constitutionalism in International Law," *Goettingen Journal of International Law*, 4, 2012, fn 53, p. 637.

[135] I am referring to the 1923 *Die Einheit des rechtlichen Weltbildes auf der Grundlage der Völkerrechtsverfassung*, Tubingen: Mohr and the 1926 *Die Verfassung der Völkerrecthsgemeinschaft*, Wien–Berlin: Springer.

[136] See, in the same sense, Anthony Carty, "Alfred Verdross and Othmar Spann: German Romantic Nationalism, National Socialism and International Law," *European Journal of International Law*, 6, 1995, pp. 82, 87, and 94 and Bruno Simma, "The Contribution of Alfred Verdross to International Law," *European Journal of International Law*, 6, 1995, pp. 37–9.

[137] See Alfred Verdross, "Le fondement du droit des gens," *Recueil des cours de l'Académie de droit international de La Haye*, 16, 1927, pp. 252–3.

[138] Ibid., p. 257.

[139] See ibid., pp. 253–6.

*impose le respect de la parole donnée.*" International law could not rest only on the autonomous will of States: it presupposed that same unity of mankind theorized by early modern Catholic theologians and later adopted by Grotius. One had to recognize that "*la doctrine classique du droit des gens surtout celle de Suarez et de Grotius renaît.*"[140]

According to Verdross' pupil Bruno Simma, his "Catholicism" indeed "provided a fitting, if not essential, foundation for his natural law philosophy as well as for his universalistic view of international law." But, Simma adds, Catholicism played a part also in Verdross' controversial political positions over the course of the 1930s, the decade in which we find him working with Scott in the Vitoria-Suárez Association. "[I]n the mid-thirties Verdross still described Mussolini as a defender of Christian values, and the National-Socialist doctrine of international law as anti-imperialistic and federalist. . . . But maybe for a person of Verdross's background and upbringing—Catholic, conservative—it was not uncommon at that time to view Fascism and National-Socialism as bulwarks against Communism."[141]

The 1937 first edition of Verdross' international law textbook[142] was permeated by a *völkisch*, German nationalist streak.[143] The language Verdross used in a letter written in March 1938, few days before the Anschluss, to the then Austrian Chancellor Kurt Schuschnigg is meaningful. It showed how Verdross saw his Christian nationalism not in opposition to Nazism in itself, but only to its anti-religious excesses. Verdross called for "cooperation between the All-German (*gesamtdeutsch*) oriented Christian groups and moderate National Socialists" to keep alive the "hope" of maintaining "assured . . . the Christian leadership . . . in Austria." This would achieve the purpose the Anschluss had in Verdross' mind: "the melting of all good Austrians into a Christian German people. Such a success might strengthen Christian elements in Germany itself where anti-Christian elements dominate within National Socialism."[144]

Following the Anschluss, the new Nazi rulers suspended Verdross from teaching for a semester. Defending his position, he did not claim to be a National Socialist, but pointed to the nationalist streak in his scholarship. Verdross' Christian nationalism puzzled the Nazi evaluators about his loyalty to the regime. This must be why, after the suspension, Verdross was allowed to return to teach international law, perceived as a more technical discipline, but not the more politically charged legal philosophy.[145]

140 Ibid., p. 283.

141 Simma, 'The Contribution of Alfred Verdross', pp. 36–7.

142 Alfred Verdross, *Völkerrecht*, Berlin: Springer, 1937.

143 See in the same sense, for instance, Jochen Von Bernstorff, *The Public International Law Theory of Hans Kelsen. Believing in Universal Law*, Cambridge: Cambridge University Press, 2010, pp. 59–60 and 282–3.

144 Quoted in Carty, "Alfred Verdross and Othmar Spann," fn 65, p. 89.

145 For an analysis of Verdross' controversial relation with National Socialism and its intellectual background see ibid.

This short survey might give a sense that, for Verdross, the Vitoria-Suárez Association was not just another professional organization. His active participation in it was particularly meaningful. Indeed, at the first operative meeting of the Association in Paris in 1934, Verdross would take it upon himself to direct, together with the Jesuit Yves de la Brière, the organization's main project: a collective volume, spanning from Augustine to Grotius, capturing the pioneers' doctrines and ideas "*qui sont vraiment devenues les bases du droit international*."[146] 1934 was not any year to start such a project: it was the year in which Scott's initiatives to outline the Catholic conception of international law came together, including the publication of his book with that same title. He was ready to lay the full evidence in front of the Curia and the Pope himself: international law belonged to the Catholic intellectual tradition.

## The Catholic Conception as a Collective Scholarly Enterprise

Scott's action of rapprochement, symbolized by the American committee for the Vitoria celebrations, bore immediate fruit. In the early 1930s, US Catholic academics and international lawyers found common ground in the name of the Spanish origin theory. Articles on Vitoria as the founder of international law appeared more and more often in Catholic publications. Among them, the 1930 pamphlet by the Dominican C. H. McKenna[147] is the perfect example of the intellectual contiguities Scott strived for, both in terms of content and institutional cooperation. In his text, titled *Francis de Vitoria, Founder of International Law*, McKenna quoted extensively from Scott's *Spanish origin* book and his *Discovery of America* speech. To quote Vitoria's *relectiones*, he adopted the English translation of the Classics edition. The pamphlet was published by two committees of the Catholic Association for International Peace. The chairman of the one on Ethics was Father John A. Ryan, while the chairman of the one on International Law and Organization was none other than Charles G. Fenwick, Scott's former pupil and sometime rival in the ASIL.

In turn, international lawyers who had previously been little interested in the history of the discipline, started challenging the received wisdom that international law had begun with Hugo Grotius.[148] For instance, Clyde Eagleton, professor of

[146] Words by Nicolas Politis as reported in *Procès-verbal—Séance de l'Assemblée de l'Association Internationale Vitoria-Suarez tenue, à Paris, le 17 octobre 1934*, vol. 342, CEIP Papers.

[147] C. H. McKenna, *Francis de Vitoria, Founder of International Law*, Washington, D.C.: Catholic Association for International Peace, 1930.

[148] Beyond his own publications, speeches, and organizing work, Scott made sure to nurture that interest by sending free copies of a number of publications on the Spanish origin, including the ones by Catholic academics and activists, to US international law professors (see, for instance, J. Edwin Young to James Brown Scott, December 29, 1932, vol. 486, CEIP Papers).

international law at New York University, wrote to thank Scott: "Really, you have gotten me so interested in the theologians and their influence upon the building of international law."[149]

Scott's vision went beyond creating a reciprocal interest and cooperation between experts in Catholic political thought and in international law. That was a basis on which to build. He saw the need for a body of work uniting expertise in both fields. Those interdisciplinary works would serve a purpose Scott had been advocating since the inception of the Classics: articulating the connection between the moral experience of centuries and current international legal doctrines. With such scholarship, international lawyers who had intuitively realized that treaties were not enough to sustain adequate reflection on the discipline would have a roadmap. For instance, rather than grasping at new versions of concepts like international community to interpret developments in international organization, they could gain insight by going at those concepts' intellectual spring: Catholic theological reflection.[150]

Scott knew and admired works of colleagues who had gone in that direction before, bringing together theological tradition and international law. For instance, he had sought the cooperation of Ernest Nys for the Classics after reading his *Les origines du droit international.*[151] Yet, that book could not fulfill the mission Scott had in mind for two main reasons. In the first place, it was published in 1894. It could have not taken into account the two Hague Peace Conferences, let alone the foundation of the League of Nations and the other postwar developments. Secondly, its method was not radical enough for Scott's purpose. Indeed, Nys tracked the evolution of thought on fundamental concepts and institutions of international law, ranging from freedom of the seas to the declaration of war. But his study was decidedly historical in nature: it carried the progress of the concepts analyzed from their origin until the seventeenth century, without reaching his present day. Scott was looking for works in which the historical progress would bear fully on the present of international relations: learned narratives depicting the trajectories between, for instance, Vitoria's *De Indis* and the Mandates of the League of Nations.[152] This kind of scholarship could go beyond giving international lawyers awareness of the rich background of their discipline. It could also convince the

[149] Clyde Eagleton to James Brown Scott, January 8, 1936, vol. 507, CEIP Papers.

[150] That Scott had started to identify what he called the moral foundations of international law almost entirely with the Catholic tradition was signaled also by a language shift. Around the turn of the decade leading into the 1930s, he started, at times, to use the concept of natural law interchangeably with that of moral foundations. He had always avoided equating them previously, most likely because of the strong Catholic connotation the idea of natural law had, which could have put off Protestants (see, for instance, James Brown to C. G. Haines, February 21, 1929, Folder 5, and June 28, 1930, Folder 11, both in Box 12, JBS Papers).

[151] Ernest Nys, *Les origines du droit international*, Brussels: Alfred Castaigne, 1894.

[152] Scott had already drawn this specific connection in his 1928 *Spanish Origin* book (see Chapter 4 of this work).

Papacy that endorsing international law was not an intrusion in politics but a natural corollary of the Catholic tradition of moral thought.

The collective book planned by the Vitoria-Suárez Association, as we have seen, was one such enterprise, conceived with the declared purpose of outlining the contribution of Scholastic theology to the most recent advancements of international law. In those years, Scott promoted other studies with the same purpose. The monographs by Camilo Barcia Trelles and John Eppstein were further examples.

The result of Camilo Barcia Trelles' stay in Washington, D.C. at the Carnegie Endowment in 1928 and 1929 was a lengthy monograph titled *Doctrina de Monroe y cooperación internacional*.[153] The book traced the origin of the Monroe Doctrine in Vitoria's work and described its evolution into the basis of the growing scope of Pan-American cooperation, pointing to the landmark codification conventions agreed upon at the 1928 Havana Conference.

Later Scott promoted the publication of the book by John Eppstein, the British founder of the Catholic Council for International Relations.[154] The book would eventually come out in 1935, under the aegis of the CEIP and the Catholic Association for International Peace, with the title *The Catholic Tradition of the Law of Nations*.[155] Scott had circulated the manuscript among CEIP leadership since 1933. He had also immediately suggested changing its working title *International Ethics* to one that would reflect its Catholic content.[156] The two years of gestation were due to a period of sickness of the author but also to doubts about the method adopted in the work. James T. Shotwell, Director of the CEIP Division of Economics and History, noted how "there were serious lapses from the standpoint of scholarship." Shotwell was convinced that the cavalier use of quotations and translations, without "the proper footnote references," undermined "[t]he only value that the book ha[d:] contain[ing] the teaching . . . of the Great Churchmen [and] the Popes . . . on questions of war and peace." The way "Mr. Eppstein wove his story out of the original material" without "having the exact text of the citations carefully translated into English," overlooked that "the formula used is important, and not merely the fact that such and such an authority spoke on such and such a question." Shotwell was mostly complaining that Eppstein did not offer precise textual references, but his criticism also entailed a larger point. Those shortcomings allowed Eppstein, an activist and not a scholar, to enlist authorities to support his points by leaving "the reader . . . not . . . sure whether the text continued Mr. Eppstein's comment or whether it was a paraphrase from an original text."[157] With these techniques, Eppstein built a narrative uniting in a single thread the New Testament to the League of Nations and the Pact of Paris, passing through the Fathers of the Church,

[153] Camilo Barcia Trelles, *Doctrina de Monroe y cooperación internacional*, Madrid: Mundo Latino, 1931.

[154] See *The Tablet*, July 5, 1924, p. 24.

[155] John Eppstein, *The Catholic Tradition of the Law of Nations*, Washington, D.C.: published for the Carnegie Endowment of International Peace by the Catholic Association for International Peace, 1935.

[156] See, for instance, George Finch to James T. Shotwell, November 29, 1933, Box 81, CEIP Papers.

[157] See James T. Shotwell to James Putnam, August 23, 1934, Box 81, CEIP Papers.

the Schoolmen, and the pronouncements *ex cathedra* of Popes up to the twentieth century. Notwithstanding the forcefully formulated objections by a senior CEIP figure like Shotwell, Scott pushed the publication of *The Catholic Tradition* through and gave it a glowing review. According to Scott, "between [the book's] covers lie[d] what should be the international law of the future, if law [was] to be looked upon as a moral and spiritual concept instead of a brutal command." After praising Eppstein's reconstructions and especially the prominent role he had reserved for Vitoria and Suárez, Scott closed the review admitting his lack of impartiality toward the subject. "Being . . . an outspoken advocate of the Catholic conception of international law, the reviewer feels no hesitancy in recommending unreservedly Mr. Eppstein excellent compendium of *The Catholic Tradition of the Law of Nations*."[158]

Scott did not only promote works of others: he was also preparing his own account of the Catholic conception of international law. He started by expanding his studies of the Catholic tradition beyond Vitoria and Suárez, taking advice from and discussing with his collaborators. For instance, in 1930, Yves de la Briére suggested that he should look into the Italian Jesuit Luigi Taparelli d'Azeglio (1793–1862).[159] Later, in 1932, Scott informed Barcia Trelles that he was studying the work of Vitoria's pupil Domingo de Soto, of another Dominican theologian, Domingo Báñez, and of two legal scholars also active in the Spanish *siglo de oro*: Fernando Vázquez de Menchaca and Diego de Covarruvias.[160]

By August 1934, Scott could inform Bustamante that he had left a "manuscript in the hands of the printer." He "ha[d] been . . . exceptionally busy [in] the [previous] few months, . . . put[ting] into shape a volume for a special purpose."[161] The following month, Scott wrote again announcing that one of the first copies of his *The Catholic Conception of International Law* was on its way to his friend in Cuba. Excitedly, he also told Bustamante that he would sail to Europe the next day,[162] for what would turn out to be the last visits to Rome and Spain of his life.

## 3. The Last Attempt: The Catholic Conception of International Law at the Vatican

### Establishing the Catholic Conception: The Genealogy of Tyrannicide and the Salamancan Theories of International Organization

The last attempt to gain the Pope's endorsement of international law took place between September 1934, when Scott visited Rome to circulate *The Catholic*

[158] James Brown Scott, "Book Review—The Catholic Tradition of the Law of Nations by John Eppstein," *Georgetown Law Journal*, 24, 1935–36, pp. 1055 and 1063.

[159] See Yves de la Briére to James Brown Scott, March 11, 1930, vol. 316, CEIP Papers.

[160] See James Brown Scott to Camilo Barcia Trelles, December 20, 1932, vol. 330, CEIP Papers.

[161] James Brown Scott to Antonio de Bustamante, August 8, 1934, Folder 24, Box 12, JBS Papers.

[162] James Brown Scott to Antonio de Bustamante, September 13, 1934, Folder 24, Box 12 JBS Papers.

*Conception* among senior figures of the Catholic Church, and July 1935 when Father Walsh met the Pontiff to discuss "the Great Project."[163]

Scott had involved several allies in order to reach as many influential figures in the Curia and the religious orders as possible. He did not expect all of them to read his book in its entirety: he prepared shorter memoranda and pointed them to specific parts of the volume, especially its preface and conclusions. But he also made it clear that his full case rested in his "*oeuvre de propagande*." With it, he "show[ed] that the Catholic conception of International Law should be and therefore must be, the accepted Law of Nations of the future if not the present, if the intercourse of nations is to be, as it must be, both moral and Christian."[164]

How then did *The Catholic Conception* differ from the 1928 *Spanish Origin*? How had Scott's account of the historical progress of international law evolved? As the subtitle[165] and the conclusions[166] made explicit, the book, while expanding to the work of other authors, was still primarily focused on Vitoria and Suárez. The basic narrative remained the same. Prompted by the discovery of America, Vitoria had founded international law out of the *relectiones De Indis* and *De Iure belli*. Later, Suárez had developed international law into a philosophical system. The fundamental concepts and themes on which Scott relied remained the same: the equality of States and individuals he saw affirmed by Vitoria in *De Indis*; the subtle distinction but fundamental closeness of natural law and *jus gentium*; the doctrine of the State as *perfecta communitas*; the law of war, depicting the prince pondering on the justice of his cause as if he was a judge; free trade as the essential content of the *ius communicandi* that kept mankind united.

Scott developed these themes in more detail and length than in the earlier work, without major variations in content. The novelty in the book was represented by two topics, which occupied, combined, the majority of its pages: the nature of sanctions in international law and the theory of tyrannicide as the forerunner of a democratic conception of the State.

In treating this latter theme Scott showcased the knowledge he had acquired by expanding his studies in the early modern history of political thought beyond the authors of the School of Salamanca.[167] He took as a starting point the rejection of the absolute power of kings articulated in the 1613 *Defensio fidei* by Suárez and his openness to the possibility of killing a tyrant if there were no other means

[163] Edmund A. Walsh to James Brown Scott, July 27, 1935, Folder 9, Box 8, JBS Papers.
[164] James Brown Scott to Wlodimir Ledóchowski, September 29, 1934, Folder 2, Box 52, JBS Papers.
[165] The subtitle was "Francisco de Vitoria, Founder of the Modern Law of Nations; Francisco Suárez, Founder of the Modern Philosophy of Law in General and in Particular of the Law of Nations: A Critical Examination and a Justified Appreciation."
[166] See Scott, *The Catholic Conception of International Law: Francisco de Vitoria, Founder of the Modern Law of Nations; Francisco Suárez, Founder of the Modern Philosophy of Law in General and in Particular of the Law of Nations—A Critical Examination and a Justified Appreciation*, Washington, D.C.: Georgetown University Press, 1934, pp. 481–94.
[167] Tyrannicide is treated ibid. in chapters V to XI, pp. 261–436.

of protecting the community. He expanded on the theory within the Counter-reformation with an account of Juan de Mariana's *De rege et regis institutione.* Mariana had taught theology in Rome to Robert Bellarmine, whose "theory of the source of power as vested in the people is the foundation of Democratic government throughout the world" and, in particular, in the United States. Indeed Scott did not lose the chance to reaffirm the Neo-Scholastic trope that "the truths that Thomas Jefferson . . . held to be 'self-evident' are to be found in the section on *De Laicis* of Cardinal Bellarmine's famous *Controversiae*."[168] Other than through the direct inspiration of Jefferson by Bellarmine, Catholic theology on tyrannicide originated modern democracy—and its most accomplished example, the United States—by inspiring a more general evolution in European political thought. In *The Catholic Conception*, Scott tracked the doctrine's life in Protestant works such as the 1579 anonymous Huguenot tract *Vindiciae contra tyrannos* and its practical tests in the tumultuous Britain of the seventeenth century. Indeed, Scott closed his survey with John Milton's defense of the deposition and decapitation of King Charles I of England. In the 1649 pamphlet *The Tenure of Kings and Magistrates*, Milton delineated an early theory of constitutionalism and separation of powers that found favor with the US Founding Fathers.[169] To find but one obvious example of how the doctrine of tyrannicide had found its way into the US Constitution, Scott pointed to the procedures it provided for the impeachment of the president and other federal officials. Turned into a "constitutional remedy," tyrannicide in this "modified form" remained "the ultimate means whereby the people, as the source of the power, may exercise that power and cause their will to prevail."[170]

In Scott's work of propaganda with the Catholic Church, the genealogy so established was even more relevant than the details and the nuances of the theory of tyrannicide. He had not only reaffirmed Bellarmine's influence on the Declaration of Independence, claimed by the US Catholics as proof of how rooted democratic sentiment and thought were in Catholic tradition; he had considerably expanded on that point following a score of intellectual and political connections. Most importantly to his plan, he had managed to bring Suárez into the picture, the thinker who he held as the establisher of the philosophy of international law. In his work, then, Scott could find a common point of origin—crucially a Catholic one—for modern political thought both in terms of domestic rule and international relations.

If his technique of argumentation on tyrannicide had been to put together a detailed genealogy building on a large body of work and events, in treating the theme of the international community and its sanctions Scott would go a different way.

[168] Ibid., pp. 425–6.

[169] On the influence of Milton on the Founding Fathers see, for instance, Preston, *Sword of the Spirit, Shield of Faith*, pp. 94–5: "One of the most important links between the Puritan Republicanism of the English Civil War and the Christian Republicanism of the American Revolution was the poet John Milton" (p. 94).

[170] Scott, *The Catholic Conception*, pp. 434 and 436.

He aimed primarily at drawing direct connections between the theories of Vitoria and Suárez and the present development of international organization.

The theme of sanctions had already been important to Scott earlier in his career, as we saw in Chapter 3. In the earliest years of the twentieth century, he had dismissed the Austinian challenge to international law with his casebook. The case-law therein stood proof of international law being applied in domestic courts and, therefore, carrying a municipal sanction, alongside the moral one of public opinion. Later, Scott treated the theme with the new urgency prompted by the Great War and the plans for the new global order in its aftermath. He stood against collective security as a form of coercive sanction that merely reproduced power relations rather than creating an international order based on justice and the equality of nations. The way forward was in strengthening the finally existing Permanent Court of International Justice and allowing it to build an authoritative body of independent decisions, which would eventually command the full obedience of nations. The United States, Scott argued, was the perfect example of a community of independent States brought together by the judicial pull of the Supreme Court.

In *The Catholic Conception*, Scott returned to the theme once again. This time, he traced it back to Vitoria and Suárez, finding in their work two different but complementary understandings of the international community and, consequently, of sanctions. Scott argued that the respective views of the Dominican and the Jesuit represented the intellectual origins of the two sides of an essential dichotomy still alive in his time. He attributed to Vitoria a vision of the international community holding the authority to consciously make law and enforce it. This was the vision behind the League of Nations, entailing "a legal and physical sanction." Suárez, however, understood the international community in looser terms, along the lines that inspired the Hague Peace Conferences, which declared the unconscious, customary development of international legal principles over the centuries. Here, "the sanction [wa]s based fundamentally . . . upon the moral principle which underlies all human relationships, good faith."[171]

Scott described what he called Vitoria's organic conception of the international community and Suárez's inorganic one in two long chapters.[172] Yet, his case was based mainly on just two passages as primary sources. He extracted Vitoria's view from a passage in the *relectio De Potestate Civili* (1528), the earliest of his surviving lectures:

> International law has not only the force of a pact and agreement among men, but also the force of a law; for the world as a whole, being in a way one single state,

[171] Ibid., p. 484.

[172] Respectively titled "The Modern Law of Nations and its Municipal Sanction" (pp. 59–125) and "Francisco Suárez—His Philosophy of Law and of Sanctions" (pp. 127–240).

> has the power to create laws that are just and fitting for all persons, as are the rules of international law. Consequently, it is clear that they who violate these international rules, whether in peace or in war, commit a mortal sin; moreover, in the gravest matters, such as the inviolability of ambassadors, it is not permissible for one country to refuse to be bound by international law, the latter having been established by the authority of the whole world.[173]

The translation of the passage itself betrayed Scott's eagerness to forge a direct connection between Vitoria and the international relations of its time. He translated the text himself, as *De Potestate Civili* had not been published in the Classics. *Ius gentium* became international law without the medium of the expression law of nations; concepts like *respublica* and *regnum* lost their differentiation and the nuances in their meaning to simply become the State.[174] From the passage so translated Scott saw "the conclusions flowing . . . that every rule of international law has a municipal sanction *in esse* or *in posse*, and that a failure to enact a municipal statute for that purpose—or to apply it if enacted—renders the state in default liable in damages."[175] Connecting Vitoria with his earlier work, Scott proceeded then to trace this principle in US court cases, ultimately in the 1887 Supreme Court judgment of *United States v. Arjona*.[176] The Justices had unanimously declared in line with the Constitution a statute criminalizing the counterfeit of foreign currency. This was because the law of nations, according to the Supreme Court, "require[d] every national government to use 'due diligence' to prevent a wrong being done within its dominion to another nation."[177] This case for Scott was the clearest expression of "the law of nations exist[ing] without an affirmative act on the part of the respective countries."[178] Nevertheless, Vitoria's passage focused on the obligation civil institutions have for such positive enactment. If that obligation had been imposed for centuries over national institutions, the creation of the League of Nations showed the promise of "a world law."[179] With the evolution of international organization, legislation enacting international law could be produced at supranational law.

After his account of Vitoria as the intellectual father of the spirit of Geneva and of the positive enactment of international rules, Scott moved to delineate the understanding of international sanctions in the work of Suárez. As main source of his analysis, he employed once again the chapters on *jus gentium* in the second book of *De legibus ac Deo legislatore*, the same ones that had found prominence

173 Francisco de Vitoria, "De Potestate Civili," in *Relectiones Morales*, Cologne and Frankfurt: Simon's edition, 1696, quoted and translated from Latin, Scott, *The Catholic Conception*, p. 59.

174 As a comparison see the English translation in Vitoria, *Political Writings*, p. 40.

175 Scott, *The Catholic Conception*, p. 59.

176 120 US 479 (1887).

177 120 US 484.

178 Scott, *The Catholic Conception*, p. 124.

179 Ibid., p. 125.

in *The Spanish Origin*.[180] As he had underlined in that earlier book,[181] Scott considered section 9 of chapter XIX[182] as the clearest description of the international community, "integrated if inorganic,"[183] in the thought of Suárez. In Scott's interpretation of the section, the Jesuit had envisioned "states . . . independent of one another and yet linked" in a "community" which was surely "political" and "social" but primarily "moral." This common bond of humanity determined the necessary existence of the interdependence of nations and of *jus gentium* to regulate it. Its rules were created, according to Suárez, by universal custom: "among the human race as a whole it was possible for laws to be introduced by the habitual conduct of nations."[184] Scott proceeded to compare the understandings of the two authors:

> With Vitoria . . . the international community is by the very existence of states an organic community, with the power to make laws to prevent the violation of the obligation which every state has by reason of its existence and membership in the community. With Suárez, the law of the international community was simply the product of "usage and tradition" rather than of "pact and agreement."[185]

Scott's next step was, like he had done with Vitoria, to connect Suárez's views with examples from US constitutional law. Suarez's description of customary law as intimately linked to the behavior and the moral sentiment of the community as a whole prompted Scott to reaffirm as a "fundamental conception of the Spanish School that the source of power is vested in the people."[186] Custom being based on generalized consensus and observance made Scott consider it as an expression of popular sovereignty. Indeed, according to Suárez, "if . . . a custom is established which is contrary to a given law, the law falls before the will of the people." This would happen anyway through the action of government: "the people does not 'actively', as Suárez says, abolish law. Rather the custom is the voice of the people demanding that 'the superior . . . abolish the law.'"[187] Scott pointed to the *de facto* rejection and scarce application of the Eighteenth Amendment to the US Constitution, forbidding the manufacture and sale of intoxicating liquors, before its formal repeal in 1933.

As he had argued over the course of his career, global public opinion would also mature and grow in influence, until any violation of international law could be

[180] See Chapter 4, section 3.

[181] See Scott, *The Spanish Origin of International Law: Lectures on Francisco de Vitoria and Francisco Suarez*, Washington, D.C.: Georgetown University Press, 1928, pp. 90–1.

[182] See Suárez, "A Treatise on Laws and God the Lawgiver," Section 9, Chapter XIX, Book II, in *Selections from Three Works*, translations by Gwladys L. Williams, Ammi Brown, and John Waldron, with revisions by Father Henry Davis, Oxford: Oxford University Press, 1944, vol. II, pp. 348–9.

[183] Scott, *The Catholic Conception*, p. 483.

[184] Suárez, "A Treatise on Laws," p. 349.

[185] Scott, *The Catholic Conception*, p. 185.

[186] Ibid., p. 234.

[187] Ibid., pp. 233–4.

avoided or punished simply by its opposition. This was the moral sanction that Scott considered foreseen in the customary *jus gentium* discussed by Francisco Suárez. This kind of theory was reflected in the form of law-making of periodic conferences, as opposed to stable international organizations like the League of Nations. Periodic conferences, such as the Hague Peace ones, were called when the conduct of nations and gradual development of legal principles were mature and established enough to be recognized and codified.

Then, Scott argued, "in point of fact the two great modern conceptions of the international community are the conceptions of Vitoria and Suárez. . . . The choice of the future lies between the two."[188] The choice itself was not Scott's pressing concern here. His message was that whichever direction international law took, it would owe its intellectual origin to at least one of those two forefathers: international law could not but be based on a Catholic conception.

## The Scott-Walsh Memorandum

In September 1934, Scott could finally plant the seed of *The Catholic Conception* in Rome. On September 26, he left a copy with Wlodimir Ledóchowski, the Father General of the Jesuits. Scott directed his attention to a footnote in his book,[189] collecting the pronouncements of Popes Leo XIII, Pius X, and Pius XI on the central role of Thomas Aquinas' work for Catholic doctrine.[190] It was a signal that, whilst himself a Protestant and a US citizen, he was writing within the Neo-Scholasticism sanctioned and promoted by the Papacy. Indeed, Scott continued, *The Catholic Conception*'s purpose was "to show by a detailed analysis that the scholastic system of International Law meets all of the legitimate needs of the International Community of our day, and that it might be developed as in the past to meet the needs of the future intercourse of nations." Scott then explained to the Father General how he could help, reaching as he had done since the beginning of his approaches to the Catholic Church for its education system. His "hope was . . . that [his] Reverence might be willing to suggest that the scholastic system of International Law should be taught in the various educational institutions of the Society of Jesus."[191] The next day, Scott was received by Monsignor Giuseppe Pizzardo, the Undersecretary of State, who "graciously accept[ed] a volume on The Catholic Conception of International Law and undertaking to present a copy to the Holy Father."[192] In thanking the Jesuit Father who had interceded for him with Pizzardo, Georgetown's John E. Grattan, Scott affirmed to have "accomplished

[188] Ibid., p. 484.
[189] See ibid., pp. 132–3.
[190] See Scott to Wlodimir Ledóchowski, September 29, 1934.
[191] Ibid.
[192] James Brown Scott to Giuseppe Pizzardo, September 29, 1934, Folder 2, Box 52, JBS Papers.

what [h]e had in mind—only a beginning to be sure but, as our French friends say, 'Ce n'est que le premier pas qui coûte.' "[193]

Scott then left for Spain to attend the periodic meeting of the *Institut de Droit International* and the opening ceremony of the *Instituto de Derecho Internacional Francisco de Vitoria*.[194] On the occasion of the latter, Scott was invited by the Spanish Minister of Education to hold a *cursillo*, a short course, of six lectures on Vitoria and Suárez. Barcia Trelles, though, wrote to him confidentially so that he would not expect too much from the event. The University of Salamanca, with the support of the *Asociación Francisco de Vitoria*, had managed to start the *Instituto* the two of them had planned since Scott's first visit of 1927. Yet, without external help, the initial budget was scarce and activities at the beginning could not be too ambitious.[195]

Scott was supposed to travel to Salamanca after attending the *Institut* meeting in Madrid. But things did not go according to plan. He and his wife Adele found themselves caught up in the events of the unsuccessful revolution of October 1934. The events originated in a miners' strike in Asturias, which spread into a workers' revolt. The revolt, harshly suppressed within two weeks by the Army under the command of future dictator Francisco Franco, took place primarily in Asturias and Catalonia. But strikes and clashes took place also in other areas of Northern Spain and, indeed, in Madrid. When the Scotts reached Madrid's train station, they had to walk to their hotel because of a taxi drivers' strike, only to be forced to remain inside for days because of shootings in the streets. It would not have been possible to reach Salamanca in any case. Train service to the city was suspended, again because of the strikes against the conservative government of Prime Minister Alejandro Lerroux. The lectures had to be canceled. Interviewed by the *Washington Post* on the misadventure, Scott took the opportunity to acknowledge the existence "of an ominous situation . . . in Europe" but he "believe[d] there w[ould] be no great war" for as long as people had direct memory of the previous one.[196]

As soon as it was safe to leave, the Scotts proceeded straight to Paris where the meeting of the *Institut de droit international* had been moved. At the same time, the first operative meeting of the *Association Internationale Vitoria-Suarez* took place. It was the meeting where the project of the association's collective book on the Scholastic foundations of the international law of day was approved. Verdross, named co-editor with De la Briére, made initial suggestions toward the realization of the project. One was to ask for financial support for his German student

193 James Brown Scott to John E. Grattan, September 29, 1934, Folder 2, Box 52, JBS Papers.

194 On the plans and preparations for Scott's 1934 trip to Spain see the correspondence and the documents in vol. 498, CEIP Papers.

195 See Camilo Barcia Trelles to James Brown Scott, June 9, 1934, vol. 498, CEIP Papers.

196 "Dr. Scott's Lectures Encounter an Obstacle in Spanish Revolt," *Washington Post*, November 12, 1934.

Friedrich August von Heydte (1907–94), so that he could assist with the publication while continuing his research on the law of nations in the Middle Ages.[197]

Scott would grant the request, through CEIP funding.[198] It was not the first time that Heydte asked for his support at Verdross' recommendation. In February 1933, Heydte sent a letter inquiring about the CEIP Fellowships in International Law.[199] He informed Scott of his publications, especially his article on Vitoria's international law which was about to appear in a journal edited by Verdross.[200] As well as his other academic achievements and working experience, he mentioned his current job as personal assistant to the renowned legal scholar Hans Kelsen at the University of Cologne. By April, Scott was able to inform Heydte that CEIP had awarded him funding.[201] Yet, political events in Germany caused Heydte to ask for further help. Kelsen had been one of the first law professors to be dismissed by the newly installed Nazi government and, with him gone, Heydte believed he had "lost all possibilities for a future career." Kelsen's Jewish background[202] surely played a part and also his ideas on law and politics, significantly far from Nazi ideology. However, Heydte presented the dismissal as a misunderstanding. The "hitleriates, which have, without doubt, the best will" dismissed Kelsen because "for long years the German and Austrian Marxists pretended that he was their partisan and, therefore, generally he passed for a Marxist."[203] Heydte's leniency toward the men who fired his mentor might be explained by the circumstance that he would join the National Socialist Party less than a month after writing the letter; he would also enter the Sturmabteilung (SA) that same year.[204] Heydte came from a staunchly nationalist and conservative background. His father, a Bavarian Baron, had served in the First World War. Heydte followed in his father's footsteps joining the Army for two years in the mid-1920s before leaving to pursue his studies in law and diplomacy. Heydte's family was also devoutly Catholic and had relations with influent members in the Church, a circumstance of interest for Scott.

Over the following months, Heydte, claiming economic difficulties because of Kelsen's dismissal and the falling value of the dollar in which the CEIP fellowships were paid, would often request and obtain advance payments, raises of his grant

[197] See *Procès-verbal—Association Internationale Vitoria-Suarez, 17 octobre 1934.*

[198] See Alfred Verdross to James Brown Scott, October 29, 1934 and James Brown Scott to Alfred Verdross, November 26, 1934, vol. 338, CEIP Papers.

[199] See Friedrich August von Heydte to James Brown Scott, February 17, 1933, vol. 384, CEIP Papers. On the CEIP Fellowship see the first call, issued in 1926, Box 54, CEIP Papers.

[200] See Friedrich August von Heydte, "Franciscus de Vitoria und sein Völkerrecht," *Zeitschrift für öffentliches recht*, 13, 1933, pp. 239–68.

[201] See James Brown Scott to Friedrich August Von Heydte, April 3, 1933, vol. 384, CEIP Papers.

[202] Kelsen converted first to Catholicism in 1905, then to Protestantism in 1912 (see Bernstorff, *The Public International Law Theory of Hans Kelsen*, p. 275).

[203] See Friedrich August von Heydte to James Brown Scott, April 20, 1933, vol. 384, CEIP Papers. Underlining in the original.

[204] See Ernst Klee, *Das Personenlexicon zum Dritten Reich*, Frankfurt am Mein: Fischer Taschenbuch Verlag, 2005.

and the renewal of it for a second year.[205] Shortly after the Paris meeting of the Vitoria-Suarez Association, Scott could finally exploit Heydte's connections within the Curia and have him check on the results of his visit in September. In November, Heydte went to Rome to continue his studies at the renewed Vatican Library, with "the . . . aim . . . to contribute towards a 'rinascimento' of th[e] catholic conception of the law of nations," following the "valuable inspirations" of Scott's "book."[206] He also reported having spoken of Scott's "ideas and plans" with senior figures of the Curia, including "an old friend of [his] father who [wa]s camerario segreto [personal chamberlain], and also a personal friend, of the pope." Heydte received the most enthusiastic response from an Austrian Bishop, Alois Hudal, who had been publicly voicing support for the Nazi cause, out of his Pan-Germanic nationalism and anti-Semitic views.[207] Hudal hoped for "a 'syllabus' of international law taken out of the work of St. Augustin, Thomas, Vitoria and Suarez, and published by the pope in a solemn declaration." Heydte "only had to say: yes, that's the idea of Professor Brown Scott too." Instead, "[t]he camerario asked" for "some written aide-memoire in order to speak to the pope by occasion."[208]

Scott replied, noticing gladly that "the Association of Vitoria and Suárez ha[d] anticipated the suggestion of the good Bishop"[209] Hudal, as it coincided with the content of the collective book. But Scott had also anticipated the request of the *camerario*: together with Father Edmund Walsh he was preparing a memo detailing the Catholic conception of international law for the senior ranks of the Church in Rome.

The idea for a new memo grew out of his renewed acquaintance with Tisserant. During his visit to Rome, Scott had been given a guided tour of the renovated Vatican Library by the Monsignor, who was by now the *de facto* head librarian with the title of Pro-Prefect. After returning to the United States, Scott wrote to promise his support and that of the Executive Committee for the renewal of CEIP funding to the Library.[210] Indeed, given the difficult financial situation of CEIP, some Trustees argued for ending the subvention now that the modernizing of the Library infrastructure was concluded. But the Vatican requested further help to continue the cataloging work and CEIP, eventually, obliged.[211]

After the assurance of his help with the Library cause, Scott informed Tisserant that he would send him a memorandum on a different cause for which he hoped

[205] See correspondence in vols. 338, 384, and 389, CEIP Papers.

[206] See Friedrich August von Heydte to James Brown Scott, November 17, 1934, vol. 338, CEIP Papers.

[207] See Peter Godman, *Hitler and the Vatican*, New York: Free Press, 2004, pp. 44–6.

[208] See Friedrich August von Heydte to James Brown Scott, November 30, 1934, vol. 338, CEIP Papers.

[209] See James Brown Scott to Friedrich August Von Heydte, December 15, 1934, vol. 338, CEIP Papers.

[210] James Brown Scott to Eugène Tisserant, November 23, 1934, Folder 3, Box 71, JBS Papers.

[211] CEIP continued granting subventions to the Library for more than another decade.

to obtain his collaboration in turn. Scott sent the short text, a few days later, in December. In seven pages, he explained how "[f]or many years, [he] ha[d] devoted himself almost exclusively to the genesis of the modern law of nations," which was "due to two noble Churchmen[,] Francisco de Vitoria [and] Francisco Suárez." After his usual explanation of their role as, respectively, founder and earliest philosopher of the law of nations, Scott asked Tisserant "to present this delicate matter to the Holy Father, in the hope that he might be willing . . . to recommend . . . the teaching of the scholastic conception of law, of international law, and of their philosophy, in Catholic institutions at large." This "would . . . greatly tend to make the law of nations . . . conform . . . to the spirit of the Novum Testamentum." Scott also remarked that he "had hoped to include . . . a series of memoranda dealing . . . with . . . the contributions . . . to international law [of] St. Augustine, St. Thomas Aquinas, Francisco de Vitoria, Francisco Suárez and St. Robert Bellarmine."[212]

The new detailed memorandum would soon reach Rome, but the Pope would receive Tisserant even before that happened, on February 15, 1935. The Monsignor offered Pius XI two books he had received from Scott, the Classics edition of Vitoria's *relectiones* and the second book titled *The Spanish Origin of International Law*, published, like *The Catholic Conception*, in 1934. Tisserant informed the Pope of Scott's help with CEIP funding for the Library and of his campaign on the Catholic conception. The Pope, reportedly, listened with attentiveness and seemed keen on following up: "*le Souverain Pontife ne manquera pas de lire tout ce que je lui ai remis et . . . Il trouvera quelque moyen d'entrer dans vos vues en quelque realization pratique.*"[213]

By March, the thirty-six-page memorandum found its way to Rome. It originated out of Scott's meeting in September 1934 with the Father General of the Jesuits who, immediately after, wrote to Walsh asking for a detailed text on the Catholic conception. Walsh obliged, sending it to Ledóchowski,[214] while Scott forwarded it to Tisserant with the request that the Pontiff be provided with this text as well.[215]

The Scott-Walsh memorandum represented the most explicit and direct explanation of the action Scott hoped for the Papacy to take and the reasoning behind it. In its introduction, the authors painted a bleak picture of Western societies during those years of political and economic uncertainty. This situation was "*la conséquence même qui existe aujourd'hui dans la pensée des hommes à travers le monde.*" This "*manque d'équilibre spirituel*" led to dangerous "*panacées douteuses et . . . doctrines contradictoires.*"[216]

[212] James Brown Scott to Eugène Tisserant, December 5, 1934, Folder 4, Box 52, JBS Papers. Underlining in the original.

[213] Eugéne Tisserant to James Brown Scott, February 16, 1935, Folder 2, Box 8, JBS Papers.

[214] Edmund A. Walsh to Wlodimir Ledóchowski, February 18, 1935, Folder 9, Box 8, JBS Papers.

[215] James Brown Scott to Eugéne Tisserant, March 6, 1935, Folder 25, Box 12, JBS Papers.

[216] James Brown Scott and Edmund A. Walsh, "Résumé du Memorandum ci-inclus," *Memorandum sur la Conception Catholique du Droit International*, Folder 1, Box 52 JBS Papers, p. 1.

The character and purpose of mankind's behavior, the authors argued, depended on the quality of thinking that sustained it. The way to improve thought and action was a return to the roots of Christian tradition and truth. Only this could preserve universal peace. Indeed, "*les accords navals pour la reduction des armaments, les pactes destinés à mettre la guerre hors la loi et l'abolition . . . des moyens matériels de conflit*" would not suffice unless human beings first found in their heart the serenity needed to reach "*une solution pacifique de leur différends, base sur la justice, le respect mutuel et la confiance réciproque.*"[217]

International law could represent such a solution only if based on natural law and not on "*des principes uniquement utilitaires.*" Only with "*un principe de cȏntrole, fondamentalement moral et, par suite, universellement applicable, affranchi de tout machiavélisme*" would mankind naturally uphold international law. "*Alors, seulement, verra-t-on la loi, en tant qu'expression de la justice, imposer le respect et mériter l'obéissance.*"[218]

The moral foundations of international law and the preservation of peace were to be found in the Catholic teachings on the subject. The authors outlined a progressive genealogy of that line of thought, flattening all differences of context and opinion among the authors. The "*germe original*" planted by Augustine had flowered in the thought of Thomas Aquinas, Vitoria, Suárez, and Bellarmine, before finding a nineteenth-century expression in the work of Luigi Taparelli d'Azeglio. The understanding of human nature of the Catholic tradition of moral thought had found "*son application moderne dans une longue suite d'Encycliques,*" published by Leo XIII, Benedict XV, and the present Pope, Pius XI. The Pontiff had offered his guidance on the economic and social issues faced by contemporary societies with his 1931 encyclical *Quadragesimo Anno*. Yet, the authors reported that many, Catholics and non-Catholics alike, were calling for his moral leadership to show the way forward "*relativement au probléme de la paix internationale.*"

Scott and Walsh had prepared their memorandum "[*p*]*our fournir une réponse pratique à cette question*" in three points. First, the memorandum contained an historical survey of the doctrines of the Catholic authorities mentioned, which could be a starting point for the drafting of an encyclical. Such an encyclical, the authors argued, would elicit warm approval from lawyers all over the world, like *Quadragesimo Anno* had done with economists and sociologists. The encyclical on international peace would then complete "*la doctrine de l'Eglise sur les deux problèmes les plus urgents de l'époque actuelle.*" Secondly, the content of the encyclical should be adopted as official doctrine to be imparted in Catholic

[217] By explicitly submitting the primacy of the moral dimension in international relations over "scientific" approaches, Scott was effectively reneging on his pre-World War stance and his criticism of the more religiously-oriented groups of the Peace Movement (see Part I).

[218] Scott and Walsh, "Résumé du Memorandum ci-inclus," p. 2.

educational institutions. This would likely lead to the emergence of a "*mouvement solidaire dans l'intérêt de la paix, car ce qui ressort des événements récents, c'est que le désarmement moral devra précéder le désarmement matériel.*" Thirdly, and lastly, the authors proposed the publication of a manual conceived precisely for the teaching of the "*conception catholique de la paix internationale ainsi que le point de vue de l'Eglise relativement au droit international.*" Luckily, a book fitting the description was almost ready. The reference was to the collective volume of the Vitoria-Suárez Association.

In recommending these measures, Scott and Walsh delivered a strong sense of urgency: it was paramount to employ all the weight of the "*influence catholique en vue de la solution d'un problème mondial qui assume de jour en jour le caractère d'une véritable crise.*"[219]

## The Catholic Conception and the Approaching War

On March 21 and 22, 1935, the two main newspapers of Washington, D.C. reported a rumor that Adolf Hitler had publicly denounced the clauses on German disarmament of the Treaty of Versailles and reinstated military conscription. This had already happened a few days before and there had been no reaction from the Pontiff. The newspapers had learned from some unspecified prelates in the Curia that this was because Pius XI was preparing an encyclical on peace. Its publication was a matter of days, it was expected on the first day of April.[220]

Yet, the encyclical would not arrive then either. On April 1, Pius XI delivered an allocution titled *Pergratus Nobis*. The allocution acknowledged the "rumor of future war, which most agitate[d] every human being and awaken[ed] terror." This led the Pope "to add an Apolostical word, as it seem[ed] required by the Pontifical charge." The repetition of the total destruction, "the renewed spilling of brother's blood" of the World War would have been such an "enormous crime and an act of madness" that the Pope refused to believe it possible, "according to the saying: *Quae contra ius fiunt, nec fieri possunt credenda sunt.*" (What happened against the law, must not be believed to have happened.) This was the only mention of law in the speech. Against "the moral impossibility of a new war," Pius XI called for faith in God and prayer.[221]

No senior figure in CEIP claimed any credit for the allocution this time round. The search for an endorsement of international law continued. In July, Walsh had an audience with the Pope to discuss the Catholic conception project outlined in the

219 Ibid., pp. 3–5.
220 See "Pope Prepares to State Stand on Reich Arms," *The Evening Star*, March 21, 1935 and "Papal Encyclical to Urge Peace," *The Washington Post*, March 22, 1935.
221 "Pergratus Nobis," *Acta Apostolicae Sedis*, vol. II, 1935, p. 132. My translation from Latin.

memo he had prepared with Scott. While showing sympathy the Pope essentially suggested that the campaign should continue without any rush to obtain results:

> The great ideas in history have come from a small group of thinkers and leaders. But to make them effective, and to have them accepted by the masses requires constant and laborious efforts. The thinkers have always been in advance of the throng. They must use very skilful [sic] means—of propaganda, of experimental statements and of publicity in order to prepare the world to accept their projects. If a project is launched prematurely, one risks failure because the mind of the people was not ripe to receive it. That is why we must carefully and patiently "publicize" the truths contained in the Memorandum of Dr. Scott and P. Walsh, by speaking of them often, by writing articles, and by a progressive preparation of the public opinion.[222]

In the same letter, Walsh reassured Scott that the "policy" of continued publicity "so wisely and clearly outlined [by] His Holiness" was already "in actual execution." He relayed that *La Civiltá Cattolica*, a Jesuit periodical founded in 1850 by Luigi Taparelli d'Azeglio, was "often used by the Vatican as an unofficial (but authoritative) mouthpiece."[223] Enrico Rosa, the editor of the journal, had already authored and published two articles on the Catholic conception of international law.

The two articles appeared in the second quarterly volume for 1935, alongside one on *Pergratus Nobis*, written by Rosa as well. On that single reference to *ius*, Rosa built an account of the allocution as an "unexpected call to natural law, extended to the international law of peoples."[224] He then began the first of the two articles referred to by Walsh, titled "Il Concetto Cattolico del Diritto dei Popoli nelle Presenti Condizioni Sociali" ("The Catholic Conception of the Law of Peoples in the Current Social Conditions"), by affirming that statesmen had heeded the call of Pius XI with the Final Declaration of the Stresa Conference, "pushing away . . . the scary prospect of war." This aversion to an easy recourse to violence was a signal of "the catholic and christian conception of law rising, . . . recognized in our days . . . and reaffirmed also by non-catholic jurists"[225] as universally applicable. Rosa's definition of the conception overlapped with Scott's:

> [I]t substantially entail[ed] that also international law . . . would always make morality and justice dominate in the relations between peoples, especially in the

[222] Edmund A. Walsh to James Brown Scott, July 27, 1935, Folder 9, Box 8, JBS Papers. The quote is Walsh's summary of the Pope's statements during their meeting.

[223] Ibid.

[224] Enrico Rosa, "La Parola di Pio XI per la Pace nel Mondo e il Diritto dei Popoli," *La Civiltá Cattolica*, 2, 1935, p. 119. My translation from Italian.

[225] Enrico Rosa, "Concetto Cattolico del Diritto dei Popoli nelle Presenti Condizioni Sociali," *La Civiltá Cattolica*, 2, 1935, pp. 239 and 241. My translation from Italian.

pacific settlement of their disputes, substituting violence or war, among individuals as well as among States. [O]nly the guidance of the Church and the triumph of the catholic conception of law could bring true peace [and] reciprocal trust among individuals and people[.][226]

Rosa finished the article with praise for CEIP and its capacity to go beyond the confessional divide with its publications promoting Catholic doctrines. In particular, Rosa mentioned Scott's *The Catholic Conception*, to which he devoted the next article on the topic. Having an entire article praising his work on the Salamancans in *La Civiltá Cattolica*[227] was not necessarily the type of direct public blessing Scott sought from the Church. Yet, a blessing it undeniably was.

Indeed, Walsh concluded the letter in which he informed Scott about his meeting with the Pope and Rosa's articles on an upbeat note: "This is substantial progress."[228] However, with the international situation rapidly deteriorating, the project soon lost any real hope of ultimate success. The results of Stresa Conference of April 1935, mentioned by Rosa, seemed to have given some stability to Europe for a short while. There, the prime ministers of Italy, France, and the United Kingdom had created a common front based on the upholding of the Locarno treaties of 1925 and a commitment to Austrian independence against Hitler's plans for its annexation. Already in the following June, the United Kingdom broke the Stresa front by entering into the Anglo-German Naval Agreement, which permitted an increase in the size of the German Navy beyond the one set in the Treaty of Versailles. The Abyssinian crisis, triggered by the Italian invasion of Ethiopia in the following October, gave a definitive sign of the ineffectiveness of the League of Nations' system of collective security.

As the Catholic conception project faded, so was Scott's health deteriorating, forcing him to reduce his professional engagements. In 1937 he was hit hard by the death of his favorite sister Jeannette, followed by his wife Adele in 1939. Notwithstanding, Scott continued his campaign until the very end. For instance, on February 21, 1938, he addressed members of the Boston College, on the occasion of the 75th anniversary of that Jesuit institution. His speech "The Catholic Conception of the State and of the Law of Nations" reaffirmed Bellarmine and Suárez as the intellectual fathers of American democracy, while Vitoria and, again, Suárez had conceived the modern understandings of the international community. In their work, Scott still found hope: "If we of today sometimes fear that the future will be dark . . . and war seems to threaten our civilization," one could follow the examples of the past's great thinkers, who "had the courage thus to look beyond their

[226] Ibid., p. 242. My translation from Italian.

[227] See Enrico Rosa, "Concetto Cattolico e Fondatori del Diritto Internazionale nelle Pubblicazioni della 'Dotazione Carnegie'," *La Civiltá Cattolica*, 2, 1935, pp. 391–402.

[228] Walsh to Scott, July 27, 1935.

own day to an enlightened future under an enlightened law—the law of Bellarmine, Suárez and Vitoria[. S]urely we of the present age should have the courage to hold fast to their dreams and to add to them our own plans for a better world."[229]

Accordingly, until the very end of his career, Scott sought the completion of the collective volume of the Vitoria-Suárez Association. Despite the continued assurances by De la Briére,[230] Heydte,[231] and Verdross[232] that the book would be ready in time for the 1936 session of the *Institut de droit international*, it would still need to overcome a series of difficulties and a few more years before it saw the light. The work proceeded in a Europe falling deeper into chaos. For instance, the 1936 meeting of the *Institut* was to be held in Madrid, an attempt to cancel out the fiasco of 1934. Instead, the hosting city was changed once again, this time to Brussels, because of the outbreak of the Spanish Civil War. Political events affected the work of the editors. At the time of the Anschluss and pending his suspension from teaching, Verdross resigned from any responsibility in the Vitoria-Suárez Association and sent all its Secretariat's documents to De la Briére.[233] In March 1939, De la Briére also informed Scott that Heydte had stopped working on the book altogether and had rejoined the German Army, leaving unfinished business behind him.[234] For instance, he had commissioned a series of translations to one Mr. Bernoud of Geneva, falsely claiming to act as an agent of CEIP in the matter. Once Heydte cut communication, Bernoud pressed his claim for payment of services rendered to CEIP through the Swiss Minister in the United States. Eventually, Scott, unwilling to use CEIP funds for unauthorized expenses and believing in the translator's good faith, decided to pay out of his own pocket.[235]

The book would be concluded by De la Briére and finally published in August 1939, under the title *Vitoria et Suarez: Contributions des théologiens au droit international moderne*.[236] Less than a month later, Germany would invade Poland, marking the beginning of the Second World War. Most copies of the book would remain in storage with the publisher Pedone for the duration of the conflict. After

[229] James Brown Scott, *The Catholic Conception of the State and of the Law of Nations. Address delivered by James Brown Scott at the Seventy-fifth Anniversary of Boston College, Boston, Massachusetts, February 21, 1938*, Folder 4, Box 55, JBS Papers.

[230] See Yves De la Briére to James Brown Scott, February 17, 1935, vol. 342, CEIP Papers.

[231] See Friedrich August von Heydte to James Brown Scott, November 15, 1935, vol. 342, CEIP Papers.

[232] See Alfred Verdross to James Brown Scott, November 24, 1934, vol. 342, CEIP Papers.

[233] See Yves De la Briére to James Brown Scott, August 11, 1939, Box 86, CEIP Papers.

[234] See Yves De la Briére to James Brown Scott, March 28, 1939, Box 86, CEIP Papers. Later in the year, Heydte participated in the German invasion of Poland, receiving the Iron Cross. He fought on many of the fronts of the Second World War. Caught in the course of a failed paratrooper mission in December 1943, he would remain in England as a prisoner of war until 1947. After the war, he continued his academic career as a professor of international law and was politically active in the Christian Social Union.

[235] The correspondence on the issue is in Box 86, CEIP Papers.

[236] *Vitoria et Suarez: Contributions des théologiens au droit international moderne. Choix de textes latins avec traduction française. Suivi de trois mémoires par l'abbé Robert Jacquin, Louis Le Fur, J.-T. Delos. Préface par James Brown Scott. Introduction par Yves de La Briére*, Paris: A. Pedone, 1939.

suffering a stroke in the winter of 1938 and the death of his wife Adele on October 15, 1939, Scott was offered retirement by the CEIP Trustees. He officially retired in June 1940, but Finch had already taken over almost all of his tasks months before. By the time Japan attacked Pearl Harbor in December 1941 and the United States entered the war, Scott's mental health had deteriorated so badly that he lacked any awareness or understanding of those events.[237]

## The Conservative Legacy of the Catholic Conception

The immediate legacy of the Catholic conception campaign was very limited, if any, among the international legal community in the United States. The shift toward privileging policy analysis within the ASIL, begun with the break of the younger generation in favor of collective security during the First World War, continued even more markedly through the Second World War and the beginning of the Cold War. This further turn away from legalism and utopianism toward political realism and international relations found its most iconic proponent in the German *émigré* Hans Morgenthau and its manifesto in his 1948 book *Politics Among Nations*.[238] In 1953, Philip C. Jessup, the professor of international law at Columbia University who had taken over from Scott as Director of the CEIP Division of International Law, wondered at the annual meeting if ASIL would soon change its "name . . . to the American Society of International Realism."[239]

The rights-based revival of natural law that Scott championed through Vitoria and Suárez found anyway a continuation in the post-Second World War era. To discern it, it is important to analyze what brought the alliance behind the Catholic conception campaign together in the first place. Scott's project seemed to appeal primarily to European conservatives and authoritarians, the kind of figures he had criticized for most of his career as representatives of an old world order that would disappear, substituted by the progressive new international law based on American democratic values. This shift was favored by a changed global context. In the interwar era, liberals and conservatives routinely found common ground in their anti-socialism and, more specifically, anti-Bolshevism. The successful revolution and the following stabilization of the Soviet Union had provided a successful model to workers' movements searching for greater social justice and equality in

[237] On the deterioration of Scott's physical and mental health from 1938 to his death on June 25, 1943, see "Testimony of George A. Finch," Folder 4, Box 71, JBS Papers.

[238] Hans Morgenthau, *Politics Among Nations: The Struggle for Power and Peace*, New York: A. A. Knopf, 1948. On the intellectual development of Morgenthau from his early legal studies to the development of international relations see Martti Koskenniemi, *The Gentle Civilizer of Nations*, Cambridge: Cambridge University Press, 2001, pp. 436–74.

[239] Philip C. Jessup, "International Law in 1953 A.D.," *Proceedings of the American Society of International Law*, 47, 1953, p. 8.

the fluid political situation of the years immediately following the Great War. In this context, the rise of nationalist right-wing dictatorships in Europe was, initially at least, saluted by American liberal elites as an antidote to the Red Scare and atheist materialism. It is within this framework that we can better understand the initial fascination with Mussolini's Fascist regime of many prominent Americans, including Nicholas Murray Butler,[240] or Scott's defense of Primo de Rivera's dictatorship on the *New York Times*.[241] Opposition to Bolshevism made it also easier for liberals and conservatives, Protestant and Catholics, to find common ground in Christian values. The gradual recognition of Nazi Germany as an enemy that could not be appeased but only defeated, the complex relation of the Catholic Church with the Nazi regime, and later, the war-time alliance with the Soviet Union, all muddled this scheme of loyalties as the 1930s progressed and the Second World War unfolded. However, it proposed itself again once the war came to an end and the common enemies of the West were again the Soviet Union and communism. And, indeed, recent revisionist works of historical research have re-described the European political projects on human rights of the early postwar period in a conservative light[242] that uncovers and emphasizes strong intellectual affinities with Scott's Catholic conception.[243] Both were characterized by a Christian understanding of natural rights, expressed through international law and construed in opposition to communism.

The basic narrative that European unification and continental judicial protection of human rights were leftist projects born of a complete reversal from the trauma of fascism has found a healthy problematization in those recent works. Their thesis is apparent if one looks at the strong opposition to those Europeanist projects on the left.[244] But it is even clearer if one looks at the main characters behind those projects. Winston Churchill, Konrad Adenauer, Alcide De Gasperi, Robert Schuman were all social conservatives. The last three were also devout Catholics who offered their religious approach to life as a primary component of their political engagement and thinking.

[240] See Adam Tooze, "When we loved Mussolini," *The New York Review of Books*, issue of 18 August 2016 and Michael Rosenthal, *Nicholas Miraculous: The Amazing Career of the Redoubtable Dr. Nicholas Murray Butler*, New York: Farrar, Straus and Giroux, 2006, *passim*.

[241] See Chapter 4.

[242] For the most in-depth analysis along these lines see Marco Duranti, *The Conservative Human Rights Revolution. European Identity, Transnational Politics, and the Origins of the European Convention*, Oxford: Oxford University Press, 2017.

[243] "If... Europeans preserved human rights, it was in the frequently Christian, 'personalist' key that allowed the concept to take on a conservative meaning as the postwar era began. Personalism provided a powerful idiom for West European incorporation of human rights[.] As time passed such personalism more and more simply rephrased anticommunism and Western unity rather than offering a philosophy of global amity" (Samuel Moyn, *The Last Utopia: Human Rights in History*, Cambridge: Harvard University Press, 2010, p. 191).

[244] See Duranti, *The Conservative Human Rights Revolution*, *passim*.

If one could argue that Scott's ideas found expression in the postwar political action for European human rights, it is more difficult to point to an intellectual lineage within the international legal profession, in its prevailing realist bent of the early Cold War. After Scott's death, only Spanish international lawyers, operating within the political environment of the Franco regime, celebrated his work on the Salamancans explicitly.[245] This was more for instrumental reasons than intellectual closeness, though. As the depiction of Vitoria as a humanitarian became a key element of the nationalist mythology,[246] claiming a foreign and non-Catholic proponent of that account had a symbolic value.

The international lawyer who maintained an explicitly Neo-Thomist approach throughout the early Cold War was Scott's ally in the Catholic conception campaign, Alfred Verdross. He remained committed to natural law for the rest of his career.[247] As part of this commitment he "argued for human rights as the necessary inference from human dignity for decades."[248] Fittingly with the ideal connection between international legal Neo-Thomism and postwar Europeanist projects, Verdross would serve as a judge of the European Court of Human Rights for eighteen years, between 1958 and 1976. While Verdross is the paradigmatic figure embodying the connection between interwar Catholic conservatism and postwar human rights initiatives, he was hardly alone among European international lawyers. As a further example, I can point to another founding member of the *Association internationale Vitoria-Suarez*, the Belgian Charles de Visscher, a judge at both the Permanent Court of International Justice and its successor, the International Court of Justice. As a rapporteur at the first postwar meeting of the *Institut de droit international* in 1947, De Visscher built a case for human rights resting on the Christian tradition and a personalist foundation. As a result the *Institut* approved a declaration affirming "*le respect des droits de la personne humaine*" as the "*base d'une restauration du droit international*."[249]

Returning to Scott, looking at his approaches to the Catholic Church points to his adoption of Vitoria and Suárez as a conservative move, signaling him as a defender of the status quo, now not only in the United States, but also with regard to Europe. Indeed, the language in his works on the Salamanca School shifted to

[245] See for instance Alejandro Herrero to George A. Finch, October 17, 1946, Folder 1, Box 66.

[246] On this phenomenon see Ignacio de la Rasilla y del Moral, "The Fascist Mimesis of Spanish International Law and its Vitorian aftermath, 1939–1953," *Journal of the History of International Law*, 14, 2012, pp. 207–36.

[247] For an analysis of Verdross' natural law theory across his career see Antonio Truyol y Serra, "Verdross et la théorie du droit," *European Journal of International Law*, 6, 1995, pp. 55–69.

[248] Moyn, *The Last Utopia*, p. 191.

[249] For the full text of the declaration see *Annuaire de l'Institut de Droit International*, Paris: A. Pedone Editeur, 1947, pp. 258–60. De Visscher's report and its discussion can be found ibid., respectively at pp. 1–13 and 142–90. On De Visscher's understanding of human rights in historical perspective in this phase see Charles de Visscher, "Human Rights in Roman Law Countries," *The Annals of the American Academy of Political and Social Science*, 243, 1946, pp. 53–9. De Visscher's 1947 initiative is commented and contextualized in Samuel Moyn's excellent overview of Christian efforts for human rights in the period (*Christian Human Rights*, Philadelphia: University of Pennsylvania Press, 2015, pp. 65–8).

integrate his typical focus on equality and popular sovereignty within the frame of a higher moral order based on godly authority and Church tradition. This was a similar integrative move to the one made through Neo-Scholasticism by American Catholics like John Ryan, except Scott reached that linguistic compromise coming from the other end of its spectrum.

The picture of Scott's Spanish origin theory, however, becomes more complicated when one considers that Scott used Vitoria and Suárez to justify many other legal and political agendas beyond closeness to the positions of the Catholic Church. One of these uses in particular, the pursuit of international equal rights for women, was a considerably radical position in the political context of the time. This project, of which I provide an account in the following and last chapter, brought Scott criticism and opposition from some of his closest collaborators within the CEIP. Even more surprisingly, it led him to publicly oppose the US government for the first time in his career, just as he was about to retire.

# 6

# Apostles of Equality: James Brown Scott and the Feminist Cause

## 1. The Making of the US Feminist Movement and the National Woman's Party

### A Room of Their Own

In 1929, novelist Virginia Woolf published the feminist essay *A Room of One's Own*. The text addressed the relationship between women and fiction, noting how the idealization of the "gentler sex" in literature was coupled with repression and denial of basic independence and education in social reality.

> Women have burnt like beacons in all the works of all the poets since the beginning of time . . . , among the dramatists; then among the prose writers[. I]f woman had no existence save in the fiction written by men, one would imagine her a person of the utmost importance; . . . as great as a man, some think even greater. . . . Imaginatively she is of the highest importance; practically she is completely insignificant. She pervades poetry from cover to cover; she is all but absent from history. She dominates the lives of kings and conquerors in fiction; in fact she was the slave of any boy whose parents forced a ring upon her finger. Some of the most inspired words, some of the most profound thoughts in literature fall from her lips; in real life she could hardly read, could scarcely spell, and was the property of her husband.[1]

Woolf then reflected on the challenges of women writers through history. Her conclusion was a clear demand, carrying both literal and figurative meaning: "Give her a room of her own and five hundred a year, let her speak her mind . . . and she will write a better book one of these days."[2] In other words, give a woman enough independence and space for expression and she will prove her ability to shape culture and society.

At the same time as Woolf was writing her essay, the members of the Inter-American Commission of Women (IACW) were indeed fighting for a room of their

[1] Virginia Woolf, *A Room of One's Own*, London: Penguin Books, 2000 [1929], pp. 44–5.
[2] Ibid., p. 93.

*Rewriting the History of the Law of Nations: How James Brown Scott Made Francisco de Vitoria the Founder of International Law*. Paolo Amorosa, Oxford University Press (2019). © Paolo Amorosa
DOI: 10.1093/oso/9780198849377.001.0001

own. The Commission had been created by the Sixth Pan-American Conference of Havana in early 1928 and given an office in Washington, D.C., in the headquarters of the Pan-American Union. After a few months, the Commission's members had been asked to temporarily vacate the premises, as they were to be used for the preparations for an upcoming Conference on arbitration. When they tried to return in February 1929, the Director General of the Union Leo Rowe refused. The Commission, he argued, was not an official organ and therefore was not entitled to office room in the headquarters.[3]

The women of the Commission were used to fighting for their space. Their chairman[4] was Doris Stevens (1888–1963), a veteran of the suffrage struggle. She had been among the women arrested for picketing the White House and had written the most popular account of that experience, *Jailed for Freedom*.[5] When the office issue broke out Stevens called on the one man who could and would help: James Brown Scott. Thanks to his intervention, within a few months the Commission had working space both at the Union and in the Carnegie Endowment for International Peace (CEIP) building.

A collaboration that would have been unlikely only a few years earlier turned out to be one of the most significant in Scott's later career. As Stevens brought Scott over to the feminist cause, he found new ways to deploy the legacy of Vitoria and the School of Salamanca in twentieth-century politics. Scott's argument that Vitoria had founded modern international law on the principle of equality fit well with the equal rights brand of feminism that Stevens championed.

Indeed, both Scott and Stevens believed in a formal understanding of equality that would purposely disregard differences. Woolf's essay, for instance, was open to criticism: her demands for equal opportunities took a form that was within the horizon of upper-middle class women but utterly unrealistic and unsuited to the needs of the ones belonging to the working class or of non-white ethnicity. In a similar fashion, equal rights feminists were the object of harsh criticism on class and racial grounds, coming especially from another group of feminists who did not agree with their approach. "Retrospectively called social feminists, these women

[3] On the office controversy see Doris Stevens to James Brown Scott, February 3, 1929, Folder 1, Box 48, JBS Papers.

[4] The use of 'chairman' to denote a title held by a woman sounds odd to twenty-first-century ears. But it was consistently used in women's organizations Doris Stevens and Alice Paul created and led. While I do not have hard evidence for this, I do think that it was a conscious choice and not just a reflection of the usage of the day, whereby language reflected that leadership positions could be held almost exclusively by men. As this chapter makes clear, equal rights feminists like Stevens and Paul believed in bettering the conditions of women by asserting their absolute equality with men, and not by underlining gender and class differences, as social feminists did. Within the equal rights frame of mind, adopting the title of 'chairman', without seeking for a differentiated word for a woman, was a coherent stance.

[5] Doris Stevens, *Jailed for Freedom*, New York: Boni and Liveright Publishers, 1920.

viewed suffrage as a tool for reform, were involved in public policy issues dedicated to the needs of working women, and advocated a feminist welfare state."[6]

This intellectual rift within the feminist movement led to open confrontations only during the 1920s. Indeed, the common goal of achieving the right to vote had kept together a large and composite coalition. Once the Nineteenth Amendment to the Constitution was ratified, establishing equal suffrage, the National Woman's Party (NWP), which counted Stevens among its leaders, chose the primary objective of its next campaign. It was another amendment to the Constitution, containing the following clause: "Men and women shall have equal rights throughout the United States and every place subject to its jurisdiction." Introduced in Congress for the first time in 1923, it came to be known as the Equal Rights Amendment (ERA). If Stevens and her allies conceived the ERA as the crowning achievement of feminism in legal terms, for social feminists it was a recipe for disaster. Indeed, such a blanket legal prescription of equality could have the effect of dismantling the protective labor legislation that set, for instance, a limit to daily working hours and a minimum wage for women.[7]

By the closing years of the 1920s the NWP had decided to pursue equal rights legislation beyond national politics and the ERA. On the legal advice and with the enthusiastic cooperation of James Brown Scott, they lobbied international Conferences for two multilateral treaties, one modeled on the ERA, the other bestowing equal nationality rights on women. Before meeting Stevens, Scott had shown no sympathy for the feminist cause and even denigrated it on occasion. Yet, once they had started working together, he would throw all the weight of his Spanish origin narrative behind the NWP's goals.

While, in Scott's mind, his alliance with the Catholic Church was a natural one, expressed since a young age, the one with the feminist movement was not. The Church was an institution that represented authority, tradition, and Christian moral values, sustained through the centuries. In opposition, Scott, had perceived feminist activism as a radical enterprise and disapproved of the militant tactics employed by the NWP. It is not surprising, then, that Scott aligned with the NWP years later, when the Party's methods of political struggle had become almost exclusively institutional and its sole guiding principle had become formal equality. Arguably, though, the effort Scott deployed for equal rights feminism did not spring solely out of common political views. The genuine personal closeness he

[6] Mary K. Trigg, *Feminism as Life's Work: Four Modern American Women through Two World Wars*, New Brunswick: Rutgers University Press, 2014, p. 8.

[7] On the ERA controversy during the 1920s see Nancy F. Cott, "Feminist Politics in the 1920s: The National Woman's Party," *The Journal of American History*, 71, 1984, pp. 43–68. On early twentieth-century protection laws in the United States see Susan Lehrer, *Origins of Protective Labor Legislation for Women, 1905–1925*, Albany: State University of New York Press, 1987. On the pursuit and achievement of protective international agreements through the International Labor Organization (ILO) in the interwar years see Carol Riegelman Lubin and Anne Winslow, *Social Justice for Women: The International Labor Organization and Women*, Durham: Duke University Press, 1990, pp. 25–53.

developed with Alice Paul (1885–1977), the most influential figure of the NWP, and, especially, Doris Stevens, also played a role. The story of how Scott enlisted Vitoria and Suárez as pioneers of the equality of sexes and a modern understanding of nationality is also the story of that friendship and of the life-long commitment of Paul and Stevens to feminism.

## Feminism and the Suffrage Movement in the United States

In the self-narration of the US feminist movement, most accounts have pointed to the Seneca Falls Convention of 1848 as the founding act. The notice advertising that event in the local newspaper of the Seneca County (New York) described it as "a convention to discuss the social, civil, and religious condition and rights of woman."[8] The two main figures of the Convention were Lucretia Mott and Elizabeth Cady Stanton, both already experienced activists within the abolitionist movement. After a lively debate, 100 people—sixty-eight women and thirty-two men—out of the 300 attending agreed to sign the Declaration of Sentiments. The Declaration was a document Stanton had modeled on the US Declaration of Independence, affirming that women had an inalienable right to suffrage. At the time, such a claim was seen as radical even among those actively supporting women's rights. Opponents favored a more gradualist approach, entailing a focus on less controversial goals such as enlarging the scope of property rights for married women, hindered by the common law doctrine of coverture. A similar dynamic, with some groups advocating radical strategies and others exercising more caution, would characterize the suffrage movement until its final success in 1920.

But, even considering the continuities, played up in order to muster the authority of the early activists, by the time women obtained suffrage the movement was different from what it was in the mid-nineteenth century. Historian Nancy F. Cott has underlined the analytical importance of realizing that feminism was a term entering into use in the United States only in the early twentieth century. This was no mere vocabulary shift, it signaled the appearance of a new set of ideas and attitudes.

> People in the nineteenth century did not say *feminism*. They spoke of the advancement or the cause of woman, woman's rights, and woman suffrage. Most inclusively, they spoke of the woman movement, to denote the many ways women moved out of their homes to initiate measures of charitable benevolence, temperance, and social welfare and to instigate struggles for civic rights, social freedom, higher education, remunerative occupations, and the ballot. Nineteenth-century

[8] *Seneca County Courier*, July 11, 1848, quoted in Judith Wellman, *The Road to Seneca Falls. Elizabeth Cady Stanton and the First Woman's Rights Convention*, Urbana: University of Illinois Press, 2004, p. 189.

women's consistent usage of the singular *woman* symbolized, in a word, the unity of the female sex. It proposed that all women have one cause, one movement. But to twentieth-century ears the singular generic *woman* sounds awkward, *the woman movement* ungrammatical.[9]

Feminism was a full-fledged ideology and involved more than a set of reforms championed by women as a social group. It entailed the rethinking and reshaping of the role of women in society and the relationships between sexes, including an experimental approach to sexuality.[10] Given its radicalism, not all women identified with feminism. Stevens, like Paul, was part of the earliest generation of activists who fully embraced feminism and brought a sense of renewed purpose into a suffrage effort that was making progress at State level but was not making headway in the US Congress. By the time Stevens and Paul met for the first time in 1913, sixty-five years had passed since the signature of the Declaration of Sentiments. Yet, women could only vote in eleven of the forty-eight States of the Union. Just seven years later, Congress would finally approve the Nineteenth Amendment to the Constitution and women gained the right to vote nationwide.

Doris Stevens was born on October 26, 1888 in Omaha, Nebraska in a staunchly Republican family of Presbyterian faith.[11] Her early years were marked by the difficult relationship between her parents. The idealistic Henry Stevens never achieved the material success his pragmatic wife, Caroline Koopman Stevens, had hoped for. Born into a Dutch family that moved to the United States when she was three, Caroline was unhappy in marriage, quite apart from the shortcomings she saw in her husband. Before meeting Henry she had wanted to become a doctor. "When her own waylaid career ambitions could not be vicariously fulfilled in a successful career for her husband, she grew bitter."[12]

Doris loved her father and appreciated his honesty and good nature. But she also understood her mother and determined that she would not live her life unfulfilled as she had done. She found the intellectual articulation of that sentiment when she moved to Ohio to attend college in 1906, the same year James Brown Scott began his collaboration with Elihu Root at the State Department. Stevens would study for four years at Oberlin College, the first to open its doors to women and African American students in the United States, starting in the 1830s. Once there, she joined the College Equal Suffrage League and started her activism for women's rights. As Mary Trigg noted, Stevens had already identified the "two key goals of the equal rights feminism to which she devoted her life: legal equality and

[9] Nancy F. Cott, *The Grounding of Modern Feminism*, New Haven: Yale University Press, 1987, p. 3.

[10] On the relationship of the woman's movement with early feminism in its diverse intellectual manifestations see Trigg, *Feminism as Life's Work*, pp. 11–15. On sexuality as a site for feminist experimentation see ibid., pp. 67–94.

[11] On Stevens' childhood and youth see ibid., pp. 29–33.

[12] Ibid., p. 30.

companionship between the sexes."[13] Her views translated into a simple and effective formula when it came to college life: "Same rules for girls and boys (Legal side), permit dancing between boys and girls (Social side)."[14]

Stevens left Oberlin in 1911 with a bachelor's degree in sociology. She briefly worked in a settlement house and, later, as a high school teacher. She continued promoting suffrage by joining the National American Woman Suffrage Association (NAWSA). Soon, she left her job to become NAWSA's organizer for Dayton County, Ohio. When Alice Paul formed the Congressional Union for Woman Suffrage, Stevens moved to Washington, D.C. to join her.

NAWSA was the largest and best-known suffrage organization in the country. Its foundation in 1890 marked the reconciliation of a rift that had plagued the woman movement for two decades.[15] Indeed, following the Civil War, the Fifteenth Amendment was added to the Constitution. Its purpose was to protect from discrimination the exercise of the right to vote by the newly enfranchised African Americans. Not all women suffragists supported the measure. The opponents did not accept the exclusive focus on race of postwar constitutional reforms. African Americans were entitled to equal voting rights but women were too. Therefore, the Fifteenth Amendment, which forbade discrimination on the basis of race but not on the basis of sex, was to be opposed, as long as women's quest for equal voting rights were ignored. The National Woman Suffrage Association, led by Elizabeth Cady Stanton and Susan B. Anthony, championed this position.

However, the American Woman Suffrage Association, led by Lucy Stone, sought the respectability it associated with a more accommodating position. Its members accepted that it was the "Negro's hour" and women could and should wait.[16] They "believed that [the vote] could be won only by avoiding issues that were irrelevant and calculated to alienate the support of influential sections of the community." The association's "leaders had no interest in organizing working women, in criticizing the churches, or in the divorce question[.] While paying lip service to the principle of a Federal woman suffrage amendment, they concentrated their practical work for the franchise within the several states."[17]

[13] Ibid., p. 32.

[14] Doris Stevens, "Autobiographical Jottings," Folder 251, Box 8, Doris Stevens Papers, Schlesinger Library, Radcliffe Institute, Harvard University, quoted in ibid.

[15] On the schism within the woman movement see Eleanor Flexner, *Century of Struggle: The Woman's Rights Movement in the United States*, Revised Edition, Cambridge: Harvard University Press, 1975 [1959], pp. 150–8; Christine Lunardini, *Alice Paul: Equality for Women*, Boulder: Westview Press, 2013, pp. 20–3.

[16] The "Negro's hour" argument was deployed in the aftermath of the Civil War by those reformers who believed that the cause of suffrage for black men should be prioritized over the cause of women, as both would be doomed to fail if pushed together. On the controversy between those reformers, on one side, and Anthony and Stanton, on the other, see Faye E. Dudden, *Fighting Chance: The Struggle over Woman Suffrage and Black Suffrage in Reconstruction America*, Oxford: Oxford University Press, 2011, pp. 61–87.

[17] Flexner, *Century of Struggle*, p. 156.

With the passing of time, a younger generation joining the suffrage movement failed to see any reason for the division, other than the clash of personalities of the older leaders. In January 1887, when a woman suffrage constitutional amendment suffered a heavy defeat in the Senate, the strategy of focusing on State campaigns gained ground.[18] 1890 saw both the foundation of NAWSA and Wyoming joining the Union as the first State recognizing women's right to vote. A successful path seemed marked, but by the time Alice Paul joined NAWSA in 1910, that momentum was lost. The organization had grown significantly, reaching 117,000 members.[19] But no State had granted suffrage to women since 1896, with the total at only four. Seven more States would join between 1910 and 1913, but for Paul it was not enough: she wanted the focus back on a suffrage constitutional amendment. She planned to pursue it through the aggressive tactics she had tested in England. Working with suffragettes between 1907 and 1909, she was arrested several times and force-fed when she started a hunger strike in prison. That past, in combination with her insistence on seeking suffrage federally, made her problematic in the eyes of NAWSA's leadership since the beginning. At first, she tried to work with them, taking over the organization's Congressional Committee, thanks to the intercession of the renowned reformer Jane Addams (1860–1935) on her behalf. Her first major undertaking was the Woman Suffrage Procession held in Washington, D.C. on March 3, 1913, the day before the inauguration of Woodrow Wilson as president. With only a few months to organize and notwithstanding the lack of cooperation from local authorities, the suffrage parade was a success. Eight thousand marchers, led by the iconic figure of Inez Milholland dressed in white and riding a white horse, flooded Pennsylvania Avenue. Male crowds physically attacked the parade, with the police often participating. Even though 200 people needed hospital treatment for injuries as a result of the disturbances, most of the marchers made it to the endpoint, close to the White House.

The organization of the parade brought the first accusations of racial bias against Paul and her allies, accusations that would often be reiterated toward the NWP in the context of the ERA campaigns of the interwar years. Southern women informed Paul that they would not march alongside black women. At the end of the day, the delegations from black organizations such as Howard University participated under a segregated arrangement: white women were in front of the parade, with the men's section providing a separation and the black groups closing the order. Paul maintained for the rest of her life that a compromise on the racial issue had been readily found by all parties involved.[20] However, *Crisis*, the periodical of

[18] On these and other developments discouraging the pursuit of a suffrage constitutional amendment in the Reconstruction period see Lunardini, *Alice Paul*, pp. 23–4.

[19] See Sara Hunter Graham, *Woman Suffrage and the New Democracy*, New Haven: Yale University Press, 1996, pp. 51–2.

[20] For an account accepting Paul's version see Lunardini, *Alice Paul*, pp. 51–3. For Paul's own telling of the issue, six decades after it happened, see Robert S. Gallagher, "'I was Arrested, Of Course . . .' An Interview with the Famed Suffragette, Alice Paul," *American Heritage*, 25(2), February 1974, p. 20..

the National Association for the Advancement of Colored People (NAACP), reported that only after significant protest were the initial plans for a fully segregated parade scrapped and individual black women allowed to march with the delegations of their State or profession.[21]

In any case, the parade brought visibility and new resources for the suffrage campaign, which the NAWSA leadership enjoyed. But Paul's success did not lead them to espouse her federal strategy or give her more liberty of action. Relations grew tense. In April, the month after the parade, Paul founded the Congressional Union (CU), an independent organization affiliated with NAWSA. By July, Doris Stevens was at her side. There she remained when in December, among growing personal and institutional rivalries, the Congressional Union and NAWSA cut all ties.

## "A Party to Free their Own Sex":[22] The Anti-Democratic Campaigns and the Birth of the National Woman's Party

Finally free from direction from NAWSA, Paul could implement the vision she had proposed when she first joined the organization, only to be shot down as too radical and counterproductive. Beside lobbying and actions to maintain visibility on the issue, the suffrage movement could count on a powerful yet untapped resource: the vote itself. The ballots of the enfranchised women in Western States could be mustered to engage in an exercise of third-party politics. The memory of the 1912 presidential election was still fresh: if the Democrats had been able to return to power with Woodrow Wilson after decades of Republican dominance, it was largely due to Theodore Roosevelt's bid as candidate of the Progressive Party, which siphoned away votes that would have likely kept the incumbent President Taft in the White House. That same electoral round provided the Democrats with solid majorities in both Houses of Congress. The party held the levers of power and could use them to take decisive legislative steps toward women's enfranchisement. Here were the two main elements of Paul's plan: the realization that even a relatively small pocket of votes could swing an election and a target on which to use that electoral pressure. Paul wanted to use women's votes to hold the ruling party responsible for its disappointing record on suffrage. This would be the price Wilson and the Democrats would pay for failing to heed the demands of the suffrage movement.

In the August of 1914, Paul laid out her plans for that year's mid-term elections in front of the Congressional Union's Advisory Council: "[T]he time has

[21] *Crisis*, 5(6), April 1913, p. 267, cited in Sheridan Harvey, "Marching for the Vote: Remembering the Woman Suffrage Parade of 1913," *American Women* section, Library of Congress website, available at https://guides.loc.gov/american-women-essays/marching-for-the-vote#note37, (last accessed July 9, 2019).

[22] Stevens, *Jailed for Freedom*, p. 35.

come when we can really go into *national* politics and use the nearly four million votes we have to win the vote for the rest of the women in the country." She was careful to note that this campaign was "absolutely non-partisan," even as it called for the boycott of one of the two major parties in favor of the other. Indeed, it required "women to lay aside all party affiliations and put suffrage before party."[23] The challenging part was spreading the message among enfranchised women in Western States. Paul handpicked the best organizers and speakers in the organization and convinced them to leave their homes for weeks, traveling westward in difficult conditions and with little resources.[24] Two CU members toured each of the nine suffrage States, making the case that a vote against Democratic candidates was a vote in favor of the federal suffrage amendment. Among them, campaigning in Colorado, was Doris Stevens. According to her account, "the Democratic leader" in the State "invited [her] politely but firmly" to desist "the day after [she] had arrived."

Undeterred by "harsh words" and "violent threats,"[25] Stevens and the other CU organizers achieved a level of success that was acknowledged by the wide public, despite the controversy their campaign had raised. Twenty-three out of forty-three Democratic candidates in the States concerned were defeated. Paul did not claim that each of those defeats was determined by women's votes. Instead, she demanded and obtained full credit only for those that were unexpected according to most predictions. "In Kansas, Colorado, Utah, Oregon, Washington, and Idaho, Democratic Party incumbents in both the House and Senate who were, by all accounts, assured of reelection lost their seats. In each of these elections, the voters, the press, and sometimes even the candidates themselves acknowledged that they went down to defeat because of the CU buzz-saw."[26]

The 1914 campaign, described by the *New York Tribune* as "the first . . . national movement of women armed to fight with political weapons for their rights,"[27] achieved several objectives. Suffrage had finally turned into a matter of primary relevance in national political discourse: the president and the Democratic Party could hardly keep brushing it off as a States' rights issue. Even more fundamentally, it proved that women just had to organize to be a political force to be reckoned with. They had hurt the Democrats in 1914, but in 1916, with the presidential elections, the stakes would be even higher. Paul had clear in mind the next step to build up on the 1914 success. The Congressional Union was ready to become something more than a lobbying group: women would have their own political party.

[23] Alice Paul quoted in Lunardini, *Alice Paul*, pp. 89–90. See also Stevens, *Jailed for Freedom*, pp. 33–4.

[24] To give an example, Sara Bard Field, campaigning in Nevada for the elections of 1916, described a small-town hotel both she and organizers in 1914 stayed at as "one big spittoon with all the cooking odors in the state for two generations collected within its walls" (quoted in Lunardini, *Alice Paul*, p. 93).

[25] Stevens, *Jailed for Freedom*, p. 35.

[26] Lunardini, *Alice Paul*, p. 95.

[27] *New York Tribune*, August 30, 1914.

The first move was to secure a stable presence for the CU in every State of the Union. The expansion was achieved quickly and effectively thanks to the exceptional organizational skills and hard work of Doris Stevens, now the executive secretary of the organization.[28] Further actions in 1915[29] seemed to open a small breach in the president's resistance. Unexpectedly, Wilson had declared that he would vote in favor of women suffrage in New Jersey. With the 1916 elections approaching, Paul called for a convention of women voters in June in Chicago to start off the campaign. Women's votes would be organized through a new organization, the National Woman's Party. Paul made clear at the outset that the Party's representation of women's interests had to boil down to the single issue of suffrage: any other concern would lower the focus and endanger the effectiveness of its action. Membership would be restricted solely to enfranchised women, with the exception of Alice Paul, named as one of the two vice-chairmen. The delegates enthusiastically approved the foundation of the Party and the undertaking of another campaign against the Democrats.

Paul, Stevens, and their allies would not be as successful as they had been two years earlier. The NWP's action led the two major parties to consider suffrage in their platforms. However, the elections' results did not push them to follow up. The Party failed to unite women against Wilson and the Democrats this time because many would not consider suffrage the only decisive factor of the presidential elections of 1916.

> The one major issue that made all the difference . . . was the war in Europe. . . . The Wilson slogan—"He Kept Us Out of War"—resonated with voters overall but especially with women. . . . Even some of CU/NWP's longtime supporters, such as Jane Addams and Crystal Eastman, were compelled to place peace before suffrage.[30]

Indeed, by comparison to his opponent, the Republican candidate Charles Evans Hughes, who would become Secretary of State and president of the American Society of International Law (ASIL) in the 1920s, seemed much more inclined to intervene in the war, with his talk of "preparedness." Political commentators agreed that this was the cause of his eventual narrow defeat, turning women to Wilson notwithstanding Hughes' coming out in favor of a suffrage amendment in August.[31] Women had swung contested mid-Western States toward Democrats. California,

[28] See Trigg, *Feminism as Life's Work*, p. 59.

[29] The main events were the first national convention of women voters in San Francisco, organized by Stevens, and the subsequent trip across the country of Sara Bard Field to deliver to Washington a pro-suffrage petition with a reported—but likely inflated—number of 500,000 signatures appended (see Lunardini, *Alice Paul*, pp. 98–102).

[30] Lunardini, *Alice Paul*, p. 110.

[31] On the vote's analysis see ibid., pp. 110–11.

where Stevens had campaigned, returned a landslide victory for the president.[32] Yet, there was also consensus that the 1916 elections could not be seen as a defeat for the NWP, quite the opposite. Neutrality in the European war might have won Wilson the presidency, but suffrage had arguably been an equally important issue during the campaign. Candidates courted women's votes and addressed the theme of nation-wide suffrage at length. The *San Francisco Examiner* remarked that suffrage could not be considered anymore "a western vagary. Nothing that has 2,000,000 votes is ever vague to the politicians."[33] Soon, the women of the NWP would provide the president with a daily reminder of suffrage's political relevance just outside the gates of the White House.

## "Jailed for Freedom": Paul, Stevens, and the Nineteenth Amendment

On Christmas Day 1916, the NWP organized a memorial function in honor of Inez Milholland. The woman who had led the suffrage parade of 1913 on a white horse would also be hailed as the first martyr of the suffrage movement in the United States. Milholland had collapsed during a campaign speech in California in October. Her last words from the podium happened to be symbolic and meaningful: "Mr. President, how long must women wait for liberty?"[34] Following the memorial, the NWP leaders went to see Wilson, who made clear that he had not changed his mind and would not use his influence in a favor of a constitutional amendment. Moreover, he suggested, with a high dose of paternalism, that their electoral campaigns had been misguided. Real change, he schooled them, came through the action of the major parties, by influencing rather than alienating their representatives. Outraged and exasperated, Paul and her allies decided they could not wait for another election. They would make sure that the president would stop dismissing them.[35]

Starting on January 10, 1917, every morning women would leave Cameron House, the seat of the CU and the NWP, and walk across the park to silently stand with banners calling the president to task in front of the White House. Their neighbor, James Brown Scott, would look at them from the windows of his office in the CEIP headquarters at Jackson Place. Not yet the staunch feminist he would become in later years, Scott showed no sympathy for the cause and expressed his annoyance about the militant nature of the protest. In one "occasional . . . remark"

[32] Contrary to the general opinion, Stevens would later argue that the NWP's campaign had been successful in siphoning votes away from the Democrats (see Stevens, *Jailed for Freedom*, pp. 46–7).

[33] Quoted in Lunardini, *Alice Paul*, p. 111.

[34] Quoted in Stevens, *Jailed for Freedom*, p. 48.

[35] For Stevens' account of the meeting with Wilson and immediately following events see ibid., pp. 52–60.

recorded by Finch, he affirmed that the suffrage movement was made of "long-haired men and short-haired women." Finch would add that "[s]ince [Scott] was nearly bald, obviously he did not include himself in the group."[36]

Scott would not be the only one to be increasingly disturbed by the picketing. In the early days of the action the establishment seemed mostly indifferent to the silent sentinels. Wilson would often tip his hat to them, passing through the gate. Yet, this attitude would quickly change once, in February, the United States severed diplomatic ties with Germany and prepared to enter the First World War. Almost all activist organizations, including the ones devoted to peace and NAWSA,[37] reacted by fully supporting the administration through the war and shelving their claims for a later date.[38] The NWP did not. In early March, around a month before the United States went to war, the Party held a convention.[39] The delegates approved a resolution that articulated their organization's unconventional stance:

> Be it resolved that the NWP, organized for the sole purpose of securing political liberty for women, shall continue to work for this purpose until it is accomplished, being unalterably convinced that in so doing the organization serves the highest interests of the country.[40]

The NWP members would pay harshly their refusal to fall into line. The silent sentinels put Wilson on the spot: their highly visible protest, enacted every day just in front of the White House, reminded the global public opinion that the United States did not provide the universal democratic rights it was waging a war in Europe for. Women were excluded. To underline this hypocrisy the picketers' banners would bear a quote from the president's war speech in the days after it was delivered: "We shall fight . . . for democracy—for the right of those who submit to authority to have a voice in their own government."[41]

Still, it was only in June, after an episode involving James Brown Scott's mentor and president of CEIP Elihu Root, that the administration decided to strike back. The president had tasked Root with heading a diplomatic mission to Russia[42] in

36 Finch, "Equal Rights for Women," unpublished text meant for Scott's biography, Folder 3, Box 69, JBS Papers, p. 5.

37 See Cott, *The Grounding*, pp. 60–1.

38 As we saw in Chapter 3, CEIP placed its resources at the government's disposal and added to its stationery the sentence "Peace through Victory."

39 Beyond declaring the Party's intention to continue suffrage action during the impending war, the Convention also dissolved the Congressional Union, integrating its unenfranchised members into the NWP.

40 Cited in Lunardini, *Alice Paul*, p. 118.

41 Ibid., p. 121.

42 See, for instance, Members of Mission to Russia Named: Elihu Root to Lead With General Hugh L. Scott, Chief of Staff, a Member," *Sacramento Union*, May 12, 1917, p. 12. See also The Mission to Russia—Introductory Note," in Elihu Root, *The United States and the War; The Mission to Russia; Political Addresses*, Collected and edited by Robert Bacon and James Brown Scott, Cambridge: Harvard University Press, 1918, pp. 87–97.

order to convince the liberal Provisional Government, installed after the abdication of Czar Nicholas II in March, to stay in the war. In his first official speech in Petrograd (Saint Petersburg), Root addressed the Council of Ministers and praised the country's democratic turn. Welcoming "the new sister in the circle of democracies," he remarked that "the Mission" had come "from a democratic republic" with "universal, equal, direct and secret suffrage."[43] The NWP immediately moved to gain political capital out of what they considered an outrageous misrepresentation by Root.

> On June 20, . . . a Russian delegation visited the White House to continue talks regarding cooperation. Paul stationed Lucy Burns and Dora Lewis outside the White House gate with an enormous banner addressed to the Russians. "President Wilson and Envoy Root are deceiving Russia . . . ," it read. "The women of America tell you that America is not a democracy. Twenty million women are denied the right to vote. . . . Tell our government that it must liberate its people before it can claim free Russia as an ally." As soon as the Russian delegation passed through the gate, all hell broke loose. Angry crowds tore the banner down, shredding it and harassing the picketers while DC police stood idly by and watched. The next morning, it was front-page news.[44]

Nonetheless, the women of the NWP continued their daily demonstrations at the White House gate. In the next few days, twenty-seven picketers would be arrested and, after refusing to pay fines, would be sentenced to spend three days in jail. Picketers arrested on July 14, including Doris Stevens, would receive unexpectedly harsh sentences of sixty days in Occoquan Workhouse, known for the terrible conditions its detainees endured.[45] Unfortunately for Wilson, the judge's zealous move angered figures of relevance for his administration. Dudley Field Malone, a long-time proponent of women's suffrage who would later become Stevens' first husband, went directly from the courtroom to the White House. A key supporter of Wilson in both his winning presidential campaigns, Malone had been rewarded first with an appointment as Assistant Secretary of State and later made Collector of the Port of the New York. He informed the president that he was resigning his position in order to defend the arrested picketers as their lawyer.[46] John A. H. Hopkins, the coordinator of Wilson's campaign in New Jersey who had just seen his wife being sentenced and taken away, was next to visit. "How would you like to have your wife sleep in a dirty workhouse next to prostitutes?"[47] he asked the president.

[43] Elihu Root, *The United States and the War*, pp. 98–9.
[44] Lunardini, *Alice Paul*, p. 121. See also Stevens, *Jailed for Freedom*, pp. 91–3.
[45] For Stevens' account of her stint at Occoquan see *Jailed for Freedom*, pp. 107–16. Stevens' book provided as well details of other activists' imprisonments.
[46] Malone's own account of the meeting can be found ibid., pp. 158–63.
[47] Quoted ibid., p. 110.

Stevens believed that, even in a wartime when any dissent was perceived as treasonous, the exaggerated punishment inflicted on the picketers had turned the tide of public opinion. "For the first time . . . our form of agitation began to seem a little more respectable than the Administration's handling of it."[48] A few days after their imprisonment, the president issued a pardon for the women at Occoquan. The picketing promptly resumed. The arrests continued through the summer and fall giving rise to growing outrage among the public, while the president refrained from commenting either on suffrage or the treatment of the picketers.[49] On October 20, it was Paul's turn to get arrested and she received the longest sentence yet, seven months at Occoquan. After she started a hunger strike, she would be repeatedly force-fed, a fate which had already befallen her in England almost a decade before, and confined to the psychiatric ward of the facility. Suffragists would begin to be physically abused and denied emergency medical treatment at Occoquan. In late November, amidst growing pressure on the administration, Paul received a visit from David Lawrence, a personal friend of the president who claimed to be there on his own initiative to inquire about her situation. Lawrence made clear that the administration was open to some kind of compromise, but Paul stated in no uncertain terms that "[n]othing short of passage of the amendment w[ould] end [the] agitation."[50] A few days later all picketers would be released. The protest and arrests continued, but from then on the women of the NWP would receive only suspended sentences. On March 4, 1918 the District of Columbia Court of Appeals would declare every arrest and convictions of the silent sentinels void.[51]

On January 9, Wilson finally came around and publicly endorsed the approval of a constitutional amendment enfranchising women nationwide. The House of Representatives voted in favor the next day, a year after the NWP had started picketing the White House, eliciting a temporary stop to the protest. Yet, the Senate would still offer resistance for over a year. On June 4, 1919, the senators finally voted in favor and the pickets could stop for good. It would take another year to obtain the necessary ratifications in thirty-six States. Finally, on August 18, 1920, the Nineteenth Amendment became part of the Constitution. Colloquially known as the Anthony Amendment, in honor of Susan B. Anthony, it made sure that "the right of citizens of the United States to vote [could] not be denied . . . on account of sex."

Historians of the suffrage movement in the United States are not in agreement over the importance of the pickets for the final success.[52] The protest of

[48] Ibid., p. 111. For an account that deemphasizes the importance of the picketing and of the NWP in general toward the achievement of suffrage see Flexner, *Century of Struggle*, pp. 292–98.

[49] See Lunardini, *Alice Paul*, p. 127.

[50] Quoted ibid., p. 131.

[51] See Flexner, *Century of Struggle*, p. 297.

[52] See and compare as examples the diverging analyses by Flexner (*Century of Struggle*, pp. 299–300) and Lunardini (*Alice Paul*, pp. 133–8).

the silent sentinels has been described in widely diverging ways. For some, it was a counterproductive exercise: its radicalism had risked undermining the sensible efforts of middle-of-the-road suffragists, the ones who had actually convinced the Wilson administration to support Congress' approval of the Anthony Amendment.[53] For others, it created the embarrassment that forced the hand of the political establishment to finally address the unjust exclusion of women from full political rights.[54] What seems undeniable is that Paul and her allies managed to keep suffrage as a key issue in the US press and public discourse, at a time in which the war could easily have suffocated any other concern.[55] In any case, the NWP's visible role in the suffrage victory would represent a pedigree on which Paul and Stevens built careers as influential feminist leaders that would last several decades more. A substantial contribution to the building of this pedigree came from the success of Stevens' own book, *Jailed for Freedom*, which she dedicated to Paul. Once the two expanded their advocacy to the international arena, their ally James Brown Scott would make sure that their clout would extend outside the United States: he published French, Spanish, and Portuguese translation of *Jailed for Freedom* paying for them out of his own pocket.[56]

Yet, the move to the realm of international law would not be a straightforward one for the NWP, immediately conceived as the next step after the achievement of national suffrage. It was quite the contrary: Paul, the strategic mind behind every key decision of the Party, would eventually decide to repeat the successful blueprint of acting as a single-issue organization. Following that model, the NWP would switch its sole dedication from suffrage to the achievement of equal rights for women. Within this single-issue mindset, devoting attention to the international was considered as a counterproductive dilution of focus and message. Efforts toward international organization were not perceived as creating

[53] Even before the passage of the Amendment, Wilson himself was trying to establish this interpretation. On September 30, 1918, the president addressed an "appeal" to the Senate in favor of the Amendment, defining it "a vitally necessary war measure" as well as "vital to the right solution of the great problems which we must settle . . . when the war is over." He was careful to note, early in the speech, that the protesters had had no influence on him whatsoever: "the voices of foolish and intemperate agitators do not reach me at all." (The full speech is reproduced in Marla J. Jarmer, "Woodrow Wilson: Women's Suffrage," in Jeffrey S. Ashley and Marla J. Jarmer (eds.), *The Bully Pulpit, Presidential Speeches, and the Shaping of Public Policy*, Lanham: Lexington Books, 2016, pp. 30–3.)

[54] Somehow contradicting the president about the effectiveness of the methods of the NWP, Representative Thaddeus H. Caraway from Arkansas told two Party activists that "all this agitation, the lobbying, the persistence never-ceasing, often to us men very irritating like grains of sand in the eyes, has nevertheless hastened your amendment by ten years" (Report of Dora Lewis and Maud Younger on Interviews with Congressmen, March 1, 1919, National Woman's Party Papers, quoted in Lunardini, *Alice Paul*, p. 138).

[55] See, in the same sense, Flexner, *Century of Struggle*, p. 297.

[56] See, for instance, Finch, "Equal Rights for Women," p. 5 and Camilo Barcia Trelles to James Brown Scott, February 9, 1933, vol. 330, CEIP Papers. On the inception of the translations project see James Brown Scott to Laura Berrien, April 30, 1929, Folder 6, Box 12, JBS Papers.

an alternative forum to further any kind of political project, including, possibly, women's rights: internationalism was a political project in itself. This view was due to internationalism still being inextricably intertwined, in the US political discourse, with the experience of the peace movement. Paul and Stevens saw peace activism,[57] like the causes of labor and race, as competing concerns that would have made the NWP's work toward the achievement of equal rights for women less effective. The turn toward internationalism of the NWP in the mid-1920s would result from the realization that the equal rights project would not come to fruition as quickly and easily as it had seemed when the enthusiasm of the suffrage victory was still fresh. By then, other feminist groups had already made their presence felt in international politics.

## 2. From the National to the International, from Suffrage to Equal Rights

### Internationalist Feminism and Early Approaches to Scott

In November 1914, British activist for women's rights Emmeline Pethick-Lawrence[58] went on a speaking tour of the United States. An article she published the next month, titled "Motherhood and War"[59] reiterated the main argument she had wanted to convey: "[t]he emancipation of women must be included in the program of those who would lay a broad foundation of constructive peace for the rebuilding of the modern world." This was because she considered "women . . . as the natural custodians of human race":

> The bed-rock of humanity is motherhood. The solidarity of the world's motherhood . . . underlies all cleavages of nationality. Men have conflicting interests and ambitions. Women all the world over . . . have one passion and one vocation, and that is the creation and the preservation of human life.[60]

[57] For a discussion of the idea that "any form of women's pacifism may be positively subversive of feminist purpose" see Jo Vellacott, "A Place for Pacifism and Transnationalism in Feminist Theory: The Early Work of the Women's International League for Peace and Freedom," *Women's History Review*, 2, 1993, *passim*, quote at p. 24.

[58] Pethick-Lawrence had been active in the same circles of the English suffrage movement as Alice Paul, working with Emmeline and Christabel Pankhurst. While Paul had taken inspiration from the Pankhursts' methods of political struggle and adapted them to the US context, Pethick-Lawrence had broken with them in the years immediately preceding her US tour because of her disapproval of those same radical forms of protest.

[59] Emmeline Pethick-Lawrence, "Motherhood and War," *Harper's Weekly*, 59, December 5, 1914, p. 542, reproduced in John Whiteclay Chambers (ed.), *The Eagle and the Dove: The American Peace Movement and United States Foreign Policy*, Syracuse: Syracuse University Press, 2nd edn, 1991, pp. 46–9.

[60] Ibid., pp. 47–8.

Pethick-Lawrence's tour sparked a flurry of activity in the United States toward a feminist peace initiative.[61] In that same month of November, suffragist Grace Hoffman White wrote to James Brown Scott, seeking advice about the draft program of the Woman's Movement for Constructive Peace.[62] Scott's reply was a couched in formal politeness but did not shy away from explicit disapproval of the project: "I do not find myself in sympathy with a number of articles in the original paper and I would ask you not to consider the revision . . . as representing my view." He asked to consider his "modification" an attempt to express "in terms of what may be called the peace movement . . . the ideas contained in [the] statement."[63]

Notwithstanding his taking distance, Scott drafted the modified text along familiar lines: on one hand, adding the focus on international adjudication that unwaveringly characterized his thinking; on the other, neutralizing the feminism that was at the center of the original proposal, consistent with his generally unsympathetic attitude in the earlier phase of his career. Of the references in the statement to an improved role for women in working toward peaceful relations, Scott left untouched only the general purpose enshrined in the first proposition: "That in behalf of Peace the democracies of the world should be reinforced by the inclusion of the mother-half of the human race in the ranks of articulate citizenship."[64] For the rest, Scott removed even the basic claim "[t]hat women should" participate and "be represented at [future] Hague Conferences."[65] Instead, he placed calls for "the study of international law" and "the peaceable settlement of the disputes . . . among peoples and nations."[66]

In other words, Scott seemed to suggest that there was no space for feminism in "proper" peace advocacy, like there was none for collective security. Paradoxically, he was making the point by excising every distinctive claim out of the purposes of an organization that was being created exactly to champion a feminist approach to peaceful international relations. Scott's disapproval of the NWP pickets a few

[61] See Karen Knop, *Diversity and Self-Determination in International Law*, Cambridge: Cambridge University Press, 2004, pp. 290–2.

[62] For a historical survey of early organizations representing women across national lines see Leila Rupp, "Constructing Internationalism: The Case of Transnational Women's Organizations, 1888–1945," *American Historical Review*, 99, 1994, pp. 1571–1660. Here I follow the story of the Woman's Peace Party and the Women's International League for Peace and Freedom as the earliest attempts at institutionalizing a feminist approach to international politics, rather than merely advancing women's rights. Given their purpose, it makes sense that these would be the first feminist organizations to search for the cooperation of a leading international law expert like James Brown Scott.

[63] James Brown Scott to Grace Hoffman White, November 20, 1914, Folder 2, Box 9, JBS Papers.

[64] "Statement of Purposes of the Woman's Movement for Constructive Peace," attached to Scott to White, November 20, 1914. The proposition can be found almost *verbatim* in Pethick-Lawrence's article, which would be published the following month (see Pethick-Lawrence, "Motherhood and War," in Chambers (ed.), *The Eagle and the Dove*, pp. 47–8). Considering also the obvious overlap, in wording and substance, of other proposals contained in the statement and in the article, it seems likely that the statement was written drawing heavily from Pethick-Lawrence's US lectures or even drafted by Pethick-Lawrence herself.

[65] Ibid.

[66] "Suggested Revision," attached to Scott to White, November 20, 1914.

years later could have been simply against the sensationalist method and the lack of patriotism of the protest. Considering that episode in connection with the modified statement of the purposes, Scott leaves us with the impression of having been against feminist politics per se during the 1910s. Nevertheless, at the end of the war and the decade, Scott received cooperation proposals from US internationalist feminists based on a different kind of approach, more congenial to his belief in formal equality as the basis of progressive law and, frankly, less controversial, due to changed political circumstances. In 1919, Scott would be approached regarding the topic of women achieving equal nationality rights. This would be the topic that, according to Finch, would prompt Scott to support a feminist project for the first time, though much later, in 1926.[67]

Between that first approach to Scott in 1914 and the later one in 1919, the Woman's Movement for a Constructive Peace had turned plans into action. On January 10, 1915, 3,000 women met in Washington, D.C. to respond to the pleas of Pethick-Lawrence and Hungarian feminist Rosika Schwimmer. Hailing from countries on the opposite sides of the conflict, both had sought the help of women in the United States to protest against the war and pressure belligerent governments into negotiating and finding a reasonable peace agreement. The meeting led to the foundation of the Woman's Peace Party (WPP) and a platform calling for a permanent Conference of neutral powers to offer continuous mediation.[68] As leaders of the new organization emerged Jane Addams elected as president, and Carrie Chapman Catt.[69] The former, primarily known as a pioneer of social work, was an iconic figure for suffragists and the progressive movement in general. As noted above, she had supported Paul against NAWSA's attempts to curtail her action. Catt, meanwhile, was Paul's main antagonist in the controversies between NAWSA and CU/NWP in that last phase of the suffrage struggle in the United States. Twice President of NAWSA (1900–04 and 1915–20), Catt also led, between 1904 and 1923, the International Woman Suffrage Alliance (IWSA), a loose federation which included, by 1914, twenty-five national suffrage associations.[70] The originators of the WPP took the opportunity of the 1915 IWSA meeting to seek European support to their initiative. Initially planned in Berlin, the meeting was moved to The Hague after the outbreak of the war. The move from a belligerent to a neutral country was at first conceived for merely practical reasons; the meeting was still supposed to discuss IWSA's routine matters and stick to suffrage.[71] It

[67] See Finch, "Equal Rights for Women," p. 8.

[68] See Chambers (ed.), *The Eagle and the Dove*, pp. 49–50. The full platform is at ibid, p. 52.

[69] Catt and Addams' speeches at WPP's organizing Convention are reproduced ibid., respectively at p. 50 and pp. 54–6.

[70] See Rupp, "Constructing Internationalism," pp. 1575 and 1587.

[71] See David S. Patterson, *The Search for Negotiated Peace: Women's Activism and Citizen Diplomacy in World War I*, London: Routledge, 2008, p. 51.

was Scottish feminist Chrystal Macmillan who took the initiative to change the meeting into a women's peace Conference.

> She proposed that the meeting discuss the subjects of international arbitration, democratic control of foreign policy, principles underlying the revision of territorial boundaries, reduction of armaments, and world organization. She also indicated that if the alliance refused to sanction such a meeting, she would urge women interested in these issues to convene one on their own.[72]

Macmillan's challenge implied the expectation that her proposal would cause controversy within the IWSA. Indeed, this was the case. "Most . . . European suffragists . . . feared the radical implications of a women's peace movement."[73] So did Catt, who kept her distance from the initiative to avoid worsening the divisions it was causing among IWSA members.[74] Addams, instead, enthusiastically accepted the invitation. She would serve as the chair of the International Congress of Women, which opened on April 28, 1915 in The Hague. Notwithstanding the controversy and the difficulty of traveling with the war ongoing,[75] 1,200 women were in attendance, coming from twelve countries, including both belligerent and neutrals. The US delegation was made of forty-seven women, most of whom were WPP members. The Hague Congress reaffirmed the basic ideas that had been behind the foundation of the WPP and Macmillan's proposal: international disputes should be settled through peaceful means; the enfranchisement of women was a fundamental step toward that goal.

> Successive generations of historians have alternately dismissed the International Congress of Women . . . as naïve radicalism and recalled it as courageous visionariness. Belittled in the press as an international ladies' party or criticized as the folly of "Pro-Hun peacettes", the Congress adopted a series of resolutions for a just peace that were later credited with inspiring President Wilson's famous "Fourteen Points". Jane Addams recorded that Wilson himself had told her that he considered the resolutions the best formulations he had seen up to that time.[76]

For all his admiration, Wilson did not follow up on the main request of the International Committee of Women for Permanent Peace, established at The Hague: a Conference of neutrals for continuous mediation.[77] Besides the US

[72] Ibid.

[73] Ibid., p. 52.

[74] See ibid., pp. 58–9. On national groups of women cutting ties with transnational peace organizations during the First World War see Rupp, "Constructing Internationalism," pp. 1587–90.

[75] On the adventurous travel of the US delegation to The Hague see Patterson, *The Search for Negotiated Peace*, pp. 62–7.

[76] Knop, *Diversity and Self-Determination*, p. 294.

[77] See the related documents in Chambers (ed.), *The Eagle and the Dove*, pp. 65–7 and 88–90.

government, delegations of women appointed by the Congress presented their plans and resolutions to the major European governments and the Pope.[78] Their advocacy would continue until the end of war and beyond: already at The Hague it had been decided to have a new Conference alongside the one that would eventually decide the peace terms, in order to exert influence on it. The second International Congress of Women would take place in Zurich in May 1919, while the Paris Peace Conference's activities were in full swing. The Congress transformed the International Committee in a permanent organization, the Women's International League for Peace and Freedom (WILPF), with Addams again at its head. The Congress discussed "an advance copy of the peace treaty." Its position was "[s]trongly critical of the treaty's terms as a betrayal of the principle of self-determination and other principles first framed by President Wilson."[79] To turn the resolutions of the Zurich Congress into action, Addams headed a delegation to Paris which met Wilson, discussed several times with his right-hand man Colonel House and had audiences with top-level officials of the major winning powers.[80]

The story of the foundation and early activity of the WILPF arguably marked a turning point for women's participation in matters of foreign policy and international law.[81] Beyond the inspiration possibly provided for Wilson's Fourteen Points, the WILPF women had managed to express through the war and the peace negotiations a clear yet articulated message of what a just peace from a feminist perspective looked like. Notwithstanding the accusations of extremism they received, they had also managed to muster support and establish themselves as interlocutors of the major players in international politics. WILPF would continue to play an important role in the new postwar world order, maintaining an intense presence in and close collaboration with the League of Nations institutional system.[82] The skills and preparation demonstrated by the WILPF leaders in their peace activities translated into growing acceptance of the organization by the mainstream.[83] A symbolic recognition of this trend would be the award of the Nobel Peace Prize to Jane Addams in 1931.[84]

As well as lobbying about the postworld order, including the case for women's suffrage as a key step toward peace, WILPF championed women to break into the male-dominated spheres of diplomatic service and international law. Some signs

[78] See Knop, *Diversity and Self-Determination*, p. 295.

[79] Ibid., pp. 295–6. For further information on the deliberations of the Zurich Congress see Vellacott, "A Place for Pacifism," pp. 31–8.

[80] See Knop, *Diversity and Self-Determination*, p. 296.

[81] Of course, women had had influential roles in foreign policy before, if in a more haphazard way and individual capacity. For a survey see Glenda Sluga and Carolyn James (eds.), *Women, Diplomacy and International Politics since 1500*, London: Routledge, 2016. On the novelty of the WILPF's approach see Vellacott, "A Place for Pacifism," pp. 32–6.

[82] Vellacott, "A Place for Pacifism," pp. 39–42.

[83] See ibid., p. 45.

[84] Only the second woman to be awarded the Peace Prize, Addams shared it that year with none other than Nicholas Murray Butler.

that the idea was gaining ground were already present during the war and the Paris Peace Conference. For instance, WILPF's own Rosika Schwimmer was named Hungarian Ambassador to Switzerland in 1918. Another example of a woman rising to a position of authority, this time as a legal expert, would be a protégée of James Brown Scott, Sarah Wambaugh. She "authored a magisterial history of plebiscites at the request of the Peace Conference," which signaled "women's suffrage as the first major difference between the pre-war and post-war plebiscites."[85] Indeed, she affirmed that "the principle of woman suffrage in all the plebiscites [had] been adopted as a matter of course by the Allies at Paris."[86] With the establishment of the League of Nations, the WILPF cultivated collaborative relations with the three women in the Assembly and the sole woman in a leadership position in the Secretariat, Dame Rachel Crowdy. In addition, WILPF lobbied constantly for further appointments of women.[87] By September 1923, an article in the *Washington Post* saluted the effectiveness of the modern administrative methods employed by the Secretariat's staff, comprising nationals of over forty nations. Yet, the key sign of a new era of international relations was in the employment of a "contingent [of] young women combining beauty and brains."[88] This sense of new openness toward women's participation to international politics, certainly to be increased but marking a distinct progress, went beyond Geneva. In that same year of 1923, a group of Latin American feminists obtained an important result at the first postwar Pan-American Conference, held in Santiago de Chile. Attending the meeting without any official capacity, they found a voice through a delegate from Guatemala. Máximo Soto Hall introduced a resolution on women's rights, which was unanimously approved by the Conference.[89] The resolution recommended to the American governments the promotion of women's education and a study of their own legal system in order to devise measures to address inequalities based on sex. It also recommended that these topics would be tackled in future Conferences featuring national delegations including women.[90]

It was on the basis of this resolution that at the next Conference, in 1928, Doris Stevens and her allies would obtain the creation of the Inter-American Commission of Women, the event that sparked Stevens' cooperation with Scott.

[85] Knop, *Diversity and Self-Determination*, p. 297.

[86] Sarah Wambaugh, *Plebiscites since the World War*, New York: Carnegie Endowment for International Peace, vol. I, 1933, p. 477.

[87] See Vellacott, "A Place for Pacifism," pp. 42–4.

[88] Constance Drexler, "Young Women Combining Beauty and Brains Serve in League Headquarters," *Washington Post*, September 9, 1923, p. 29. See also Florence Brewer Boeckel, "Women in International Affairs," *Annals of the American Academy of Political and Social Science*, 143, 1929, pp. 230–48.

[89] See, for instance, Francesca Miller, *Latin American Women and the Search for Social Justice*, Hanover: University Press of New England, 1991. pp. 94–5; K. Lynn Stoner, *From the House to the Streets: The Cuban Woman's Movement for Legal Reform, 1898–1940*, Durham: Duke University Press, 1991, p. 187.

[90] For the text of the resolution see James Brown Scott, "Inter-American Commission of Women," *American Journal of International Law*, 24, 1930, p. 759.

Yet, until then, neither had taken the opportunity to participate in the movement that was increasingly connecting feminism and women's rights with international politics and institutions. The trajectories of their political thinking over the course of the 1920s, detailed in the two following subsections, would bring them together. As I noted above, for Stevens this trajectory would be represented by the repurposing of the NWP from its dedication to suffrage to the championing of an equal rights constitutional amendment. Scott, on the other hand, would slowly discover his alignment to feminist positions through a change of heart with regard to the discriminatory effects of US nationality law. The month before the Zurich Conference, in March 1919, WILPF's Juliet Barrett Rublee, in Paris to follow the Peace Conference, approached Scott to direct his attention to the plight suffered during the war by US women who had married nationals of enemy powers, especially Germans.[91] According to the legislation then in force, women who married foreigners automatically lost their US citizenship, even if they kept residing in the country. Of course, this brought legal restrictions even before the United States joined the war, but it was common for an expatriated woman to just continue living her everyday life unaware that marriage had deprived her of her native nationality. This changed with the declaration of war: women married to citizens of the Central Powers would be declared enemy aliens by the government and their properties confiscated.[92] Possibly Rublee did not know that Scott, during his time at the State Department, had been instrumental in the approval of the 1907 Expatriation Act, the piece of the legislation that had determined the situation she was denouncing.

## Scott and the Principle of Independent Nationality

The position of women under US nationality law changed significantly over the course of the nineteenth century and the beginning of the twentieth. In the early years of the Republic men and women acquired and lost US citizenship in the same ways.[93] US citizenship could be acquired at birth, either by *jus soli* (birth on

[91] See Juliet Barrett Rublee to James Brown Scott, April 12, 1919, Folder 1, Box 48, JBS Papers.

[92] See Candice Lewis Bredbenner, *A Nationality of Her Own: Women, Marriage and the Law of Citizenship*, Berkeley: University of California Press, 1998, p. 68.

[93] See, in the same sense, Virginia Sapiro, "Women, Citizenship and Nationality: Immigration and Naturalization Policies in the United States," *Politics and Society*, 13, 1984, p. 6. It is worth bearing in mind that, in this historical phase, up to the aftermath of the Civil War, US citizenship would be restricted to "free white persons," as affirmed by the earliest US Naturalization Act (1790) and restated by the Supreme Court in the infamous *Dred Scott* case of 1857 (60 US 393). There is another important consideration to add: while US citizenship was regulated by the general principles here described, key aspects such as who could be included and which rights and duties it entailed would remain uncertain and contested for most of the nineteenth century (see, for instance, Nancy F. Cott, "Marriage and Women's Citizenship in the United States, 1830–1934," *American Historical Review*, 103, 1998, pp. 1444–51).

the national territory) or *jus sanguinis* (birth to a citizen parent).[94] Later in life, one could voluntarily acquire US citizenship through a process of naturalization. The potential loss of citizenship also operated under the same rules for men and women. In the 1830 Supreme Court case *Shanks v. Dupont*, Justice Joseph Story restated that "marriage with an alien, whether friend or enemy, produce[d] no dissolution of the native allegiance of the wife." In any case, "[t]he general doctrine" at the time, Story continued, "[wa]s that no person c[ould], by any act of their own, without the consent of the government, put off their allegiance and become aliens."[95] In other words, no voluntary decision, including prolonged or even permanent residence abroad, could determine an automatic change of nationality.

The process of curtailing women's nationality rights by making their citizenship dependent on that of their husbands began in the 1850s. To be sure, the principle of family unity, which demanded simplification and uniformity of the legal regimes applicable to a married couple and their children, found an expression in the US legal system through the common law doctrine of coverture. Arising from the legal fiction that spouses are a single person, coverture "dictated that a married woman generally could not sue or be sued, sign contracts or wills, or possess property."[96] Yet, the doctrine's field of operation was that of private rights; it did not extend to political rights and US nationality law. In practice, foreign women who had married US citizens would generally be accorded naturalization. But naturalization was still always the consequence of an application, never the automatic effect of a legal rule.

Section 2 of the Naturalization Act of 1855 changed this state of affairs. It determined that "[a]ny woman . . . married to a citizen of the United States, and who might herself be lawfully naturalized shall be deemed herself a citizen."[97] This

[94] It is to be noted, though, that only the father could pass on citizenship *jure sanguinis* to legitimate children.

[95] *Shanks v. Dupont*, 28 US 242 (1830). It was only in 1868 that the US Congress moved beyond the concept of perpetual allegiance and recognized the right to voluntary expatriation (see Bredbenner, *A Nationality of Her Own*, pp. 19–20.)

[96] Bredbenner, *A Nationality of Her Own*, p. 19. The seminal description of the doctrine was penned in the eighteenth century by William Blackstone: "By marriage, the husband and wife are one person in law: that is, the very being or legal existence of the woman is suspended during the marriage, or at least is incorporated into that of the husband: under whose wing, protection, and cover, she performs every thing" (*Commentaries on the Laws of England*, vol. I, 1st edn, Oxford: Clarendon Press, 1765, p. 430). In 1946, historian Mary Beard, a founding member of the NWP who broke with Paul and Stevens in the 1920s, published a detailed criticism of Blackstone's formulation. One key accusation was that Blackstone and other late systematizers, had failed to give account of the rich and complex legal tradition in which the principle was commonly mitigated by equity arrangements. This false representation was particularly detrimental because of the enormous influence Blackstone's *Commentaries* had as a law textbook, carrying "dicta . . . later accepted as true and binding by generations of lawyers and judges in England and the United States" (Mary Ritter Beard, *Woman as Force in History: A Study in Traditions and Reality*, New York: The MacMillan Company, 1946, p. 95). This is why Beard charged Blackstone with "extinguish[ing] the married woman's personality" (ibid., p. 78). For the full argument see ibid., pp. 78–95.

[97] The trend toward derivative citizenship for women upon marriage had started in France with the Code Napoleon of 1804. The US statute was modeled upon a British one enacted in 1844. See, for instance, Sapiro, "Women, Citizenship and Nationality," pp. 7–9.

provision "bestowed on the foreign wives of Americans the ambiguous distinction of being the first and only group of adults to receive United States citizenship derivatively."[98] In an era of anxiety about increasing immigration, coinciding with the peak of popularity for the nativist Know-Nothing Party,[99] the measure drew surprisingly little attention. Evidently, the automatic concession of citizenship to a class of immigrant women did not pose a threat: it did not entail the right to vote and to directly influence US politics. Congress could congratulate itself for a move that spared wives of citizens the hurdle of the process of naturalization and the legal disabilities linked to alienage.

> Few of the country's lawmakers could imagine that the foreign-born woman naturalized by marriage suffered from the incontestable forfeiture of her premarital citizenship. She had become, after all, . . . an American. [T]he conveyance of citizenship to the citizen's wife cost the giver and receiver little, if anything—a view that persisted until the ratification of the Nineteenth Amendment forced a reassessment of the accuracy of that equation. [T]he . . . legislators . . . refus[ed] to concede that marital naturalization was fundamentally a policy of coercion rather than choice[.] In reality, it was a nod to male prerogative, the power of the federal government and the principles of international comity. . . . Even female reformers failed then to ponder the ominous implications of this naturalization policy; the leaders of the woman's rights movement, most of whom were U.S. citizens by birth, viewed naturalization policies as an issue outside their sphere of concern.[100]

The lack of reaction to the Naturalization Act of 1855 is in stark contrast with the opposition generated by the Expatriation Act of 1907. In section 3, it affirmed "[t]hat any American woman who marries a foreigner shall take the nationality of her husband." This provision, in combination with the Act of 1855, made the citizenship of every married woman in the United States dependent on her husband's. The doctrine of coverture had, by this time, virtually lost any relevance to private legal relations. Congress gave it a new life as a key principle of US nationality law.

The provision, like others in the Act,[101] reflected renewed anxieties about immigration and the allegiance of newcomers to the body politic: meaningfully, the number of new permanent residents in the United States had reached an

[98] Bredbenner, *A Nationality of Her Own*, p. 15. The Act excluded from derivative citizenship women who were racially ineligible for naturalization and, following a later amendment, women who belonged to "sexually immoral classes" (see ibid., pp. 16–17).

[99] See Sapiro, "Women, Citizenship and Nationality," p. 8.

[100] Bredbenner, *A Nationality of Her Own*, pp. 16 and 42. For a detailed analysis of the implications of section 2 of the Naturalization Act of 1855 see ibid., pp. 15–22.

[101] See, for instance, section 2 providing for the automatic loss of citizenship of naturalized persons in consequence of residence abroad.

unprecedented peak of 1,285,349 in 1907.[102] Yet, the enactment of section 3 was presented as a technical endeavor, with the goal of streamlining and clarifying citizenship policies. Indeed, the 1855 Act had introduced in the US legal system the concept of dependent citizenship but left unregulated the status of American women married to aliens. Between 1855 and 1907, notwithstanding unsettled policies in the State Department and contradictory court rulings,[103] some agreed upon principles emerged. Mere marriage to an alien was not tantamount to a declaration of expatriation if it was not followed by removal from the United States. Even then, the citizenship of the woman married to an alien and residing abroad seemed to be suspended rather than revoked: she was not entitled to a passport or diplomatic protection, but she would acquire full rights again once her marriage ended or she returned to the United States.[104] Scott and the other architects of the 1907 Expatriation Act did not only contribute to a dramatic change of this state of affairs; they even denied it was ever in place by playing up the relevance of the few judicial decisions that deprived resident women married to foreigners of their nationality.

On July 3, 1906 Robert Bacon, Acting Secretary of State while Root was in South America, named a board of experts tasked with the production of a report on the country's nationality law and its reform. The three members of the board were James Brown Scott, then Solicitor at the State Department, David Jayne Hill, US Minister to the Netherlands, and Gaillard Hunt, the chief of the Department's Passport Bureau.[105] In December, the board delivered its report, containing an impressive survey of US and foreign nationality statutes and judgments plus a series of recommendations the Congress would follow closely in drafting the Act.[106] In

[102] See Bredbenner, *A Nationality of Her Own*, p. 5. "The basic objective of the Expatriation Act of 1907 was a reduction in the number of Americans who, in the eyes of the federal government, had compromised their citizenship status by maintaining or establishing foreign ties of some type. The expatriation of women with alien spouses was only one strategy adopted by the government in pursuit of that goal (ibid., p. 57).

[103] For an analysis of the conflicting policies in that period see Edwin Borchard, "The Citizenship of Native-Born American Women who Married Foreigners before March, 2, 1907, and Acquired a Foreign Domicile," *American Journal of International Law*, 29, 1935, pp. 396–422. See also Bredbenner, *A Nationality of Her Own*, pp. 58–9; Sapiro, "Women, Citizenship and Nationality," pp. 9–10; Cott, "Marriage and Women's Citizenship," pp. 1459–61; Linda K. Kerber, *No Constitutional Right to Be Ladies*, New York: Hill and Wang, 1998, pp. 33–41.

[104] See, for instance, the explanation of Secretary of State James Blaine to the William Walter Phelps, US Minister to Germany (February 1, 1890, in *Foreign Relations of the United States*, 1890, p. 302): "The view has been taken by this Department in several cases that the marriage of an American woman to a foreigner does not completely divest her of her original nationality. Her American citizenship is held for most purposes to be in abeyance during coverture, but to be susceptible of revival by her return to the jurisdiction and allegiance of the United States."

[105] As we saw in Chapter 3, the cooperation between Scott and Hunt would continue in the closing years of the First World War. Together they produced an edition of James Madison's notes of the Constitutional Convention, one of what I have called Scott's Armistice Day books. In Chapter 5, I also mentioned Hunt as the author of an article tracing the connection between Thomas Jefferson and Robert Bellarmine in 1917, before this became commonplace in the 1920s.

[106] *Report on the Subject of Citizenship, Expatriation, and Protection Abroad*, Document No. 326, 59th Congress, 2nd Session, Washington: Government Printing Office, 1906. For a review contemporary to

relation to married women, the authors of the report affirmed that coverture applied generally to nationality law. This principle was already enshrined in the 1855 Act for foreign women marrying US citizens; in the same way a statute should affirm unequivocally "[t]hat an American woman who marries a foreigner shall take, during coverture, the nationality of her husband."[107] After all, the principle was already established in the judicial orientation they considered "sounder . . . from the standpoint of comity and the avoidance of conditions of dual allegiance."[108] Indeed, implementing the principle of family unity through a general application of derivative marital citizenship, detrimental as it was to women's rights, responded to certain practical needs of legal rationalization. In an increasingly globalized yet strongly nationalistic age, it was one of the most obvious and direct ways to reduce the number of individuals with double citizenship and the requests of diplomatic protection they could generate. It also had the effect of overcoming conflicts of applicable law to marital relationships. In any case, the case-law analysis used in the report to support derivative marital citizenship was misleading. The claim of an existing judicial orientation that already deprived resident women married to foreigners of their US citizenship was built on a single judgment based on peculiar facts, namely *Pequignot v. Detroit* (1883).[109] Arbitrarily, Scott and his colleagues decided to give that one exception the same weight as the established interpretation followed by all other courts.[110]

The report had treated the matter of the nationality of married women in the technical language of legal analysis. However, when he commented on the 1907 statute after its adoption, Scott would betray a degree of prejudice that could have influenced his position. The only motivations he conceived for a marriage between a foreign man and an American woman were exploitation by the former and gullibility of the latter.

> It is a noticeable fact that American young women of beautiful parts and ample fortunes have insisted on conferring themselves and their purses upon impecunious foreigners. The union ordinarily ends by mutual separation or by the action of the divorce court. The young woman has experience, the foreigner has the purse. What is the status of this woman? As long as the married relation remains

the report see Frederick Van Dyne, "Review—Report on the Subject of Citizenship, Expatriation, and Protection Abroad," *American Journal of International Law*, 1, 1907, pp. 548–53.

---

[107] *Report on the Subject of Citizenship*, p. 3.

[108] Ibid., p. 33. See also pp. 152–3.

[109] 16 Fed. 211. The case regarded a French woman, who had been residing permanently in the United States since she was six years old. She had acquired US citizenship through her first husband. After the termination of her first marriage, she remarried to a Frenchman residing in the United States but not intending to pursue naturalization. The court in this case declared Mrs. Pequignot an alien.

[110] See in the same sense, with a review of relevant judgments, Bredbenner, *A Nationality of Her Own*, pp. 58–60.

> she is a foreigner. . . . Any doubt previously existing as to the status of such a person is set at rest by §3 of the [1907 Expatriation A]ct[.][111]

The passage makes for stunning reading, considering Scott's later feminist advocacy. Yet, nationalist prejudice could explain also why women's rights organizations did not immediately react to the enactment of marital expatriation. After all, they had never protested in the five decades in which derivative citizenship had already been imposed on immigrant women. Likely, many suffragists shared the widespread prejudice against American women who married foreigners,[112] which Scott had voiced in his editorial. An organized response began to emerge when the connection of marital expatriation and suffrage became patent.

> In states where women had gained the vote, foreign born women naturalized by marriage were able to register to vote while native-born women with alien husbands were turned away. Leaders of the woman suffrage movement protested that the government had once again invited a group of foreign-born residents to exercise a fundamental political right still denied most native-born women[.][113]

In any case, the issue did not achieve prominence in public discourse until the case of Ethel Mackenzie reached the Supreme Court in 1915.[114] Born and raised in California, she married Gordon Mackenzie, a British subject, in 1909. In those years she had been involved in the campaign to enfranchise women in California, which eventually achieved success in 1911. While acting as an organizer in the following drive to register women to vote in the State, she realized that, because of her marriage, she could not obtain the registration for herself. Mackenzie's lawyer argued that she had neither expressly consented to be deprived of her citizenship nor placed herself under the jurisdiction of the British government. It was a violation of due process. The Supreme Court agreed that "a change of citizenship cannot be arbitrarily imposed . . . without the concurrence of the citizen." Yet, this was not the case with section 3, as marriage was "a condition voluntarily entered into, with notice of the consequences." In addition, the Court found the rationale of the provision justified, adopting yet another dubious affirmation of the historical pervasiveness of coverture.

[111] James Brown Scott, "Editorial Comment—The New Citizenship Law," *American Journal of International Law*, 1, 1907, pp. 459–60. On the prejudice against transnational marriages in the United States in this period in general, see Bredbenner, *A Nationality of Her Own*, pp. 61–3.

[112] See, in the same sense, Bredbenner, *A Nationality of Her Own*, p. 64. On the general attitude of suffragists toward immigrants see ibid., pp. 47–9.

[113] Ibid.

[114] *Mackenzie v. Hare*, 239 US 299 (1915).

> The identity of husband and wife is an ancient principle of our jurisprudence. It was neither accidental nor arbitrary, and worked in many instances for her protection. There has been, it is true, much relaxation of it, but in its retention, as in its origin, it is determined by their intimate relation and unity of interests, and this relation and unity may make it of public concern in many instances to merge their identity, and give dominance to the husband. It has purpose if not necessity in purely domestic policy; it has greater purpose, and, it may be, necessity, in international policy. And this was the dictate of the act in controversy. Having this purpose, has it not the sanction of power?

Suffragists were outraged at the decision but accepted that the only way to obtain a reversal was through Congress, not the judiciary. Yet, this avenue was also complicated. Several members of Congress had made clear that they would not be keen on revising marital expatriation legislation until women had achieved nationwide suffrage, given the deep connection of the two issues.[115] Suffragists and the media contributed to this identification of citizenship and right to vote, which created blind spots over the other legal disadvantages women deprived of citizenship could suffer.

Indeed, the Mackenzie case had had the merit of producing legal commentary and public awareness on derivative citizenship. However, its media coverage presented it as an issue affecting only the right to vote of women belonging to privileged classes.[116] The inaccuracy of this picture became clear with the entrance of the United States into the First World War. Native-born resident women married to citizens of the Central Powers were registered as enemy aliens; 25 million of the 56 million dollars confiscated by the federal government and held by the Alien Property Custodian were owned by these formerly citizen women.[117] Later Congressional debates featured stories of the distortions and misery section 3 had caused during the war. A woman married to an Austrian miner, killed in a work accident in the State of Washington, had the workmen's compensation seized and was left without means of sustenance. The daughter of a veteran severely injured in the Civil War was forbidden to continue her volunteer work in the Red Cross because she had refused, for religious reasons, to divorce the German husband she had been estranged from for years.[118] Nonetheless, the wartime anxiety toward foreigners prevented these women from receiving sympathy and their plight from summoning the political will for a corrective legislative action. After all, the common opinion went, by marrying an alien they had showed a lack of patriotic character.

[115] Bredbenner, *A Nationality of Her Own*, p. 67.
[116] Ibid., pp. 68–70.
[117] See ibid., p. 72.
[118] See Helen Irving, *Citizenship, Alienage and the Modern Constitutional State: a Gendered History*, Cambridge: Cambridge University Press, 2016, pp. 139–40.

The end of the war and the ratification of the Nineteenth Amendment created the conditions for reform. Anti-immigrant sentiments made independent nationality preferable now that a woman's US citizenship brought with it the right to vote. The legal *status quo* deprived a group of native-born, often educated and patriotic women of the ballot and gave it to immigrants who often did not speak a word of English.[119] Nativist anxieties required a reversal.[120] Moreover, the pressure applied by women's rights organizations could now count on nation-wide enfranchisement to back up their requests to Congress.[121] Still, the first action of the legislators to restore independent nationality for married women would be one of compromise, which left in place several problematic effects of the 1907 Expatriation Act.

The Cable Act of 1922 abolished marital naturalization and expatriation. Foreign women married to US citizens retained the privilege of a simplified and quicker process of naturalization, becoming eligible after only one year of residence rather than the regular five. Moreover, women were finally able to apply for naturalization independently of their husbands. American-born women could retain their pre-marital citizenship, but were still presumed to have renounced it if they resided for two years in their husband's country or five years in any other foreign country. Another significant vestige of derivative citizenship was represented by the extension to the spouse of the still-standing racial exclusions from naturalization.

> A woman's ability to pursue naturalization or maintain U.S. citizenship remained contingent on her spouse's eligibility for naturalization. If he could not be naturalized for any reason, she could not; and if she was a citizen, she was denationalized for wedding a man ineligible for citizenship and could not seek repatriation until the termination of the marriage. . . . One of the most shocking consequences of the country's race-based naturalization policies was the permanent denationalization of native-born women of color. The American-born woman not identified as Caucasian or of African descent who married an alien ineligible for naturalization lost her U.S. citizenship permanently.[122]

The initial reaction of American Society of International Law (ASIL) members to the Cable Act was critical but not because of those shortcomings. In a short editorial comment published in the *American Journal of International Law* (AJIL) in 1923, Jesse S. Reeves pointed to the principle of independent nationality itself as the problem. He "traced back" marital derivative citizenship "to the Code of Justinian[.

[119] For a concrete example of frustration on this point see Bredbenner, *A Nationality of Her Own*, pp. 80–1.

[120] The legislative result of the immigrant scare of the early 1920s were the harsh restrictions to new arrivals of the 1921 Quota Act and the 1924 Immigration Act.

[121] On the connection between the Nineteenth Amendment and the Cable Act, see, for instance Sapiro, "Women, Citizenship and Nationality," pp. 12–13.

[122] Bredbenner, *A Nationality of Her Own*, pp. 97–8.

T]he Expatriation Act of 1907" had finally made "the law of the United States fit in with the laws passed on the subject by practically all other civilized states of the world."[123] With the Cable Act, the United States had placed itself outside of the order guaranteed by the international application of the principle of family unity, thereby generating cases of statelessness and double nationality. Reeves knew who to blame: the "many women's organizations" exploiting the wave of the Nineteenth Amendment. This was reflected in "[t]he Congressional debate" from which "the Cable bill" resulted: it "displayed . . . not a little confusion . . . as to the right to vote, United States citizenship, and American nationality."[124] Reeves closed his comment remembering with nostalgia the now surpassed opinion of the Supreme Court in *Mackenzie v. Hare*: "The identity of husband and wife . . . has purpose, if not necessity, in purely domestic policy; *it has greater purpose and, it may be, necessity, in international policy*."[125]

The following year, Cyril D. Hill presented a different perspective to the AJIL readers. He considered the move toward the principle of independent nationality as positively progressive. Indeed, the principle of "family unity" was based on the fading assumption that "the ties which unite husband and wife . . . result from motives and desires of a political nature." Instead, especially in the globalized twentieth century, "[m]arriage and citizenship are two institutions, separate and distinct. Never in the history of the world did they have less in common than they do today."[126] Hill did not deny the shortcomings of the Cable Act. It left women marrying US citizens stateless pending naturalization, as other nations had generally retained the principle of family unity in their legislation. "The independent attitude of the United States ha[d] created . . . international confusion [by] granting independent citizenship to the women of one country." Yet, several initiatives elsewhere pointed to a worldwide reflection inspired by the Cable Act: "We see that the international situation is sensed and is being considered by many agencies, home and foreign legislative bodies, by national and international associations, and by many individuals."

Hill advocated a cautious approach: "Surely it seems inadvisable at the present time that women of every country, under present conditions, should be given independent citizenship." In any case, the times were ripe for "a matter assuming so vital a role in international affairs" to obtain "the sincere consideration of an international tribunal or conference."[127] The unspoken conclusion of Hill's reasoning,

[123] Jesse S. Reeves, "Editorial Comment—Nationality of Married Women," *American Journal of International Law*, 17, 1923, p. 98. For a contemporary critical reaction to the Cable Act by a prominent ASIL member see Richard W. Flournoy Jr., "The New Married Women Citizenship Law," *Yale Law Journal*, 33, 1923, pp. 159–70.

[124] Ibid., p. 99.

[125] Quoted ibid., p. 100 (italics by Reeves).

[126] Cyril D. Hill, "Citizenship of Married Women," *American Journal of International Law*, 18, 1924, p. 723.

[127] Ibid., pp. 735–6.

for all its cautiousness and gradualism, was clear. Independent nationality, if not the present, was likely to be the future. From this perspective, the Cable Act had not necessarily made the United States a troublemaker of the international order. History could prove the country to be, once more, a pioneer of progress and equality.

The debate over independent nationality was played out at the 1926 ASIL annual meeting. The discussion was lively and chaotic, with several key members of the Society, representing its various souls, weighing in. Attorneys and State Department officials kept providing practical examples of difficult solution, claiming that the Cable Act had exacerbated the strain that transnational marriages brought on the effectiveness of nationality laws and their international coordination. Richard W. Flournoy Jr., Assistant Solicitor at the State Department and successor of Gaillard Hunt as chief of the Passport Bureau, was careful to disassociate himself from the Act: "I had nothing to do with it myself. I would have vetoed it."[128] Academics engaged with the practitioners, linking their practical remarks with historical and theoretical reflections on the relevant principles. Manley O. Hudson, for instance, challenged the established notion that dual nationality was a major source of legal headaches. This was even truer for women, who did not risk being called for military service by two different nations, as could happen to men. "What is there objectionable about her having both [nationalities]? What would be the practical inconvenience of such confusion? I do not see such confusion arising to any great extent, and I do not know what its practical inconveniences are for a woman."[129]

Edwin Borchard tried to keep the conversation orderly by offering a solution that would retain family unity as a rule "without impairing the woman's freedom."

> The Cable Act, I think, would have created much less confusion than it has if it had been left in such form, that the nationality of the wife shall follow that of the husband, provided she does not, by some affirmative act, indicate her desire to the contrary. That would, I think, have preserved all the liberty that most of the women would like.[130]

Borchard's attempt to maintain the focus on concrete proposals of reform of the Cable Act failed. Following speakers kept jumping between different problems, topics, and perspectives. The only notable achievement of the sessions was to underline once more how complex the treatment of nationality law was, with its ramifications and underlying political assumptions. Still, the ideological divide surrounding the nationality of married women, relevant as it was to legislative

128 ASIL Proceedings, 20, 1926, p. 99.
129 Ibid., pp. 91–2.
130 Ibid., p. 91.

choices, remained in the background for almost the entirety of the debate. Only occasionally did it resurface under the technical language of legal arguments. Henry B. Hazard of the Naturalization Bureau at the Department of Labor took it for granted that a nation founded on equality like the United States could not but proceed in the direction taken by the Cable Act. "Consideration of the woman's political and citizenship status in the United States leads to the belief that the present principle of independent status is too strongly grounded to justify the hope that international benefits from uniformity would be looked upon as outweighing national wishes."[131] In opposition, an authoritative member of the old guard like George Wickersham, former Attorney General under President Taft, was deeply offended by the Cable Act as a tearing of the seams of society. "It does seem quite extraordinary that one of the first products of the newly conferred franchise of women, should have been the enactment of such a measure . . . contributing . . . powerfully towards the destruction of that unity of the marriage relation which for centuries has been considered the foundation stone of the state."[132]

James Brown Scott's single utterance in the debate was in stark contrast with that of Wickersham, his associate since the times of the campaign for international adjudication with the ASJSID. So much so that Scott's position was more progressive than that of younger colleagues like Borchard or even Hudson. It was an unequivocal endorsement of the international campaign of women's rights organizations for independent nationality. The intervention also seemed, intentionally or not, timed for maximum effect. Scott spoke at the closing of the last of three days in which the nationality of married women was debated. Over a dozen speakers had participated, alternating for hours long lecture-like speeches and tirades with quick back-and-forth on the most specific of legal details. All of them had been men with the single exception of Hope K. Thompson, who had made a couple of short remarks.[133]

Scott unexpectedly seized on an off-hand remark of another ASIL member, expressing the sudden realization that "women" might want "to speak for themselves" on the several proposals put forward for the regulation of their citizenship. Scott added that "women" were not only "competent to speak for themselves[:]

[131] Ibid., p. 85.

[132] Ibid., p. 126.

[133] Originally from Canada, Thompson was a lawyer based in Philadelphia. She was possibly the first active female member of the ASIL. Indeed, she had been published in the AJIL already in 1919, but her gender was concealed by the use of initials: her book review was signed H.K. Thompson. ASIL would officially open its membership to women only the following year in 1920. The decision at the founding to admit "any man of good moral character" would determine the denial of membership to high-profile figures such as Jane Addams. The ASIL's archive preserves the application of an Isabelle Bridge, turned down by Scott as late as 1916. Until 1917, women were not even allowed to participate to ASIL banquets as guests (see Frederick L. Kirgis, *The American Society of International Law's First Century 1906–2006*, Leiden/Boston: Martinus Nijhoff Publishers, 2006, p. 12, and for further details on ASIL's attitude toward women in its early years, Alona E. Evans and Carol Per Lee Plumb, "Women and the American Society of International Law," *American Journal of International Law*, 68, 1974, pp. 290–3).

they ha[d]."[134] To present "The Women's Point of View," he decided to read a short text with that title published in that same year by the Brazilian feminist Bertha Lutz.[135] Scott, through Lutz, found the legal views of women enshrined in the IWSA draft Convention on the nationality of women, approved by the association in 1923. The Convention, presented by Chrystal Macmillan at the International Law Association that same year, translated into nationality rules the principle of equality between sexes.[136] Lutz remarked that legal authorities such as André Weiss, the French judge at the Permanent Court of International Justice, and Alejandro Álvarez, had endorsed the IWSA proposal. Lutz also adopted the general principles on nationality of another supporter of independent citizenship, the Argentinean international lawyer Estanislao Zeballos. The first principle set individual autonomy as the key criterion: "Nationality is a self-determined right." Scott approved Zeballos' formulation and asked a rhetorical question: "Could there be a more logical or more legal sanction than these principles, especially Nos. 6 and 8 [safeguarding individuals from changes of nationality imposed by the State against their will], of the woman's point of view?"

Scott set forth a motion, later approved, to include the paragraph by Lutz restating the Zeballos principles in the record of the ASIL meeting as the "statement of the views of women, from an accredited representative . . . so that it may not be unilateral but bilateral." Closing his intervention, Scott shared Lutz' conclusion, affirming both the principle of independent citizenship and the progressive leadership of the Americas in its coming worldwide implementation.

> [T]he rule that makes a married woman follow the nationality of her husband is no longer absolute and . . . , on the contrary, the exceptions are fast becoming the rule. [T]he forward tendency is to confer independent citizenship on women, principally in the American continent[.] Encouraged by the fact that several of these Republics . . . already ensure the inviolability of the nationality rights of their women; that others are at present remodeling their codes and institutions, and that liberality and progress are essential features of the American continent, we hope and feel assured that the day is not distant when the independent citizenship

134 ASIL Proceedings, 20, 1926, p. 142.

135 The full article is Bertha Lutz, "Nationality of Married Women in the American Republics," *Bulletin of the Pan-American Union*, 1926, pp. 392–9. The excerpt read by Scott is its conclusion at pp. 397–9.

136 Macmillan had sent a letter to Scott (Chrystal Macmillan to James Brown Scott, August 29, 1923, Folder 1, Box 48, JBS Papers) attaching the text of the Convention and asking for feedback. To the best of my knowledge, Scott did not take any initiative in response until his intervention at the 1926 ASIL Meeting. For further detail on the draft Convention and Macmillan's campaign see Karen Knop and Christine Chinkin, "Remembering Chrystal Macmillan: Women's Equality and Nationality in International Law," *Michigan Journal of International Law*, 22, 2001, especially pp. 524–7. For Macmillan's contemporary perspective on the subject see Chrystal Macmillan, "Nationality of Married Women: Present Tendencies," *Journal of Comparative Legislation and International Law*, 7, 1925, pp. 142–54.

of married women will be a uniform and universally adopted principle in the whole of the Western Hemisphere.[137]

Emma Wold of the NWP, a new member of the ASIL, took the floor last. In her defense of the equal status of women as citizens and denunciation of the shortcomings of the Cable Act in this respect, she took a moment to thank Scott for highlighting women's point of view as stated by Lutz.[138] This event marked both the first alignment of Scott with the positions of the NWP and, overall, his first endorsement of the cause of women's rights.[139] It is interesting to note that the 1926 ASIL meeting took place while Scott's first course on the founders of international law was underway. The theme of America spearheading the full implementation of equal rights was key to both the historical and the feminist enterprise. By the time Scott met Stevens at the 1928 Pan-American Conference of Havana, he had written his first book on Vitoria and Suárez. As we have seen, his Spanish origin narrative had matured in the decade following the First World War, as a response to the demise of the old European regime and a pedigree for the new liberal and American-led world order. In a similar fashion, the NWP had spent the 1920s figuring out its new identity and narrative after the suffrage victory.

## The National Woman's Party in the 1920s: From Suffrage to Equal Rights

The NWP had represented a minimal portion of the suffrage movement in terms of number of members. Nonetheless, it had managed to achieve results and prominence beyond its size, because of the dramatic and radical nature of its methods. That same militant attitude had made the NWP membership particularly heterogeneous. Alongside a liberal and bourgeois core, it attracted women from the working class, the political left, and black communities.[140]

The new direction Alice Paul and her close collaborators pushed through[141] would reduce further and reshape the membership of the Party.[142] In July 1920,

[137] ASIL Proceedings, 20, 1926, p. 144–5.

[138] Ibid., p. 148.

[139] See Finch, "Equal Rights for Women," p. 8. Finch adds that Scott was not involved with the 1922 Act, even if its proponent, the Congressman from Ohio John L. Cable, had been his student at George Washington University, graduating in 1909. In any case, the two would later cooperate in reforming the Cable Act and removing the remaining legislative discriminations toward women in matters of nationality.

[140] On the attractiveness the early NWP had for women of the labor movement see Cott, "Feminist Politics," pp. 43–4 and Trigg, *Feminism as Life's Work*, pp. 54 and 56. On the reasons black women favored the NWP approach to the suffrage struggle see Cott, "Feminist Politics," p. 50.

[141] On Paul's authoritarian leadership style see Cott, "Feminist Politics," p. 45.

[142] At the height of the suffrage struggle the NWP had between 35,000 and 60,000 members. During the 1920s, the membership never exceeded 10,000 (see ibid., p. 55).

just before the ratification of the Nineteenth Amendment, Paul had already found the new goal in "the passage of a blanket enactment to remove all discriminations against women in existing legislation."[143] This was the practical meaning the NWP leadership had given to women's full equality with men. It was only at the Party's Convention, in February 1921, that the exclusive and exclusionary nature of the endeavor became evident to its later opponents. In the lead-up to the event, Mary White Ovington, a white socialist who had been a founding member of the NAACP, stressed the importance of including a black woman as a speaker. Black vote was violently suppressed in the South. As an organization devoted to equal suffrage, Ovington argued, the NWP should take up the issue. Emma Wold denied the request on behalf of Paul.

> Wold . . . explained that the convention could give the podium only to groups with legislative programs for women or with feminist aims. . . . Since Mary C. Talbert of the National Association of Colored Women's Clubs, the speaker whom Ovington recommended, represented a group with a "racial", not "feminist", intent, she could not be featured. . . . She encouraged the appointment of black delegates who could speak from the floor.[144]

The rights of black women was just the first issue to be sacrificed on the altar of equality. At the Convention, a minority report argued for the Party to turn toward pacifism and disarmament. Crystal Eastman, a socialist lawyer, presented a more articulated program of reforms to liberate women, spanning from birth control and sexual morality to marriage, divorce, and inheritance.[145] Both proposals were voted down. Notwithstanding the vocal protests by Eastman and others about the undemocratic attitude of the NWP leadership, the majority resolution, embracing the program of removing women's legal disabilities, had the genuine support of most delegates.[146] The outcome prompted defections and criticism of left-wing members. Addressing merely legal disabilities, "felt chiefly by women of property," could not get "women . . . liberated" as it failed to "get at the root of the matter." Others complained that the newly instated higher membership fees turned the NWP into "a conservative, property-holding, upper-crust group," an "aristocratic affair."[147]

143 Quoted in Peter Geidel, "The National Woman's Party and the Origins of the Equal Rights Amendment," *The Historian*, 42, 1980, p. 562.

144 Cott, "Feminist Politics," p. 51.

145 For the text of Eastman's resolution and her criticism of Paul's post-suffrage "normalization" see Crystal Eastman, "Alice Paul's Convention," *The Liberator*, 37, April 1921, pp. 9–10.

146 See ibid., pp. 48–9 and Geidel, "The National Woman's Party," pp. 565–6.

147 NWP members quoted in Cott, "Feminist Politics," p. 49. On the Convention and the criticism directed at it see also Susan D. Becker, *The Origins of the Equal Rights Amendment: American Feminism between the Wars*, Westport: Greenwood Press, 1981, pp. 17–18.

Still, the initial action of the NWP toward equality legislation was not as uncompromising with the instances of social feminists as it would later become. NWP leaders scoured State codes for rules based on sex discrimination and drafted a model blanket bill to be introduced in State legislatures. The model bill listed six legislative areas where inequality was to be addressed, but also contained a safeguard clause for protective legislation. As Paul explained early in the campaign to the Massachusetts NWP chairman, she did not "want to interfere in any way with the so called welfare legislation . . . protecting women from night work and from too long hours of labor, even though this legislation may not be equal for men and women." Indeed, the Equal Rights Bill championed by the NWP and passed by the Wisconsin legislature in June 1921, preserved the "special protection and privileges which [women] now enjoy for the general welfare." The bill also followed closely the model list, providing "women" with "the same rights . . . as men in the exercise of suffrage, freedom of contract, choice of residence for voting purposes, jury service, holding office, holding and conveying property, care and custody of children and in all other respects."

By the autumn, Paul had changed her position: "I do not believe in special protective labor legislation for women. . . . I think that enacting labor laws along sex lines is erecting another handicap for women in the economic struggle."[148] This shift was likely favored by the influence that, according to historian Nancy Cott, Gail Laughlin had on Paul.[149] Laughlin, a lawyer from Maine, as chair of the NWP Lawyers Committee began producing draft bills, including a federal amendment, without a safeguard clause. Going forward the positions of both the NWP and social feminists became more rigid and antithetical, especially after a failed attempt at a compromise between disagreeing women's organizations in December 1921.[150] During the course of 1922, a score of prominent figures and associations, including the successor of NAWSA, the National League of Women Voters (NLWV), came out unequivocally with their opposition to blanket equal rights bills.[151] At the same time, Laughlin took the lead in quashing all remaining dissenting voices within the NWP. Her legal reasoning was two-fold. First, the proposed equal rights legislation would not give freedom of contract a wider space of application than it already had under the Constitution and the statutes in force. Secondly, it was the protective legislation, and not freedom of contract, which was preventing women from competing in the job market. "If women can be segregated as a class for special legislation under any line," Laughlin's argument went, "the same classification can be used for special restrictions along any other line which may, at any time, appeal to the caprice or prejudice of our legislatures." It was this legislation treating women

[148] Quoted in Cott, "Feminist Politics," p. 57.
[149] See ibid.
[150] On this meeting see ibid., pp. 57–8 and Geidel, "The National Woman's Party," p. 570.
[151] See, for instance, Geidel, "The National Woman's Party," pp. 572–4.

as a class that was threatening to stop "the advancement of women in business and industry" and consign them "to the lowest worst paid labor."[152]

In April 1923, *Equal Rights*, the NWP's journal, applauded the decision of the Supreme Court in the case of *Adkins v. Children's Hospital*.[153] Upholding its 1905 judgment in *Lochner v. New York*, the Court voided a District of Columbia law mandating a minimum wage for women and children as a violation of freedom of contract. By standing behind this decision, the NWP aligned with the formal understanding of equality of Langdellian legal theory[154] that had been championed by James Brown Scott and the ASIL's other founders.[155] It might be worth noting that the Chief Justice at the time was one of those lawyers, former US President William Howard Taft. From this perspective, Crystal Eastman's accusation at the 1921 NWP Convention that the majority's narrow focus on legal formalism was "old-fashioned" found confirmation. According to her, "nobody that has a thread of modern feminism w[ould] care a rap"[156] about such an endeavor.

Yet, it was exactly this exclusive focus on the elimination of legal discrimination based on sex that allowed NWP members to claim they were actual feminists while their opponents were just reformers.[157] In addition to the single-issue focus, the NWP soon returned to another feature of the victorious suffrage campaign: the primary, if not exclusive, insistence on a federal amendment. Indeed, besides the victory in Wisconsin, the NWP State campaigns for blanket equality bills or elimination of specific discriminatory rules had achieved little or none success. In July 1923, Paul announced the new direction. She claimed Susan B. Anthony's legacy by organizing a NWP Convention in Seneca Falls, on the 75th anniversary of the one that had marked the symbolic beginning of the woman's movement.[158] There she presented a constitutional amendment of her own drafting, which was unanimously approved: "Men and women shall have equal rights throughout the United States and every place subject to its jurisdiction." There was no safeguard clause, no list of legislative areas to address. The NWP demanded full constitutional equality for women without any limitation or qualification. The ERA would be introduced in Congress for the first time in December 1923.

The national struggle between equal rights feminists and supporters of protective legislation soon spilled into the international women's rights movement. When, in 1925, the NWP sought membership in IWSA, its application was rejected because of the opposition of the NLWV.[159] In turn, the rejection prompted

[152] Quoted in Cott, "Feminist Politics," p. 59

[153] See ibid., p. 62. The reference for the case is 261 US 525.

[154] See Chapter 3.

[155] See Chapter 1.

[156] Quoted in Cott, *The Grounding*, p. 70.

[157] See, for instance, the quote in Becker, *The Origins*, p. 171.

[158] On the historical legacy of the 1848 Convention, including its influence on 1923 NWP event see Lisa Tetrault, *The Myth of Seneca Falls: Memory and the Women's Suffrage Movement, 1848–1898*, Chapel Hill: University of North Carolina Press, pp. 181–99.

[159] On the controversy see Becker, *The Origins*, pp. 166–8.

the resignation from IWSA of the Six Point Group, a British feminist equal rights organization, led by Lady Margaret Rhondda. Rhondda had already been cooperating with the NWP as a member of its international advisory committee, created in June 1925. The creation of the committee was an effect of the newly found enthusiasm of the NWP for internationalism. Now that the Party had a well-defined post-suffrage strategy, its leadership no longer believed international activities were a distraction, rather they were the path to increased influence and effectiveness. In any case, the NWP had internationalism in its pedigree: its attitude during the Great War proved that it was ready to put feminism above patriotism when it counted.

It was Rhondda who suggested to Paul, in 1926, that they start a campaign for an international equal rights treaty. The NWP leader immediately drafted one, modeled on the ERA. "For the next decade Paul spent most of her time outside the US attempting to sell the treaty to feminists, the Pan-American Union, the League of Nations and the International Labor Office (ILO)."[160]

While Paul concentrated on the League of Nations and Europe, Stevens would become the main figure of the NWP equal rights work in Latin America and at the Pan-American Union. The NWP had first looked at Latin America with interest in the context of the effort to achieve equal nationality rights for women in US law. After the passage of the Cable Act, the NWP realized that progress toward equal citizenship was being made and nationality law was an area that promised further success. It was also an issue on which equal rights and social feminists managed to find some alignment and loose cooperation, at least through the 1920s. Notwithstanding their diverging understandings of the significance of citizenship for women, both groups lobbied to remove the same discriminatory nationality rules.[161]

A handful of American Republics had gone further in terms of equal citizenship than the United States had done with the Cable Act or did not have a discriminatory nationality law in the first place.[162] By the mid-1920s, this had convinced some US feminists that American governments might be more willing to listen to their arguments than European ones.[163] Almost by chance, the NWP would beat the NLWV to this advocacy opportunity. As I have noted above, a resolution of the 1923 Pan-American Conference, obtained through the lobbying of Latin American feminists, urged the governments of the continent to follow up on women's rights issues and include women in the official proceedings. Already in 1924, Bertha Lutz, the Brazilian feminist quoted by Scott at the 1926 ASIL meeting, searched for support in the United States ahead of the next Conference in 1928 in Cuba. Writing

[160] Carol Miller, "'Geneva—the Key to Equality': Inter-war Feminists and the League of Nations," *Women's History Review*, 3, 1994, p. 221.
[161] See Bredbenner, *A Nationality of Her Own*, pp. 155–7.
[162] See ibid., pp. 195 and 197.
[163] See ibid., p. 197.

to Carrie Chapman Catt, Lutz urged the NLWV to send representatives. "Catt, however, thought that the trip to Havana would be too costly and the expense not worth the potential outcome, discounting the importance of Pan American feminism and viewing it as secondary in the promotion of women's rights on the international scene."[164]

The NWP would learn about the event much later and respond with an opposite, enthusiastic approach. In December 1927, Cuban feminist and lawyer Flora Díaz Parrado visited the NWP headquarters in Washington, D.C., asking the Party to join Latin American women's rights activists at the Conference. Parrado called on sisterhood and claimed that the participation of US feminists would give a boost to the suffrage struggle of the Cuban women.[165] Jane Norman Smith, the NWP chairman at the time, wrote to member Margaret Lambie regretting their late discovery: "It is such a pity that we did not know about it sooner for it is very important."[166] Indeed, the event was scheduled to start in the following month of January. Notwithstanding the short time for preparations, the NWP dispatched Smith, Muna Lee, Valentine Winters, and Doris Stevens to Havana. There Stevens met James Brown Scott and presented him with the equal rights treaty they would go on to champion together.

## 3. Scott and the International Equal Rights Campaign

### The 1928 Pan-American Conference and the Beginning of the Scott–Stevens Collaboration

The Sixth Pan-American Conference took place between January 16 and February 20, 1928. The women of the NWP spent their initial efforts in Havana lobbying the US delegates, finding them only "preoccupied with detecting and countering anti imperialism."[167] It was in the course of one of these attempts that Stevens met

[164] E. Sue Wamsley, "Constructing Feminism Across Borders: The Pan American Women's Movement and the Founding of the Inter-American Commission of Women," in Pernilla Jonsson, Silke Neunsinger, and Joan Sangster (eds.), *Crossing Boundaries: Women's Organizing in Europe and the Americas, 1880s–1940s*, Uppsala: Uppsala Universitet, 2007, p. 69.

[165] On Parrado's visit and her case to NWP members see Ellen Carol DuBois, "A Momentary Transnational Sisterhood: Cuban/U.S. Collaboration in the Formation of the Inter-American Commission of Women," in Alessandra Lorini (ed.), *An Intimate and Contested Relation: The United States and Cuba in the Late Nineteenth and Early Twentieth Centuries*, Firenze: Firenze University Press, 2005, pp. 86–7.

[166] Quoted in Wamsley, "Constructing Feminism," p. 69.

[167] Diane Elizabeth Hill, *International Law for Women's Rights*, unpublished PhD dissertation, University of California at Berkeley, 1999, p. 31. On the patronizing attitude shown to Stevens by Charles Evans Hughes, Secretary of State and ASIL President see Bredbenner, *A Nationality of Her Own*, pp. 200–1. On the international legal implications of the political tensions surrounding the Conference see Arnulf Becker Lorca, *Mestizo International Law: A Global Intellectual History 1842–1933*, Cambridge: Cambridge University Press, 2014, pp. 343–9.

Scott: by February 1 she had followed up with a letter asking him to consider the NWP's attached proposal for an equal rights treaty and offer his "eminent legal opinion."[168]

The NWP envoys found better fortune with Cuban delegates. Stevens made a good impression on Orestes Ferrara, the Cuban Ambassador to the United States. More crucially, she gained the ear of the President of the Conference, Scott's friend and associate Antonio de Bustamante.[169] This would be instrumental for the feminists' agenda. Indeed, the governments and the Pan-American Union had not followed up on the resolution approved at the previous Conference of 1923. There was no space in the official program of the Conference for women's rights. But on February 7, Bustamante favored a motion to add a "Plenary meeting . . . with extra-official character" to allow "the representatives of the various feminist associations" to illustrate "their viewpoints on the matter of civil and political rights for woman."[170] Moreover, Bustamante agreed to preside over the session, attended by a third of the Conference delegates and a "thousand local women" who "poured into the hall, galleries and stairwells [of] the University's Aula Magna"[171] to demonstrate their demand of suffrage. Stevens was among the speakers.

On February 18, the Conference followed up on the event by unanimously approving the resolution that established the Inter-American Commission of Women, widely considered as "the first inter-governmental body to deal with women's issues."[172] The unofficial but ever-present theme of the Conference had been the soothing of Latin American discontent with the hegemonic actions of the United States. At the same time, the US delegation sought to secure and reinforce that hegemony. In line with this attitude, the governing board of the Pan-American Union would shortly later appoint the most visible feminist representative from the United States, Doris Stevens, as chairman of the new institution.

According to later accounts of the NWP, approved by Scott, he had been[173] "stirred by Doris Stevens' appeal for treaty action on women's rights in the special plenary session." Her speech had been the trigger for his commitment to "the abolition of discriminations based on sex" and the achievement of "equality

[168] Doris Stevens to James Brown Scott, February 1, 1928, Folder 1, Box 48, JBS Papers.

[169] See Dubois, "A Momentary Transnational Sisterhood," p. 87.

[170] "Motion—Invitation to Women's Associations to Present their Views relative to the Rights of Women," Sixth International Conference of American States, February 7, 1928, in James Brown Scott (ed.), *The International Conferences of American States, 1889–1928: A Collection of the Conventions, Recommendations, Resolutions, and Motions adopted by the First Six Conferences of the American States, and Documents relating to the Organization of the Conferences*, Oxford: Oxford University Press, 1931, p. 324.

[171] Dubois, "A Momentary Transnational Sisterhood," p. 89.

[172] Nitza Bercovich, *From Motherhood to Citizenship: Women's Rights and International Citizenship*, Baltimore: Johns Hopkins University Press, 1999, p. 81. For Stevens' account of the establishment of the Commission and the roles of Bustamante and Maurtua in it, see Stevens to Scott, February 3, 1929.

[173] "James Brown Scott," attached to Edith Houghton Hooker to James Brown Scott, June 29, 1934, Folder 1, Box 49.

by international action." His private correspondence shortly after the Havana Conference tells a different story. Writing to his sister Mary, Scott joked about his referring to a married woman with her husband's surname, fearing he would only be able to do that "until the forty-eleventh amendment to the Constitution shall determine that women are to keep their own names upon marriage, and that husbands shall renounce theirs in favor of their wives'. From what I have seen of the Equal Right [sic] leaders in Habana I begin to fear for the few we have left," he added referring to Stevens and her NWP colleagues. "From my experiences in Habana," he concluded, "they have already become our 'masters.'"[174] In the detailed account of the Conference Scott published in the April issue of the AJIL, he made no mention of the feminists' action or of the creation of the IACW.[175]

By 1929, Scott's opinion on Stevens and the NWP had changed completely. Most likely, Scott was swayed by two realizations. First, he recognized the political affinities between him and the NWP leaders: their brands of equality coincided, their projects could be advanced together and support each other. Secondly, he had been impressed by the legal skills Stevens and Paul had shown in their initial work for the IACW. Beyond their direct experience with the lobbying of legislatures and legislative action, both sought an academic background in law. Starting her studies in 1922, Paul obtained several degrees. In 1928, the American University awarded her a doctorate in Civil Laws.[176] In 1929, Stevens began her studies in international law and foreign policy at Columbia.

The resolution that instituted the Commission had tasked it with "the preparation of juridical information . . . to enable the [next] Conference of American States to take up the consideration of the civil and political equality of women in the continent."[177] Stevens and Paul began working on a study of the legal status of women in the Americas, to build a case for their equal rights treaties. By July, the Commission had agreed to focus on nationality issues. Consulting with Scott on the topic, they found a common, radical approach diverging from the mainstream of international lawyers and diplomatic operators. Stevens, Paul, and Scott naturally began to work together.

This came at a crucial moment when several approaches and initiatives were jockeying to gain influence in view of the League of Nations Codification

[174] James Brown Scott to Mary Scott, March 15, 1928, Folder 4, Box 70, JBS Papers.

[175] See James Brown Scott, "The Sixth Pan American Conference," *American Journal of International Law*, 22, 1928, pp. 351–62.

[176] Nancy Cott has drawn a connection between Paul's law studies in the 1920s and "her aims [being] framed . . . more and more abstractly and legalistically." Along with this trend, "the NWP campaign for equal rights devolved into a practice of exclusiveness and a defense of the status quo with regard to everything but the gender question. . . . As a result of its construction of the gender imperative, the NWP made equal rights an abstract goal, because placing it in the context of social reality would have required stands on social and political issues that affected women but that were not strictly gender questions" (Cott, "Feminist Politics," pp. 65 and 67–8).

[177] "Resolution—Inter-American Commission of Women," in Scott (ed.), *The International Conferences of American States*, p. 408.

Conference, called for 1930. Nationality, alongside territorial waters and State responsibility for damages to foreigners, had been chosen as subjects for codification at the Conference in The Hague. In November 1927, Manley Hudson had started a preparatory project, known as the Harvard Research in International Law,[178] with the purpose of researching and drafting treaties on the topics of the Conference. Hudson assembled a group of top-level experts including Borchard, Flournoy, Wickersham, and James Brown Scott.

Scott was part of the working group on nationality led by Flournoy. In May 1928, Scott wrote him a letter to explain his general views on the subject.[179] He was aware he was proposing "a somewhat drastic method" to streamline nationality laws worldwide and instate a uniform global standard. His formula rested on two basic ideas: first, the adoption of *ius soli* as the single mode of acquisition of nationality at birth; second, the adoption of nationality rules based on full individual equality.

Scott remarked how the differentiation between nationality by place of birth (*ius soli*) and nationality derived from parents (*ius sanguinis*) had deep and sensible historical roots. Countries of emigration, primarily European ones, had preferred *ius sanguinis*, to maintain a connection with nationals living abroad and allow them to pass their nationality on to their children. Countries of immigration, primarily American ones, had preferred *ius soli* as a means of assimilation of residents with foreign roots. The co-existence of these two principles naturally created situations of double nationality; the fact that most countries gave preference to one of the principles, but also applied the other under more limited circumstances, further complicated the legal picture.

"Each of the two worlds is correct from its standpoint, and the conflict is inevitable. If the conflict is to be resolved, one or the other of the principles must give way," Scott affirmed. "Which shall it be? Speaking as an American, I would say the jus sanguinis; and the underlying reason for preferring the locality of birth to nationality through blood is that the nationality of the country of birth is acquired with the elimination of any other nationality."[180] In other previous and later publications, Scott had also provided *ius soli* with an authoritative pedigree, tracing it back to Vitoria's *De Indis*. "The acceptance of this principle, which [Vitoria] lays down as a rule of law, would give to each human being—man, woman or child—one and only one nationality; . . . in a word, it would equally obviate statelessness and double nationality."[181]

This simplification of the rules and adoption of *ius soli* would lead to and achieve another development: "the elimination of 'sex'" and derivative nationality

[178] For details on the Harvard Research and its inception see James T. Kenny, "Manley O. Hudson and the Harvard Research in International Law 1927–1940," *The International Lawyer*, 11, 1977, pp. 319–29.

[179] James Brown Scott to Richard W. Flournoy, Jr., May 15, 1928, Folder 3, Box 12, JBS Papers.

[180] Ibid.

[181] Scott, *The Spanish Origin of International Law: Francisco de Vitoria and his Law of Nations*, Oxford: Oxford University Press, 1934, pp. 286–7.

"from the statute book." Scott added that "the effect of this triumph on the part of womankind—which [he] personally regard[ed] as as desirable as it [was] inevitable" would not generate trouble if parents were of different nationalities under a *ius soli* regime, while it could under *ius sanguinis*. In his view, independent nationality and *ius soli* were the combined elements of the global nationality "law of the future." The "suggestion . . . that the husband and wife should be of the same nationality . . . is generally made by the husband, and is a remnant of the old law. The more modern legislation, which permits the wife to retain her nationality is the order of the day, and is inconsistent with former views and practise [sic]."[182]

Times were not ready, though, for the Harvard Research to fully accept Scott's proposals. In the months leading to the presentation of the final draft Convention on nationality of the Harvard Research, set for April 1929, Scott and Stevens teamed up to push for the inclusion of a full right to independent citizenship for women. Realizing they were on the losing side of the argument, they decided together to publish Scott's letter to Flournoy to seek support.[183] The Harvard Research went in a different direction in any case. Scott and Stevens objected to Article 19 of the draft Convention on nationality,[184] which read: "A woman who marries an alien shall, in the absence of a contrary election on her part, retain the nationality which she possessed before marriage."[185] While more progressive than the law in force in most countries, this article still provided for an exception to independent nationality, which put women in the position to renounce their nationality in consequence of a momentary, possibly impulsive, decision.

On May 27, Stevens informed Scott that she had decided to form a Committee on Nationality of the IACW, headed by Paul and alternative to the one of the Harvard Research.[186] Scott approved and applauded the initiative.[187] After all, Stevens had already proven that her skills could compare with those of the Harvard experts: she had pointed out several errors of translations in a collection of nationality laws prepared by Hudson and Flournoy, just in time for it to be revised before being published by the CEIP.[188] Scott motivated Stevens further in the pursuit of

[182] Scott to Flournoy, March 15, 1928.

[183] See Doris Stevens to James Brown Scott, February 19, 1929, Folder 7, Box 8, JBS Papers. The letter was published as James Brown Scott, "International Status of Married Women," *Advocate of Peace through Justice*, 91, March 1929, pp. 137–40. Scott also asked Stevens if it would have been helpful to enlist the help of the NLWV. She replied negatively, informing Scott that "they did not do Pan American work as we did, . . . they did not confine themselves to feminist work as we did." (Quoted in Bredbenner, *A Nationality of Her Own*, p. 205.)

[184] See James Brown Scott to Doris Stevens, February 26, 1929, Folder 6, Box 48, JBS Papers.

[185] Research in International Law—Harvard Law School, "Nationality, Responsibility of States, Territorial Waters: Draft of Conventions Prepared in Anticipation of the First Conference on the Codification of International Law, The Hague, 1930," *American Journal of International Law*, Special Supplement to vol. 23, April 1929, p. 16.

[186] See Doris Stevens to James Brown Scott, May 27, 1929, Folder 1, Box 48, JBS Papers. See also Bredbenner, *A Nationality of Her Own*, p. 204.

[187] See James Brown Scott to Doris Stevens, May 29, 1929, Folder 6, Box 48, JBS Papers.

[188] See Richard W. Flournoy, Jr. to James Brown Scott, received April 24, 1929, Folder 1, Box 48, JBS Papers and James Brown Scott to Doris Stevens, April 26, 1929, Vol. 314, CEIP Papers. The book

equal rights through treaties by pointing out the domestic advantages of this international route.[189] Scott pointed to constitutional history and Supreme Court caselaw[190] to argue that civil and political rights fell within the treaty making power of the United States. An international equal rights treaty would represent the law of the land, leaving no constitutional recourse to States after its ratification in the Senate. At the end of the day, it would have the same effect as an equal rights constitutional amendment.[191]

Through the spring and summer of 1929, Scott enlarged significantly the scope of his cooperation with Stevens, beyond the direct pursuit of equal nationality treaty law. He introduced her to the professional circles he valued the most. For instance, Scott presented Stevens—and Paul[192]—with a lifetime ASIL membership. He established good working relations between the American Institute of International Law—later making Stevens its first woman member[193]—and the IACW.[194]

Most crucially here, Scott took steps to connect his newfound commitment to equal rights for women with his campaign on the Spanish origin of international law. As we saw in the previous chapter, Scott included Stevens in the committee for the celebrations of Vitoria planned for 1932 in Salamanca. Scott extended the invitation with the explicit understanding that celebrating Vitoria meant also advancing international justice and equal rights for all, including women, in the present. Stevens accepted enthusiastically:

> It is hard to conceive of any more delightful task than to help honour the memory of Francisco de Vitoria, and in so doing to hasten justice and peace in the international community. Naturally I am deeply stirred to learn that on this occasion

was eventually published as Richard W. Flournoy, Jr. and Manley O. Hudson (eds.), *A Collection of Nationality Laws of Various Countries as Contained in Constitutions, Statutes and Treaties*, Oxford: Oxford University Press, 1929.

---

189 See especially the correspondence between Scott and Stevens over the spring and summer of 1929 in Folder 6, Box 48, JBS Papers.

190 See *Missouri v. Holland*, 252 US 416 (1920). Another judgment Scott considered a key foundation for his interpretation was *People v. Gerke*, decided by the Supreme Court of California in 1855 (5 Cal. 381).

191 Scott would develop the full argument in his 1934 ASIL Presidential Address, with explicit reference to the effects of the possible ratification of the 1933 Montevideo Equal Rights Treaty: see James Brown Scott, "Treaty-Making under the Authority of the United States," *ASIL Proceedings*, 28, 1934, pp. 2–34. George Finch would later criticize the trend of enlarging the scope of the treaty-making power and pointed to the campaign for the equal rights treaty at the 1928 Pan-American Conference as its beginning: see George Finch, "The Need to Restrain the Treaty-Making Power of the United States within Constitutional Limits," *American Journal of International Law*, 57, 1954, pp. 62–3.

192 See Alice Paul to James Brown Scott, April 24, 1929, Folder 1, Box 48, JBS Papers.

193 See, for instance, Muna Lee, "Equal Rights Approved by American Institute of International Law," *Equal Rights*, November 28, 1931.

194 See, for instance, James Brown Scott to Doris Stevens, May 27, 1929, Folder 6, Box 48, JBS Papers.

> the rights of men and women through international equality shall be discussed and furthered on this spot, the cradle of international law.[195]

In response, Scott, who had by now taken on the role of Stevens' law teacher and mentor, sent her, in view of her participation to the committee, the Classics edition of Vitoria's *relectiones*, "thought . . . to have founded the modern law of nations."[196]

The fusion of Scott's commitments to, on one hand, women's rights and his collaboration with Stevens and, on the other, the Spanish origin of international law and Vitoria's equality found a highly symbolic moment on October 12, 1929, Columbus Day. In front of the members of the *Institut de droit international*, gathered for the first time in the United States at Briarcliff Lodge, New York, Scott recited his speech *The Discovery of America and Its Influence on International Law*.[197] He described how Columbus' discovery had created the conditions for Vitoria to conceive a modern, truly universal, law of nations. The recent 1928 Pan-American Conference, which had created the IACW and was held in Cuba, an island on which Columbus set foot during its first voyage to the New World, had maintained the promise of an American continent at the forefront of progress with its successful codification of several international legal topics.[198] Alongside Scott, the Secretary of Sessions for the meeting took the floor. Indeed, choosing a venue outside Europe was not the only first since the 1873 foundation of the *Institut* happening that year. For the first time, the Secretary was a woman, Doris Stevens.[199] Her speech complemented Scott's perfectly, elaborating on the meaning of the Discovery.[200] She reminded the all-male membership of the *Institut* that the day's celebration would not have been possible without the wisdom of a woman, Isabella of Castile. It had been by chance that she had been able to support Columbus and change the world's history forever: in the first place, women had been accepted as rulers only when situations of force majeure had eliminated all viable male candidates;[201] secondly, her husband and co-ruler, Ferdinand of Aragon had had the foresight not

[195] Doris Stevens to James Brown Scott, April 25, 1929, Folder 8, Box 7, JBS Papers.

[196] James Brown Scott to Doris Stevens, May 1, 1929, Folder 5, Box 12, JBS Papers.

[197] See "Discours prononcé par M. James Brown Scott, en qualité de Président de l'Institut de Droit International: La Découverte de l'Amérique et son Influence sur le Droit International," *Annuaire de l'Institut de Droit International*, Paris: A. Pedone Editeur, vol. II, 1929, pp. 67–103.

[198] I have analyzed the content of the speech in detail in the previous chapter.

[199] See the press release in Folder 14, Box 33, JBS Papers.

[200] It was Paul who first suggested that Scott include Stevens in the speakers for the Columbus Day event. Laura Berrien of the NWP had the intuition, approved by Scott, to suggest to her that she speak on the woman who had had a most crucial role in the discovery: "Isabella the Catholic [who] sent [Columbus] westward[. B]ecause of this intervention Vitoria was able to formulate the modern law of nations, there would be something lacking if the appreciation of America as a Continent were not voiced on that occasion" (see James Brown Scott to Alice Paul, July 2, 1929, Folder 14, Box 33 JBS Papers).

[201] See Doris Stevens, *Toast à Isabelle porté par Miss Doris Stevens, President de la Commission Interamericaine des Femmes au Banquet de l'Institut de Droit International à Briarcliff Lodge, Briarcliff Manor, New York, à l'Occasion de l'Anniversaire de Christophe Colomb, le 12 Octobre 1929*, Folder 17, Box 32, JBS Papers, pp. 3–4.

to oppose her, even if personally he did not approve of Columbus' plans.[202] "*Voilà une occasion où un homme et une femme ont exercé une autorité égale, au bénéfice de toute l'humanité*,"[203] Stevens commented.

The moral she drew out of the story was clear: in a present where men seemed to offer less resistance, it was time to include women in power and decision-making, so that the achievements of an Isabella would be more a regular occurrence than a singularity dictated by chance. Stevens concluded with an appeal:

> Nos rêves sont les mêmes. Nous voulons tous un monde où règneront la justice internationale, l'ordre, l'égalité. En somme, qu'est-ce que la communauté mondiale? Des hommes et des femmes, pas autre chose[.] C'est tout. Il n'y a rien d'autre. . . . Embarquons-nous ensemble pour une noble expédition de découverte. Voyons quel trésor nous pouvons trouver ensemble.[204]

On that same day, the *Institut* had approved a meaningful document, which proved that Stevens' appeal found some sympathy within the international legal community. The adoption of the *Déclaration des Droits Internationaux de l'Homme* followed a lively discussion, orderly though not free of controversy.[205] The members of the *Institut* were aware that they were issuing a document of a pretty general and abstract character.[206] At the same time, they realized that this was not a routine resolution and that they were taking a bold and novel approach. Hans Wehberg pointed out that this was "*la première fois qu'une association scientifique s'occupe des droits de l'homme au point de vue international*."[207] The implications left several members of the *Institut* uncomfortable. Since the advent of constitutionalism in the eighteenth century, rights had been conceived as universal in the realms of philosophy and natural law but enforceable as positive rules of law within national legal systems. The Declaration suggested that individual rights could be guaranteed by positive rules of international law, understood before the Great War as a system concerning only the rights and duties of States. Indeed, Jan Kosters asked the rapporteur, André Mandelstam, if he intended the Declaration to reflect existing law, "*droit international actuel*," or it envisaged future law, "*jus constituendum*." For Kosters, the first option was simply not conceivable: "*Le droit international positif ne vise que les droits des Etats*."[208] Mandelstam refused to reply by picking one of

[202] See ibid., pp. 5–6.
[203] Ibid., p. 6.
[204] Ibid., pp. 6–7.
[205] The full discussion is at pp. 110–38 of the *Annuaire de l'Institut de Droit International*, II, 1929.
[206] Indeed, Frederic Coudert, a New York corporate lawyer, gave as the reason for his abstention the Declaration's lack of practical value. He added, though, that he would not have approved it anyway, even if it had been effective and enforceable, because in that case it would have also been dangerous. See ibid., p. 137.
[207] Ibid., p. 114.
[208] Ibid., p. 133.

Kosters' two alternatives; instead, he came up with a third category: the Declaration was new law, "*droit nouveau, réclamé par la conscience juridique des peuples.*"[209] Scott concurred: "*la déclaration internationale des droits de l'homme, qu'on viens de voter, est la constatation solennelle d'un nouvel esprit d'un nouveau monde.*"[210]

Faced with Scott and Mandelstam's idealist stance, Kosters raised another hard-nosed argument: what about colonies? On one hand, Kosters reasoned, the international rights of the Declaration would obviously have to apply in a colonial context, considering that they were the positive transposition of the universal rights recognized to every human being by natural law. On the other, it would be practically impossible to square the Declaration's provisions with colonial reality and "*accorder à des races indigènes tous les droits de l'homme et notamment l'admissibilité des indigenes a tous les emplois.*"[211] Pressed by Kosters' considerations, Mandelstam had to admit that the new law was not universal after all. Even if Article 4 of the draft Declaration prohibited discrimination based on race, without qualifications or exception, Mandelstam explained that, "*dans l'esprit de la Commission, les indigènes des colonies ne sont pas visés.*"[212]

A similar discussion arose with regard to discrimination based on sex. Arrigo Cavaglieri wondered if the drafting Commission had intended to force States to award the right to vote to women and open to them all public offices.[213] Mandelstam replied that he was convinced of the full equality of sexes under the law. Even if "*certains Etats n'ont pas encore sanctionné cette égalité, cela ne saurait empêcher l'Institut de la proclamer, s'il la croit, . . . conforme á la conscience juridique du monde contemporain.*"[214] Nevertheless, Article 4 of the Declaration raised concerns among the members exactly because it was the most concrete of the draft. Rather than simply prohibiting discrimination in principle, it pointed to specific rights which could not be restricted on the basis of sex, race, language, or religion, the most controversial being access to all public functions. James Brown Scott carried the day with a signature move: remove controversial effects and proclaim the abstract principle anyway. He proposed to remove the words "*accés aux emplois public, fonctions et honneurs.*" After all, Scott argued, that was not a right: States could choose civil servants as they wanted.[215] Thanks to Scott's intervention the article could pass, if with a relatively close vote, thirty-one to twenty-two.[216] The Declaration as a whole went through much more comfortably, with just one contrary vote and a dozen abstentions.[217] Notwithstanding its equivocal genesis, Scott

209 Ibid., p. 134.
210 Ibid., p. 137
211 Ibid., p. 115. See also Niboyet at p. 124 and Kosters at p. 125.
212 Ibid., p. 125.
213 See ibid., p. 124.
214 Ibid., p. 126.
215 See ibid., p. 126.
216 See ibid., p. 127.
217 See ibid., p. 138. For the full text of the Declaration as approved see ibid., pp. 298–300.

would keep returning to the Declaration as a milestone in the campaign toward equal rights for women. For instance, during the following year, he would use it to criticize the outcome of the League of Nations Codification Convention of The Hague.[218]

## "Unprogressive Codification of Nationality at The Hague"

Doris Stevens was determined to attend the Hague Codification Conference as prepared as possible. She spent the summer of 1929 in Europe, consulting and strategizing with feminist leaders, including Margaret Rhondda and Chrystal Macmillan, and discussing the merits of equal nationality in public events.[219] She also campaigned for the appointment of women as delegates for the Conference.[220]

In the meantime, the IACW research on nationality laws proceeded well in the United States under the direction of Paul. Scott continued to offer help, providing resources and expertise.[221] On September 5, Paul wrote to Dora Sedgwick Hazard, a long-time friend of Jeannette Scott who had first organized the NWP in Syracuse and central New York State. She thanked her for having offered to introduce her to Scott years before, when the NWP did not yet engage in international activity. Now that the cooperation Hazard had wished to facilitate had finally come to pass, Paul told her that Scott's "help ha[d] been greater and more valuable—by far—than that of any other one individual."[222] Scott had also made possible the organization of the first Conference of the IACW, to be held in February 1930 as preparation for the Hague Conference, which would begin in March. Stevens had first contacted to State Department, asking support to organize the event in Washington, D.C., but this had met with a refusal.[223] Scott alerted his Cuban contacts and vouched to the Cuban government the official status of the IACW,[224] a status that had been put in doubt by the Director of the Pan-American Union Leo Rowe when he had tried to take away the Commission's office space.

[218] See, for instance, James Brown Scott, "Nationality," *American Journal of International Law*, 24, 1930, pp. 560–1.

[219] See Muna Lee, "The Inter-American Commission of Women: A New International Venture," originally in *Pan-American Magazine*, October 1929, reprinted in Jonathan Cohen (ed.), *A Pan-American Life: Selected Poetry and Prose of Muna Lee*, Madison: The University of Wisconsin Press, 2004, p. 223.

[220] See Bredbenner, *A Nationality of Her Own*, pp. 202–3.

[221] See, for instance, "Resolution—Tribute to the Carnegie Endowment for International Peace," First Conference of the Inter-American Commission of Women, February 24, 1930, in Scott (ed.), *The International Conferences of American States*, p. 505.

[222] Alice Paul to Dora Sedgwick Hazard, September 5, 1929, Folder 1, Box 48, JBS Papers.

[223] See Francis White to Doris Stevens, March 8, 1929, Folder 6, Box 48, JBS Papers.

[224] See the correspondence between Scott and Stevens in Folder 6, Box 48, JBS Papers.

The presentation of the report of the Nationality Committee was the highlight of the IACW gathering in Havana.[225] It analyzed the nationality laws of eighty-four countries and recommended the adoption of an equal nationality treaty as an end to discrimination against women in matters of citizenship.[226] In praising the volume, Scott did not miss the chance to remark how more precise and complete it was than the one prepared by the Harvard Research: "The documents contained in the treatises prepared by our masculine experts are full of incredible errors, which have been corrected by feminine industry and exactitude." This achievement was further proof of the "faith" Scott already had "in the capacity of woman." It was time for women to participate directly in determining the nationality laws that affected them. Therefore, Scott renewed the request to the "Governments of all the Americas [to] appoint women delegates to take part in the Conference of The Hague [so] that equality may be introduced into the world."[227] The IACW issued a more specific resolution, asking the president of the United States to appoint Doris Stevens as a plenipotentiary for the Codification Conference.[228]

The selection of delegations was an early sign that the Hague Conference would not be rich in success for women's rights organizations. Only two women, one from Germany, Marie-Elisabeth Lüders, the other from the United States, were appointed as full delegates. The US delegate Ruth B. Shipley, head of the Passport Division of the State Department, was not connected to the women's rights movement.[229] President Hoover did, however, appoint an NWP member for a minor position in the delegation: Emma Wold would act as a technical advisor in The Hague. These two appointments were made against the advice of Manley O. Hudson, who "had made it clear" to the administration "that he did not want women to be officially part of the delegation."[230]

Once the Conference opened, on March 13, it soon became clear that there was no room for an agreement on territorial waters and State responsibility. Therefore, the stakes to achieve any kind of compromise on nationality became higher: the League of Nations and the participating governments could not afford to close the Conference without a treaty to show for it. The delegate of Chile, Miguel Cruchaga

[225] For the program of the Conference and the resolutions it approved see Scott (ed.), *The International Conferences of American States*, pp. 500–6. A later copy of the report, revised for the 1933 Montevideo Conference, can be found in Folder 5, Box 49, JBS Papers.

[226] See Hill, *International Law for Women's Rights*, pp. 129–32.

[227] James Brown Scott, "Miss Paul's Golden Book," in James Brown Scott, *Observations on Nationality*, Oxford: Oxford University Press, 1931, pp. 95–6.

[228] See Scott (ed.), *The International Conferences of American States*, p. 503.

[229] Historian Ellen DuBois has called Shipley an "antifeminist" (see Ellen DuBois, "Storming The Hague: the 1930 Campaign for Independent Nationality for Women Regardless of Marital Status," *Tijdschrift voor Genderstudies*, 4, 2003, p. 20). Somewhat contradicting Dubois' assessment is the fact that Shipley proposed to the Conference a resolution for the further study of equal nationality (see, for instance, David Hunter Miller, "The Hague Codification Conference," *American Journal of International Law*, 24, 1930, pp. 682–3.)

[230] Bredbenner, *A Nationality of Her Own*, pp. 206–7.

introduced Paul's equal nationality treaty as a resolution, on behalf of the NWP and the IACW. It was quickly defeated. After that, the goal of women's rights activists at The Hague was to make sure that the Conference would not crystallize and reaffirm the principle of derivative citizenship for women in international law. The officers of the Conference did not make their job easy. The President of the Conference, Theodorus Heemskerk, barred them from the Peace Palace, making it impossible for them to lobby the delegations at the event's venue.[231] The exception was Nicolas Politis who, in his capacity as Chairman of the Nationality Committee, gave women activists a chance to be heard, "merely [as] an act of courtesy."[232] In her speech at the hearing, held on April 1, Stevens made public that many delegates had already told her that she could not change their mind. Defiantly, she reminded them that they had no merit for the privilege and power they held: it was "a mere accident that we were born women and you were born men."[233]

The draft Convention that emerged out of the Conference's discussions accepted and assumed the principle of dependent nationality of married women: it only sought to coordinate different national laws so that their combination would not determine cases of statelessness as result of marriage. For instance, its Article 8 prescribed that "[i]f the national law of the wife causes her to lose her nationality on marriage with a foreigner, this consequence shall be conditional on her acquiring the nationality of the husband."[234] Scott would argue later in the year that a much simpler way to avoid statelessness, and guarantee equality at the same time, would have been to leave "woman's nationality . . . not affected by marriage,"[235] a principle already accepted in a constantly growing number of national legal systems. On April 4, Stevens sent a cable to Paul in Washington, D.C., informing her that the Convention on Nationality would pass: "The leaders are agitated over our pressure but we have lost."[236] Still, she suggested another course of action. There were still goals to achieve by lobbing the US government and Congress. That was the reason why Paul had stayed back. She had started "by canvassing senators

[231] See, ibid., p. 210. Scott had sent Heemskerk an introduction to Stevens and her activities, which apparently failed to gained his benevolence (see Scott to Theodorus Heemskerk, March 17, 1930, Folder 8, Box 12, JBS Papers.)

[232] Quoted in Bredbenner, *A Nationality of Her Own*, p. 211.

[233] See ibid. At the opening of the Conference, Scott sent a cable to Politis introducing Stevens and telling him that he hoped for "the adoption of [the] equality resolution or nothing" with regard to the "nationality [of] women" (James Brown Scott to Nicolas Politis, March 7, 1930, Folder 8, Box 12, JBS Papers). On April 11, Politis replied that, given "the ultraconservative spirit . . . in this Conference," what had been "obtained"—for instance Article 9, which allowed married women to retain their nationality in case of naturalization of the husband during marriage—was "the maximum that could be reached" (letter in Folder 6, Box 6, JBS Papers).

[234] "Convention on Certain Questions Relating to the Conflict of Nationality Laws," in "Conference for the Codification of International Law—Final Act," *American Journal of International Law*, Supplement, 24, 1930, p. 193.

[235] James Brown Scott, "Unprogressive Codification of Nationality at The Hague," *Women Lawyers' Journal*, 18, 1930, p. 39.

[236] Doris Stevens to Alice Paul, April 4, 1930, Folder 8, Box 7, JBS Papers.

tirelessly,"[237] making sure that, even if the administration eventually signed the unequal Convention, there would be no majority for ratification. In any case, the US government had already been skeptical of the opportunity of regulating nationality through international law, but did not advertise this position for diplomatic reasons. Leaving open the possibility of accession to a nationality treaty allowed the United States to participate in the negotiations and influence the drafting process.[238] Once the final draft was set, the US delegation had more than one reason to be unhappy with it. It was not only incompatible with the Cable Act, it also forbade expatriation unless the person already possessed or would receive as a consequence another nationality.[239] This was a sensitive point for the United States, who were not ready to give up the unfettered possibility to deprive of nationality citizens who had left the country for good. The administration preferred not to advertise this position either, as it was a possible source of tension with immigrant communities and their countries of origin.[240] Therefore, the issue of independent nationality became the point of contention the US government highlighted the most among its several perplexities about the Convention.[241] The United States could have signed the Convention with significant reservations as many other countries did, but the NWP and its allies mounted a relentless campaign for the government to take a stand and vote against. Scott did his part. Throughout the duration of the Conference, he had repeatedly made his case for equal nationality and explained the dangers of a discriminatory convention in letters to State Department officials,[242] US Senators,[243] Latin American diplomats,[244] and delegations at The Hague.[245] On the day of the final vote, Scott, John Cable, and representatives of the NWP and the National Association of Women Lawyers went to the White House to make a final appeal to President Hoover.[246] Doris Stevens described the

237 Bredbenner, *A Nationality of Her Own*, p. 210.

238 See ibid., pp. 207–8.

239 See Article 7, "Convention on Certain Questions Relating to the Conflict of Nationality Laws," p. 193.

240 See Bredbenner, *A Nationality of Her Own*, pp. 211–12.

241 It should be noted that after the United States' negative vote on the Convention, Acting Secretary of State Joseph Cotton released a statement offering expatriation and equality as equivalent motivations, both being "principles . . . firmly embedded in our law" (quoted ibid., p. 214). This was possibly an attempt to counteract the criticism leveled at the administration for having its hand forced by what Cotton called the "feminine lobby." For instance, Manley Hudson would later affirm that the government was "more intent upon mollifying a section of its own public opinion than upon grappling with the very real problems which exist today and which the convention is designed to solve" (Manley O. Hudson, "The Hague Convention of 1930 and the Nationality of Women," *American Journal of International Law*, 27, 1933, p. 122).

242 See, for instance, James Brown Scott to Wilbur Carr, dateable to early April 1930, Folder 8, Box 12, JBS Papers.

243 See, for instance, James Brown Scott to Claude A. Swanson, April 4, 1930, and James Brown Scott to William E. Borah, April 7, 1930, Folder 9, Box 12, JBS Papers.

244 See, for instance, James Brown Scott to Tirso Mesa, April 8, 1930, Folder 9, Box 12, JBS Papers.

245 See, for instance, James Brown Scott to Miguel Cruchaga, April 7, 1930, Folder 9, Box 12, JBS Papers.

246 See Bredbenner, *A Nationality of Her Own*, p. 213 and Finch, "Equal Rights for Women," p. 19.

decisive moment: "There was exhilaration in the air. . . . The nationality convention was . . . the only document to come out of the conference. All of a sudden David Hunter Miller, head of the US delegation went to the platform and announced that the USA would not sign."[247] This would be the only dissenting vote: the other forty countries would all sign the Convention. Yet, the isolated stand of the United States allowed Scott and NWP to spin a triumphant narrative, along familiar lines, out of what was an ostensible setback for equal nationality. Less than two weeks after the vote, Anna Kelton Wiley, Chairman of the NWP, put into words this interpretation of the events of the Conference in a letter to James Brown Scott:

> Instead of the final outcome at The Hague being a defeat, it is really a moral victory. "Forty to One" will become a by-word for the feminists of the United States. It makes one think of the Pass of the Thermopylae with the United States playing the role of Leonidas, with this difference. The dying courage of Leonidas stirred all Greece; the living courage of the United States at The Hague, we hope, will stir the world from its ancient prejudice against women.[248]

The step from moral victory to moral superiority of the new world over old Europe was short. Alva Belmont, the NWP's main financial backer, depicted Europeans hanging on to "the old world subjection of women" as the last remnant of their disappearing *ancien régime*:

> These men have lost their slaves. They have lost their serfs. They have lost their dominion over the working class. They still think they can dominate women. It terrifies them to think that in the future women mean to govern themselves[.][249]

Conveniently overlooking that Latin American governments had signed the Convention, Scott wrote of a "Western Continent, conceived in liberty, . . . insist[ing] upon equality in law."[250]

The narrative of moral superiority prompted "a surge of home support for the rejection of the convention," which, in turn, helped to spur Congress into action and remove two of the provisions of the Cable Act still inspired by dependent citizenship. In 1930, the clause expatriating women married to foreigners and residing abroad was repealed. In 1931, it was the turn of the barring from citizenship of women married to aliens ineligible for naturalization to disappear from the books.[251]

[247] Quoted in DuBois, "Storming The Hague," pp. 23–4. For Miller's own account of the Conference see Miller, "The Hague Codification Conference."
[248] Anna Kelton Wiley to James Brown Scott, April 23, 1930, Folder 2, Box 9, JBS Papers.
[249] Quoted in Bredbenner, *A Nationality of Her Own*, p. 215.
[250] Scott, "Nationality," p. 560.
[251] See Bredbenner, *A Nationality of Her Own*, p. 215.

The events of The Hague also spurred further international initiatives by Stevens, Paul, and Scott. Paul moved to Geneva to follow up and maintain pressure on the League of Nations. Initially she relied on a recommendation that Ruth Shipley of the US delegation had introduced at the Codification Conference, calling for further "study of . . . the principle of equality of sexes in matters of nationality."[252] The joint action of women's rights activist group led to the establishment, in 1931, of a Women's Consultative Committee on Nationality to support the League in that further examination. The Committee took several initiatives to reopen the discussion but "[m]ost of the governments opposed any fresh examination of the matter."[253] The best that could be achieved was an Assembly resolution in 1932, which simply affirmed "that the coming into force of Articles 8 to 11"—the ones in the Convention dealing with the nationality of married women—"would in no way prejudice further concerted international action [and] place any restriction upon . . . any state that may desire to give further effect in its nationality laws to the principle of the equality of the sexes."[254]

The effectiveness of the Women's Committee was not only marred by the opposition of governments but also by its own internal disagreements, which exacerbated when Paul sought to expand its purview beyond nationality issues to the general legal status of women. Indeed, if a shaky alignment could be found around independent citizenship, equal rights and social feminists could find no other common position. The Committee's lack of unity made it incapable of exerting any significant influence in a campaign already waged against difficult odds.[255] Paul never lacked the support of James Brown Scott, constantly lobbying in favor of all her initiatives.

Around this time, in the early 1930s, Scott was producing his maximum effort in both his major projects, one for women's equality and the other rewriting the history of his discipline. Naturally, he began increasingly to draw an explicit connection between his feminist activism and the Salamancan origins of international law. For instance, he sent a telegram to the Spanish permanent delegate to the League of Nations, Salvador de Madariaga, explaining that support for Paul would be a natural expression of his country's tradition: "I URGE YOUR SUPPORT . . . ALICE PAUL'S RESOLUTION . . . WE HOPE SPANISH LEADERSHIP HUMAN RELATIONSHIPS IN ACCORDANCE VITORIA'S PROGRESSIVE LAW NATIONS."[256]

[252] "Conference for the Codification of International Law—Final Act," p. 229.

[253] Hudson, "The Hague Convention of 1930," p. 119. On the detail of those initiatives see ibid., pp. 118–20.

[254] The resolution is reproduced ibid., pp. 119–20.

[255] On the Women's Consultative Committee and its internal divisions see, for instance, Miller "Geneva—The Key to Equality," pp. 227–32 and Leila Rupp, *Worlds of Women: The Making of an International Women's Movement*, Princeton: Princeton University Press, 1997, pp. 41 and 147–8.

[256] James Brown Scott to Salvador de Madariaga, January 25, 1932, Folder 3, Box 48, JBS Papers.

Scott also promoted the two causes in parallel within the *Institut de droit international*. In the 1929 meeting in the United States, he had saluted Vitoria as the founder of modern international law and promoted the *Déclaration des Droits Internationaux de l'Homme*. In criticizing the outcome of the Hague Conference, Scott had offered the Declaration as proof that, in addition to the American continent as a whole, the global community of international lawyers also stood for progressive values. "[L]iberty and equality, which is the perfection of liberty, have not merely penetrated the statesmen of the Western World but also the leaders of international opinion of all the nations. In behalf of this seemingly extravagant assertion, I am happy to vouch the Declaration of the Rights of Man [that] expressly excludes from its six articles all discriminations."[257]

However, the discussion around the Declaration, described in the previous section, and the criticism Scott received from colleagues, paint a more complicated picture. For instance, Jan de Louter, a renowned Dutch international lawyer who had recently cooperated with Scott on the Classics edition of Van Bynkershoek's *Quaestionum juris publici*,[258] wrote him a letter expressing his disappointment. He condemned not only Scott's commitment to equal nationality but also his use of Vitoria as champion of his individualist views:

> I fear that your American horror of all that seems or sounds conservative, spec. in the question of the nationality of "married women" has shut your eyes for the high value and strong arguments in favor of the unity of law in the family, the real historical basis of Christian Society, now more and more despised and loosening to the detriment of mankind. Finally I well enough can agree with you in the glorification or hero-worship of Fr. Vitoria . . . , but I cannot share your exultation of the individual man-woman or (oder) child, and most universal phenomena[.][259]

At the next session of the *Institut*, in 1931 in Cambridge, Scott first proposed the foundation of the *Association internationale Vitoria-Suarez*. He also obtained the creation of a commission studying the nationality of married women and the appointment as rapporteur, alongside Albert de Lapradelle. Scott's parallel work continued at the 1932 Oslo meeting. The draft statutes were approved and the Vitoria-Suarez association officially founded. With regard to equal nationality, Scott presented his detailed report in which he rebuffed all major legal and theoretical arguments against the principle.[260] For instance, with regard to unity of the family, he reminded his colleagues that it could not be reduced to a common

257 Scott, "Nationality," p. 560.

258 Cornelius Van Bynkershoek, *Quaestionum juris publici libri duo*, translated into English by JAN de Louter, Oxford: Oxford University Press, 1930 [1737].

259 Jan de Louter to James Brown Scott, February 23, 1931, vol. 323, CEIP Papers.

260 The report was signed by both Scott and Lapradelle. *De facto*, it was Scott who wrote it, with Lapradelle approving his draft (see the documents in Folder 26, Box 32, JBS Papers and the correspondence in vol. 325, CEIP Papers). For the final version of the report see James Brown Scott and Albert de Lapradelle, "Nationalité de la femme mariée—Report," *Annuaire de l'Institut de Droit International*,

citizenship shared by its members: "*L'unité de la famille est chose d'esprit et non de droit.*"[261] He concluded the report by affirming once again that the principles establishing an effective and progressive universal standard for nationality law were all found at the origin of international law, in Vitoria's *De Indis: ius soli*, accessible naturalization for residents and individual equality.[262] At first Scott hoped to obtain a resolution fully endorsing independent citizenship for married women but, meeting resistance, he gradually watered down the wording and reduced the ambition of the text.[263] The resolution eventually approved by the *Institut* opened by recommending that States respect and maintain the unity of the family as much as possible. The operative part was limited to two suggestions with regard to the effects of marriage on nationality. In the first place, the nationality of one spouse could be extended to the other only with her/his consent. Secondly, if spouses had different nationalities, States should provide for fast and simple procedures of naturalization so that each of the spouses could join the citizenship of the other.[264]

At the end of the day, neither within the League of Nations nor the *Institut*, would Scott and his allies ever come close to obtaining meaningful support for the kind of blanket equality treaty, modeled on the ERA, which they sought. However, fittingly with Scott's narrative on the discovery of America as the birth of the progressive law of nations, they would finally succeed at the following Pan-American Conference, held in Montevideo in 1933.

## Victory at Montevideo: Scott and the Stevens Treaties

The defeat at The Hague provided Scott and Stevens with an opportunity to start a deeper discussion with Latin American governments over equal nationality. Latin American States had signed the Nationality Convention at the Codification Conference, but it was not too late to prevent their ratification. The two proceeded with a concerted action. In July 1930, Stevens, in her capacity as Chairman of the IACW, sent a communication to the Ministers of Foreign Affairs of all State members of the Pan-American Union. The main item was a questionnaire on their respective legal systems. Its function was to gather information for further studies on the legal status of women that the Commission was undertaking in view of the following Pan-American Conference. Stevens suggested that "the Ministers refrain from action"[265] in the meantime: the fact that the Codification Conference itself

Paris: A. Pedone Editeur, 1932, pp. 1–24. The related discussions and revisions of the resolution are ibid., pp. 24–64 and 530–48.

261 Scott and Lapradelle, "Nationalité de la femme mariée," p. 5.
262 See ibid., pp. 22–3.
263 See Finch, "Equal Rights for Women," p. 24.
264 For the text of the resolution see *Annuaire de l'Institut de Droit International*, 1932, p. 564.
265 James Brown Scott to Doris Stevens, July 2, 1930, Folder 12, Box 12, JBS Papers.

had recommended additional study on the nationality of married women called for prudence.

Scott contributed by cultivating his vast network in the foreign policy establishment of the American continent. As soon as rumors emerged that a country was taking preliminary steps toward ratification, he intervened with opposing arguments. As well as educating his correspondents on the diplomatic and legal issues involved,[266] Scott kept reminding them of the responsibility of the Americas' moral and progressive leadership. So he did, for instance, with the Cuban Secretary of State:

> The Western World . . . is breaking down barriers which have separated classes and it has begun the process of according to individuals, as such, equal rights, equal duties and equal privileges. I ask if Cuba would not confess its faith in . . . equal right, to the extent of withholding its approval of the Convention on Nationality and refraining from submitting the Convention to the Republic for its ratification.[267]

Scott also proceeded to align the positions of the American Institute of International Law (AIIL) with those of the IACW. In October 1931, the Governing Board of the Institute named Stevens as its first woman member, filling the seat left open by the commanding figure of Elihu Root. In the same session, the board also recommended for approval at Montevideo an equal rights treaty and an equal nationality treaty. Both had a single substantial article. The former, adopting the language Paul had devised for the ERA, provided that in the "jurisdiction" of "Contracting States . . . men and women shall have equal rights throughout the territory." With the latter, "the Contracting Parties agree[d] there shall be no distinction based on sex in their law and practice relating to nationality."[268] In view of the Montevideo Conference, Stevens was also named the Institute's rapporteur on the civil and political equality of men and women.[269]

On November 4, 1933, Scott spoke before the Convention of the NWP of the prospective "adoption . . . by the Conference at Montevideo," taking place the following month, of "these two epoch-making projects." He showed faith in the ability of the women of the IACW to obtain their approval, which "would . . . dedicate the Republics of the vast American continent to equality as they are already dedicated

[266] See, for instance, the memorandum sent to the Mexican Ambassador to the US, April 14, 1930, Folder 14, and the correspondence with Brazilian diplomats and the US Ambassador in Brazil, Folder 17, October and November 1931, Box 12, JBS Papers. Beyond the personal letters, Scott also sent a memorandum to all American Ministers of Foreign Affairs in the summer of 1931 as President of AIIL (see "Second letter to Ministers of Foreign Affairs—Draft," June 10, 1931, Folder 4, Box 49, JBS Papers).

[267] James Brown Scott to Rafael Martínez Ortíz, June 27, 1930, Folder 11, Box 12, JBS Papers.

[268] See Muna Lee, "Equal Rights Approved by American Institute of International Law."

[269] See, for instance, James Brown Scott to Doris Stevens, November 7, 1933, and James Brown Scott to Victor Maurtua, November 10, 1933, vol. 332, CEIP Papers.

to liberty." He closed his speech with a plea to "God" to "bless the American women" who would soon "join battle far, far to the south at Montevideo under the light of the Southern Cross."[270] A few days later, Scott sent a letter to the Secretary of State Cordell Hull, appointed to the position by Franklin Delano Roosevelt, who had assumed the US presidency earlier in the year and had been Scott's student at Columbia Law School. Scott's letter, over forty pages long, sought to enlighten Hull on his positions on every topic to be addressed by the upcoming Conference. With regard to "the political and civil rights of women," Scott retraced for Hull the events and the steps forward of recent years, ranging from the initiatives within the Pan-American machinery to the League of Nations and the *Institut de droit international*. The Secretary of State could contribute to an "immense victory of right over inequality": he just had to instruct "the Chairman of the American Delegation" at Montevideo to "advocate the acceptance of six lines, three on equal rights and three on equal nationality in the projects to be presented by Miss Stevens."[271]

Not surprisingly though, the United States' delegation initially opposed both recommendations. The equal rights treaty was perceived—correctly—as an attempt by the NWP to force the hand of national institutions toward the ERA. With regard to equal nationality, what Paul considered a reversal of the US policy at The Hague was really not: the State Department had consistently preferred not to be bound in matters of nationality by a treaty, whatever its approach and content.[272]

The United States brought a woman delegate to Montevideo, Sophonisba Breckinridge. She would join the battle but on the opposite side of Stevens and the NWP. Breckinridge, a professor at the University of Chicago who had published extensively on the social, legal, and economic condition of women in the United States, took the floor before the Third Committee of the Conference, tasked with addressing the civil and political rights of women. She explained in detail why she, the government she represented, and "several groups of organized women," including the League of Women Voters, considered the initiatives of equal rights feminists misguided.

> [W]hile equality should enter into the solution as a guiding principle, it is not enough since equality may be obtained by selecting the less advantageous situation[. T]here are two groups of women, whose interests apparently in conflict are, in fact, identical[.] The woman of general professional attainments who feels the irksome restrictions imposed sometimes by law, sometimes by prejudice, needs and desires emancipation from those restrictions. While no treaty of equality will persuade a client or a patient to employ a woman rather than a man,

[270] James Brown Scott, "The Inter-American Commission of Women Reports at Montevideo—Address before the Biennial Convention of the National Woman's Party, Wilmington, Delaware, November 4, 1933," Folder 1, Box 49, JBS Papers.

[271] James Brown Scott to Cordell Hull, November 7, 1933, vol. 335, CEIP Papers.

[272] See Bredbenner, *A Nationality of Her Own*, pp. 233–4.

> it is not unnatural that such women might think to find assistance in some such device. On the other hand, the women at the bottom of the occupational ladder, weak bargainers . . . , find almost the only basis of effective equality in such protection from undue exploitation as is provided by legislation restricting hours, prohibiting night work, prescribing conditions of safety and decency in work places[.][273]

The proposal for an equal rights treaty was declined. The Conference resolved that it could not "impose" such blanket "binding obligations . . . without curtailing the sovereign rights of the different States."[274] Nevertheless, the delegations of four States—Cuba, Ecuador, Paraguay, and Uruguay—decided to sign the treaty.[275]

The equal nationality treaty received much wider support. Several countries had announced that they would sign it before the Conference opened. The United States would eventually change its course and join them. Once the intention of the government not to sign became public knowledge during the opening days of the Conference, supporters of the treaty mounted a vehement campaign of protest. The only women's organization that supported the administration in this phase was the NLWV. Even though they promoted and campaigned for independent citizenship, "the NLWV's leaders were too distracted by the obvious textual similarities between the nationality treaty and the . . . equal rights amendment to assess the merits of the nationality treaty independently. [It] had to be arrested because it could serve as the means towards . . . the abolition of all laws based on sex."[276]

The NLWV remained isolated in its position. The protest went beyond feminists and reformers, receiving support from most of the nation's press. Indeed, the general perception was that not signing in Montevideo was not a consistent prosecution of the US policy at The Hague: rather it was a betrayal of the spirit of that earlier decision taking a stand for women's rights.[277] Beyond the public pressure, there were other circumstances that favored reconsideration by the administration. Refusing to sign a treaty so strongly supported by Latin American countries did not fit with the "good-neighbor" policy Roosevelt had committed to. Moreover, the United States had little to lose in terms of new obligations: the Cable Act, with its recent modifications, already prescribed full equality in almost every aspect of domestic nationality law. Notwithstanding the objections of the State Department, Roosevelt instructed the delegation to switch position. On December 26, 1933,

273 "Seventh International Conference of American States, Third Committee, Civil and Political Rights of Women—Minutes and Antecedents," Folder 1, Box 49, JBS Papers, pp. 14–15.

274 Resolution quoted in Finch, "Equal Rights for Women," p. 28.

275 For the full text of the treaty see James Brown Scott, "The Seventh International Conference of American States," *American Journal of International Law*, 28, 1934, p. 221.

276 Ibid., p. 217. See also pp. 235–7.

277 See also Bredbenner, *A Nationality of Her Own*, pp. 234–5.

nineteen American countries, including the United States, signed the equal nationality treaty.[278]

Scott and the NWP celebrated the outcome of the Montevideo Conference as a turning point in history.[279] Anna Kelton Wiley affirmed that Scott, Paul and Stevens were among the "few mortals . . . given the great joy of victory due to their own labors" and deserving "the gratitude of hosts of people." She also expressed her own personal gratitude to Scott: "Our two leaders are quite peerless in this great triumph but without your great knowledge, great sympathy and great personality this event could not have taken place."[280]

Scott was ready to place elsewhere the credit for the equality conventions by coining for them the name of Stevens Treaties.[281] He opened his account of the Montevideo Conference on the AJIL, by analyzing those two documents and commenting on their importance:

> At Montevideo there was established a great and illuminating precedent. In achieving equality by international agreement, our American women, whether consciously or not, have given to the future law of nations its inevitable and enduring direction; and the future law of nations will it not be the result of the collaboration of enlightened men and women?[282]

Scott continued by celebrating the Montevideo Conference as a step forward with regard to two more crucial aspects of the progressive development of international law. Alongside individual equality, American States had committed to the equality of States and recognized the moral roots of the law of nations in the foundational role of Francisco de Vitoria. With regard to States' equality, Scott praised the recognition in treaty law of the principle of non-intervention, enshrined in Article 8 of the Convention on the Rights and Duties of States, signed at Montevideo.[283] In any case, Scott argued, this represented only the legal translation of the Monroe Doctrine that the United States had consistently applied. "The policy is not of yesterday or the day before; it is the 'traditional' policy of these

[278] For the official text of the treaty see "Seventh International Conference of American States—Final Act," *American Journal of International Law*, Supplement, 28, 1934, pp. 62–3

[279] See, for instance, James Brown Scott, "Conflict and Victory: The Inter-American Commission of Women at Montevideo," *Equal Rights*, January 13, 1934, also preserved in draft in Folder 5, Box 49, JBS Papers.

[280] Anna Kelton Wiley to James Brown Scott, December 21, 1933, Folder 3, Box 48, JBS Papers.

[281] See, for instance, Scott, "The Seventh International Conference," pp. 220–1 and James Brown Scott, "Our American Women in Action," *Women Lawyer's Journal*, 21, 1934, p. 16.

[282] Scott, "The Seventh International Conference," p. 222.

[283] For the full official text of the Convention and the US reservation see "Seventh International Conference of American States—Final Act," pp. 75–8. For accounts of the international legal implications and political context surrounding the approval of the Convention and, in general, the Montevideo Conference see Becker Lorca, *Mestizo International Law*, pp. 327–52 and Juan Pablo Scarfi, *The Hidden History of International Law in the Americas: Empire and Legal Networks*, Oxford: Oxford University Press, 2017, pp. 147–68.

United States of America."[284] True, the United States had signed the Convention with a reservation covering all its eleven substantial articles; but, according to Scott, the terms of the reservation left no doubt to his country's continuing commitment to the principle: "The United States Government is as much opposed as any other government to interference with the freedom, the sovereignty, or other internal affairs . . . of the governments of other nations."[285] Soon enough, Scott affirmed, "President Roosevelt's policy of the 'good neighbor' [would] be found . . . to accord with . . . the . . . convention, and . . . the President himself w[ould] direct the unreserved signature of the United States to this splendid, forward-looking, and indeed law-making, convention."[286]

Finally, Scott informed his readers of the unanimous approval of the following resolution:

> The Seventh International Conference of American States, *Resolves*: To recommend that a bust of the Spanish theologian, Francisco de Vitoria, be placed in the headquarters of the Pan American Union, in Washington, as a tribute to the professor of Salamanca who, in the sixteenth century, established the foundations of modern international law.[287]

With this resolution, Scott held, "twenty-one American republics, successors of the barbarian 'principalities' . . . discovered by Columbus[,] ha[d] declared" Vitoria's *relectiones* to have founded "their . . . international law"[288] of the day. Essentially, this was the first official recognition of the pedigree Scott had incessantly advocated for in the previous years.

Scott clearly saw the decisions of the Seventh Pan-American Conference as a vindication of his life's work; he recognized the role of Stevens in the achievement of that goal. The triumph of Montevideo would be completed on May 24, 1934, the day that arguably represented the peak of the Scott-Stevens collaboration for women's equality. On that day, the US Senate ratified the equal nationality treaty and President Roosevelt signed into law the Dickstein-Copeland bill, originally drafted by Alice Paul.[289] In consequence of its enactment, all rules in US nationality law applied equally to men and women.

[284] Scott, "The Seventh International Conference," p. 224. On Scott's understanding of the Monroe Doctrine and the principle of equality of States in American international law see Chapter 2.

[285] "Seventh International Conference of American States—Final Act," p. 78.

[286] Scott, "The Seventh International Conference," p. 229.

[287] Reprinted ibid. The bust of Vitoria would be placed in the headquarters of the Pan-American Union only thirty years later, in 1963 (see Juan Pablo Scarfi, "Reconfiguraciones del saber jurídico: James Brown Scott reflota la obra de Vitoria desde Estados Unidos en años de entreguerras," in Ricardo D. Salvatore (ed.), *Los Lugares del Saber*, Rosario: Beatriz Viterbo Editora, 2007, p. 285).

[288] Scott, "The Seventh International Conference," p. 230.

[289] See Bredbenner, *A Nationality of Her Own*, pp. 238–42.

As we saw in the previous chapter, in that same year, Scott published *The Catholic Conception*. In its final page he drew a direct line between the Stevens Treaties and the theology of Salamanca:

> As Suárez stood for equality of men and women, Victoria, by adopting the principle of *jus soli*, necessarily stood for the principle of nationality. Appropriately the New World has taken up the equal and single nationality of Victoria and the larger equality of Suárez at the Seventh of the Pan American Conferances [sic] held in Montevideo in 1933, when the American Republics adopted an equal nationality convention without a dissenting vote, and a quadruple equal rights treaty.[290]

## Vitoria and the Equal Rights Treaties: The Unbearable Lightness of Scott's Equality

The successes Scott and Stevens achieved in 1933 and 1934 came when their positions of influence were already in jeopardy. In January 1933, all NWP-led activities, including the IACW, had lost their main source of financial support with the death of Alva Belmont, who had bankrolled the Party since its foundation. The limited funding Scott had been able to give for the IACW legal reports through the Division of International Law of CEIP also came to an end. The Trustees had initially indulged Scott's venture into feminist activism. However, they "decided to discontinue the Endowment's financial support" when Scott gave the cause "what they considered undue importance and prominence."[291]

Both the positions of the AIIL and the IACW within the Pan-American system came under attack at Montevideo. The AIIL lost the semi-official role as advisor to the Pan-American Union for the codification of international law it had enjoyed since the mid-1920s. By 1933, the Institute had not held a plenary session in years. It was not considered able to represent the views of American international lawyers as a professional group. The equal rights projects at Montevideo "produced some outspoken dissatisfaction with the methods of the Institute in formulating its recommendations. They were said to be not the considered judgment of the organization as a whole, but the proposals of a few of its most active members,"[292] Scott and his closest allies.[293] As a result, the Montevideo Conference created an

[290] Scott, *The Catholic Conception*, p. 494.

[291] Finch, "Equal Rights for Women," p. 1.

[292] George A. Finch, "The American Institute of International Law," unpublished text meant for Scott's biography, Folder 3, Box 69, JBS Papers, p. 37.

[293] The accusation was not new: Alejandro Álvarez had already questioned Scott's autocratic choices with regard to the subjects of codification projects and their designated rapporteurs (see, for instance, Alejandro Àlvarez to James Brown Scott, July 27, 1929, vol. 313, CEIP Papers).

official machinery for codification that supplanted the AIIL. It recommended the American republics create their own national codification commission, while the Pan-American Union would have its committee of experts and a juridical section to take care of the administrative aspects of the process.[294]

The IACW was, however, confirmed by the Conference, despite a US-led attempt to secure its suppression.[295] The primary goal of the Roosevelt administration was not to get rid of the Commission in and for itself, but to get rid of Stevens. Indeed, the leading women in the administration were social feminists and supported protective legislation. Among them were figures like Frances Perkins, Secretary of Labor and first woman to be appointed to the US cabinet, and the First Lady, Eleanor Roosevelt, whose "disagreements with the NWP were public knowledge."[296] The growing opposition to Stevens' leadership among Latin American feminists facilitated the moves against her.[297] At the following Pan-American Conference, held in Lima in 1938, the IACW was reformed, allowing the United States to appoint a new representative. On February 1, 1939, Mary Winslow of the Women's Trade Union League, a social feminist, was chosen to replace Stevens.[298]

Notwithstanding the increasingly precarious nature of their efforts for women's equality, the collaboration between Scott and Stevens did not end there. Rather, it took a more personal turn.[299] Most crucially here, Stevens' initiative determined a highly symbolic event that has marked Scott's legacy. Thanks to her, the deep

294 For an account of the hostility toward the AIIL and its ouster see Finch, "The American Institute," pp. 34–40.

295 See Finch, "Equal Rights for Women," pp. 26 and 34.

296 Bredbenner, *A Nationality of Her Own*, p. 236. The US press speculated that the initial opposition of the United States to the equal nationality treaty at Montevideo had been directly inspired by Eleanor Roosevelt, an accusation she forcefully rejected (see ibid.).

297 As examples, one can point to the growing wedge between the NWP and Cuban feminists (see Dubois, "A Momentary Transnational Sisterhood," p. 90) or the accusations made by Bertha Lutz that Stevens was swaying delegates with flirtation and sexual offers (see Leila Rupp, "Sexuality and Politics in Early Twentieth Century: The Case of the International Women's Movement," *Feminist Studies*, 23, 1997, pp. 577 and 594).

298 See Becker, *The Origins*, pp. 184–6 and Finch, "Equal Rights for Women," pp. 33–7. Scott, close to retirement and in declining health, enlisted Bustamante in an unsuccessful campaign to fight the decision (see James Brown Scott to Antonio de Bustamante, May 18, 1939, Folder 31, Box 12, JBS Papers). They argued that, as Stevens had been appointed by the Pan-American Union, the United States had no legal control over her membership and chairmanship of the IACW (see, for instance, James Brown Scott to Cordell Hull, June 29, 1939, Folder 32, Box 12, JBS Papers). Scott sought the support of the Foreign Ministries of the American republics (see the model letter in Folder 32, Box 12, JBS Papers), the Pan-American Union (see Leo Rowe to James Brown Scott, February 2, 1929, Folder 5, Box 48, JBS Papers) and members of the US Congress. It was the first time Scott had challenged a decision of the US government in such an open and official manner.

299 For instance, when, in November 1937, Scott's sister Jeannette, known artist and early member of the NWP, died, Stevens took the initiative to write an obituary for her and publish it in the *New York Times* (see Doris Stevens, "Jeannette Scott, Art Leader, Dies," *New York Times*, November 17, 1937, p. 23). Scott was so impressed and grateful that he asked Stevens to prepare a book recounting Jeannette's life and collecting reproductions of her most valued works (see Doris Stevens, *Paintings and Drawings of Jeannette Scott*, privately printed for James Brown Scott, 1940).

intellectual connection Scott had developed with Vitoria found a visual expression we can still admire today on the walls of the Justice Department building.

The United States Department of Justice had moved through several temporary locations since its creation in 1870. Finally, in 1935, its dedicated building, which is still home to the Department today, was completed. The Treasury Department Art Program invested considerably in decorating the interior with murals "depict[ing] scenes of daily life from throughout American history and symbolic interpretations or allegorical themes relating to the role of justice in [American] society."[300] The artist Boardman Robinson was tasked with painting a series of eighteen panels depicting the Great Codifiers of the Law, which would surround the staircase leading to the building's Great Hall. Robinson compiled an initial list of subjects, including sixteen individuals and two legal texts, with the assistance of two legal luminaries, Roscoe Pound and Supreme Court Justice Harlan Fiske Stone. The texts selected for a depiction of their signing were the Magna Charta and the American Constitution, drawing a narrative of the universal role of Anglo-American constitutionalism that Scott had himself championed.[301]

The list of individual codifiers covered a wide array of figures; each of them belonged in some capacity to the received tradition of Western legal thought. The roster ranged from sacred figures like Moses and Jesus Christ to US legal icons such as John Marshall and James Kent. Doris Stevens, "a long-time friend and former neighbor" of Robinson, protested: the list lacked "a giver of the law of nations." When she mentioned Francisco de Vitoria, Robinson said he had never heard of him and that he would need a portrait as model. Stevens replied that there was no portrait of the Dominican but not to worry: she would "introduce [Robinson] to the scholar who is an authority on him. [T]he image of Dr. Scott w[ould] do very well. He resembles a friar and he is passionately trying to bring about a renascence of Victoria." In November 1935, Stevens made the introduction: the two "got on like a couple of kittens; Robinson sketched [Scott's] head and hands."[302] Scott also proposed elements for the composition of Vitoria's panel: "an atlas disclosing America, and a scroll upon which is the inscription 'Derechos, Iguales de Hombres y Mujeres, under which I . . . would . . . put the simple initials 'D. S.'"[303] By the end of this first conversation, not only Vitoria, but also Grotius and Thomas Aquinas had made the list and gained their mural at the Justice Department.[304]

[300] "Building Overview—U. S. Department of Justice Building." Available at http://gsa.gov/portal/ext/html/site/hb/category/25431/actionParameter/exploreByBuilding/buildingId/321 (last accessed August 3, 2017).

[301] See Chapter 3.

[302] Doris Stevens to George Finch, November 28, 1944, Folder 6, Box 48, JBS Papers.

[303] James Brown Scott to Boardman Robinson, November 8, 1935, Folder 25, Box 12, JBS Papers. In the completed panel Vitoria is looking at America on a globe, not an atlas, and the paper next to him on the floor does not bear any inscription.

[304] See ibid.

When, in 1937, Robinson completed the paintings and Scott could finally see them, he was delighted:

> Words fail me to express my appreciation of the magnificent mural of Franciscus de Victoria[.] I do not think there could have been conceived a finer setting for this founder of the law of nations and from the bottom of his heart the unworthy one whose likeness Victoria bears on the walls of the Department of Justice thanks you for the most perfect portrait that he has ever had, painted by you at the suggestion, I am happy and proud to say, of the always thoughtful and gracious Doris Stevens, who never, as you know, fails as a friend.[305]

The figure bears the name and the Dominican robes of a sixteenth-century Spanish theologian. Yet its features are those of the twentieth-century international lawyer who turned him into a prophet of progressive international law and equal rights. The fingers pointing at the American continent on a globe are Scott's. Robinson's mural is the most extreme and patent expression of a conflation of identities and projects carefully built by Scott and his associates.

For instance, Bustamante had bestowed on Scott a monicker that "spontaneously came to [his] lips . . . to characterize" his friend's "enthusiastic, heartfelt and indisputable defense of the rights of the woman." He was "[t]he Apostle of Equality."[306] The title, with its religious connotation, would have been an even better fit for the character of Vitoria that Scott had constructed for his Spanish origin argument. In this narrative, both were Apostles of Equality, agents of an inevitable progress toward a utopia of universal rights. Indeed, Scott had portrayed the approval of the equal rights treaties he sponsored at Montevideo as simply the "logical . . . conclusion" of "the principle of equality . . . fundamental to both . . . Victoria and . . . Suárez."[307]

This conflation of Scott and Vitoria, of early modern Catholic theology and interwar feminist activism, prompts a series of considerations over Scott's Spanish origin. Providing the equal rights treaties with a Salamancan historical pedigree served a key ideological function: it turned the cause and its eventual success into an act of providence or, at the very least, into a metapolitical event, operating beyond the realm of everyday government affairs. This last alternative depended on Scott's usual ambiguity: as we have seen, Scott always walked the line between the religious and the secular when describing the foundations of international law. The principle of equality, embodied by Vitoria, was no different. At times, Scott's Vitoria is an enlightened modern liberal and his equality a human aspiration. At

[305] James Brown Scott to Boardman Robinson, December 8, 1937, Folder 10, Box 63, JBS Papers.

[306] Antonio de Bustamante, "El apostol de la igualdad," preface to James Brown Scott, *El progreso del derecho de gentes*, Madrid: Espasa-Calpe, 1936, also available in draft in Folder 9, Box 2, JBS Papers, my translation from Spanish.

[307] Scott, *The Catholic Conception*, p. 493.

others, the Dominican's translation of Christian morality into a universal legal system appeared as a God-inspired event for mankind's redemption.

Scott suggested that the equal rights treaties participated in such eschatological function. He did so even in the AJIL, the forum where he normally stuck to more technical legal language. In a passage of his account of the Montevideo Conference, he contrasted the unanimous approval of the equal nationality treaty with its rejection in 1930 in The Hague. The passage, until that point couched in matter-of-fact language, is closed by a Biblical sentence, which Scott neither introduced or elaborated on: "The stone which the builders refused is become the headstone of the corner."[308] If this was just a rhetorical figure employed by a religious man who liked to quote the Scriptures, it was certainly a loaded one. Originally found in the Book of Psalms (188:22), the sentence is repeated by Peter in the Acts (4:8–12). "Filled with the Holy Spirit," the first among the apostles explained to the Jewish leaders that Jesus was the stone they rejected but God had made the cornerstone of salvation: "Salvation is found in no one else, for there is no other name under heaven given to mankind by which we must be saved." By the simple addition of this quote, Scott placed the equal nationality treaty outside the normal operation of transactional politics. Again adopting a biblical reference, he affirmed that the "action" of the four countries that had signed the equal rights treaty had made of "all America . . . the land of promise."[309] The choice between supporting the treaties and rejecting them was a moral one with metaphysical implications; it was a choice between salvation and damnation, good and evil.

The eschatological and providential dimension of Scott's narrative was problematic in both historiographical and political terms, ultimately making his arguments unpersuasive. With regard to the first aspect, he claimed to write as an historian. In bestowing the role of founder of international law on Vitoria, he affirmed to be restoring a correct and objective view of the history of the discipline. Vitoria had been passed over in favor of Grotius because of prejudice, while Scott, employing the *relectiones* as primary evidence, was setting the historical record straight. This rationalist stand could be squared with Scott's view of history as animated by the unfolding of democracy and equality: it was a teleological form of narration quite common within the modern historical tradition. Scott placed himself outside of historical argumentation and into a fully religious vision with his implication that equality was a matter of salvation. It was not just a human goal but the millenarian coming of the end of history.[310] Only within this dogmatic mind-frame, did Scott's direct connection, breaking historical context to the point of utter non-relevance, become conceivable. Vitoria teaching the implications of the discovery of America

[308] Scott, "The Seventh International Conference," p. 221.

[309] Ibid., p. 222.

[310] On the distinction and similarities between organicist history-writing and religious accounts see Hayden White, *Metahistory: The Historical Imagination in Nineteenth-Century Europe*, Baltimore: The Johns Hopkins University Press, 1973, pp. 15–16.

for the administration of the sacrament of penance in the sixteenth century; Scott and Stevens pushing controversial feminist treaties within international institutions in the twentieth: it was all the same God's work. Crucially, Scott did not even try to build a logical case for this equivalence: he simply evoked the principle of equality as the self-evident link. Accepting this proposition did not require any rational conviction. It called exclusively for a leap of faith.

This leads to the second aspect of Scott's connection between Vitoria and the equal rights treaties that I find problematic. Placing the treaties outside the realm of political confrontation clashed with the reality surrounding them and their proponents. The debate on equal rights could not plausibly be reduced to a moral choice between progress and reaction, justice and oppression. As Sophonisba Breckinridge had explained with clarity at Montevideo, the NWP's credo that women would achieve social equality through blanket equal rights legislation was widely contested, not just in the political discourse at large, but among women and feminist activists. The equal nationality treaty at least responded—in spirit, but not in method—to an aspiration shared within the women's rights movement. The equal rights treaty, instead, was perceived as the attempt of elitist upper-class professionals to gain privileges at the expense of working-class and non-white women, to whose plight they seemed to be oblivious or indifferent.[311]

Scott never acknowledged this point, not even as the divide between social and equal rights feminists turned increasingly from one of ideas and personalities into one of partisanship. In 1928, the same year in which Scott first met Stevens, the NWP made a fundamental change in its strategy for presidential elections. Before the adoption of the Nineteenth Amendment, the NWP had urged enfranchised women to vote against the Democrats, the party in power, for their failure to enact the right of suffrage nationwide. It was arguably a vote for women, rather than in favor of a political side. This argument was much more difficult to plausibly make when the NWP leaders decided to endorse the Republican candidate, Herbert Hoover. Hoover had not endorsed the ERA, but the NWP leadership argued that a Republican victory was the best chance for its approval. They maintained this position when Hoover stated that he would not change the protective legislation already in force.[312]

The endorsement of Hoover, a decision made by a small number of Party leaders behind closed doors,[313] accelerated the decline of the NWP and heightened its internal divisions. Voices in favor of democratization of the Party governance did not lead to reform but only to harsh confrontations and defections.[314] As the NWP

311 To be clear, I am not implying that equal rights arguments had no merit whatsoever. Rather I find correct the social feminist argument that the NWP, by claiming that the equal rights approach was the only truly feminist one, failed to address the complexity of the issues connected to the quest for women's rights. On this point see, for instance, Cott, "Feminist Politics," pp. 57–62.

312 On the NWP's endorsement of Hoover, its implications and consequences see ibid., pp. 62–4.

313 See Becker, *The Origins*, p. 94.

314 See Cott, "Feminist Politics," pp. 63–4.

grew weaker and its leadership isolated, the Party also lost the rather cooperative relationship it had enjoyed with the US government when the Democrats regained power. Having openly sided with the Republicans, the NWP had a hard time gaining any support from the Roosevelt administration, which, as we have seen, also featured several high-profile social feminists. Like the endorsement of the Republican ticket in 1928, the contemporaneous decision to start an international equal rights campaign came from the very top. Paul and Stevens pursued it in their own terms, running, respectively, the Women's Consultative Committee on Nationality and the IACW as independently as they could.[315]

Looking at it from this point of view, the campaign for the equal rights treaties appears to be the self-referential action of a restricted elitist group rather than a popular quest for universal justice. Yet, it was also the impressive effort of activists who dedicated their lives to improving the social conditions of women and managed, alongside many other friendly and competing groups, to put women's rights on the agenda of international politics for the first time. A complete and fair account of the campaign should encompass both these perspectives.

With his participation, Scott, claiming the authority of Vitoria and Suárez, took an uncompromising stand for women's equality and feminism, against the opposition and backlash of his professional network. However, the brand of feminism he championed overlooked, by design, any other social injustice. The organization he allied with, the NWP, fell prey to partisan interests and internal squabbles. Its single-minded effort for legislation calling abstractly for a formal equality of rights appeared a long way off meaningfully addressing the problems and aspirations of most women. Within this context, Scott's association of the equal rights treaties with the universal morality of a saint-like figure like the Vitoria in his books could not but sound increasingly hollow.

[315] Eventually, Paul and Stevens developed a rivalry and severed their relationship. Mary Trigg traces their early disagreements to 1931 when Paul felt overshadowed by the growing identification of the equal rights treaties campaign with Stevens in the press (see Trigg, *Feminism as Life's Work*, pp. 155–6). After Scott's retirement, in 1941, they had their final confrontation, occasioned by a long-standing dispute over Alva Belmont's inheritance. Stevens participated in a failed take-over of the NWP, including an occupation of its headquarters (see Lunardini, *Alice Paul*, pp. 160–2.) After leaving the NWP, Stevens' politics moved further right and her immediate goal became to oppose the welfare measures of the New Deal. She did not hide the fact that she was at least partly motivated by her disdain for the administration and the woman she blamed for her removal from the IACW: Eleanor Roosevelt (see Trigg, *Feminism as Life's Work*, p. 164).

# Concluding Remarks. The Legacy of James Brown Scott and the Responsibilities of International Legal History

My primary intention in telling the story of James Brown Scott's historical project has been clear to me since the beginning. The goal was to embark on a journey of professional self-reflection, providing insight into the activity of international lawyers concerned with the past of the discipline. To begin with, there is the realization that our unquestioned assumption that Vitoria is a fundamental early figure for the legal discourse we study depends, in fact, on the politics and preferences of a colleague, active before the Second World War, who had, at least for a time, fallen into oblivion. The assessment of Vitoria's legacy, as carried by Scott's narrative, has led Antony Anghie to reflect on the structural, constraining elements of international legal discourse to describe its persistent oppressiveness, as I noted in the introduction. This approach is politically opposite but intellectually specular to Scott's own as they both focused on continuity and necessity. Scott, of course, was much more extreme in his views and less nuanced in his history-writing: he presented freedom and equality as timeless concepts, inevitably bound to rule human relationships. In his account, Vitoria was the prophet who had pointed to those natural laws, Suárez the intellectual master who developed that inspired intuition into principles that explained the past and predicted the future. Scott's international legal history was ultimately fatalist and deterministic.

However, I set out to clarify that the inception of the Spanish origin narrative, against the intentions of its author, also tells us about the role of contingency and individual agency in the history of international law.[1] The repurposing of sixteenth-century Salamancan theology into the moral and intellectual foundations of a universalist legal order shaping up in the twentieth century was determined, as this book shows, by a series of professional events and choices which marked James Brown Scott's life. The Spanish origin was based on Scott's Langdellian legal education and its exceptionalist implications. It complemented his earlier project on US constitutional history, as they both presented the development of the international organization entwined with the progressive spirit of the

[1] On the importance of a proper consideration of both necessity and contingency in international legal scholarship see Susan Marks, "False Contingency," *Current Legal Problems*, 62, 2009, pp. 1–21.

*Rewriting the History of the Law of Nations: How James Brown Scott Made Francisco de Vitoria the Founder of International Law*. Paolo Amorosa, Oxford University Press (2019). © Paolo Amorosa
DOI: 10.1093/oso/9780198849377.001.0001

American continent. The scientific element of this narrative combined naturally with its reliance on providence, building upon the harmonious view of religion and science that characterized Scott's Presbyterian upbringing. His conviction that international law should be based on a universal Christian moral authority brought him closer to the Catholic Church and its institutions of higher education in the United States. This closeness gave him the chance to be involved in the Neo-Scholastic revival taking place at Georgetown and other Catholic universities, a participation that provided him with the intellectual means to hone his argument connecting Salamancan theology, American democracy, and international organization. The Spanish origin was later shaped by the concrete projects Scott associated with it, determining which aspects of the work of Vitoria and Suárez he emphasized and related to twentieth-century international law. He remarked how the foundations of the discipline rested on natural law and just war theory to appeal to the Roman Curia. In the context of the promotion of women's equality through treaty, Scott relied on Vitoria's universalism to affirm that civil and political rights and non-discrimination provisions belonged not only to the sphere of national legal systems but also to international law. While the Spanish origin resonated with Scott's background, expertise, and political sensibility, he probably would not have dedicated himself so significantly to it if his position within the American Society of International Law (ASIL) had not been in a declining trajectory. In a way, he was cornered deeper into the study of the history and moral foundations of international law by the rise of the younger generation with their realist bent; yet, his commitment to the project and belief in its importance were enthusiastic and unwavering.

Drawing attention to the contingency of Scott's life circumstances and related choices, pointing to his agency in reshaping international legal history, is not a mere exercise in historical revision or a philosophical statement about the nature of historical inquiry. It is key because agency brings with it responsibility. The history of mankind is not only about predetermined laws and irresistible principles, which dictate inevitable outcomes, as Scott seemed to believe. Individual actions matter, the work of an international lawyer could shape discourse and influence society in ways that are intuitively recognizable if not always intended and measurable. This consideration points to the necessity of reconsidering certain images of our profession, at the same time self-aggrandizing and de-responsibilizing, that we have come to recognize and accept. When we think of ourselves as the "priesthood" of a technical discipline, operating in a legal sphere separated from politics, or as the members of a universal invisible college,[2] depositaries of "the legal conscience of

[2] Anthea Roberts has recently paraphrased the famous characterization by Oscar Schachter, depicting international lawyers as an "invisible college dedicated to a common intellectual enterprise" (Oscar Schacter, "The Invisible College of International Lawyers," *Northwestern University Law Review*, 72, 1977, p. 217). She claims instead that, given the diverse approaches to the discipline due to cultural differences and national traditions she details in her book, the profession would be better defined as a

the civilized world,"[3] we deny our role as situated, engaged, and self-aware political actors. Self-awareness carries with it the immersion of historical narratives about international law into the general discourse of global politics; it also counteracts the temptation of retreating into a realm of timeless ideas bearing little grip on the stakes of concrete social arrangements. This is not to say that we should avoid addressing the large concepts that provided the foundations of Scott's international law like democracy, equality, or human rights. They are structural elements of our current political language, their use is necessary for participation in any meaningful conversation on fundamental international legal issues. The challenge lies in appreciating their historicity and conceptual evolution, learning the work they can do from previous uses in their peculiar contexts and articulating how they could be redeployed in innovative fashion for transformative goals.

Among these large concepts, the intellectual legacy of Scott's Spanish origin relates more closely and specifically to current human rights discourse. The persisting purchase of associating Vitoria with the modern beginning of international law is intimately linked with the growing pervasiveness of rights language in recent decades in all branches of the discipline.[4] Vitoria's *De Indis* naturally evokes questions we have been and are still facing in connection to the rise of human rights approaches to international law. Does the formal recognition of universal human rights contribute to a fairer global order or does it represent a deceptive justification of a *status quo* based on oppression and exploitation?

Certainly, the story of the rights projects Scott associated with Vitoria and Suárez shows how the purity of universal formal principles is easily lost when facing political realities. At the same time as Scott was asserting the close link of Scholastic theology with the rise of American egalitarian democracy, he associated with international lawyers of authoritarian convictions like Verdross and Von Heydte, dictators like Spain's Primo de Rivera and the most outspoken Nazi supporter in the Roman Curia, Bishop Alois Hudal.

If Scott was ready to compromise his democratic values in order to ally with powerful figures and influential colleagues, he would not be so accommodating about the conflicting understandings of equality within the women's rights movement: he remained unwaveringly loyal to the formalist views he shared with Doris

divisible college (see Anthea Roberts, *Is International Law International?*, Oxford: Oxford University Press, 2017).

[3] The *Institut de Droit International* was founded with the explicit ambition of embodying that conscience (see Martti Koskenniemi, *The Gentle Civilizer of Nations*, Cambridge: Cambridge University Press, 2001, p. 41). This ambition was often renewed and evoked by members in later decades (see, for instance, Mandelstam in *Annuaire de l'Institut de Droit International*, Paris: A. Pedone Editeur, vol. II, 1929, p. 134).

[4] On the ubiquitousness and versatility of human rights see, for instance, Conor Gearty and Costas Douzinas, "Introduction," in Conor Gearty and Costas Douzinas (eds.), *The Meanings of Rights: The Philosophy and Social Theory of Human Rights*, Cambridge: Cambridge University Press, 2014, pp. 1–10.

Stevens and Alice Paul. The National Woman's Party (NWP) campaign Scott contributed to, claiming to be the translation into legal action of true feminism, refused to accept that women's social instances could be better served by goals other than a blanket recognition of equal rights. What Scott was presenting as a crusade sanctioned by the universalism of the Salamanca theologians, on behalf of the female half of mankind, turned out to be representative of only a small privileged minority of the US feminist movement.

Scott's combination of contradictory actions glossed over by triumphant progressive narratives is, by now, a familiar scheme, apt to describe the trajectory of human rights in recent decades. For all the good the human rights movement has sought and achieved, it has become commonplace to criticize it for its "normalization" into a regime. David Kennedy has put forward the best-known formulation of this argument. He has famously wondered if human rights, aiming to be part of the solution, have instead become "part of the problem."[5] This development could be considered a somehow natural consequence of the success of human rights language and its mainstreaming. As human rights became a vernacular buttressing the everyday workings of national and global bureaucracies, courts, and institutions, it was bound to lose some of its rebellious edge and connection to transformative politics. This evolution becomes especially problematic when coupled with historical accounts providing *carte blanche* legitimacy to human rights as such, blinding us to dark sides and shortcomings. In recent years, the historiography on rights language in international law has been enriched by texts providing more complex and varied perspectives.[6] Yet, traditional narratives celebrating the rise of human rights as an expression of the relentless progress of mankind still appear and have purchase,[7] reinforcing simplistic approaches that offer "humanization" as a panacea to any shortcoming international law might have, as if the legal content of humanity was not, as well, a matter of political contention.[8] Fittingly with Scott's

[5] See David Kennedy, "The International Human Rights Movement: Part of the Problem?," *European Human Rights Law Review*, 3, 2001, pp. 245–67 and David Kennedy, "The International Human Rights Regime: Still Part of the Problem?,' in Rob Dickinson, Elena Katselli, Colin Murray, and Ole W. Pedersen (eds.), *Examining Critical Perspectives on Human Rights*, Cambridge: Cambridge University Press, 2013, pp. 19–34.

[6] For instance, Samuel Moyn in his *The Last Utopia* has directed our attention to the novelty of the human rights culture as we know it, placing its explosion in the 1920s. Marco Duranti has instead described the establishment of the European postwar human rights system as a conservative project (*The Conservative Human Rights Revolution*). Taina Tuori has looked further back, providing an account of rights language in the work of the League of Nations' Permanent Mandates Commission (*From League of Nations Mandates to Decolonization: A History of the Language of Rights in International Law*, Helsinki: Unigrafia, 2016). These diverse genealogies come together to provide a better sense of the complex and varied nature of rights projects in international law in the last century. This book aims to contribute to that enterprise.

[7] As a relatively recent example see Lynn Hunt, *Inventing Human Rights*, New York: W. W. Norton & Company, 2007. For an insightful general criticism of the "textbook narrative of human rights" see Miia Halme-Tuomisaari and Pamela Slotte, "Introduction," in Miia Halme-Tuomisaari and Pamela Slotte (eds.), *Revisiting the Origins of Human Rights*, Cambridge: Cambridge University Press, 2015, pp. 1–36.

[8] See for instance, Antônio A. Cançado Trindade, *International Law for Humankind: Towards a New Jus Gentium*, Leiden: Brill, 2010 and Ruti Teitel, *Humanity's Law*, Oxford: Oxford University Press,

faith-based approach, the intensity of belief associated with human rights practice, embodied in those triumphant historical accounts, has led several commentators to liken human rights to a religion.[9] The risk here is treating human rights as ends in themselves rather than as a means to achieve concrete political and social goals like freeing political prisoners, protecting minorities from discrimination, and, generally, holding governments and institutions to higher standards of behavior and accountability.

Scott's Spanish origin narrative, indeed, can be considered as a model for later celebratory narratives of human rights, emphasizing abstract principles and legislative successes, leaving aside setbacks and controversy. This scheme has also been useful to sustain governance practices that seek legitimacy by adopting human rights justifications instead of or alongside with, for instance, the contested language of economics. Indeed, in analyzing Scott's Spanish origin, realizing what he left out might be as important as being aware of what was included. Scott presented the relevance of Salamancan theology in connection to civil and political rights, the construction of global institutions, and a moral approach to international relations. What he did not address was their rich and articulated economic thought. This move had long-lasting consequences. Since then, international lawyers have searched for the thought of Salamanca scholars relevant to our discipline almost exclusively in the limited part of their production Scott had commented on or decided to include in the Classics of International Law series.[10]

This is not to say that Scott was not interested in global economics and international trade, quite the contrary. He assumed, in his reconstruction of Vitoria's capacious *ius communicandi*, that the right to free trade was the fundamental element bringing together mankind on a global scale. Scott emphasized the cooperative side of free trade but left out a key implication about its imposition, already drawn implicitly by Vitoria and explicitly by Suárez. Conceiving commercial relations as crucial to the unity of mankind made the removal of any opposition to trade morally justified, if not required, even through war, if necessary.[11] In the late eighteenth century and the early decades of the twentieth, Latin Americans knew

2011. In his review of Teitel's book, Martti Koskenniemi elaborates on the open-endedness of humanity discourse in international law (*Ethics & International Affairs*, 26, 2012, pp. 395–8).

[9] For a review of texts on international law adopting this *topos* and the opposition it sparked see Immi Tallgren, "The Faith in Humanity and International Criminal Law," in Martti Koskenniemi, Mónica Garcia-Salmones Rovira and Paolo Amorosa (eds.), *International Law and Religion: Historical and Contemporary Perspectives*, Oxford: Oxford University Press, 2017, p. 335 fn. 6.

[10] It was only recently that an international lawyer, Martti Koskenniemi, put forward the argument that Salamancan economic thought and "vocabulary of private rights[,] enabl[ing] the universal ordering of international relations by recourse to private property, contract, and exchange," was the "real Spanish contribution" of the school to modern political thinking (see Martti Koskenniemi, "Empire and International Law: The Real Spanish Contribution," *University of Toronto Law Journal*, 61, 2011, p. 1).

[11] I have drawn the implications of Scott's commentary of trade and just war in Vitoria and Suárez in Chapter 4 section 3.

all too well that assertions of the right of free trade made in the United States could see them on the receiving end of military imposition.[12]

In Scott's Spanish origin narrative, free trade was a vague notion equated to just and peaceful relations. But, looking elsewhere, it is easy to realize that for him and his Carnegie Endowment for International Peace (CEIP) colleagues, the expression "free trade" signaled a detailed system of economic prescriptions and recipes, inscribed in their larger liberal political ideology. In 1937, when many were already predicting the coming of a new war in Europe, the trustees of the Endowment released to the public their "program for peace." The resolution called for "[t]he conclusion of multilateral agreements, open to 'all comers', stimulating international trade" with "[t]he deliberate inclusion . . . of the most-favored-nation clause." It further contained a list of measures, including prescriptions of monetary policy, tending toward "the reduction of excessive barriers to trade." The resulting "increase of trade" would determine "the appeasement of nations."[13]

The basic thinking behind the CEIP program of peace is aligned with the fundamental principles sustaining the current international trade law regime. The success of the CEIP views on trade and the international order has been complemented by a growing trend of translating economic formulas into rights language, following Scott's blueprint whereby *ius communicandi* stood for twentieth-century free trade ideology, while rule of law and freedom of contract stood for the illegality of any measure of labor protection. Indeed, in recent years, international financial institutions such as the World Bank and the International Monetary Fund have resorted more and more often to presenting their conditional measures for aid and lending as best practices of governance responsive to human rights standards and the rule of law.[14]

The issue here is not, in itself, the evolution of the discourse of global politics and the rationalization of governance practices. It is the circumstance that human rights language has come to stand for and offer legitimacy to a specific set of economic practices and their encompassing ideology, often imposed on national

[12] For an account of US economic interventions abroad up to the Spanish-American War see Howard Zinn, *A People's History of the United States*, London: Longman, 1980, pp. 290–306. For a general historical overview of US imperialism, mentioning the several interventions in Latin America in the period examined see Frank Ninkovich, *The United States and Imperialism*, Malden: Blackwell Publishers, 2001. Alongside interventions, the United States exercised pressure through legal means giving rise to a system of "international arbitration [that] served as an instrument of muscular diplomacy" geared toward "trade liberalization and investment protection" (Alan Nissel, "The Duality of State Responsibility," *Columbia Human Rights Law Review*, 44, 2012, pp. 797–8).

[13] "CEIP Program for Peace," Press Release, January 2, 1937, Box 257, CEIP Papers.

[14] On the larger ideological implications of this trend see, for instance, Costas Douzinas, "Seven Theses on Human Rights: (3) Neoliberal Capitalism & Voluntary Imperialism," *Critical Legal Thinking*, May 23, 2013, available online at http://criticallegalthinking.com/2013/05/23/seven-theses-on-human-rights-3-neoliberal-capitalism-voluntary-imperialism/ (last accessed July 10, 2019). For an historically oriented evaluation of the connected rise of human rights and neoliberalism see Samuel Moyn, "A Powerless Companion: Human Rights in the Age of Neoliberalism," *Law and Contemporary Problems*, 77, 2014, pp. 147–69.

communities without a real investigation of the potential local consequences.[15] Too often concepts like rule of law, democracy, equality, and human rights act as thought-stoppers rather than rallying points for discussing inclusive, pluralistic, and transformative politics. Scott's Spanish origin has contributed to this phenomenon by turning those concepts into unquestionable moral truths inscribed into international law centuries ago by the founding figure of Francisco de Vitoria. This powerful pedigree of messianic progress blessed, by simple association, Scott's choices and enterprises and rendered moot, in his eyes, the addressing of conflicting conceptions and political opposition.

With this study I have aimed to make those enterprises and their social stakes evident, reclaiming the key concepts Scott took possession of through Vitoria, and offering a contribution to the historical understanding of their uses in the practice of international law. Indeed, historical narratives could have the effect of obfuscating the politics of international law, as I have argued about Scott's Spanish origin, but they could also spark and enlighten productive conversations, providing further knowledge and perspectives. The key to maintaining the critical and responsible approach to international legal history I have called for is not to fall into rigid delimitations between disciplinary boundaries. In turn, this stance would lead to a retreat into conceptual purity and disregard of a close analysis of practice. Anne Orford has made a forceful formulation of this point.

> Once the history and philosophy of a discipline are abstracted and treated as distinct from its practice, a politically engaged vision of that practice is much harder to realise. In the case of international law, historians seek to import the conviction that historical methods provide the only form of interpretive practice that can produce an adequate knowledge of the past, not only for historians but also for international lawyers. The effect of the argument that historical method should replace legal method as the means of engaging with the past of international law means that critical practitioners lose the capacity to intervene in development of the law. As a result, international lawyers who have been trained in the techniques and languages of international law are asked to give up their responsibility for creating a less repressive future for the field.[16]

However, together with Orford, I argue that it is possible to overcome these limitations and build histories of international law seeking understanding of the past

[15] For instance, Anne Orford has built a convincing case, showing how measures of institutional reform and economic liberalization imposed by international institutions substantially contributed to the instability leading to the hostilities and humanitarian crises in the former Yugoslavia and Rwanda in the 1990s (see Anne Orford, *Reading Humanitarian Intervention*, Cambridge: Cambridge University Press, 2003, pp. 82–125).

[16] Anne Orford, "International Law and the Limits of History," in Wouter Werner, Marieke de Hoon, and Alexis Galán (eds.), *The Law of International Lawyers: Reading Martti Koskenniemi*, Cambridge: Cambridge University Press, 2017, pp. 311–12.

and a politically engaged view of the future. This requires an integrative approach, encompassing a "critical engagement with the substance of international legal doctrines, the history and sociology of the profession, and the political situation of the international lawyer."[17] This captures the ambition with which I have described Scott's Spanish origin, with the hope that this work has offered a contribution to our understanding of what it means to be an international lawyer.

[17] Ibid., p. 312. Orford uses this formula to describe the approach behind Martti Koskenniemi's *The Gentle Civilizer*.

# Bibliography

## Archival Collection

Carnegie Endowment for International Peace Papers, Butler Library, Rare Books and Manuscript Collection, Columbia University, New York, N.Y.
James Brown Scott Papers, Lauinger Library, Booth Family Center for Special Collections, Georgetown University, Washington, D.C.

## Serials

Advocate of Peace
American Journal of International Law
Annuaire de l'Institut de Droit International
Carnegie Endowment for International Peace Year Book
Civiltá Cattolica
Foreign Relations of the United States
International Conciliation
Proceedings of the American Society of International Law
Recueil des cours de l'Académie de droit international de La Haye

## Newspapers

*ABC* (Madrid, Spain)
*El Adelanto* (Salamanca, Spain)
*La Libertad* (Madrid, Spain)
*La Prensa* (New York)
*New York Times*
*New York Tribune*
*Sacramento Union*
*Washington Evening Star*
*Washington Post*

*Rewriting the History of the Law of Nations: How James Brown Scott Made Francisco de Vitoria the Founder of International Law*. Paolo Amorosa, Oxford University Press (2019). 
DOI: 10.1093/oso/9780198849377.001.0001

Adams, Brooks. *The Gold Standard: An Historical Study*, Boston: Alfred Mudge & Son, 1894.
——. *The Law of Civilization and Decay. An Essay on History*, New York: MacMillan & Company, 1895.
——. "The Spanish War and the Equilibrium of the World," in *The Forum*, August (1898): 641–51.
——. *America's Economic Supremacy*, New York: The MacMillan Company, 1900.
——. *The Emancipation of Massachusetts: The Dream and the Reality*, Boston and New York: Houghton Mifflin Company, 1919 [1887].
Adams, Charles Francis (ed.), *The Works of John Adams*, vol. 4, Boston: Charles C. Little and James Brown, 1851.
Álvarez, Alejandro. *The Monroe Doctrine: Its Importance in the International Life of the States of the New World*, New York: Oxford University Press, 1924.
Amorosa, Paolo. "James Brown Scott's International Adjudication between Tradition and Progress in the United States," *Journal of the History of International Law* 17 (2015): 15–46.
——. "Messianic Visions of the United States: International Law, Religion, and the Cuban Intervention, 1898–1917', in Martti Koskenniemi, Mónica García-Salmones Rovira, and Paolo Amorosa (eds.), *International Law and Religion: Historical and Contemporary Perspectives*, Oxford: Oxford University Press, 2017, 433–53.
Anghie, Antony. *Imperialism, Sovereignty and the Making of International Law*, Cambridge: Cambridge University Press, 2004.
——. "The Evolution of International Law: Colonial and Postcolonial Realities," *Third World Quarterly* 27 (2006): 739–53.
Armitage, David. "The International Turn in Intellectual History," in Darrin M. McMahon and Samuel Moyn (eds.), *Rethinking Modern European Intellectual History*, Oxford: Oxford University Press, 2014, 232–52.
Association internationale Vitoria-Suarez, *Vitoria et Suarez: Contributions des théologiens au droit international moderne. Chox de textes latins avec traduction française. Suivi de trois mémoires par l'abbé Robert Jacquin, Louis Le Fur, J.-T. Delos. Préface par James Brown Scott. Introduction par Yves de La Briére*, Paris: A. Pedone, 1939.
Austin, John. *The Province of Jurisprudence Determined*, London: John Murray, 1832.
Aveling, Francis. "The Neo-Scholastic Movement: A Retrospect and a Prospect," *American Catholic Quarterly Review* XXXI (1906): 19–33.
Ayala, Balthazar. *De iure et officiis bellicis et disciplina military libri III*, edited by John Westlake, Washington, D.C.: Carnegie Institution, 1912 [1582].
Barcia Trelles, Camilo. "Francisco de Vitoria et l'École moderne du Droit international," *Recueil des cours de l'Académie de droit international de La Haye* 17 (1927): 133–337.
——. *Doctrina de Monroe y cooperación internacional*, Madrid: Mundo Latino, 1931.
Becker Lorca, Arnulf. "Alejandro Álvarez Situated: Subaltern Modernities and Modernisms that Subvert," *Leiden Journal of International Law* 19 (2006): 879–930.
——. *Mestizo International Law. A Global Intellectual History 1842–1933*, Cambridge: Cambridge University Press, 2014.
Becker, Susan D. *The Origins of the Equal Rights Amendment: American Feminism between the Wars*, Westport: Greenwood Press, 1981.
Belda Plans, Juan. *La Escuela de Salamanca y la renovación de la teología en el siglo XVI*, Madrid: Biblioteca de Autores Cristianos, 2000.
Bellamy, Edward. *Looking Backward: 2000–1887*, Boston: Ticknor and Company, 1888.
Bercovich, Nitza. *From Motherhood to Citizenship: Women's Rights and International Citizenship*, Baltimore: Johns Hopkins University Press, 1999.

Bernstorff, Jochen von. *The Public International Law Theory of Hans Kelsen. Believing in Universal Law*, Cambridge: Cambridge University Press, 2010.

——. "Georg Jellinek and the Origins of Liberal Constitutionalism in International Law," *Goettingen Journal of International Law* 4 (2012): 659–75.

——. "International Law and Global Justice: On Recent Inquiries into the Dark Side of Economic Globalization," *European Journal of International Law* 26 (2015): 279–93.

Bevans, Charles I. (ed.), *Treaties and Other International Agreements of the United States of America 1776–1949*, vol. 6 Canada-Czechoslovakia, Washington, D.C.: Department of State Publications, 1971.

Blackstone, William. *Commentaries on the Laws of England*, vol. I, 1st edn, Oxford: Clarendon Press, 1765.

Bloodworth, Jeffrey. "For Love or for Money?: William McKinley and the Spanish-American War," *White House Studies* 9 (2009): 135–57.

Boeckel, Florence Brewer. "Women in International Affairs," *Annals of the American Academy of Political and Social Science* 143 (1929): 230–48.

Borchard, Edwin. "The Resurrection of International Law," *Proceedings of the American Society of International Law* 17 (1923): 61–70.

——. "The Citizenship of Native-Born American Women Who Married Foreigners before March, 2, 1907, and Acquired a Foreign Domicile," *American Journal of International Law* 29 (1935): 396–422.

Bredbenner, Candice Lewis. *A Nationality of Her Own: Women, Marriage and the Law of Citizenship*, Berkeley: University of California Press, 1998.

Brett, Annabel. "Francisco de Vitoria and Francisco Suárez," in Anne Peters and Bardo Fassbender (eds.), *Oxford Handbook of the History of International Law*, Oxford: Oxford University Press, 2012, 1086–92.

Butler Nicholas Murray, *Across the Busy Years*, vol. II, New York: Scribner's Sons, 1940.

Calo, Zachary. "'The Indispensable Basis of Democracy': American Catholicism, the Church-State Debate, and the Soul of American Liberalism, 1920–1929," *Virginia Law Review* 91 (2005): 1037–73.

Campbell, John P. "Taft, Roosevelt, and the Arbitration Treaties of 1911," *The Journal of American History* 53 (1966): 279–98.

Cançado Trindade, Antônio A. *International Law for Humankind: Towards a New Jus Gentium*, Leiden: Brill, 2010.

Carnegie, Andrew. "Wealth," *North American Review* 148 (1889): 653–664.

Carrington, Paul D. "Hail! Langdell!," *Law and Social Inquiry* 20 (1995): 691–760.

Carty, Anthony. "Alfred Verdross and Othmarr Spann: German Romantic Nationalism, National Socialism and International Law," *European Journal of International Law* 6 (1995): 78–97.

Cassidy, Lewis Cochran. "James Brown Scott: A Citizen of the World," *New York University Law Quarterly Review* 9 (1931–32): 49–60.

Castagna, Luca. *A Bridge across the Ocean: The United States and the Holy See between the Two World Wars*, Washington, D.C.: The Catholic University of America Press, 2014.

Cavallar, Georg. "Vitoria, Grotius, Pufendorf, Wolff and Vattel: Accomplices of European Colonialism and Exploitation or True Cosmopolitans?," *Journal of the History of International Law* 10 (2008): 181–209.

Coates, Benjamin. *Transatlantic Advocates: American International Law and U.S. Foreign Relations, 1898–1919*, unpublished PhD dissertation, Columbia University, 2010.

——. "'Upon the Neutral Rests the Trusteeship of International Law': Legal Advisers and American Unneutrality," in Johan Den Hertog and Samuël Kruizinga (eds.), *Caught in the*

*Middle: Neutrals, Neutrality and the First World War*, Amsterdam: Amsterdam University Press, 2011, 35–52.

——. *Legalist Empire. International Law and American Foreign Relations in the Early Twentieth Century*, Oxford: Oxford University Press, 2016.

Cobbett, Pitt (ed.), *Leading Cases and Opinions on International Law*, London: Stevens and Haynes, 1885.

Cohen, Nancy. *The Reconstruction of American Liberalism, 1865–1914*, Chapel Hill: The University of North Carolina Press, 2002.

Corvin, Edward S. "Book Review. The United States of America: A Study in International Organization," *University of Pennsylvania Law Review* 69 (1921): 393–4.

Cott, Nancy F. "Feminist Politics in the 1920s: The National Woman's Party," *The Journal of American History* 71 (1984): 43–68.

——. *The Grounding of Modern Feminism*, New Haven: Yale University Press, 1987.

——. "Marriage and Women's Citizenship in the United States, 1830–1934," *American Historical Review* 103 (1998):1440–74.

Dennis, William C. "International Organization: Executive and Administrative. Some Supposed Objections to a League for Peace," *Proceedings of the American Society of International Law* 11 (1917): 96.

de Visscher, Charles. "Human Rights in Roman Law Countries," *The Annals of the American Academy of Political and Social Science* 243 (1946): 53–9.

Dodge, David Low and others, *Memorial of Mr. David L. Dodge*, Boston: S. K. Whipple & Co., 1854.

Douzinas, Costas. "Seven Theses on Human Rights: (3) Neoliberal Capitalism & Voluntary Imperialism," *Critical Legal Thinking*, May 23, 2013. Available at http://criticallegalthinking.com/2013/05/23/seven-theses-on-human-rights-3-neoliberal-capitalism-voluntary-imperialism/.

Dubin, Martin David. "The Carnegie Endowment for International Peace and the Advocacy for a League of Nations, 1914–1918," *Proceedings of the American Philosophical Society* 123 (1979): 344–68.

DuBois, Ellen Carol. "Storming The Hague: The 1930 Campaign for Independent Nationality for Women Regardless of Marital Status," *Tijdschrift voor Genderstudies* 4 (2003): 18–29.

——. "A Momentary Transnational Sisterhood: Cuban/U.S. Collaboration in the Formation of the Inter-American Commission of Women," in Alessandra Lorini (ed.), *An Intimate and Contested Relation: The United States and Cuba in the Late Nineteenth and Early Twentieth Centuries*, Firenze: Firenze University Press, 2005, 86–7.

Dudden, Faye E. *Fighting Chance: The Struggle over Woman Suffrage and Black Suffrage in Reconstruction America*, Oxford: Oxford University Press, 2011.

Dumenil, Lynn. "The Tribal Twenties: 'Assimilated' Catholics' Response to Anti-Catholicisim in the 1920s," *Journal of American Ethnic History* 11 (1991): 21–49.

Duranti, Marco. *The Conservative Human Rights Revolution: European Identity, Transnational Politics, and the Origin of the European Convention*, Oxford: Oxford University Press, 2017.

Eastman, Crystal. "Alice Paul's Convention," *The Liberator* 37 (April 1921): 9–10.

Eppstein, John. *The Catholic Tradition of the Law of Nations*, Washington, D.C.: published for the Carnegie Endowment of International Peace by the Catholic Association for International Peace, 1935.

Evans, Alona E. and Carol Per Lee Plumb. "Women and the American Society of International Law," *American Journal of International Law* 68 (1974): 290–3.

Fenwick, Charles. "International Organization—Judicial," *Proceedings of the American Society of International Law* 11 (1917): 64–75.
——. "An Outline of the Problems Presented in the Further Development of International Law," *Proceedings of the American Society of International Law* 17 (1923): 47–52.
——. "International Law: The Old and the New," *American Journal of International Law* 60 (1966): 475–83.
Fernández Sebastián, Javiér and Juan Francisco Fuentes. "Conceptual History, Memory, and Identity: An Interview with Reinhart Koselleck," *Contributions to the History of Concepts* 2 (2006): 99–127.
Finch, George A. "James Brown Scott, 1866–1943," *American Journal of International Law* 38 (1944): 183–217.
—— . "The Need to Restrain the Treaty-Making Power of the United States within Constitutional Limits," *American Journal of International Law* 57 (1954): 57–82.
—— and William E. Butler (eds.), *Adventures in Internationalism: A Biography of James Brown Scott*, Clark: Lawbook Exchange, 2012.
Fitzmaurice, Andrew. "The Problem of Eurocentrism in the Thought of Francisco de Vitoria," in José María Beneyto and Justo Corti Varela (eds.), *At the Origins of Modernity. Francisco de Vitoria and the Discovery of International Law*, Cham: Springer International Publishing, 2017, 77–93.
——. "Context in the History of International Law," *Journal of the History of International Law* 20 (2018): 5–30.
Flexner, Eleanor. *Century of Struggle: The Woman's Rights Movement in the United States*, revised edn, Cambridge: Harvard University Press, 1975 [1959].
Flick, Lawrence F. "What the American has got out of the Melting Pot from the Catholic," *The Catholic Historical Review* 11 (1925): 407–30.
Flournoy, Richard W. Jr., "The New Married Women Citizenship Law," *Yale Law Journal* 33 (1923): 159–70.
——. and Manley O. Hudson (eds.). *A Collection of Nationality Laws of Various Countries as Contained in Constitutions, Statutes and Treaties*, Oxford: Oxford University Press, 1929.
Foner, Eric. *The Story of American Freedom*, New York: W. W. Norton, 1998.
Frazer, Gregg L. *The Religious Beliefs of America's Founders*, Lawrence: Kansas University Press, 2012.
Gallagher, Robert S. "'I was Arrested, Of Course . . . ' An Interview with the Famed Suffragette, Alice Paul," *American Heritage* 25 (1974): 17–24.
Gamarra Chopo, Yolanda. "La ilusión española de la Sociedad de Naciones," in Yolanda Gamarra Chopo and Carlos Fernández Liesa (eds.), *Los orígenes del Derecho internacional contempóraneo: Estudios conmemorativos del Centenario de la Primera Guerra Mundial*, Zaragoza: Institución Fernando el Católico, 2015, 289–96.
Gearty Conor and Costas Douzinas. "Introduction," in Conor Gearty and Costas Douzinas (eds.), *The Meanings of Rights: The Philosophy and Social Theory of Human Rights* Cambridge: Cambridge University Press, 2014, 1–12.
Geidel, Peter. "The National Woman's Party and the Origins of the Equal Rights Amendment," *The Historian* 42 (1980): 557–82.
Gladstone, William E. *Gleanings of Past Years, 1843–78*, vol. 1, London: John Murray, 1879.
Gleason, Philip. "Neo-Scholasticism as Intellectual Ideology," *U.S. Catholic Historian* 7 (1988): 401–11.
Gorak, Jan. *The Making of the Modern Canon: Genesis and Crisis of a Literary Idea*, London: Athlone, 1991.

Gordon, Robert W. "Historicism in Legal Scholarship," *Yale Law Journal* 90 (1980–81): 1017–56.

——. "Critical Legal Histories," *Stanford Law Review* 36 (1984): 57–125.

——. "The Past as Authority or as Social Critic: Stabilizing and Destabilizing Functions of History in Legal Argument," in Terrence J. McDonald (ed.), *The Historic Turn in the Human Sciences, Ann Arbor: Michigan University Press*, 1996, 339–67.

Graham, Sara Hunter. *Woman Suffrage and the New Democracy*, New Haven: Yale University Press, 1996.

Green, Steven K. "The Blaine Amendment Reconsidered," *American Journal of Legal History* 36 (1992): 38–69.

Grey, Thomas C. "Langdell's Orthodoxy," *University of Pittsburgh Law Review* 45 (1983–84): 1–53.

Gross, Linda P. and Theresa R. Snyder, *Philadelphia's 1876 Centennial Exhibition*, Charleston: Arcadia Publishing, 2005.

Grotius, Hugo. *De jure belli ac pacis libri tres*, vol. I, Washington, D.C.: Carnegie Institution, 1913.

——. *De jure belli ac pacis libri tres*, vol. II, Oxford: Oxford University Press, 1925.

Haggenmacher, Peter. *Grotius et la Doctrine de la Guerre Juste*, Geneva: Graduate Institute Publications, 1983.

Halme-Tuomisaari, Miia and Pamela Slotte, "Introduction," in Miia Halme-Tuomisaari and Pamela Slotte (eds.), *Revisiting the Origins of Human Rights*, Cambridge: Cambridge University Press, 2015, 1–36.

Harrington, James. *The Commonwealth of Oceana*, London: John Streater, 1656.

Hepp, John. "James Brown Scott and the Rise of Public International Law," *Journal of the Gilded Age and Progressive Era* 7 (2008): 151–79.

Hernández, José M. *Cuba and the United States: Intervention and Militarism, 1868–1933*, Austin: University of Texas Press, 1993.

Hill, Cyril D. "Citizenship of Married Women," *American Journal of International Law* 18 (1924): 720–36.

Hill, Diane Elizabeth. *International Law for Women's Rights*, unpublished PhD dissertation, University of California at Berkeley, 1999.

Hindman, E. James, "The General Arbitration Treaties of William Howard Taft," *The Historian* 36 (1973): 52–65.

Hudson, Manley O. "International Legislation," *Proceedings of the American Society of International Law* 17 (1923): 52–5.

——. *Cases and Other Materials on International Law*, St. Paul: West Publishing Company, 1929.

——. "The Hague Convention of 1930 and the Nationality of Women," *American Journal of International Law* 27 (1933): 117–22.

Humphreys, Robert Arthur. "Presidential Address: Anglo-American Rivalries and the Venezuela Crisis of 1895," *Transactions of the Royal Historical Society* 17 (1967): 142–6.

Hunt, Gaillard. "The Virginia Declaration of Rights and Cardinal Bellarmine," *The Catholic Historical Review* 3 (1917): 276–89.

——. and James Brown Scott (eds.), *The Debates in the Federal Convention of 1787 which Framed the Constitution of the United States of America reported by James Madison*, Oxford: Oxford University Press, 1920.

Hunt, Lynn. *Inventing Human Rights*, New York: W. W. Norton & Company, 2007.

Hunter, Ian. "The Figure of Man and the Territorialisation of Justice in 'Enlightenment' Natural Law: Pufendorf and Vattel," *Intellectual History Review* 23 (2013): 289–307.

Ireland, John. "The Catholic Church and Civil Society," in John Irealnd, *The Church and Modern Society. Lectures and Addresses*, New York: D.H. McBride & Co., 1903, 25–66.

——. "The Dogmatic Authority of the Papacy: The Encyclical on Modernism', *The North American Review* 187 (1908): 486–97.
Irving, Helen. *Citizenship, Alienage and the Modern Constitutional State: A Gendered History*, Cambridge: Cambridge University Press, 2016.
Janis, Mark. *The American Tradition of International Law: Great Expectations, 1789–1914*, Oxford: Oxford University Press, 2004.
Jarmer, Marla J. "Woodrow Wilson: Women's Suffrage", in *The Bully Pulpit, Presidential Speeches, and the Shaping of Public Policy*, edited by Jeffrey S. Ashley and Marla J. Jarmer, Lanham: Lexington Books, 2016, 27–40.
Jessup, Philip C. *Elihu Root*, New York: Dodd, Mead & Company, 1938.
——. "International Law in 1953 A.D.," *Proceedings of the American Society of International Law* 47 (1953): 8–15.
Kahn, Paul W. "Reason and Will in the Origins of American Constitutionalism," *Yale Law Journal* 98 (1989): 449–517.
——. *Political Theology: Four New Chapters on the Concept of Sovereignty*, New York: Columbia University Press, 2011.
——. "Law of Nations at the Origins," in Martti Koskenniemi, Mónica García Salmones-Rovira, and Paolo Amorosa (eds.), *International Law and Religion: Historical and Contemporary Perspectives*, Oxford: Oxford University Press, 2017, 414–32.
Kenny, James T. "Manley O. Hudson and the Harvard Research in International Law 1927–1940," *The International Lawyer* 11 (1977): 319–29.
Kennedy, David. "The Move to Institutions," *Cardozo Law Review* 8 (1987): 841–988.
——. *International Legal Structures*, Baden-Baden: Nomos, 1987.
——. "The International Human Rights Movement: Part of the Problem?," *European Human Rights Law Review* 3 (2001): 245–67.
——. "The International Human Rights Regime: Still Part of the Problem?," in Rob Dickinson, Elena Katselli, Colin Murray, and Ole W. Pedersen (eds.), *Examining Critical Perspectives on Human Rights*, Cambridge: Cambridge University Press, 2013, 19–34.
Kent, James. *Commentaries on American Law*, vol . I, New York: O. Halsted, 1826.
Kerber, Linda K. *No Constitutional Right to Be Ladies*, New York: Hill and Wang, 1998.
Kimball, Bruce A. "The Langdell Problem: Historicizing the Century of Historiography, 1906–2000s', *Law and History Review* 22:2 (2004): 335–7.
——. *The Inception of Modern Professional Education. C.C. Langdell, 1826–1906*, Chapel Hill: The University of North Carolina Press, 2009.
Kirgis, Frederic L. *The American Society of International Law's First Century 1906–2006*, Leiden/Boston: Martinus Nijhoff Publishers, 2006.
Knop, Karen and Christine Chinkin, "Remembering Chrystal Macmillan: Women's Equality and Nationality in International Law," *Michigan Journal of International Law* 22 (2001): 523–85.
Knop, Karen. *Diversity and Self-Determination in International Law*, Cambridge: Cambridge University Press, 2004.
Koselleck, Reinhart. "The Temporalization of Concepts," *Finnish Yearbook of Political Thought* 1 (1997): 16–24.
Koskenniemi, Martti. "Between Commitment and Cynicism: Outline for a Theory of International Law as Practice," in *Collection of Essays by Legal Advisers of States, Legal Advisers of International Organizations and Practitioners in the Field of International Law*, New York: United Nations, 1999, 495–523.
——. *The Gentle Civilizer of Nations*, Cambridge: Cambridge University Press, 2001.
——. *From Apology to Utopia: The Structure of the International Legal Argument*, Cambridge: Cambridge University Press, 2005 [1989].

——. "The Ideology of International Adjudication and the 1907 Hague Conference," in Yves Daudet (ed.), *Topicality of the 1907 Hague Conference, the Second Peace Conference/Actualité de la Conférence de La Haye de 1907, Deuxième Conférence de la paix*, Leiden/Boston: Brill, 2008, 127–52.

——. "International Law and *raison d'état*: Rethinking the Prehistory of International Law," in *The Roman Foundations of the Law of Nations: Alberico Gentili and the Justice of Empire*, edited by Benedict Kingsbury and Benjamin Straumann, Oxford: Oxford University Press, 2010, 297–339.

——. "Empire and International Law: The Real Spanish Contribution," *University of Toronto Law Journal* 61 (2011): 1–36.

——. "Histories of International Law. Dealing with Eurocentrism," *Rechtsgeschichte* 19 (2011): 152–77.

——. "Book Review—Humanity's Law by Ruti G. Teitel," *Ethics & International Affairs* 26 (2012): 395–8.

——. "Vitoria and Us," *Rechtsgeschichte* 22 (2014): 119–38.

Kosters, Jean. *Les Fondements du Droit des Gens*, in *Bibliotheca Visseriana*, vol. VI, Leiden: Brill, 1925.

Kuehl, Warren F. and Lynne K. Dunn, *Keeping the Covenant: American Internationalists and the League of Nations, 1920–1939*, Kent: The Kent State University Press, 1997.

Landauer, Carl. "The Ambivalences of Power: Launching the American Journal of International Law in an Era of Empire and Globalization," *Leiden Journal of International Law* 20 (2007): 325–58.

Langdell, Christopher Columbus (ed.), *A Selection of Cases on the Law of Contracts with References and Citations . . . Prepared for Use as a Text-Book in Harvard Law School*, Boston: Little, Brown, 1870.

——. (ed.), *A Selection of Cases on the Law of Contracts with References and Citations . . . Prepared for Use as a Text-Book in Harvard Law School*, Boston: Little, Brown, 1871.

Lansing, Robert. *The Peace Negotiations, A Personal Narrative*, Boston: Houghton Mifflin Company, 1921.

Lee, Muna. "Equal Rights Approved by American Institute of International Law," *Equal Rights*, November 28, 1931.

——. "The Inter-American Commission of Women: A New International Venture," originally appeared in Pan-American Magazine, October 1929, reprinted in Jonathan Cohen edited, *A Pan-American Life: Selected Poetry and Prose of Muna Lee*, Madison: The University of Wisconsin Press, 2004.

Legnano, Giovanni da. *De bello, de repraesaliis et de duello*, edited by Thomas Erskine Holland, Washington, D.C.: Carnegie Institution, 1917 [1477].

Lehrer, Susan. *Origins of Protective Labor Legislation for Women, 1905–1925*, Albany: State University of New York Press, 1987.

Leopold, Richard W. *Elihu Root and the Conservative Tradition*, Boston: Little, Brown and Company, 1954.

Longfield, Bradley J. *Presbyterians and American Culture: A History*, Louisville: Westminster, John Knox Press, 2013.

Lunardini, Christine. *Alice Paul: Equality for Women*, Boulder: Westview Press, 2013.

Lutz, Bertha. "Nationality of Married Women in the American Republics," *Bulletin of the Pan-American Union* (1926): 392–9.

Macmillan, Chrystal. "Nationality of Married Women: Present Tendencies," *Journal of Comparative Legislation and International Law* 7 (1925): 142–54.

Maine, Henry Sumner. *Ancient Law: Its Connection to the Early History of Society and Its Relation to Modern Ideas*, London: John Murray, 1861.
Marchand, C. Roland. *The American Peace Movement and Social Reform, 1889–1918*, Princeton: Princeton University Press, 2015 [1973].
Marks, Susan. "False Contingency," *Current Legal Problems* 62 (2009): 1–21.
Marotta, Gary. "The Economics of the American Empire," in *The American Economist* 19 (1975): 34–7.
Matarese, Susan M. *American Foreign Policy and the Utopian Imagination*, Amherst: University of Massachusetts Press, 2001.
McCartney, Paul T. *Power and Progress: American National Identity, the War of 1898, and the Rise of American Imperialism*, Baton Rouge: Louisiana State University Press, 2006.
McCullough, Matthew. *The Cross of War: Christian Nationalism and U.S. Expansion in the Spanish-American War*, Madison: The University of Wisconsin Press, 2014.
McKenna, C. H. *Francis de Vitoria, Founder of International Law*, Washington, D.C.: Catholic Association for International Peace, 1930.
McNamara, Patrick. *A Catholic Cold War: Edmund A. Walsh, S. J., and the Politics of American Catholic Anticommunism*, New York: Fordham University Press, 2005.
Miller, Carol. "'Geneva—The Key to Equality': Inter-war Feminists and the League of Nations," *Women's History Review* 3 (1994): 219–45.
Miller, David Hunter. "The Hague Codification Conference," *American Journal of International Law* 24 (1930): 674–93.
Miller, Francesca. *Latin American Women and the Search for Social Justice*, Hanover: University Press of New England, 1991.
Morgenthau, Hans. *Politics Among Nations: The Struggle for Power and Peace*, New York: A. A. Knopf, 1948.
Moyn, Samuel. *The Last Utopia. Human Rights in History*, Cambridge: Harvard University Press, 2012.
——. "A Powerless Companion: Human Rights in the Age of Neoliberalism," *Law and Contemporary Problems* 77 (2014): 147–69.
——. *Christian Human Rights*, Philadelphia: Pennsylvania University Press, 2015.
——. "Legal Theory Among the Ruins," ssrn.com/abstract=2817067 (2016), later published in Justin Desautels-Stein and Christopher Tomlins (eds.), *In Search of Contemporary Legal Thought*, Cambridge: Cambridge University Press, 2017.
——. *Not Enough: Human Rights in an Unequal World*, Cambridge: Belknap Press, 2018.
Neuman Gerald L. and Tomiko Brown-Nagin (ed.), *Reconsidering the Insular Cases:*
*The Past and Future of the American Empire*, Cambridge: Harvard University Press, 2015.
Ninkovich, Frank. *The United States and Imperialism*, Malden: Blackwell Publishers, 2001.
Nissel, Alan. "The Duality of State Responsibility," *Columbia Human Rights Law Review* 44 (2012): 793–858.
Nurnberger, Ralph Dingman. *James Brown Scott: Peace Through Justice*, unpublished PhD dissertation, Georgetown University, 1975.
Nuzzo, Luigi. *Il linguaggio giuridico della conquista. Strategie di controllo nelle Indie spagnole*, Napoli: Jovene, 2004.
——. *Origini di una Scienza: Diritto Internazionale e Colonialismo nel XIX Secolo*, Frankfurt am Main: Klostermann, 2012.
Nys, Ernest. *Les origines du droit international*, Brussels: Alfred Castaigne, 1894.
Orford, Anne. *Reading Humanitarian Intervention: Human Rights and the Use of Force in International Law*, Cambridge: Cambridge University Press, 2003.
——. "In Praise of Description," *Leiden Journal of International Law* 25 (2012): 609–25.

——. "The Past as Law or History? The Relevance of Imperialism for Modern International Law," *NYU Institute for International Law and Justice Working Paper Series* 2 (2012): 1–17.

——. "On International Legal Method," *London Review of International Law* 1 (2013): 166–97.

——. "International Law and the Limits of History," in Wouter Werner, Marieke de Hoon, and Alexis Galán (eds.), *The Law of International Lawyers. Reading Martti Koskenniemi*, Cambridge: Cambridge University Press, 2017, 297–320.

Pagden, Anthony. "The School of Salamanca," in George Klosko (ed.), *Oxford Handbook of the History of Political Philosophy*, Oxford: Oxford University Press, 2011, 247–55.

Papadaki, Marilena. "The Government Intellectuals: Nicolas Politis—An Intellectual Portrait," *European Journal of International Law* 23 (2012): 221–31.

——. "Nicolas Politis, une approche biographique," *Monde(s)* 7 (2015): 45–64.

Parfitt, Rose. "The Spectre of Sources," *European Journal of International Law* 25 (2014): 297–306.

Parsons, William Barclay. *Engineers and Engineering in the Renaissance*, Baltimore: The Williams and Wilkins Company, 1939.

Patterson, David S. "Andrew Carnegie's Quest for World Peace," *Proceedings of the American Philosophical Society* 114 (1970): 371–83.

——. *The Search for Negotiated Peace: Women's Activism and Citizen Diplomacy in World War I*, London: Routledge, 2008.

Pena González, Miguel Anxo. *La Escuela de Salamanca. De la Monarquía hispanica al Orbe católico*, Madrid: Biblioteca de Autores Cristianos, 2009.

Pereña, Luciano. *La idea de justicia en la conquista de América*, Madrid: Mapfre, 1992.

Pérez, Louis A Jr. *Intervention, Politics and Revolution in Cuba, 1913–1921*, Pittsburgh: University of Pittsburgh Press, 1978.

——. "Incurring a Debt of Gratitude: 1898 and the Moral Sources of United States Hegemony in Cuba," *American Historical Review* 104 (1999): 356–98.

——. *Cuba in the American Imagination: Metaphor and the Imperial Ethos*, Chapel Hill: University of North Carolina Press, 2008.

Pethick-Lawrence, Emmeline. "Motherhood and War," *Harper's Weekly*, 59, December 5, 1914, 542, reproduced in John Whiteclay Chambers (ed.), *The Eagle and the Dove: The American Peace Movement and United States Foreign Policy*, Syracuse: Syracuse University Press, 2nd Edition, 1991, 46–9.

Peters, Anne and Bardo Fassbender (eds.). *Oxford Handbook of the History of International Law*, Oxford: Oxford University Press, 2012.

Phillimore, Lord Walter. "Scheme for the Permanent Court of International Justice," *Transactions of the Grotius Society* 6 (1920): 89–98.

Preston, Andrew. *Sword of the Spirit, Shield of Faith. Religion in American War and Diplomacy*, New York: Alfred A. Knopf, 2012.

*Proceedings at the Laying of a Wreath on the Tomb of Hugo Grotius*, The Hague: Martinus Nijhoff, 1899.

*Proceedings of the Third American Peace Congress held in Baltimore, Maryland, May 3 to 6, 1911*, Eugene Noble (ed.), Baltimore: William & Wilkins Company, 1911.

Rasilla, Ignacio de la. "The Fascist Mimesis of Spanish International Law and its Vitorian aftermath, 1939–1953," *Journal of the History of International Law* 14 (2012): 207–36.

Rasulov, Akbar. "Bringing Class back into International Law—A Response to Professor Chimni," ssrn.com/abstract=1675447 (2008), later published in *Finnish Yearbook of International Law* 19 (2008): 243–94.

Reeves, Jesse S. "Editorial Comment—Nationality of Married Women," *American Journal of International Law* 17 (1923): 97–100.

——. "The Life and Work of Hugo Grotius," *Proceedings of the American Society of International Law* 19 (1925): 48–58.
Reibstein, Ernest. *Die Anfänge des neueren Natur- und Völkerrechts. Studien zu den 'Controversiae illustres' des Fernandus Vasquius (1559)*, Bern : Verlag Paul Haupt, 1949.
*Report on the Subject of Citizenship, Expatriation, and Protection Abroad*, Document No. 326, 59th Congress, 2nd Session, Washington: Government Printing Office, 1906.
Reuter, Frank T. *Catholic Influence on American Colonial Policies, 1898–1904*, Austin: University of Texas Press, 1967.
Richberg, Donald R. "The Rise and Fall of the Green Bag," *Green Bag* 18 (1906): 465–7.
Riegelman Lubin, Carol and Anne Winslow. *Social Justice for Women: The International Labor Organization and Women*, Durham: Duke University Press, 1990.
Rietzler, Katharina. "Philanthropy, Peace Research, and Revisionist Politics: Rockefeller and Carnegie Support for the Study of International Relations in Weimar Germany," *GHI Bulletin Supplement* 5 (2008): 61–79.
——."Before the Cultural Cold Wars: American Philanthropy and Cultural Diplomacy in the Inter-war Years," *Historical Research* 223:84 (2011): 148–64.
Ritter Beard, Mary. *Woman as Force in History: A Study in Traditions and Reality*, New York: The MacMillan Company, 1946.
Rupp, Leila. "Constructing Internationalism: The Case of Transnational Women's Organizations, 1888–1945," *American Historical Review* 99 (1994): 1571–1600.
——. "Sexuality and Politics in Early Twentieth Century: The Case of the International Women's Movement," *Feminist Studies* 23 (1997): 557–605.
——. *Worlds of Women: The Making of an International Women's Movement*, Princeton: Princeton University Press, 1997.
Roberts, Anthea. *Is International Law International?*, Oxford: Oxford University Press, 2017.
Root, Elihu. "The Need of Popular Understanding of International Law," *American Journal of International Law* 1 (1907): 1–3.
——. "The Sanction of International Law," in *Addresses on International Subjects by Elihu Root*, collected and edited by Robert Bacon and Scott, James Brown. Cambridge: Harvard University Press, 1916, 25–32.
——. *Addresses on Government and Citizenship*, collected and edited by Robert Bacon and Scott, James Brown. Cambridge: Harvard University Press, 1916.
——. *The Military and Colonial Policy of the United States: Speeches and Reports*, collected and edited by Robert Bacon and Scott, James Brown. Cambridge: Harvard University Press, 1916.
——. *The United States and the War; The Mission to Russia; Political Addresses*, collected and edited by Robert Bacon and James Brown Scott, Cambridge: Harvard University Press, 1918.
——. "Letter of the Honorable Elihu Root to Senator Henry Cabot Lodge Regarding the Covenant of the League of Nations," *American Journal of International Law* 13 (1919): 596–602.
——. "Opening Address," *Proceedings of the American Society of International Law* 15 (1921): 1–13.
Rosenthal, Michael. *Nicholas Miraculous: The Amazing Career of the Redoubtable Dr. Nicholas Murray Butler*, New York: Farrar, Straus and Giroux, 2006.
Ross, Dorothy. *The Origin of American Social Sciences*, New York: Cambridge University Press, 1991.
Rossi, Christopher. *Broken Chain of Being: James Brown Scott and the Origins of Modern International Law*, The Hague: Kluwer Law International, 1998.

Ryan, John A. *A Living Wage: Its Ethical and Economic Aspects*, New York: The MacMillan Company, 1906.

——. *Distributive Justice: The Right and Wrong of our Present Distribution of Wealth*, New York: The MacMillan Company, 1916.

Sapiro, Virginia. "Women, Citizenship and Nationality: Immigration and Naturalization Policies in the United States," *Politics and Society* 13 (1984): 1–26.

Scarfi, Juan Pablo. "Reconfiguraciones del saber jurídico. James Brown Scott reflota la obra de Vitoria desde Estados Unidos en años de entreguerras," in Ricardo D. Salvatore (ed.), *Los Lugares del Saber. Contextos locales y redes transnacionales en la formación del conocimiento moderno*, Rosario: Beatriz Viterbo Editora, 2007, 269–93.

——. *El imperio de la ley James Brown Scott y la construcción de un orden jurídico interamericano*, Buenos Aires: Fondo de Cultura Económica, 2014.

——. *The Hidden History of American International Law: Empire and Legal Networks in the Origins of the Inter-American System, 1890–1942*, Oxford: Oxford University Press, 2017.

Schachter, Oscar. "The Invisible College of International Lawyers," *Northwestern University Law Review* 72 (1977): 217–32.

Scott, James Brown. (ed.). *Cases on International Law Selected from Decisions of English and American Courts with Syllabus and Annotations*, Boston: Boston Book Company, 1902 [re-issued in 1906 by West Publishing].

——. "The Place of International Law in Legal Education," in *Transactions of the Twenty-Sixth Annual Meeting of the American Bar Association, held at Hot Springs, Virginia, August 26, 27 and 28, 1903*, Philadelphia: Dando Printing and Publishing Company, 1903, 583–94.

——. "The Study of the Law," *The American Law School Review* 2 (1906): 1–10.

——. "Editorial Comment—The New Citizenship Law," *American Journal of International Law* 1 (1907): 459–60.

——. "History of the Organization of the American Society of International Law," *Proceedings of the American Society of International Law* 1 (1907): 23–39.

——. "The Legal Nature of International Law," *American Journal of International Law* 1 (1907): 831–66.

——. "The Nature of the Government in Cuba," *American Journal of International Law* 1 (1907): 149–50.

——. "The Pontifical letter of June 11, 1911 on International Peace," *American Journal of International Law* 5 (1911): 707–9.

——. "Introduction," in William Ladd, *An Essay on a Congress of Nations*, New York: Oxford University Press—American Branch, 1916, v–vii.

——. *The American Institute of International Law: its Declaration of the Rights and Duties of Nations*, Washington, D.C.: The American Institute of International Law, 1916.

——. *The Status of the International Court of Justice*, Oxford: Oxford University Press, 1916.

——. "Lester H. Woolsey, the New Solicitor for the Department of State," *American Journal of International Law* 11 (1917): 645–6.

——. "International Organization: Executive and Administrative," *Proceedings of the American Society of International Law* 11 (1917): 101–18.

——. "The Platt Amendment—Recommendations of Habana Concerning International Organization," in American Institute of International Law, *The Recommendations of Habana Concerning International Organization. Address and Commentary by James Brown Scott*, New York: Oxford University Press, 1917.

——. "Introduction," in James Brown Scott (ed.) *Judicial Settlement of Controversies between States of the American Union: Cases Decided in the Supreme Court of the United States*, Oxford: Oxford University Press, 1918, xvii–xxvii.
——. *James Madison's Notes of Debates in the Federal Convention of 1787 and their Relation to a More Perfect Society of Nations*, New York: Oxford University Press, 1918.
——. *Judicial Settlement of Controversies between States of the American Union: An Analysis of Cases Decided in the Supreme Court of the United States*, Oxford: Oxford University Press, 1919.
——. *The United States: A Study in International Organization*, Oxford: Oxford University Press, 1920.
——. "Aim and Purpose of an International Court of Justice," *Annals of the American Academy of Political and Social Science* 96 (1921): 100–7.
——. "Editorial Comment—A Permanent Court of International Justice," *American Journal of International Law*, 15 (1921): 52–5.
——. *Cases on International Law Principally Selected from Decisions of English and American Courts*, St. Paul: West Publishing, 1922.
——. "Cuba and the United States: Exchange of Ambassadors and of Views," *American Journal of International Law* 18 (1924): 119–24.
——. "Supplemental Preface," in Alejandro Álvarez, *The Monroe Doctrine: Its Importance in the International Life of the States of the New World*, New York: Oxford University Press, 1924, unnumbered page between vi and vii.
——. "The Isle of Pines and the Solidarity of Pan-America," *Advocate of Peace through Justice* 87:4 (1925): 228–32.
——. "Grotius' De Jure Belli ac Pacis Libri Tres: The Work of a Lawyer, Statesman and Theologian," *American Journal of International Law* 19 (1925): 461–8.
——. *Cuba, la América Latina, los Estados Unidos*, Habana: El Siglo XX, 1926.
——. "Asociación Francisco de Vitoria," *American Journal of International Law* 22 (1928): 137–8.
——. "The Sixth Pan American Conference," *American Journal of International Law* 22 (1928): 351–62.
——. *El origen español del derecho internacional moderno*, Valladolid: Talleres tipográficos Cuesta, 1928.
——. *The Spanish Origin of International Law: Lectures on Francisco de Vitoria and Francisco Suarez*, Washington, D.C.: Georgetown University Press, 1928.
——. "The Sixth International Conference of American States, Held at Habana, January 16–February 20, 1928: A Survey," *International Conciliation* 12 (1928–29): 277–349.
——. "The Treaty between Italy and the Vatican," *Proceedings of the American Society of International Law* 23 (1929): 13–23.
——. *The Discovery of America and its Influence on International Law; The Four Hundredth Anniversary of Francisco de Vitoria's Disquisition "De Indis" of 1532—Address of Mr. James Brown Scott Delivered at Catholic University, February 25, 1929*, Washington, D.C., 1929.
——. "Inter-American Commission of Women," *American Journal of International Law* 24 (1930): 755–62.
——. "Nationality," *American Journal of International Law* 24 (1930): 560–1.
——. "Unprogressive Codification of Nationality at The Hague," *Women Lawyers' Journal* 18 (1930): 4–43.
——. *El descrubimiento de América y su influjo en el derecho internacional*, Madrid: Tipografía de Archivos, 1930.

——. "International Arbitration: Address of Mr. James Brown Scott before the Sunset Club, Los Angeles, California, 1897," MS 1207, Harvard Law School Library Special Collections.
——. "Miss Paul's Golden Book," in *Observations on Nationality*, edited by James Brown Scott, Oxford: Oxford University Press, 1931, 95–6.
——. "Remarks at Luncheon in Celebration of the 25th Anniversary of the Society," *Proceedings of the American Society of International Law* 25 (1931): 242–3.
——. "St. Robert Bellarmine and our Political Heritage," *Georgetown College Journal* LX (1931): 19–31.
——. "The Progress of International Law during the last Twenty-Five Years," *Proceedings of the American Society of International Law* 25 (1931): 2–34.
——. (ed.). *The International Conferences of American States, 1889–1928: A Collection of the Conventions, Recommendations, Resolutions, and Motions adopted by the First Six Conferences of the American States, and Documents relating to the Organization of the Conferences*, Oxford: Oxford University Press, 1931.
—— and Albert de Lapradelle. "Nationalité de la femme mariée—Report," *Annuaire de l'Institut de Droit International*, Paris: A. Pedone Editeur (1932): 1–24.
——. "Our American Women in Action," *Women Lawyer's Journal* 21 (1934): 16.
——. "The Modern Law of Nations and its Municipal Sanctions," *Georgetown Law Journal* XXII (1934): 131–206.
——. "The Seventh International Conference of American States," *American Journal of International Law* 28 (1934): 219–30.
——. "Treaty-Making under the Authority of the United States," *Proceedings of the American Society of International Law* 28 (1934): 2–34.
——. *The Catholic Conception of International Law: Francisco de Vitoria, Founder of the Modern Law of Nations; Francisco Suárez, Founder of the Modern Philosophy of Law in General and in Particular of the Law of Nations—A Critical Examination and a Justified Appreciation*, Washington: Georgetown University Press, 1934.
——. *The Spanish Origin of International Law: Francisco De Vitoria and his Law of Nations*, Oxford: Oxford University Press, 1934.
—— and Walter H. E. Jaeger (eds.), *Cases on International Law*, St. Paul: West Publishing, 1937.
——. *Law, the State, and the International Community*, New York: Columbia University Press, 1939.
Sewell, Mike. "Humanitarian Intervention, Democracy, and Imperialism: The American War with Spain, 1898, and After," in Brendan Simms and David J. B. Trim (eds.), *Humanitarian Intervention: a History*, Cambridge: Cambridge University Press, 2011, 302–22.
Shinohara, Hatsue. *US International Lawyers in the Interwar Years: A Forgotten Crusade*, Cambridge: Cambridge University Press, 2012.
Simma, Bruno. "The Contribution of Alfred Verdross to International Law," *European Journal of International Law* 6 (1995): 33–54.
Sinclair, Upton. *The Goose Step: A Study of American Education*, Pasadena: published by the author, 1923.
Skinner, Quentin. "Meaning and Understanding in the History of Ideas," *History and Theory* 8 (1969): 3–53.
——. *Visions of Politics*, vol. I: Regarding Method, Cambridge: Cambridge University Press, 2002.
Skouteris, Thomas. *The Notion of Progress in International Law Discourse*, The Hague: T.M.C. Asser Press, 2010.

Sluga, Glenda and Carolyn James (eds.). *Women, Diplomacy and International Politics since 1500*, London: Routledge, 2016.

Snow, Freeman. *Cases and Opinions on International Law with Notes and a Syllabus*, Boston: Boston Book Co., 1893.

Spiermann, Ole. "'Who Attempts too Much Does Nothing Well': the 1920 Advisory Committee of Jurists and the Statute of the Permanent Court of International Justice," *British Yearbook of International Law* 73 (2003): 187–260.

Stein, Peter. *Legal Evolution: The Story of an Idea*, Cambridge: Cambridge University Press, 1980.

Stephanson, Anders. *Manifest Destiny: American Expansionism and the Empire of Right*, New York: Hill and Wang, 1995.

Stevens, Doris. *Jailed for Freedom*, New York: Boni and Liveright Publishers, 1920.

——. *Paintings and Drawings of Jeannette Scott*, privately printed for James Brown Scott, 1940.

Stoner, K. Lynn. *From the House to the Streets: The Cuban Woman's Movement for Legal Reform, 1898–1940*, Durham: Duke University Press, 1991.

Stott, Annette. *Holland Mania: The Unknown Dutch Period in American Art & Culture*, Woodstock: Overlook Press, 1998.

Suárez, Francisco, *Selections from Three Works*, vol. II, Oxford: Oxford University Press, 1944.

Tallgren, Immi. "The Faith in Humanity and International Criminal Law," in Martti Koskenniemi, Mónica Garcia-Salmones Rovira, and Paolo Amorosa (eds.), *International Law and Religion: Historical and Contemporary Perspectives*, Oxford: Oxford University Press, 2017, 334–62.

Teitel, Ruti. *Humanity's Law*, Oxford: Oxford University Press, 2011.

Tetrault, Lisa. *The Myth of Seneca Falls: Memory and the Women's Suffrage Movement, 1848–1898*, Chapel Hill: University of North Carolina Press.

The League to Enforce Peace, *Enforced Peace: Proceedings of the First Annual National Assemblage of the League to Enforce Peace*, New York: League to Enforce Peace, 1916.

Thompson, Philip M. *Between Science and Religion: The Engagement of Catholic Intellectuals with Science and Technology in the Twentieth Century*, Lanham: Lexington Books, 2009.

Tomlins, Christopher. "After Critical Legal History: Scope, Scale, Structure," *Annual Review of Law and Social Science* 8 (2012): 31–68.

——. "Historicism and Materiality in Legal Theory," in Maksymilian Del Mar and Michael Lobban (eds.), *Law in Theory and History*, London: Bloomsbury, 2016, 58–83.

Torriente, Cosme de la. "La Obra del Mejor Amigo de Cuba," in James Brown Scott, *Cuba, la América Latina, los Estados Unidos*, La Habana: Cuba, 1926, 397–424.

Trigg, Mary K. *Feminism as Life's Work: Four Modern American Women through Two World Wars*, New Brunswick: Rutgers University Press, 2014.

Truyol y Serra, Antonio. "Verdross et la théorie du droit," *European Journal of International Law* 6 (1995): 55–69.

Tuori, Taina. *From League of Nations Mandates to Decolonization: A History of the Language of Rights in International Law*, Helsinki: Unigrafia, 2016.

Ulloa Sotomayor, Alberto. *Derecho Internacional Público (Curso Universitario)*, Lima: Sanmartí y cía, impresores, vol. I, 1926.

——. "El Profesor Brown Scott y la situación de Cuba," *Revista de Ciencias Jurídicas y Sociales* 1 (1927): 397–9.

Van Bynkershoek, Cornelius. *Quaestionum juris publici libri duo*, translated into English by Jan de Louter, Oxford: Oxford University Press, 1930 [1737].

Van Dyne, Frederick. "Review—Report on the Subject of Citizenship, Expatriation, and Protection Abroad," *American Journal of International Law* 1 (1907): 548–53.

Van Ittersum, Martine Julia. *Profit and Principle: Hugo Grotius, Natural Rights Theories and the Rise of Dutch Power in the East Indies, 1595–1615*, Leiden: Brill, 2006.

——. "Hugo Grotius: The Making of a Founder of International Law," in Anne Orford and Florian Hoffmann (eds.), *Oxford Handbook of the Theory of International Law*, Oxford: Oxford University Press, 2016, 82–100.

Van Vollenhoven, Cornelis. *Grotius and Geneva, lectures delivered in Columbia University, July 1925*, in *Bibliotheca Visseriana*, vol. VI, Leiden: Brill, 1926.

Vanderpol, Alfred. *La guerre devante le Christianisme (ouvrage suivi d'une traduction du "De jure belli" de François de Vitoria)*, Paris: A. Tralin, 1911.

Vellacott, Jo. "A Place for Pacifism and Transnationalism in Feminist Theory: The Early Work of the Women's International League for Peace and Freedom," *Women's History Review* 2 (1993): 23–56.

Verdross, Alfred. *Die Einheit des rechtlichen Weltbildes auf der Grundlage der Völkerrechtsverfassung*, Tubingen: Mohr, 1923.

——. *Die Verfassung der Völkerrecthsgemeinschaft*, Wien—Berlin: Springer, 1926.

——. "Le fondement du droit des gens," *Recueil des cours de l'Académie de droit international de La Haye*, 16 (1927): 247–323.

——. *Völkerrecht*, Berlin: Springer, 1937.

Vitoria, Francisco de. *Relectiones: De Indis and De Jure Belli*, Ernest Nys (ed.), Washington, D.C.: Carnegie Institution, 1917 [1696].

——. *Political Writings*, Anthony Pagden and Jeremy Lawrance (eds.), Cambridge: Cambridge University Press, 1991.

Wambaugh, Sarah. *Plebiscites since the World War*, New York: Carnegie Endowment for International Peace, 1933.

Wamsley, E. Sue. "Constructing Feminism Across Borders: The Pan American Women's Movement and the Founding of the Inter-American Commission of Women," in Pernilla Jonsson, Silke Neunsinger, and Joan Sangster (eds.), *Crossing Boundaries: Women's Organizing in Europe and the Americas, 1880s–1940s*, Uppsala: Uppsala Universitet, 2007, 51–73.

Wertheim, Stephen. "The Wilsonian Chimera: Why Debating Wilson's Vision Hasn't Saved American Foreign Relations," *White House Studies* 10:4 (2011): 343–59.

——. "Reading the International Mind: International Public Opinion in Early Twentieth Century Anglo-American Thought," in Daniel Bessner and Nicolas Guilhot, *The Decisionist Imagination: Sovereignty, Social Sciences and Democracy in the 20th Century*, New York: Berghahn Book, 2019, 27–49.

Wheaton, Henry. *Elements of International Law with a Sketch of the History of the Science*, Philadelphia: Carey, Lea & Blanchard, 1836.

——. *Elements of International Law*, edited by Richard Henry Dana Jr., Boston: Little, Brown, and Company, 8th edn, 1866.

White, Andrew Dickson. *Autobiography*, New York: Century Co., 1905.

White, Hayden. *Metahistory. The Historical Imagination in Nineteenth-Century Europe*, Baltimore: The Johns Hopkins University Press, 1973.

Whiteclay Chambers, John (ed.). *The Eagle and the Dove: The American Peace Movement and United States Foreign Policy*, Syracuse: Syracuse University Press, 2nd edn, 1991.

Wickersham, George W. *The Supreme Court of the United States, a Prototype of a Court of Nations*, in *Proceedings of the American Society for Judicial Settlement of International Disputes* 3 (1913): 17–43.

Witt, John Fabian. *Lincoln's Code: The Laws of War in American History*, New York: Free Press, 2012.

Woolf, Virginia. *A Room of One's Own*, London: Penguin Books, 2000 [1929].
Wright, F. E. "Biographical Memoir of Robert Simpson Woodward, 1849–1924," *National Academy of Sciences of the United States of America—Biographical Memoirs*, vol. XIX (1937): 1–24.
Zapatero, Pablo. "Legal Imagination in Vitoria: The Power of Ideas," *Journal of the History of International Law* 11 (2009): 221–71.
Zasloff, Jonathan. "Law and the Shaping of American Foreign Policy: From the Gilded Age to the New Era," *New York University Law Review* 78 (2003): 239–373.
Zimmerman, Warren. *First Great Triumph*, New York: Farrar, Straus and Giroux, 2002.
Zinn, Howard. *A People's History of the United States*, London: Longman, 1980.
Zouche, Richard. *Juris et judicii fecialis, sive juris inter gentes, et quaestionum de eodem explicatio*, Thomas Erskine Holland (ed.), Washington, D.C.: Carnegie Institution, 1911 [1650].

# Index

Note: *For the benefit of digital users, indexed terms that span two pages (e.g., 52–53) may, on occasion, appear on only one of those pages.*



*Rewriting the History of the Law of Nations: How James Brown Scott Made Francisco de Vitoria the Founder of International Law*. Paolo Amorosa. Oxford University Press (2019). 
DOI: 10.1093/oso/9780198849377.001.0001